Interstate
Relations

Interstate Relations

The Neglected Dimension of Federalism

Joseph F. Zimmerman

PRAEGER

Westport, Connecticut
London

Library of Congress Cataloging-in-Publication Data

Zimmerman, Joseph Francis, 1928–
   Interstate relations : the neglected dimension of federalism /
Joseph F. Zimmerman.
     p. cm.
   Includes bibliographical references and index.
    ISBN 0-275-95614-8 (alk. paper). — ISBN 0-275-95615-6 (pb. : alk.
paper)
    1. Interstate relations—United States.   I. Title.
JK2445.I57Z55   1996
321.02′3′0973—dc20   96-2209

British Library Cataloguing in Publication Data is available.

Library of Congress Catalog Card Number: 96–2209
ISBN: 0-275-95614-8
    0-275-95615-6 (pbk.)

First published in 1996

Praeger Publishers, 88 Post Road West, Westport, CT 06881
An imprint of Greenwood Publishing Group, Inc.

Printed in the United States of America

The paper used in this book complies with the
Permanent Paper Standard issued by the National
Information Standards Organization (Z39.48-1984).

10 9 8 7 6 5 4 3 2 1

Contents

Preface   vii

1   Relations between States   1

2   Referee Role of the Supreme Court   17

3   Interstate Compacts and Agreements   33

4   Full Faith and Credit   59

5   Privileges and Immunities   87

6   Rendition of Fugitives from Justice   103

7   Interstate Economic Protectionism   117

8   Interstate Competition for Tourists, Sports Franchises,
    and Business Firms   141

9   Interstate Tax Revenue Competition   161

10 Formal and Informal Interstate Cooperation   185

11 Model for Improved Interstate Relations   213

Bibliography   237

Index   259

Preface

Dual sovereignty is a central characteristic of the U.S. federal system and involves powers exercisable by Congress and state legislatures. The latter may use these concurrent powers and other reserved powers to cooperate with each other or to create regional or national problems.

The erection of trade barriers by states between 1781 and 1788, under the Articles of Confederation and Perpetual Union, was a primary reason for the convening of the 1787 Constitutional Convention in Philadelphia to revise the articles. Based on this historical fact, one would anticipate that interstate relations would be featured prominently in the literature on the federal system. A review of the literature is disappointing, as such relations generally have been neglected with the principal exception of law review articles examining certain legal aspects of the relations. Literature focusing on the politics of interstate relations is sparse and typically old.

Improved communications and transportation systems in the post–Civil War period promoted mobility of citizens and development of multistate and, more recently, multinational corporations. The lack of uniform state statutes on a wide variety of subjects creates serious problems for citizens traveling to other states and for corporations. Although organized efforts have been made since 1892 to harmonize diverse state laws, nonuniformity characterizes statutes on numerous subjects.

The failure or inability of states to solve several important transboundary problems has resulted in increasing congressional preemption of their regulatory authority since 1965. Preemption during the past three decades has produced significant changes in the nature of the federal system in general and relations between states in particular. Congress currently is debating several bills, including product liability ones, that upon enactment would remove more regulatory powers from states. Additional preemption clearly will impact negatively the ability of states to use their respective discretionary powers to solve problems on a cooperative basis with sister states and the balance of powers between Congress and the states.

This book has two primary purposes. The first is to provide detailed information on and to analyze the various facets of interstate relations. The second purpose is to stimulate research on important but neglected interstate issues. The principal theme of this book is the need for new approaches to resolve disputes between states and to promote economic development for the benefit of citizens of all states. The concluding chapter contains a detailed model for improved relations among sister states.

Collecting information for this book was a difficult task because of the lack of current publications on many aspects of interstate relations. Numerous individuals and organizations responded generously to my requests for information. While it is not possible to acknowledge individually each contributor, a special debt of gratitude must be expressed to colleague Ronald M. Stout who examined the manuscript chapters very carefully and offered important suggestions for their improvement. A debt of gratitude also is owed to Brian R. Haak for research assistance and to Addie Napolitano for typing the manuscript. Any errors of fact or misinterpretations, of course, are solely my responsibility.

1

Relations between States

The division of political power in a federal system, between the national government and the states, automatically produces relations between the latter. These relations may be cooperative as manifested by interstate compacts, uniform state laws, reciprocity statutes, administrative agreements, and regional and national associations of state government officials. On the other hand, such relations can be hostile. A 1964 front page headline in *The New York Times* was entitled "Iowa is Called Aggressor State: Nebraska Fears Shooting War."[1] This dispute, resolved peaceably, involved the Missouri River which serves as the boundary line between the two states and has shifted its course periodically.

Interstate relations involve an important spectrum of economic, political, and social matters, yet there has been relatively little academic interest in the subject for more than fifty years. *The Annals* has published special issues devoted to intergovernmental relations and federalism. The 1940 issue contained six articles on interstate relations, but the number of articles on this subject declined to two in the 1974 issue and to zero in the 1990 issue.[2] This academic neglect is surprising since the economic and political health of the nation is dependent upon comity in interstate relations.

ORIGIN OF THE FEDERAL SYSTEM

A foreign observer of the U.S. federal system probably would conclude that interstate relations generally are chaotic and the national government possesses only limited authority to create order out of the chaos. One cannot deny the fact that the lack of uniformity of policy in many fields, resulting from general state autonomy in these fields, causes serious problems for numerous business firms and individuals, as highlighted in subsequent chapters. To understand current interstate relations, it is essential to review briefly the Articles of Confederation and Perpetual Union and the U.S. Constitution relative to the complexities of the sharing of sovereignty by Congress and the states.

The federal system evolved out of a confederate system. The Declaration of Independence of 1776 made formal a revolutionary war by colonies against the British Crown which erupted in 1775. The war involved thirteen newly declared independent states, and there was no national government. However, there was a Continental Congress, composed of delegates from the states, which provided central direction for the war effort. The Congress recognized the need for a national government, but rejected a unitary government because it was too centralized and the people had rebelled against such a government. The only existing alternative governance system, exemplified by Switzerland and the United Netherlands, was a confederacy.

The Continental Congress in 1777 drafted the Articles of Confederation and Perpetual Union and submitted them to the states for ratification. The articles provided for a league of amity, but would not become effective unless ratified by all states. The articles were ratified by eight states in 1778 and by four additional states in 1779.

Ratification was delayed for four years by disputes relative to title to lands west of the states. The British Crown made grants of land to the West without limit, but these grants were countered by the Mississippi Valley claims of the French Government. Connecticut, for example, claimed what today is Illinois, Indiana, and northern Ohio, and Virginia's claims were more extensive and included most of Illinois, Indiana, and Ohio, and parts of northern Michigan, Minnesota, and Wisconsin. Disputes over boundaries continue to this day and are examined in Chapter 2.

To resolve the boundary disputes, the Continental Congress in 1780 proposed that the lands in question should be ceded to the national government to be created by the articles to be "disposed of for the common benefit of the United States and be settled and formed into distinct states which shall become members of this Federal Union, ..."[3] The terms federal and confederal were used interchangeably during this time period.[4]

New York and Virginia responded in 1781 by ceding the lands they claimed, and other states followed suit soon thereafter. The ceding of lands led to speedy ratification of the articles by the thirteenth state, Maryland. The articles interestingly authorized Canada to join the confederation. The Congress, created by the articles, enacted the Northwest Ordinance of 1787 admitting parts of the northwest territories as states when the population of each part reached 50,000 and abolishing slavery within the new states.[5]

Article II was the heart of the new fundamental document and stipulated that "each state retains its sovereignty, freedom, and independence," and all powers not delegated to the unicameral Congress. Each state was authorized to send two to seven delegates to the Congress, but had only one vote.

The Congress was authorized to borrow and coin money, declare war, establish a postal system and standards of weights and measures, negotiate treaties with other nations, and regulate relations with the Indian tribes. The word government does not appear in the articles and there was no executive or judicial branch. Article III referred to interstate relations by describing the confederation as "a firm league of friendship with each other."

The lack of two major powers foredoomed the Congress to impotence. The articles did not authorize the Congress to tax or regulate interstate commerce. Consequently, it had to rely upon the willingness of individual states to send funds and was powerless to strike down interstate trade barriers.

Martin Diamond wrote that "neither the friends nor the enemies of the Confederation regarded the articles as having created any kind of government at all, weak or otherwise."[6] The Congress was empowered to appoint a presiding officer, termed president, for a term not exceeding one year during a three-year period and a committee of the states composed of one delegate from each state. The committee met during the recess of the Congress and was granted several powers, including borrowing money, raising an army, building a navy, coining money, declaring war, et cetera.

Constitutional Convention

The inadequacy of the articles as an effective governing document for a nation was apparent by 1785 when Maryland and Virginia officials reached an agreement relative to navigation and trade on the Potomac River and the Chesapeake Bay. In ratifying the agreement, Virginia proposed extension of the compact to all states and invited all states to send delegates to a conference to be held in Annapolis in 1786 to devise a uniform system of commerce and trade.

Although nine states appointed delegates to attend the conference, only the delegates of five states participated in the deliberations. Delegate Alexander Hamilton of New York drafted a resolution, approved by the delegates, memorializing the Congress to call a convention to meet in May 1787 in Philadelphia to examine needed revisions in the articles. On February 21, 1787, the Congress approved a resolution calling a convention. All states sent delegates to the convention except the state of Rhode Island and Providence Plantations.

The poor condition of interstate relations was a contributing factor to the replacement of the Articles of Confederation and Perpetual Union by the U.S. Constitution. A number of observers also attributed the decision to replace the articles to the fear that the United Kingdom might seek to regain control of its former colonies and to the Spanish threat to the Southwest.[7]

Governor Edmund Randolph of Virginia on May 29, 1787, proposed fifteen resolutions which would serve as the basis for a new national government with powers similar to those of the government of the United Kingdom.[8] These resolutions sparked five days of debate relative to whether the articles should be amended or replaced. A decision was made by a vote of six to one to replace the articles. The delegates of five states had not arrived by the time of the vote.

As is well known, the constitution contains several compromises between the large and small states, northern and southern states, and eastern and western states. The end product was a new system of governance based upon a geographical distribution of political powers between the Congress and the states with each possessing sovereignty relative to its exclusive powers. Congress was granted enumerated powers, including levying taxes, borrowing money, coining money, establishing post offices and post roads, and raising and supporting armies and a navy, among other powers. The inability of the Congress under the articles to prevent states from following mercantilistic policies, which brought interstate trade to a nearly complete standstill, was rectified by granting Congress broad powers to regulate interstate commerce, foreign commerce, and trade with the Indian nations.[9] As explained in subsequent chapters, the U.S. Supreme Court generally interprets the interstate commerce clause as enabling the Congress to enact statutes with almost no limits. To date, however, the Congress has played a minimalist intervention role with respect to interstate relations, preferring to leave the settlement of disputes to the courts rather than fashioning a general policy under its powers to preempt state regulatory authority.[10]

All powers not delegated to the Congress or prohibited are reserved to the states and the people as the Tenth Amendment to the U.S. Constitution attempts to make clear. These residual or reserved powers are undefinable except in the broadest of terms. The most important power of the states, other than the power to tax, is the police power which enables states to regulate persons and property to protect and promote public convenience, health, morals, safety, and welfare. This power is employed on occasions to create interstate trade barriers. Although an extremely broad power, its use is limited by the Due Process of Law clause of the Fourteenth Amendment to the U.S. Constitution and the Interstate Commerce clause.

It is important for the reader to recognize that not all powers delegated by the U.S. Constitution to the Congress are exclusive powers. Unless the constitution specifically prohibits states from exercising a power, such as the power to coin money, states are free to utilize concurrent reserved powers, such as borrowing funds, establishing courts, and levying taxes. This division and sharing of powers is referred to as dual sovereignty.

Several reserved powers, such as the power to tax, are not subject to preemption by the Congress unless they create interstate trade barriers. Other powers, such as the power to abate environmental pollution, may be exercised by the states until or unless the Congress decides to preempt totally or partially the regulatory powers of the states. The latter on occasion recognizes that a problem cannot be solved on the basis of the full cooperation by sister states and calls upon Congress to exercise its power of preemption as illustrated by the Commercial Motor Vehicle Safety Act of 1986.[11]

INTERSTATE CONSTITUTIONAL PRINCIPLES

The U.S. Constitution contains seven important provisions relating to interstate relations. The drafters of the fundamental document employed general terms without definitions which necessitate that courts in particular cases determine the applicability of the provisions. The U.S. Supreme Court in resolving constitutional disputes does not define constitutional terms and acts on a case-by-case basis.

Legal Equality

The U.S. Constitution establishes a union in which each state is legally equal to every other state. Vermont and Kentucky were admitted to the Union on March 4, 1791, and June 1, 1792, respectively, with no conditions. Vermont specifically was admitted "as a new and entire member of the United States of America."[12] In 1796, Congress declared Tennessee to be "one of the United States" which was "on an equal footing with the original states in all respects whatsoever."[13] The two newest states, Alaska and Hawaii, possess the same reserved powers guaranteed by the Tenth Amendment as any of the original thirteen states. The only distinction which the constitution makes among states is the number of representatives in Congress and presidential and vice presidential electors, a distinction based upon population.

The Congress occasionally imposed on a territory, seeking admission to the Union as a state, conditions with which it must comply prior to admission. If the conditions concern federal property in the new state, or grants of land or money to the state to be used for specific purposes, the conditions are enforceable judicially.[14]

If a condition prohibits a state from making a change in its government or internal organization, the territory, after admission to the Union as a state, may ignore the prohibition. The Oklahoma territory, for example, was required to establish Guthrie as the capitol as a condition of admission to the Union. Subsequent to admission, the state legislature moved the capitol to Oklahoma City, and the legislature's authority to move the capitol was upheld by the U.S. Supreme Court in 1911 which opined:

"This Union" was and is a union of states, equal in power, dignity, and authority, each competent to exert that residuum of sovereignty not delegated to the United States by the Constitution itself. To maintain otherwise would be to say that the Union, through the power of Congress to admit new states, might come to be a union of states unequal in power, as including states whose powers were restricted only by the Constitution, with others whose powers had been further restricted by an act of Congress accepted as a condition of admission.[15]

Interstate Suits

It was argued at the Constitutional Convention that there was no need for a national judiciary since state courts could adjudicate national as well as state controversies. Advocates of a national judiciary, however, maintained that reliance upon state courts might result in the issuance of different interpretations of the same constitutional or congressional statutory provision, thereby promoting national disunity.

Experience with interstate disputes under the Articles of Confederation and Perpetual Union convinced the drafters of the U.S. Constitution that a judicial forum for settling such disputes must be established. Section 1 of Article III of the constitution established the U.S. Supreme Court and Section 2 grants it jurisdiction "in law and equity," over all "controversies between two or more states; . . . ."

Section 1 also authorizes the Congress to establish inferior courts. As explained in Chapter 2, the U.S. Supreme Court does not always accept jurisdiction over an interstate dispute when requested by a state that is a party to the dispute.

The drafters of the Constitution assumed that no state could be sued by a private citizen without its consent since the common law provided the king (state) can do no wrong and hence there are no grounds for a suit. The U.S. Supreme Court in 1793, however, interpreted Section 2 of Article III of the constitution as permitting a citizen of South Carolina to sue Georgia even though a citizen could not sue his own state.[16] This decision generated state pressure on the Congress to propose the Eleventh Amendment, prohibiting such suits, which was quickly ratified by three-fourths of the states and became effective in 1795.

The Supreme Court plays a crucial role in interstate relations because of its constitutional responsibility to adjudicate interstate disputes and interpret the U.S. Constitution and statutes. Chapter 2 explains the exercise of the court's original jurisdiction when one state seeks to sue another state, Chapters 3 and 4 analyze the court's role relative to full faith and credit guarantees and privileges and immunities guarantees, and Chapters 7 and 9 highlight the court's actions to strike down interstate trade barriers and exportation of taxes by a state.

Interstate Compacts

An interstate compact is a valuable mechanism for promoting interstate cooperation or centralizing certain powers on a regional basis for purposes of regulation or construction and operation of physical facilities, such as bridges and tunnels. Article VI of the Articles of Confederation and Perpetual Union authorized states to enter "into any treaty, confederation, or alliance" provided Congress gave its consent. The 1785 interstate compact between Maryland and Virginia, governing use of the Potomac River and Chesapeake Bay, was one of the several compacts approved by the Congress under the articles.

Section 10 of Article I of the U.S. Constitution contains a similar provision because the drafters of the constitution recognized the desirability of interstate cooperation and the possibility that compacts could disrupt the Union. Hence, compacts were authorized provided Congress gives its formal consent to each compact. As explained in Chapter 3, the U.S. Supreme Court has opined that not all compacts require the formal consent of the Congress in order to become effective. Furthermore, there is no constitutional restriction upon the authority of a state to conduct its relations with other states on the basis of reciprocity or for administrative officials of sister states to enter into cooperative agreements.

Full Faith and Credit

To what extent must one state observe the statutes, judicial proceedings, and records of other states? Although no constitution existed until the Articles of Confederation and Perpetual Union became effective in 1781, the Continental

Congress in 1777 approved a resolution that each state should grant full faith and credit to the statutes, judicial proceedings, and records of other states. The resolution subsequently was incorporated into the articles and into the U.S. Constitution.

The constitutional principle, incorporated in Section 1 of Article IV, was designed to establish a national legal system to promote interstate intercourse and national unity. Unfortunately, full faith and credit are not always extended by individual states to citizens who move to their states, thereby creating jurisdictional disputes. For example, the clause generally has been ineffective in guaranteeing that a child support obligor makes complete and timely payments to the custodial parent residing in another state. Chapter 4 examines the Full Faith and Credit clause in detail.

Privileges and Immunities

The framers of the U.S. Constitution sought to establish interstate citizenship by including in Section 2 of Article IV a guarantee that "the citizens of each state shall be entitled to all privileges and immunities of citizens of the several states." The terms privileges and immunities are not defined in the constitution, but the U.S. Supreme Court over the decades has struck down as violative of the guarantee those state laws advantaging their citizens over citizens of other states. The court, however, has excluded certain beneficial services and political privileges from the protection of the clause. Chapter 5 explores this guarantee in detail and also notes that the Fourteenth Amendment to the U.S. Constitution contains a guarantee of privileges and immunities.

Interstate Rendition

Interstate rendition involves a process similar to the one established by extradition treaties between nations providing for the return of a fugitive from justice from the asylum nation to the requesting nation. Section 2 of Article IV of the U.S. Constitution incorporates a rendition provision nearly identical to the rendition provision in the Articles of Confederation and Perpetual Union. In contrast to nations which cannot be forced to return a fugitive from justice to the requesting nation, the governor of a state must return a fugitive provided the fugitive fled from the requesting state. Rendition is the subject of Chapter 6.

Internal Free Trade

The mercantilistic actions of individual states between 1781 and 1787 convinced the drafters of the U.S. Constitution that the Congress must be granted authority to regulate commerce among the several states, and such authority was included in Section 8 of Article I. Furthermore, Section 10 of Article I forbids states to levy import or export duties except to finance their inspection activities, with any surplus dedicated to the U.S. Treasury or to "lay any duty of tonnage."

To prevent discrimination against individual states and to promote internal free trade, Section 9 of Article I forbids the Congress to give preference "to the ports of one State over those of another; nor shall vessels bound to, or from, one state, be obliged to enter, clear, or pay duties in another." Chapter 7 explores states' use of their police, license, proprietary, and tax powers to create interstate trade barriers.

The Interstate Commerce clause clashes relatively often with the states' broad police power to regulate in order to promote public health, convenience, safety, morals, and welfare, leading to court challenges of state statutes and regulations. In general, as described in greater detail in subsequent chapters, the courts give broad scope to the interstate commerce power.

Of particular importance in terms of generating recent interstate disputes are attempts by individual states to export their taxes to business firms and residents of other states, and to require mail-order firms to collect the use tax imposed by their states in conjunction with the sales tax. Severance taxes on minerals exported to other states are a major source of interstate controversies and are examined in Chapter 9. States also engaged in competition to attract industrial firms by offering tax abatements and loans as inducements to the firms. This competition at times results in poor interstate relations as explained in Chapter 8.

The lack of uniform trade policies in many regulatory areas places burdens upon multistate business firms. These burdens can be removed through reciprocity, congressional preemption of state regulatory authority, and congressional employment of cross-over sanctions and tax credits to promote national uniformity—subjects explored in Chapters 7 and 9.

INDIAN NATIONS

A federal system is described aptly as an *Imperium in Imperio* (an empire within an empire). As noted, the U.S. Government is sovereign relative to its constitutionally delegated powers, and each state is sovereign relative to its reserved powers that are not subject to congressional preemption. The system of governance within a state with federally recognized Indian tribes also can be described as an *Imperium in Imperio* since each tribe has sovereignty over its respective reservation as provided by treaties entered into by the U.S. Government with individual tribes. In consequence, a state lacks sovereignty over an Indian reservation.

To what extent can an Indian tribe decide the benefits of tribe membership without supervision by the U.S. Government? The U.S. Supreme Court in 1978 in *Santa Clara Pueblo v. Martinez* rejected an equal protection of the laws challenge by ruling a tribe possesses sovereign immunity and only a tribal court could decide the issue.[17]

Various treaties exempt Native Americans residing on reservations from payment of state and local government taxes and fees, and also may exempt the Native Americans from state licensing requirements. As explained in Chapter 9, sales of alcohol, motor fuels, and tobacco products to non-Indians on reservations have triggered disputes with state governments concerned with the loss of state tax revenues.

Approximately fifty-three million acres of land are held in trust by the United States for Indian tribes, with the Navajo reservation occupying nearly sixteen million acres of land in Arizona, New Mexico, and Utah. The United States in 1778 entered into its first treaty with an Indian tribe—the Delawares. The U.S. Constitution, ratified in 1788, delegates authority to Congress "to regulate commerce ... with the Indian tribes; ...." Congress in 1790 enacted the first statute pertaining to Indian tribes, and the U.S. Supreme Court in 1832 in *Worcester v. Georgia* started to clarify the legal status of the relationships between the United States, states, and Indian tribes under the U.S. Constitution and treaties entered into by the U.S. Government with various Indian tribes.[18] The court in this case ruled that Congress possesses exclusive power to regulate commerce with the Indian tribes, and states lack authority in Indian country unless delegated authority by Congress.

Relations between a state and Indian reservations remain ill-defined in the closing years of the twentieth century with a growing number of controversies brought to the courts for resolution. Increasingly, tribes are seeking federal recognition which would grant them sovereignty over certain matters which currently are subject to the jurisdiction of the state government.[19] The attempts to gain federal recognition have been stimulated by the Indian Gaming Regulatory Act of 1988 which has resulted in 78 tribes in 19 states signing 100 tribe-state compacts concerning gambling on reservations.[20] Table 1.1 contains details on the gaming compacts.

Gambling on Reservations

The National Association of Attorneys General at its 1985 annual meeting approved a resolution calling upon Congress to authorize states to regulate gambling on Indian reservations. Continuing controversies involving such gambling induced Congress to enact the Indian Gaming Regulatory Act of 1988 which classifies gaming as Class I, II, and III. Class I includes social games conducted for prizes of minimal value that are engaged in as part of tribal celebrations and ceremonies. Class II consists of games of chance, such as bingo and lotto, which are regulated by tribal governments with oversight by the National Indian Gaming Commission, a U.S. Government agency. Class III games are regulated jointly by tribal governments and the concerned state government under provisions of a state-tribal agreement.

The 1988 act does not mandate that a state must permit tribal governments to conduct a specific game, but does authorize a tribal government to engage in the same types of gaming activities that are conducted by other organizations in the state. The act authorizes the governor of a state to enter into a compact with an Indian tribe. The Kansas Supreme Court, in 1992, however, held that the Governor of Kansas lacks authority to bind the state to a compact under the Indian Gaming Regulatory Act.[21] The value of such a contract to an Indian tribe is illustrated by the Oneida Indian Nation offering to share gaming profits with the state if New York Governor George E. Pataki will sign a compact with the Nation allowing it to operate a casino in Monticello which is ninety miles north of New York City and

Table 1.1
Status of Indian Gaming Compacts

The Indian Gaming Regulatory Act(IGRA), enacted in 1988, provides a legal framework for the establishment and operation of gaming on Native American lands. As of Nov. 19, 1993, 100 tribal-state compacts, involving 19 states and 78 tribes, have been approved. The progress in implementing IGRA has occurred primarily through cooperation between states and tribes, and in some cases through court decisions in litigation.

State	Number of Tribes	Number of Tribes with Compacts	State Lottery	Bingo
Alabama	1	0		
Alaska	220	0		■
Arizona	20	12	■	■
Arkansas	0	0		
California	95	5	■	■
Colorado	2	2	■	
Connecticut	1	1	■	
Delaware	0	0	■	
Florida	2	0		
Georgia	0	0	■	■
Hawaii	0	0		
Idaho	4	2	■	■
Illinois	0	0	■	
Indiana	1	0	■	
Iowa	1	3	■	■
Kansas	3	0	■	■
Kentucky	0	0	■	
Louisiana	3	3	■	■
Maine	4	0	■	■
Maryland	0	0	■	
Massachusetts	1	0	■	■
Michigan	7	7	■	■
Minnesota	6	11	■	■
Mississippi	1	1		■
Missouri	1	0	■	
Montana	7	4	■	■
Nebraska	4	1	■	■
Nevada	17	1		■
New Hampshire	0	0	■	■
New Jersey	0	0	■	■
New Mexico	22	0		■
New York	7	1	■	■
North Carolina	1	1		■
North Dakota	4	5	■	■
Ohio	0	0	■	■
Oklahoma	35	1		■
Oregon	9	0	■	■
Pennsylvania	0	0	■	■
Rhode Island	1	0	■	■
South Carolina	0	0		■
South Dakota	8	8	■	■
Tennessee	0	0		■
Texas	3	0	■	■
Utah	4	0		■
Vermont	0	0	■	■
Virginia	0	0		
Washington	26	9	■	■
West Virginia	0	0	■	■
Wisconsin	11	11	■	■
Wyoming	2	0		■

Source: Governors' Bulletin, December 6, 1993, insert page.

100 miles south of the Nation's reservation.[22] The 1988 act allows a tribe to operate a casino outside its reservation provided the U.S. Secretary of the Interior and the governor of the state approve.

State-Indian Disputes

The loss of tax revenue resulting from sales on Indian reservations is a perennial cause of concern to state governments, and the federal courts often are called upon to resolve disputes. In 1993, for example, the U.S. Supreme Court opined that Oklahoma could not levy income taxes or motor vehicles taxes on tribal members who live in "Indian country."[23] The latter includes reservations, dependent Indian communities, and Indian allotments.[24] In 1995, the Court held that Oklahoma may not tax motor fuels sold by the Chickasaw Nation in Indian country, but may tax the income of all persons, Indians and non-Indians, residing outside Indian country.[25]

Writing in *The National Law Journal*, Robert N. Clinton maintained that the purpose of the Indian commerce clause is to prevent state government encroachment on the authority of Congress to regulate Indian affairs and criticized the U.S. Supreme Court for ruling "that a state in many contexts possess inherent power to tax and regulate nonmember activities in Indian country without congressional delegation of authority."[26] States, of course, disagree with Clinton's contention and argue that they have authority to tax sales to nonmembers on Indian reservations.

Many Indian reservations are located in the arid west and disputes arise between Indian tribes, the U.S. Government, and states relative to water. In 1908, the U.S. Supreme Court ruled in *Winters v. United States* that when Congress established Indian reservations it reserved water for them.[27] This ruling conflicts with the water laws of states. After years of litigation, the federal government decided to employ negotiations to end water disputes in places of litigation. Daniel McCool studied the results of the negotiations and concluded:

1. Negotiations may or may not be as time-consuming as litigation; in most cases it has proven to be a complicated process that can take years to bear fruit.

2. The settlements are often quite expensive. In some cases, they are more costly than a litigated settlement....

3. Many settlements have failed to achieve finality and certainty.

4. Negotiation, like litigation, is risky and may result in unexpected negative outcomes.

5. Negotiation does offer the potential for substantive, flexible agreements that can be tailored to specific situations.

6. Negotiation is, by nearly all accounts, more humane. Indian-Anglo relations have long been fraught with high-intensity conflict; any process that can help alleviate that hostility while still maintaining respect for each party's interests is an achievement.[28]

Available evidence suggests that states with Indian reservations will continue to have disputes with tribes relative to the sales of tax exempt products on reservations to non-Indians as explained in Chapter 9, and arid states will experience difficulties in resolving conflicts over water rights with Indian tribes.

INTERSTATE DYNAMICS

The nature of interstate relations has changed dramatically over the decades. There was little interstate cooperation during the early decades, in part because of the relative lack of need for such cooperation. Disputes between states were more common and typically involved boundary issues generated by imprecise colonial land grants. The rapid development of new means of transportation and communications, in conjunction with increasing industrial development and urbanization during the post–Civil War period, increased the need for uniform or parallel state statutes and interstate cooperation, but also produced more disputes between sister states.

The drafters of the U.S. Constitution foresaw the need for cooperation by sister states and, as noted, authorized them to enter into compacts with each other provided Congress granted its consent. Nevertheless, the compact device was little used until the twentieth century, and no interstate development or regulatory agency was created by a compact until the third decade of the twentieth century as explained in Chapter 3.

The nature of interstate problems in the U.S. federal system today is complex and diverse. States often discover it is in its respective interest to work cooperatively to solve a common problem. In 1994, for example, it was discovered that 425 residents of Newark, New Jersey, who were collecting welfare payments in Newark, also were collecting welfare payments in nearby New York City.[29] This revelation induced Governor Mario M. Cuomo of New York on March 6, 1994, to write to Governor Christine Todd Whitman of New Jersey to inform her that the New York State Commissioner of Social Services would contact his counterpart in New Jersey and other border states to examine methods of preventing individuals from welfare double-dipping.[30] Currently, New York State is exchanging computer tapes of welfare benefit recipients with Connecticut, District of Columbia, Florida, New Jersey, Pennsylvania, Vermont, and Virginia.[31]

It is apparent that individual state boundaries do not encompass completely a number of important problems and that states have broad powers whose exercise can have major extraterritorial repercussions. These facts over the years have led to numerous proposals to reduce the number of states by forming larger regional states with a geographical scale sufficient to permit each state to solve most problems internally.

Proposals to establish such states have an attractive rational basis, but unfortunately are politically naive. It is unrealistic to suggest the replacement of existing states since the constitution guarantees the territorial integrity of each state and such replacement would require either a constitutional amendment or the consent of the Congress and each concerned state since.[32]

Chapters 2–10 describe and analyze in detail the constitutional rules governing relations between two or more states; treatment of sojourners by a state; extraterritorial validity of a state's statutes, records, and judicial proceedings; interstate disputes and methods employed to resolve them; various aspects of multistate

cooperation; state competition for industry and tax revenues; and lingering transboundary problems.

It is apparent that certain interstate problems can be solved only by the Congress.
In 1993, for example, it was discovered that many debtors, including felons, who
filed for bankruptcy protection were able to shelter millions of dollars in assets
from seizure by the U.S. Bankruptcy Court by establishing residence in Florida
where a state statute forbids the seizure of a person's legal residence and certain
other assets—including annuities and pensions—in a bankruptcy proceeding.[33]
The Florida State Legislature has not placed a limit on the Homestead Exemption,
and residences worth several million dollars are protected. Although Congress
preempted state court adjudication of bankruptcy proceedings in 1898, Congress
has allowed individual state legislatures to determine whether a homestead and
certain other exemptions should be exempt from seizure.[34] This interstate problem
involving debtors in states, such as New York, sheltering assets in other states can
be solved only by the Congress.

The process of congressional enactment of formulas for the distribution of funds
to states commonly generates lobbying by regional groupings of states with one
region opposed to a specific proposed formula and another region in favor of the
proposal. In 1995, the northern states opposed a Republican proposal to replace
seven categorical welfare grant programs by a block grant with no state-matching
requirements because funds would be shifted from the northern states to southern
and western states.[35]

The concluding chapter assesses current interstate relations and presents a model
for improving such relations to enhance the full economic and social development
of the fifty states. In particular, the model outlines the roles that the Congress,
states, and associations of state government officials can play in harmonizing the
policies of the states, while promoting the advantages of policy diversity associated
with a federal system, and encouraging cooperative and conjoint actions.

The model is a political document, but does not outline a role for the two major
political parties because they are decentralized organizations that have become
progressively weaker in recent decades. The parties are incapable of acting as
centralizing forces to promote interstate cooperation or congressional preemption
to solve multistate problems.

Chapter 2 is the first substantive chapter and examines the role of the U.S.
Supreme Court in resolving interstate disputes. Subsequent chapters highlight
three other important court functions: use of the dormant Interstate Commerce
clause to invalidate mercantilistic state statutes and regulations, interpretation of
the scope of congressional preemption statutes, and deciding whether a congressional preemption statute is *ultra vires*.

NOTES

1. Donald Janson, "Iowa is Called Aggressor State: Nebraska Fears Shooting War,"
The New York Times, July 26, 1964, pp. 1 and 24.

2. W. Brook Graves, ed., "Intergovernmental Relations in the United States," *The Annals*, January 1940, pp. 1–218; Richard H. Leach, ed., "Intergovernmental Relations in America Today," *The Annals*, November 1974, pp. 1–169; and John Kincaid, ed., "American Federalism: The Third Century," *The Annals*, May 1990, pp. 11–152.

3. Henry S. Commager, ed., *Documents of American History to 1898*, 8th ed. (New York: Appleton-Century-Crofts, 1968), Vol. I, p. 120.

4. For information on the differences between a confederation and a federation, see Joseph F. Zimmerman, *Contemporary American Federalism: The Growth of National Power* (Leicester: Leicester University Press, 1992), pp. 4–7.

5. Commager, *Documents of American History*, Vol. I, pp. 128–32.

6. Martin Diamond, "What the Framers Meant by Federalism" in Robert A. Goldwin, ed., *A Nation of States: Essays on the American Federal System*, 2nd ed. (Chicago: Rand McNally, 1974), p. 29.

7. William H. Riker, *Federalism: Origin, Operation, Significance* (Boston: Little, Brown and Company, 1964), pp. 17–20.

8. Max Farrand, ed. *The Records of the Federal Convention of 1787* (New Haven: Yale University Press, 1966), Vol. II, p. 24.

9. *U.S. Constitution*, Art. I, §8.

10. Joseph F. Zimmerman, *Federal Preemption: The Silent Revolution* (Ames: Iowa State University Press, 1991).

11. *Commercial Motor Vehicle Safety Act of 1986*, 100 Stat. 3207, 49 U.S.C.A. §521 (1995 Supp.). States were unable to solve the problem of commercial vehicle drivers holding operator licenses from several states and continuing to drive after a state suspended or revoked a license. The congressional statute makes it a federal crime for an operator of a commercial vehicle to hold more than one operator license.

12. 1 Stat. 191.

13. 1 Stat. 491.

14. *Sterns v. Minnesota*, 179 U.S. 223 (1900), and *Ervien v. United States*, 251 U.S. 41 (1919).

15. *Coyle v. Smith*, 221 U.S. 559 at 619 (1911).

16. *Chisholm v. Georgia*, 2 U.S. 415 (1793).

17. *Santa Clara Pueblo v. Martinez*, 436 U.S. 47 (1979).

18. 1 Stat. 137, and *Worcester v. Georgia*, 31 U.S. 515 (1832). See also 19 Stat. 200, 25 U.S.C.A. §261 (1983).

19. See David E. Wilkins, "Breaking Into the Intergovernmental Matrix: The Lumbee Tribes' Efforts to Secure Federal Acknowledgment," *Publius*, Fall 1993, pp. 123–42.

20. *Indian Gaming Regulation Act of 1988*, 102 Stat. 2467, 25 U.S.C.A. §2710 (1995 Supp.). See also Anne M. McCulloch, "The Politics of Indian Gaming: Tribe/State Relations and American Federalism," *Publius*, Summer 1994, pp. 99–112.

21. *State ex rel. Stephan v. Finney*, 836 P.2d 1169 (Kan. 1992).

22. James Dao, "Indians Offer State a Share of Monticello Casino Profits," *The New York Times*, March 2, 1995, p. B6.

23. *Oklahoma Tax Commission v. SAC and Fox Nation*, 113 S.Ct. 1985 (1993).

24. 62 Stat. 757, 18 U.S.C.A. §1151 (1984).

25. *Oklahoma Tax Commission v. Chickasaw Nation*, 115 S.Ct. 2214 at 2217 (1995).

26. Robert N. Clinton, "Once Again, Indian Tribes are Losing Ground," *The National Law Journal*, December 19, 1994, p. A21.

27. *Winters v. United States*, 207 U.S. 564 (1908).

28. Daniel McCool, "Intergovernmental Conflict and Indian Water Rights: An Assessment of Negotiated Settlements," *Publius*, Winter 1993, p. 101.

29. Seth Faison, "Newark Residents Accused of Taking New York Welfare," *The New York Times*, March 2, 1994, pp. 1 and B2.

30. Letter available in the Executive Chamber, Albany, NY 12224.

31. "Pataki Unveils Plan to Fight Welfare Recipients' Double-Dipping," *Times Union* (Albany, N.Y.), September 10, 1995, p. D-4.

32. *United States Constitution*, Art. IV, §3.

33. Larry Rohter, "Rich Debtors Finding Shelter Under a Populist Law," *The New York Times*, July 25, 1993, pp. 1 and 26.

34. *An Act to Establish a Uniform System of Bankruptcy of 1898*, 30 Stat. 544, 11 U.S.C.A. §1 (1993). See also the *Bankruptcy Act of 1933*, 47 Stat. 1467, 11 U.S.C.A. §1 (1993).

35. Elizabeth Schwinn, "Moynihan Sees States Warring over Welfare," *Times Union* (Albany, N.Y.), July 22, 1995, pp. 1 and A-8.

2

Referee Role of the Supreme Court

A distinguishing feature of federalism in the United States is a dual judicial system—national courts and state courts. Numerous types of cases can be brought in either the United States courts or in state courts, and the Congress has enacted a statute allowing these types of cases to be removed from national courts to state courts or vice versa.[1] A second congressional statute assigns exclusive jurisdiction to the U.S. District Court over suits brought by a citizen of one state against a citizen of another state (diversity of citizenship) if the amount in controversy is $50,000 or more.[2]

As noted in Chapter 1, the framers of the U.S. Constitution were convinced by experience under the Articles of Confederation and Perpetual Union of the need for a national supreme court which, among other duties, would hear suits by one or more states against one or more states. Section 2 of Article III of the constitution recognizes states as semisovereign units and grants the Supreme Court nonexclusive original (trial) jurisdiction over interstate disputes. Although this jurisdiction cannot be increased, the Congress in 1789 made this jurisdiction exclusive.[3] The court under Section 2 of Article III also has original but not exclusive jurisdiction over other cases in which a state is a party.

The framers recognized that suits between citizens of different states might result in state courts favoring their own citizens, and a neutral appellate tribunal should be available to review such decisions. Furthermore, it was apparent that state legislatures might enact laws discriminating against other states that violate provisions of the U.S. Constitution, and it would be essential to have a supreme national tribunal with authority to adjudicate such cases.

DISCRETIONARY ORIGINAL JURISDICTION

In contrast to congressional establishment of a procedure for implementing the Constitutional Interstate Rendition clause (see Ch. 6), Congress has not enacted a statute governing the invocation of the Supreme Court's original jurisdiction or its procedures.

The constitutional grant of original jurisdiction in certain cases to the Supreme Court is discretionary in nature and the court may decline to accept jurisdiction when one state seeks to sue another state. In 1905, the court stressed that a suit by a state against a second state must be of serious magnitude if the court is to be persuaded to exercise its original jurisdiction.[4]

The court between 1789 and April 1, 1993, issued decisions in 172 original jurisdiction cases.[5] In 1983, the court opined it possesses "substantial discretion to make case-by-case judgments as to the practical necessity of an original forum in the court of particular disputes within constitutional jurisdiction," and in 1992 stressed its judgments relative to its case-by-case jurisdiction rest upon prudential and equitable standards.[6]

In contrast to other trial courts where a plaintiff may file a complaint with the clerk of the court, a Supreme Court rule provides that a plaintiff state first must seek the court's expressed permission to file an original jurisdiction suit by filing a motion and a supporting brief with the court.[7] The respondent state also files a brief with the court. Upon receipt of such a motion, the court typically appoints a special master to receive evidence from the parties and to prepare a report with recommendations relative to facts and law.

To prevent overburdening the court with such suits, it has opined its original jurisdiction will be invoked sparingly, and the court encourages the parties to settle their disputes outside its judicial forum.[8] If the parties do not reach a settlement based on the master's report, the parties submit briefs to the court which also hears oral arguments prior to determining whether to exercise original jurisdiction. In contrast to an appeal from the decision of a trial court, the Supreme Court does not necessarily defer to the facts reported by the master.[9] Former Chief Judge Vincent L. McKusick of the Maine Supreme Court, who has served as a special master, is convinced "the court is ill-suited" to find facts or "to fashion and enforce the remedial orders that in some situations are necessary or appropriate."[10]

Prior to invoking its original jurisdiction, the court examines the party states to determine whether the complainant state is only a nominal party, the controversy is justiciable, and the case is an appropriate one.

The Parties

The court investigates the character of the parties to a controversy to determine whether each state is a genuine party. In 1972, the court refused to invoke its original jurisdiction in response to a motion to file a complaint by Illinois against a city in another state because a city is not a state, although it is a political subdivision of a state.[11] The court also denied permission to Puerto Rico to sue Iowa seeking issuance of a writ of mandamus ordering the rendition of a fugitive from justice to Puerto Rico, possibly because the writ would be served upon the governor and not the state.[12]

Similarly, the court summarily denied Oklahoma's motion to file a complaint against Arkansas because the latter was only a nominal party and the real parties were codefendent municipalities and private corporations who allegedly were polluting waters flowing into Oklahoma.[13]

The court also seeks to determine whether the complainant state has standing to bring suit as a state in its proprietary capacity or as *parens patriae* (father of its people), a right the court first established in 1900 in *Louisiana v. Texas.*[14] It must be noted that the Eleventh Amendment to the U.S. Constitution prohibits the filing of a suit by a citizen of one state against another state without its expressed consent. In 1971, Pennsylvania's challenge of a New Jersey community income tax was denied because the suit was "nothing more than a collectivity of private suits against New Jersey for taxes withheld from private parties."[15] The court emphasized a state may sue as *parens patriae* provided "its sovereign or quasi-sovereign interests are implicated and it is not merely litigating as a volunteer for the personal claims of its citizens."[16]

The Seabrook Case.   The levying by the 1991 New Hampshire General Court (state legislature) of a statewide *ad valorem* property tax of 0.64 percent on the Seabrook Nuclear Power Plant—owned by twelve utilities including ones in other states—was challenged by Connecticut, Massachusetts, and Rhode Island which sought to invoke the court's original jurisdiction by alleging that the tax and related tax credit were unconstitutional. None of the three states levies an *ad valorem* statewide property tax on nuclear power plants located in their respective states or offers a tax credit against their business profits taxes for the property taxes paid on the Seabrook plant.

In view of the fact that the tax was levied on private utility companies and not upon the plaintiff states, the motion for leave to file a complaint invoking the court's original jurisdiction immediately raised the question whether the states had the right to invoke the court's original jurisdiction.

The southern New England states sued in their proprietary capacity as consumers of electricity generated at the plant and in their capacity as *parens patriae* representing their citizens who consume electricity generated at the plant. The states argued the tax violated (*i*) the supremacy clause of the U.S. Constitution by contravening the Tax Reform Act of 1976 which prohibits the taxing of electricity in a discriminatory manner, (*ii*) the commerce clause by imposing an undue burden on interstate commerce, (*iii*) the Fourteenth Amendment by depriving the states and their citizens of equal protection of the laws, and (*iv*) the privileges and immunities clause.[17] The heart of the complaint was that New Hampshire, while levying the new tax on the Seabrook plant, did not levy a property tax on non-nuclear power electrical generating stations.

New Hampshire responded by maintaining that (*i*) the plaintiff states lacked standing to sue, (*ii*) the suit was premature as the tax had not yet been passed through to consumers, (*iii*) an alternative forum could provide relief, (*iv*) any injury would not be substantial, and (*v*) plaintiffs would not prevail on the merits of their suit.[18]

The court rejected the New Hampshire answer brief by granting the plaintiff states' motion.[19] On April 27, the court appointed McKusick as a special master to investigate the dispute and report to the court. Upon recommendation of the special master, the Supreme Court granted the motion of the involved out-of-state utilities to intervene in the case.[20]

On December 30, 1992, Special Master McKusick released a report containing his recommended conclusions of law which favored the plaintiff states. He concluded that the case was an appropriate one for the Supreme Court's original jurisdiction and that New Hampshire's "changed circumstance" argument is "an argument on the merits rather than an assertion of a jurisdictional flaw."[21] The special master also noted there was no alternative forum for this suit which raises issues the Supreme Court never considered.[22]

Stunned by the special master's report, New Hampshire officials commenced to examine amendment of the power plant property tax and its linked tax credit in order to reach an out-of-court settlement with the public utility companies. On April 14, 1993, New Hampshire and the out-of-state owners of the power plant reached an agreement. The U.S. Supreme Court had scheduled oral arguments in the case for April 19, 1993. On April 16, 1994, the General Court enacted into law the agreement reached with the out-of-state owners, and on the same day the Supreme Court dismissed the case.[23]

The negotiations leading to the out-of-court settlement of the dispute suggest that Connecticut, Massachusetts, and Rhode Island were acting *parens patriae* for their electric utility companies and not *parens patriae* for all citizen consumers of electricity in their states. All negotiations for the settlement were conducted by New Hampshire Senior Assistant Attorney General Harold T. Judd with attorneys representing the electric utility companies.[24] Although a representative of an attorney general of one of the plaintiff states would attend a negotiation meeting, the representative was not an active participant in the meeting. Mr. Judd reported: "If the other states were not acting *parens patriae*, why did they let us keep the $35 million we had collected?"[25] He also noted there is no commitment by New Hampshire not to reenact the tax credit in the future.

It is difficult to escape the conclusion that this suit should have been dismissed by the U.S. Supreme Court, and the concerned electric utilities should have sought relief in the U.S. District Court.

Justiciable Controversy

The court also examines an interstate controversy closely to determine whether its nature is justiciable and thus makes its adjudication by a law court necessary. In 1940, the court opined:

In order to constitute a proper controversy under original jurisdiction, it must appear that the complaining state has suffered a wrong through the action of the other state, furnishing ground for judicial redress, or is asserting a right against the other state which is susceptible of judicial enforcement according to the accepted principles of the common law or equity systems of jurisprudence.[26]

In 1966, the court in *Delaware v. New York* denied Delaware's motion for leave to file a complaint seeking to enjoin the "state unit" (winner receives all votes) Electoral College Voting System.[27] The denial appears to have been based upon the nonjusticiability of the controversy.

The court takes cognizance of a suit raising the possibility of a large number of suits in equity involving mutually exclusive claims. A 1939 decision involved four states each claiming the right to levy an estate tax. If each state could levy a tax, the estate would be exhausted. Hence, the court exercised its original jurisdiction on the ground the dispute was a justiciable one.[28]

In a somewhat similar case, the court in 1978 opined the suit over the domicile of decedent Howard Hughes was not a justiciable interstate controversy and the issue should be litigated in each of the involved states.[29] Four years later, however, the court invoked its original jurisdiction in the case as the result of a later motion to file a complaint in which those in charge of executing the estate of the decedent maintained that adverse decisions in California and Texas would lead to the exhaustion of the entire estate by state and federal inheritance taxes.[30]

The court also bases its denials on non-ripeness and mootness. Relative to the former, four justices dissented from the Hughes decision by opining the controversy was not ripe because the two states had not obtained unsatisfied tax judgments.[31]

In 1981, the court summarily denied without prejudice California's suit to enjoin Texas and four other states from quarantining the former's fruits and vegetables to prevent the spread of the Mediterranean fruit fly.[32] The controversy was mooted by discontinuance of the quarantines.

Appropriateness

The Supreme Court applies appropriateness as a third criterion for determining whether to exercise original jurisdiction. Because of its crowded calendar, the court will approve a state motion for leave to file a complaint only if the court concludes the case is an appropriate one for the exercise of original jurisdiction. Specifically, the court has developed three tests of appropriateness.

The court in 1971 employed the appropriateness criterion for the first time in a suit by a state against a corporation and subsequently extended the criterion to three interstate controversies.[33] Three factors are considered by the court: parties to the suit, seriousness of the subject matter, and existence of an alternative forum.

The court is most apt to exercise its original jurisdiction if both parties are states in their sovereign capacities. Traditionally, the court has exercised its original jurisdiction in boundary and water rights controversies because states are parties and the controversies are serious. On the other hand, the court denied summarily California's motion to file a complaint against West Virginia alleging breach of contract relative to scheduled football games between San Jose State University and the University of West Virginia which the court would have had to adjudicate on the basis of state law.[34] A state court was the appropriate forum for such a suit.

The third factor—an alternative form—is designed to limit use of original jurisdiction on the ground the controversy can be adjudicated by another court. In 1976, the court denied Arizona's motion to file a complaint against New Mexico because Arizona public utilities and an Arizona political subdivision had filed suit in a New Mexico court raising the identical question regarding the U.S. Constitution.[35]

Similarly, the court denied Louisiana's motion to file a complaint against Mississippi because Louisiana had intervened in a suit between private parties in a Louisiana court with respect to whether an island in the Mississippi River was in Louisiana or Mississippi.[36]

In a law review article, McKusick deduced that the existence of an alternative forum apparently was the major reason the court summarily denied motions by one state to sue another state in approximately one-half of the cases "and was a significant factor in every case where the court published an opinion explaining its reason for rejecting the suit as inappropriate for its original jurisdiction."[37] He concluded that the court's gatekeeping rules have made its original jurisdiction "almost as discretionary as its certiorari jurisdiction over appellate cases, . . ."[38]

ENFORCEMENT OF DECREES

It is apparent that certain original case judgments, such as one establishing boundaries between states and domiciles of decedents, are self-executing. Enforcement problems, however, may arise relative to judgments that are not self-executing.

The ability of the Supreme Court to enforce its decrees has been the subject of controversy since the 1793 Georgia State Legislature reacted to the court's decision allowing a citizen of South Carolina to sue Georgia by threatening to hang any person complying with the decision.[39]

In 1860, Chief Justice Taney in *Kentucky v. Dennison* dismissed Kentucky's petition for issuance of a writ of mandamus directing the governor of Ohio to return a fugitive from justice by opining that "the federal government . . . has no power to impose on a state officer, as such, any duty whatever and compel him to perform it. . . ."[40]

In 1918, however, the court in *Virginia v. West* Virginia ruled a state is subject, under the constitution, to the judicial power and the court can "enforce the judgment by resort to appropriate remedies."[41] The case involved a 1906 suit by Virginia against West Virginia and a $12 million judgment obtained by Virginia in 1915. West Virginia failed to satisfy the judgment and Virginia prayed for issuance of a writ of mandamus. West Virginia complied with the court's judgment in 1919 and the question of enforcement became moot.

It remains unclear whether the court can direct a state to exercise its discretionary legislative powers and the court recognizes this restraint by granting extensions of time for a state to comply with a decree. It also should be noted that the constitution (Art. IV, §4) guarantees each state a republican form of government, and this guarantee appears to rule out the use of the contempt power to force a state legislature to take a specific action.

INTERSTATE SUITS

The states, by ratifying the U.S. Constitution, relinquished their sovereignty relative to delegated powers and became quasi-sovereign governments. Although a state is not an international juristic person, the Supreme Court wrote in 1902 that it sits as an international tribunal in interstate suits and applies "federal law, state law, and international law, as the exigencies of the particular case may demand."[42] Five years later, the court reemphasized its 1902 opinion by explaining that interstate relations are governed by international law.[43]

The court, however, has not explained its reference to international law or its application to interstate disputes. It is apparent, however, that interstate compacts are similar to international treaties. In 1934, the court opined that interpretation of a provision of an interstate compact requires use of rules of treaty construction, including diplomatic correspondence but not verbal statements of treaty negotiators.[44]

The court in effect has developed an interstate common law that is a synthesis of the common law and international law. A note in the *Stanford Law Review* commented:

The decision of the court to apply an interstate substantive law appears to be a sound one. The alternative would be a set of choice-of-law rules referring the court to the internal law of a state which stands in a certain relation to the transaction. However, interstate controversies typically involve acts having consequences beyond the borders of any one state. Automatically looking to a given state's law would be to impose the law of one "quasi-sovereign" on another—a policy which seems repugnant to the underlying philosophy of the original jurisdiction.[45]

The court opined in 1906 that rules established by its decisions in interstate suits were reversible only by the court, constitutional amendment, or compact ratified by Congress.[46]

McKusick reported that between October 1, 1961, and April 25, 1993, the court adjudicated twenty-two boundary cases, sixteen right-to-water cases, two water abatement cases, three state escheat of unclaimed property cases, three state taxes cases, eight state regulation cases, and four miscellaneous cases.[47]

Boundary Suits

The boundaries of a state are delineated in state statutes, but such delineation does not require a neighboring state to recognize such boundaries.[48] The early boundary disputes were the product of vague land grants from the Crown and surveyors' errors. New Hampshire, for example, interpreted the Mason Grant of 1629 as giving the state title to land west of the Connecticut River, but New York claimed the same territory. The Congress in 1791 settled this dispute by admitting the disputed territory to the Union as the state of Vermont.

In 1799, the Supreme Court in *New York v. Connecticut* for the first time established a boundary line between states.[49] The court in 1927 settled a boundary dispute between Mexico and Texas on the basis of a condition established by the Congress for the admission of the New Mexico Territory to the Union as a state.[50] Congress had enacted a statute in 1850 establishing the boundary between Texas and New Mexico and made acceptance of the boundary a condition of admission for the New Mexico Territory which accepted the boundary and incorporated it into its state constitution.

Rivers historically have served as boundaries between states, but disputes arise because of natural changes in the course of rivers and disagreement as to where the boundary line is in the river. In 1984, the court in *Louisiana v. Mississippi* held that the live thalweg in the Mississippi River's navigable channel was the boundary line.[51] The thalweg rule, developed in international law, posits that the original flow of a stream continues to be the boundary between nation states when the river changes into a new channel.

The court in this case noted that the definition of thalweg is not precise and that the court in *Louisiana v. Mississippi* in 1906 had viewed the term as "the middle or deepest or most navigable channel."[52] The deepest or most navigable channel is not necessarily alike. Since the parties agreed that the boundary is defined by the thalweg and traffic on the river defines the thalweg, the court had to determine only the normal course of traffic by vessels. This rule has become part of the interstate common law developed by the court for establishing interstate river boundaries. In 1995, the court agreed to hear Mississippi's challenge of the special master's finding that the thalweg had shifted, as river currents had eroded parts of an island and built it up elsewhere, thereby merging the island into the Louisiana river bank.[53]

The court also settles boundary disputes in accordance with the doctrine of acquiescence. For example, the court ruled in favor of California in a dispute with Nevada in 1980 because Nevada did not object to the boundary line for a century.[54] Eleven years later in *Illinois v. Kentucky*, the court opined that Kentucky to justify its boundary claim on the basis of acquiescence "would need to show by a preponderance of the evidence ... a long and continuous possession of, and assertion of sovereignty over, the territory...." Kentucky was unable to provide such evidence.[55]

A boundary dispute can be settled by an interstate compact approved by the Congress (see Ch. 3). New Hampshire in 1973 filed suit against Maine, but the states in 1974 signed an interstate agreement settling the dispute which was approved by the Supreme Court.[56] Similarly, North Carolina and South Carolina reached an agreement to settle a boundary dispute and sought the approval of the Congress for the agreement.[57]

Boundary disputes are also the source of other interstate disputes. The Portsmouth Naval Shipyard is located on an island in the middle of the Piscataqua River which serves as the boundary between New Hampshire and Maine. Maine levies a personal income tax and New Hampshire does not. Maine claims the island and levied its income tax on workers at the Shipyard. New Hampshire objected, and in 1990 the U.S. Department of Justice advised the Navy to stop withholding the income taxes from New Hampshire workers until the boundary dispute is resolved.[58]

Water Suits

These suits involve pollution of streams flowing into another state and the allocation of river water between two or more states. Sewage became a major interstate problem as the United States urbanized and municipalities continued to dispose of sewage in lakes and rivers. Early in the twentieth century a drainage canal of the Chicago Sanitary District emptied sewage into a tributary of the Mississippi River which served as a water supply for Missouri municipalities. Missouri sued Illinois in 1906 seeking the enjoining of the use of the canal for sewage disposal purposes. The court ruled that Missouri would have to offer proof of the deleterious effects of the canal discharge before the court would enjoin Illinois.[59]

A state adversely affected by water pollution originating in another state today has an alternative to suing the offending state. The federal Clean Water Act and implementing U.S. Environmental Protection Agency (EPA) regulations established minimum water quality standards throughout the United States.[60] A state adversely affected by a discharge of pollutants from an upstate river, for example, may seek EPA's assistance to require the offending state to comply with national water quality standards.

Historically, water allocation disputes were settled in accordance with the doctrine of riparian rights or the doctrine of prior apportionment. The former holds that priority to the use of water is determined by ownership of the adjoining property. The latter assigns priority to the first user of the water.

The court developed the doctrine of equitable apportionment to resolve water allocation disputes by providing for the sharing of interstate waters.[61] The Colorado River originates in the Rocky Mountains in Colorado and flows through Utah to form the Arizona boundary line with Nevada and California. Although the river is a large one which made possible the development of southern California, the great demands placed upon the river by neighboring states produced a dispute over water allocation.

Arizona sued California in 1952 contending that southern California was consuming more river water than the six other states with access to the water combined. The suit involved a 1922 interstate compact allocating the river's waters. The court in *Arizona v. California* in 1963 generally ruled in favor of Arizona when the water flow is normal, but authorized the U.S. Secretary of the Interior to allocate the water when the flow drops below normal.[62] This suit was the fifth one involving the river.

A similar controversy involved Nebraska, Colorado, and Wyoming with respect to water rights to the North Platte River. The court in 1945 entered a decree establishing interstate priorities on the river and apportioning the flow of a portion of the river during the irrigation season. Nebraska in 1986 sought an order for enforcement of the decree and injunctive relief. A special master, appointed by the court in 1987, supervised pretrial proceedings and discovery and filed his report with the court in 1992. In *Nebraska v. Wyoming*, the court in 1993 held that the decree did not grant Nebraska rights to excess waters of the Laramie River that empty into the North Platte River, and to the extent that Nebraska sought to modify the decree instead of its enforcement, a higher standard of proof showing substantial injury was required.[63]

This controversy is a continuing one. In 1995, the court allowed Nebraska to challenge Wyoming's actions relative to a tributary of the North Platte River, but denied Wyoming's request for leave to file a counter claim and a cross claim for relief under the 1945 decree.[64] The court wrote: "Simply put, Wyoming seeks to replace a simple apportionment scheme with one in which Nebraska's share would be capped at the volume of probable beneficial use, presumably to Wyoming's advantage."[65]

The court in *Texas v. New Mexico* in 1987 settled a dispute involving the 1949 Pecos River Compact which divides the river's water between New Mexico and Texas without specifying the amount to be delivered to Texas annually by New Mexico.[66] Article III(a) of the compact stipulates that "New Mexico shall not deplete by man's activities the flow of the Pecos River at the New Mexico–Texas state line below an amount which will give to Texas a quantity of water equivalent to that available to Texas under the 1947 condition."

Texas engaged in fruitless negotiations with New Mexico for many years prior to filing an original action in the court in 1974. In 1980, the court adopted the report of the special master containing a new inflow–outflow manual for determining the amount of water that Texas should receive.[67] Four years later, the court approved the inflow–outflow methodology recommended by the special master.[68] Both sides took exception to the special master's 1984 report. New Mexico argued that she was not obligated to deliver water that she was under no obligation to refrain from using. The court ruled in favor of Texas and opined that its remedy was not limited to prospective relief and could provide monetary relief. The case was returned to the special master to determine whether New Mexico should be given the choice of a monetary remedy.

The court in 1992 in *Arkansas v. Oklahoma* resolved a Clean Water Act controversy.[69] EPA issued a discharge permit to the city of Fayetteville in Arkansas in response to its 1985 request pursuant to the National Pollution Discharge Elimination System established by the Act. The discharge from the city's sewage treatment plant entered the Illinois River twenty-two miles upstream from the border between Arkansas and Oklahoma. Oklahoma challenged the permit before the agency and later before the Supreme Court on the ground the discharge violated Oklahoma's water-quality standards.

The agency's administrative law judge concluded that the discharge had a *de minimis* impact on Oklahoma's waters. The court upheld the issuance of the permit by the agency and opined its interpretation of Oklahoma's water-quality standards warranted substantial deference.

Delaware, New Jersey, and Pennsylvania engaged in a dispute with New York for many years relative to the amount of water to be discharged into the Delaware

River from New York City reservoirs in the Catskill Mountains. These states were bound by a 1954 Supreme Court decree on water releases. Instead of reopening the suit, the plaintiff states and New York accepted the invitation of the Delaware River Basin Commission, created by a federal–interstate compact, to enter into good faith discussions to establish procedures and criteria for the management of the river's waters. After three years of such negotiations, the states reached agreement in 1983 for water management to meet needs until the year 2000.[70]

Tax Suits

Attempts by states to export taxes have been relatively common as illustrated by New Hampshire's general property tax levied on the Seabrook Nuclear Power Plant which was described and analyzed in a preceding section. In 1981, the court in *Maryland v. Louisiana* invalidated Louisiana's "first use tax" levied on natural gas extracted from wells in the Gulf of Mexico and processed in the state.[71] The tax was invalidated because it was levied on gas extracted from areas belonging to all citizens of the United States and was passed on to consumers in other states.

A relatively novel suit was brought by Wyoming against Oklahoma challenging under the Interstate Commerce clause an Oklahoma statute requiring coal-fired electric-generating plants in the state to burn a mixture of coal whose contents included a minimum of 10 percent coal mined in the state. Wyoming maintained it suffered harm as its revenue from a severance tax on coal decreased as Oklahoma utilities, which had been using only Wyoming coal, reduced their purchases of Wyoming coal in order to comply with the Oklahoma statute. The court in *Wyoming v. Oklahoma* in 1992 opined the statute violated the Interstate Commerce clause.[72] Interestingly, Justice Clarence Thomas in his dissent raised the question of *parens patriae* by writing "the primary dispute here is not between the states of Wyoming and Oklahoma, but between the private Wyoming mining companies and the state of Oklahoma, whose statute reduced the companies' sales to Oklahoma utilities."[73] He added that any state under the court's ruling will be able to proceed directly to the court if it can demonstrate that any tax revenue loss, even a *de minimis* one, is attributable to the action of another state.

Bona Vacantia Suits

All states have enacted an escheats or unclaimed property law providing that securities, interest, dividends, real property, and wages not claimed after a stipulated number of years are deemed to be abandoned and title reverts to the state.[74]

The court in *Texas v. New Jersey* in 1965 rendered a milestone decision establishing standards relative to the right of a state to take title to unclaimed property.[75] The primary rule holds that "fairness among the states requires that the right and power to escheat the debt should be accorded to the state of the creditor's last known address as shown by the debtor's books and records."[76] The secondary rule which awards the right to claim abandoned property to the debtor state recognizes that the primary rule will not resolve all escheat disputes because there may be no record of any address of the owner, or the last known address is in a state without an escheat statute. Hence, the secondary rule awards the right to escheat to the debtor's state of corporate domicile subject to a claim by a state with a superior right to escheat under the primary rule.

In 1972, the court in *Pennsylvania v. New York* adjudicated competing claims for proceeds of the Western Union Company resulting from its inability to locate the payees of money orders or to refund the money to the senders because the company did not record the addresses of the senders of money orders.[77]

The primary rule seldom applies to such funds since the addresses of payees were not known. Application of the secondary rule, according to several states, would result in the state of Western Union Company's domicile receiving a much larger share of the unclaimed funds. These states recommended a rule authorizing the state of the place of purchase to escheat under the primary rule. The court rejected this recommendation and adhered to its 1965 decision in *Texas v. New Jersey*.

In 1993, the court in *Delaware v. New York* adjudicated a controversy involving unclaimed securities.[78] Delaware alleged that $360 million in unclaimed dividends, interest, and other securities distributions were wrongfully escheated by New York. The special master, appointed by the court, recommended that the court award the right to escheat to the state in which the principal executive offices of the issuers of the securities are located. Both states objected to this recommendation.

The court held that the precedent established in *Texas v. New Jersey* required it to determine that the state in which the intermediary holding the securities is located has the right to escheat funds belonging to owners who cannot be located. The court remanded the case to the special master and noted that "if New York can establish by reference to debtors' records that the creditors who were owed particular securities distribution had last known addresses in New York," its right to escheat under the primary rule will supersede Delaware's right under the secondary rule.

SUMMARY AND CONCLUSIONS

The U.S. Supreme Court has interpreted its referee role in interstate disputes to be a discretionary one, and a state seeking to invoke the court's original jurisdiction has the burden of proof to persuade the court to exercise such jurisdiction. In deciding whether to exercise its original jurisdiction, the court seeks to determine whether the plaintiff state is a party in its own behalf and not a nominal party, the dispute is justiciable, and the case is an appropriate one.

The court has opined that it sits in interstate suits as an international tribunal but has not explained its reference to international law. Over the decades, the court has developed an interstate common law blending the English common law and international law.

Interstate suits most commonly involve boundaries and rights to water. Because of the complexity of these cases, the court appoints a special master to take evidence from the party states and prepare recommendations. The process often takes several years before a decision is rendered, and the court encourages the party states to settle their disputes through good faith negotiations.

Interstate disputes also can be resolved through interstate and federal–state compacts, negotiations, reciprocity (see Ch. 10), and congressional preemption. Congress possesses the power to amend or repeal interstate common law established by the court, thereby obviating the need for the court to adjudicate many controversies. Congress, however, has been reluctant to legislate a solution to many controversies, and the court has had to rely upon dormant commerce clause jurisprudence to resolve them. This type of jurisprudence involves the court basing its decisions on the clause in the absence of a congressional statute on the subject of the controversy. Chapter 3 explores the first of these alternative dispute reconciliation mechanisms.

NOTES

1. *Removal of Causes Act of 1920*, 41 Stat. 554, 28 U.S.C.A. §1441 (1995).

2. *Justice Improvement Act of 1988*, 102 Stat. 4646, 28 U.S.C.A. §1332 (1992 Supp.).

3. *Judiciary Act of 1789*, 1 Stat. 73 at 80–81. See also 36 Stat. 1156, 28 U.S.C.A. §1251(a) (1993). The Act also grants the Supreme Court authority to promulgate necessary rules for the conduct of business in U.S. courts.

4. *Missouri v. Illinois*, 200 U.S. 496 (1905).

5. "The Original Jurisdiction of the United States Supreme Court," *Stanford Law Review*, July 1959, pp. 665–719, and Vincent L. McKusick, "Discretionary Gatekeeping: The Supreme Court's Management of Its Original Jurisdiction Docket Since 1961," *Maine Law Review*, Vol. 45, 1993, p. 188.

6. *Texas v. New Mexico*, 462 U.S. 554 at 570 (1983), and *Wyoming v. Oklahoma*, 112 S.Ct. 789 at 798 (1992).

7. *United States Supreme Court Rule 17*.

8. See *Arizona v. New Mexico*, 425 U.S. 794 (1978), and *California v. Southern Pacific Company*, 457 U.S. 229 (1985).

9. Dissent of Justice William H. Rehnquist in *Maryland v. Louisiana*, 451 U.S. 725 at 765 (1981).

10. McKusick, "Discretionary Gatekeeping," p. 193.

11. *Illinois v. City of Milwaukee*, 406 U.S. 91 (1972).

12. *Puerto Rico v. Iowa*, 464 U.S. 1034 (1984).

13. *Oklahoma v. Arkansas*, 460 U.S. 1020 (1983).

14. *Louisiana v. Texas*, 176 U.S. 1 (1900).

15. *Pennsylvania v. New Jersey*, 426 U.S. 660 at 666 (1976).

16. *Ibid.*, p. 665.

17. *United States Constitution*, Art. I, §8; Art. IV, §2; Art. VI; and Fourteenth Amendment, and *Tax Reform Act of 1976*, 90 Stat. 1914, 15 U.S.C.A. §391 (1993 Supp.).

18. *Connecticut et al. v. New Hampshire. Answer of Defendant State of New Hampshire*, March 24, 1992.

19. *Connecticut, Massachusetts, and Rhode Island v. New Hampshire*, 112 S.Ct. 2951–62 (1992).

20. *Ibid.*

21. *Connecticut, Massachusetts, and Rhode Island: Report of the Special Master*, December 30, 1992, p. 16.

22. *Ibid.*, p. 17.

23. *Connecticut, Massachusetts, and Rhode Island v. New Hampshire*, 113 S.Ct. 1837 (1993).

24. Telephone interview with New Hampshire Senior Assistant Attorney General Harold T. Judd, October 22, 1993.

25. *Ibid.*

26. *Massachusetts v. Missouri*, 308 U.S. 1 at 15 (1940).

27. *Delaware v. New York*, 385 U.S. 895 (1966).

28. *Texas v. Florida*, 306 U.S. 398 (1939).

29. *California v. Texas*, 437 U.S. 601 (1978).

30. *California v. Texas*, 457 U.S. 164 (1982).

31. *California v. Texas*, 457 U.S. 164 (1982).

32. *California v. Texas*, 454 U.S. 886 (1981).

33. *Ohio v. Wyandotte Chemicals Corporation*, 401 U.S. 493 at 499 (1971); *Arizona v. New Mexico*, 425 U.S. 794 at 796–7 (1976); *California v. West Virginia*, 457 U.S. 1027 (1981); and *Louisiana v. Mississippi*, 488 U.S. 990 (1988).

34. *California v. West Virginia*, 475 U.S. 1027 (1981).

35. *Arizona v. New Mexico*, 425 U.S. 794 (1976).

36. *Louisiana v. Mississippi*, 488 U.S. 990 (1988).

37. McKusick, "Discretionary Gatekeeping," p. 202.

38. *Ibid.*

39. *Chisholm v. Georgia*, 2 Dallas 419 (1793).

40. *Kentucky v. Dennison*, 65 U.S. 66 at 107 (1860).

41. *Virginia v. West Virginia*, 246 U.S. 565 U.S. at 600 and 605 (1918).

42. *Kansas v. Colorado*, 185 U.S. 125 at 146 (1902).

43. *Kansas v. Colorado*, 206 U.S. 46 at 97 (1907).

44. *Arizona v. California*, 292 U.S. 341 at 359–60 (1934).

45. "The Original Jurisdiction of the United States Supreme Court," pp. 682–3.

46. *Missouri v. Illinois*, 200 U.S. 496 at 520 (1906).

47. McKusick, "Discretionary Gatekeeping," pp. 207–15.

48. See, for example, *New York State Law*, §§2–7 (McKinney 1984).

49. *New York v. Connecticut*, 4 U.S. 3 (1799).

50. *New Mexico v. Texas*, 275 U.S. 279 (1927).

51. *Louisiana v. Mississippi*, 466 U.S. 96 (1984).

52. *Louisiana v. Mississippi*, 202 U.S. 1 at 49 (1906).

53. *Mississippi v. Louisiana*, 115 S.Ct. 1310 (1995).

54. *California v. Nevada*, 447 U.S. 123 (1980).

55. *Illinois v. Kentucky*, 111 S.Ct. 1877 at 1881 (1991).

56. "New Hampshire Goes to High Court in Lobster Dispute," *The New York Times*, June 7, 1973, p. 43, and "230-Year Border Fight Settled by Maine and New Hampshire," *The New York Times*, July 11, 1974, p. 18.

57. "North Carolina–South Carolina Seaward Boundary Agreement," *Congressional Record*, September 29, 1981, pp. H 6667-8.

58. "Justice Department Sides with NH Workers at Shipyard . . . If It's Not in Maine," *The Union Leader* (Manchester, N.H.), October 24, 1990, pp. 1 and 16.

59. *Missouri v. Illinois*, 200 U.S. 496 (1906).

60. *Clean Water Act of 1977*, 91 Stat. 1566, 33 U.S.C.A. §1251 (1986 and 1994 Supp.). For details on congressional establishment of minimum national standards, see Joseph F. Zimmerman, *Federal Preemption: The Silent Revolution* (Ames: Iowa State University Press, 1991).

61. *Kansas v. Colorado*, 206 U.S. 46 (1907).

62. *Arizona v. California*, 373 U.S. 546 (1963).

63. *Nebraska v. Wyoming*, 113 S.Ct. 1689 (1993).

64. *Nebraska v. Wyoming*, 115 S.Ct. 1933 (1995).

65. *Ibid.*

66. *Texas v. New Mexico*, 482 U.S. 124 (1987).

67. *Texas v. New Mexico*, 446 U.S. 540 (1980).

68. *Texas v. New Mexico*, 467 U.S. 1238 (1984).

69. *Arkansas v. Oklahoma*, 112 S.Ct. 1046 (1992).

70. News Release from the Office of Governor Mario M. Cuomo of New York, February 23, 1983.

71. *Maryland v. Louisiana*, 451 U.S. 725 (1981).

72. *Wyoming v. Oklahoma*, 112 S.Ct. 789 (1992).

73. *Ibid.* at 811.

74. For an example, see the *New York Abandoned Property Law*, §511 (McKinney 1991).

75. *Texas v. New Jersey*, 379 U.S. 674 (1965).

76. *Ibid.* at 680-1.

77. *Pennsylvania v. New York*, 407 U.S. 206 (1972).

78. *Delaware v. New York*, 113 S.Ct. 1550 (1993).

3

Interstate Compacts and Agreements

Horizontal intergovernmental relations are of great importance in the U.S. federal system although they typically are overshadowed in the media by vertical inter- governmental relations. Interstate compacts and agreements are formal methods of interstate cooperation and settlement of disputes. They are traceable in origin to disputes between British colonies which were settled by litigation or negotiations leading to an agreement that was submitted to the Crown for approval.[1] Use of a compact to resolve a dispute relieves the U.S. Supreme Court of the burden of adjudicating an interstate dispute as described in Chapter 2.

The drafters of the Articles of Confederation and Perpetual Union were aware that bilateral and multilateral compacts could be employed to solve interstate dis- putes and allow cooperative action to solve problems not coinciding with bound- aries of a single state. Hence, they included Article VI stipulating that "no two or more states shall enter into any treaty, confederation, or alliance without the consent of the United States in Congress assembled, specifying accurately the pur- pose for which the same is to be entered into, and how long it shall continue." The requirement of congressional consent was included in the articles to ensure that two or more states would not enter into an agreement that would split the confed- eracy or be directed against other states. A number of compacts were entered into under the articles with the consent of the unicameral Congress, including a 1785 compact entered into by Maryland and Virginia establishing rules for navigation and fishing on the Chesapeake Bay and the Potomac River.

Numerous boundary disputes were raging when delegates to the Philadelphia Convention were drafting the U.S. Constitution. They recognized that interstate compacts were capable, among other things, of resolving such disputes, but also could cause problems for the Union. Interestingly, delegates did not debate the interstate compact clause and the authors of the *Federalist Papers* only made a passing reference to it. Although an interstate compact is similar to an international treaty, the constitution makes an important distinction between the two.

Article I, Section 10 of the constitution absolutely forbids states to enter into any alliance, confederation, or treaty but authorizes them to enter into compacts with each other or a foreign state with the consent of Congress. The ability of states to enter into compacts also may be restricted by national government treaties with foreign nations, congressional statutes, and state constitutions which may contain provisions limiting the freedom of the states to act.

The constitution's compact clause is similar to the compact clause in the articles and, by negative implication, authorizes states as equals to enter into legally binding compacts subject to a possible congressional veto. Felix Frankfurter and James M. Landis wrote in 1925 that "by putting this authority for state action in a section dealing with restrictions upon the states, the significance of what was granted has probably been considerably minimized."[2]

An approved compact establishes a contractual relationship between the signatory states which is protected from impairment by the contract clause of the constitution.[3] In common with an international treaty, a compact supersedes conflicting state laws and hence compacting states surrender part of their respective sovereignty.

The drafters of the compact clause viewed it as providing flexibility for the new federal system in solving regional problems by the cooperative exercise of reserved powers, thereby negating the need for Congress to exercise delegated powers to solve the problems. Hence, the compact instrument was included in the constitution as a tool for defining, approaching, and solving interstate problems without congressional intervention.

An interstate compact establishes what is essentially a uniform law in the party states on a given subject, but differs in origin from uniform laws which do not require congressional consent. The latter are enacted by state legislatures adopting model uniform laws drafted by the National Conference of Commissioners of Uniform Laws, a topic examined in Chapter 10. A compact authorizing a state to give its laws extraterritorial effect must comport with the Due Process of Law clause, according to a 1877 U.S. Supreme Court decision in *Pennover v. Neff*.[4]

The compact device is capable of being employed by states as corporate entities on a permanent, temporary, or standby basis, and to establish a developmental or regulatory agency to exercise powers on an interjurisdictional basis, achieve economies of scale, and solve interstate coordination problems. Frederick L. Zimmermann and Mitchell Wendell wrote in 1951 that "after a century and more of narrowly restricted use, the interstate compact has begun to show an unsuspected versatility."[5]

NEGOTIATION AND RATIFICATION

The constitution contains no required procedures for the preparation of an interstate compact, and the negotiation of a compact differs significantly from the negotiation of an international treaty by the president of the United States. The governors of the states typically play no direct role in negotiating compacts.

All compacts until 1930 were drafted by joint commissions whose members were appointed by the concerned governors. More recently, *ad hoc* arrangements have led to the adoption of compacts. For example, the Interstate Commission on Crime—composed of attorneys general and other state officers—negotiated the Compact on Parolees and Probationers without specific legislative authorization. Regional governors' conferences also have produced compacts, including the Southern Regional Education Compact.

The federal Low Level Radioactive Waste Policy Act of 1980 made the states responsible for the disposal of such wastes and encouraged the states to enter into interstate disposal compacts for submittal to Congress for approval.[6] The National Conference of State Legislatures played an active role in promoting the formation of nine such compacts.

The subject of a proposed compact determines the degree of difficulty state officials will encounter during the negotiation phase. If the compact addresses a common and relatively simple problem, negotiators may be able to reach a speedy agreement. This type of compact is illustrated by a mutual aid forest fire compact and is the exception, since most proposed compacts deal with complex problems and issues.

A proposed interstate compact typically involves important administrative, financial, substantive, and technical questions. Negotiators lack authority to commit state funds to solving future problems, and the state constitution may require voter approval before certain actions can be taken. Although one might assume that a bilateral compact would be easier to negotiate than a multilateral compact, experience often has revealed the reverse. It required twelve years for California and Nevada to negotiate a bilateral interstate water rights allocation compact.

If a proposed compact necessitates a long-term commitment of funds, negotiators tend to be cautious in reaching an agreement. State negotiators may discover that their state legislatures will not approve a compact unless special provisions for legislative oversight are included in the compact. Article X of the Port Authority of New York and New Jersey Compact, for example, requires the Authority to submit a comprehensive plan for its activities to the New Jersey and New York state legislatures for approval prior to its implementation. Similarly, article XI requires that development plans "supplementary to or amendatory of any plan theretofore adopted" must be submitted to the two state legislatures for approval prior to implementation. And article XVI grants the governor of New York and the governor of New Jersey each a veto power over any action taken by the Port Authority Commissioners. This power has been exercised occasionally. In 1990, the decision of the commissioners to raise tolls on the Hudson River tunnels and George Washington Bridge was rescinded due to the threat by the governors to veto the increase.[7]

Assuming the compact negotiators reach an agreement on the wording of a compact, they typically must seek the enactment of the compact into state law by their respective state legislatures. Many of the political concerns raised during the negotiation process arise again during legislative consideration of a proposed compact. New Jersey and New York avoided this problem by enacting statutes in 1921 providing the Port of New York Authority compact "when signed and sealed by the Commissioners of each State as hereinbefore provided and the Attorney General of the State of New York and the Attorney General of New Jersey shall become binding upon the" two states.[8]

Furthermore, all governors may veto a compact enacted by the state legislature. Assuming the proposed compact overcomes these obstacles, it still may not become operational unless it is a self-executing one. The New York State Legislature enacted the nonself-executing Interstate Compact for the Supervision of Parolees in 1936, but the state's participation in the compact did not become effective until 1944 because of the refusal of Governor Herbert H. Lehman to execute the compact.

In 1955, Wallace R. Vawter reported that four and three-quarter years was the average time required for negotiating, ratifying, and securing the consent of Congress for a compact.[9] He also reported that it required an average of six and three-quarter years for thirty natural resources compacts to become effective, and eight and three-quarter years for nineteen river management control compacts to become effective.

The expenditure of large amounts of time does not always pay off, as states repeatedly have set out to establish a compact only to fail after years of effort. A number of proposed interstate compacts—including the Interstate Tobacco Compact, New England Development Authority Compact, Interstate Crime Compact, and Potomac River Basin Compact—failed to be enacted by the requisite number of states. The proposed Potomac River Compact—between Maryland, Virginia, and District of Columbia—was laid to rest in 1976 when the negotiators were unable to reach agreement after ten years of active promotion. Although the Delaware River Basin Compact became effective in 1961, two proposed Delaware River Basin Compacts failed to gain approval in the 1920s, and a similar proposed compact in the 1950s died in a Pennsylvania Senate Committee after being approved by the other states and the Pennsylvania House of Representatives. The New England Pollution Compact, approved by the Vermont State Legislature, did not become effective because the governor of Vermont vetoed it on the ground that the legislature failed to include in the compact a pledge to abate existing pollution.

It is difficult to disagree with the conclusion of Zimmermann and Wendell that "there are weaknesses and difficulties in the use of the interstate compact. The most obvious difficulty is the necessity for securing agreement among several jurisdictions."[10]

CONGRESSIONAL CONSENT

The purpose of the congressional consent requirement is to protect the Union by controlling collective actions of the states. The framers of the consent provision were particularly concerned with boundary compacts because various states claimed wide tracts of land in the western United States and such compacts might affect the balance of power in the federal system. In common with the dormant interstate commerce clause, the compact clause can be employed by courts to invalidate state actions in violation of the clause in the face of inaction by Congress.

Types of Congressional Consent

The constitution does not establish a procedure for congressional consent for compacts or its nature. In practice, Congress has given its consent prior and subsequent to the signing of a compact, and the consent may be a blanket approval for all compacts dealing with a specified subject or may be specific to a given compact. Congress, for example, in the Weeks Act of 1911 gave its consent in advance to states to form compacts "for the purpose of conserving the forests and water supply" of compacting states.[11] More recently, Congress granted permission in advance to states to form interstate compacts to develop and operate airport facilities.[12]

The Supreme Court in *Green v. Biddle* in 1823 explained that the constitution does not specify the mode or form of congressional consent.[13] The suit involved a congressional statute referring to the Virginia–Kentucky Interstate Compact of 1789 and consenting to the admission of Kentucky to the Union. Kentucky had challenged the compact on the ground it lacked congressional consent. The court subsequently in *Florida v. Georgia* in 1854 emphasized that a boundary agreement reached by the two states would be invalid unless approved by Congress.[14]

In *Virginia v. Tennessee*, the Supreme Court in 1893 made it clear that congressional consent was not required for all types of compacts to become effective by opining consent was required only for compacts tending to increase "the political power or influence" of the party states and to encroach "upon the full and free exercise of federal authority."[15] The two states had approved a boundary compact early in the nineteenth century, but had not obtained the consent of Congress. Virginia sought to have the compact nullified and a new boundary line established. The court held that congressional reliance upon the compact's terms for revenue and judicial purposes constituted implied consent. Hence, compacts can be approved by Congress by implication as well as expressed consent.

This decision made a distinction between political compacts requiring consent of Congress and nonpolitical compacts that become effective without such consent. The court in this case provided the following example:

If ... Virginia should come into possession and ownership of a small parcel of land in New York which the latter State might desire to acquire as a site for a public building, it would hardly be deemed essential for the latter State to obtain the consent of Congress before it would make a valid agreement with Virginia for the purchase of the land.[16]

The Multistate Tax Compact was challenged in *United States Steel Corporation v. Multistate Tax Commission* in 1978 on the ground the compact had not received congressional approval, but the Supreme Court rejected the challenge and opined the compact did not "authorize the member states to exercise any powers they could not exercise in its absence...."[17]

The Northeastern Interstate Forest Fire Protection Compact, consented to by Congress in 1949, is distinctive in providing that any Canadian province contiguous to a compact state may become a member of the compact with the consent of Congress.[18]

Nonpolitical compacts often are submitted to Congress, and it can withhold its consent. The 1921 Port of New York Authority Compact was submitted to Congress because bond counsels advised that the congressional imprimatur would make the Authority's bonds more attractive to conservative investors who were not accustomed to a new organizational innovation—an interstate public authority. Congress granted its consent.

Congress can grant its consent without a time limit, but occasionally has placed a sunset clause in its consent resolution. The Interstate Oil and Gas Compact of 1935 and the Atlantic States Marine Fisheries Compact of 1942 were subject to such a clause, but these restrictions later were removed by Congress.[19] Interstate compacts entered into under the Low Level Radioactive Waste Policy Act of 1980 are subject to a five-year approval provision.[20]

Congress can attach conditions to its approval of a compact as an implied power. Chief Justice Charles Evans Hughes wrote in 1937 in *James v. Dravo* Contracting Company that "it can hardly be doubted that in giving consent Congress may impose conditions."[21] In enacting the Boulder Canyon Project Act of 1928, Congress consented to the Colorado River Compact subject to specified conditions and approval of the modified compact by California and five of the other six concerned states.[22] In approving the Wabash Valley Compact in 1959 and the Washington Metropolitan Area Transit Regulation Compact in 1960, Congress required each compact agency to publish specified information and data.[23] In addition, Congress in consenting to the Wabash Valley Compact in Section 5 specifically reserved the right to amend or repeal its consent.

Similarly, the U.S. Court of Appeals in *Tobin v. United States* in 1962 opined that Congress may attach conditions to compacts and the U.S. Supreme Court denied a petition in this case for an issuance of a writ of certiorari.[24]

Zimmermann and Wendell in 1976 stressed that many compacts do not require congressional consent and added:

A busy Congress, in a world of crisis, is hard-pressed even to perform its duties as a national legislature. Consent bills for interstate compacts dealing with issues in the realm of state activity, law, and administration, with interstate jurisdictional problems and with the settlement of interstate equities, normally serve only to clutter congressional calendars and complicate and obstruct interstate cooperation.[25]

Effects of Congressional Consent

When Congress gives its consent to a compact by an act or joint resolution, it is subject to a presidential veto. The failure of the proposed Connecticut River and Merrimack River flood control compacts to be approved in the 1930s has been attributed to the threat of a presidential veto. In 1939, President Franklin D. Roosevelt refused to approve a joint resolution granting consent in advance to states to enter into compacts pertaining to fishing in the Atlantic Ocean and wrote "it would be unwise" to grant such consent "in connection with subjects described only in broad outline....."[26] In 1942, President Roosevelt vetoed the Republican River Compact, but subsequently approved a modified compact.[27]

The Supreme Court in 1938 ruled in *Hinderlider v. La Plata River* and *Cherry Creek Ditch Company* that congressional consent to a compact does not make it equivalent to a United States treaty or statute.[28] In 1940 in *Delaware River Joint Toll Bridge Commission v. Colburn*, however, the court opined that a compact consented to by Congress "involves a federal 'title, right, privilege, or immunity' which when explicitly identified and claimed in a state court may be reviewed here on certiorari....."[29]

In 1994, the U.S. Supreme Court in *Hess v. Port Authority Trans-Hudson Corporation* held that a bistate agency created by an interstate compact with the consent of Congress is not cloaked with the immunity from suit in a federal court granted to states by the Eleventh Amendment to the U.S. Constitution.[30] The five-member majority opinion stressed that subjecting a self-financing interstate compact agency to suit in the U.S. District Court does not subject a state treasury to vulnerability. In other words, such an agency is entitled to immunity from suit only if the state provides funds for judgments against the agency.

A revolutionary decision involving the compact clause was rendered by the Supreme Court in *Cuyler v. Adams* in 1981: A compact becomes federal law when Congress grants its consent.[31] Until this decision was rendered, federal courts were bound since 1874 to accept the interpretation of state law by the state's highest court.[32] By deeming that congressional consent transforms an interstate compact into federal law, the Supreme Court in Cuyler was free to interpret the concerned Pennsylvania statute and ignore the interpretation of the statute by the Pennsylvania Supreme Court.

Congressional consent suggests Congress possesses the authority to enforce compacts, yet enforcement generally is left to the courts. Individuals and states may challenge in a state or U.S. court the validity of a compact or seek to have its obligations enforced. Although the Eleventh Amendment prohibits a citizen of one state to sue another state without its consent, a citizen can challenge a compact or its execution in a state or national court against an individual or in a proceeding to prevent a government officer from enforcing a compact.[33] Such a suit brought in a state court could be removed to the U.S. District Court under provisions of the Removal of Causes Act of 1920 because the state court "... might conceivably be interested in the outcome of the case....."[34]

What effect does an approved compact have on an existing congressional statute containing inconsistent provisions? The congressional consent could be interpreted as repealing the conflicting provisions of the prior statute. If Congress grants blanket consent to a compact and subsequently enacts a statute conflicting with the compact, the consent for the latter would be repealed except to the extent to which rights, protected by the Fifth Amendment, have become vested.

The U.S. Supreme Court occasionally is called upon by one or more states to interpret an interstate compact. Kansas in 1985, for example, brought an original action against Colorado to resolve several disputes involving the Arkansas River

Company. In 1995, the court unanimously opined that (*i*) Kansas had failed to provide evidence that Colorado had not obeyed reservoir operating principles and which alleged failure resulted in the "material depletion" of river flow, (*ii*) Colorado's winter water-storage program did not materially deplete usable stateline river flows in violation of the compact, (*iii*) the compact's article permitting beneficial development included replacement of centrifugal with turbine pumps and increased pumping wells existing prior to the compact, and (*iv*) the special master was reasonable in replying upon reports issued by the U.S. Geological Survey and the Colorado State Legislature in reaching his conclusion relative to the largest amount of precompact pumping in Colorado.[35]

COMPACT AMENDMENT AND TERMINATION

Attempts to amend a compact may encounter the same difficulties as ones encountered during the negotiations leading to entrance of states into a compact. Not only must all party states agree to an amendment, but the consent of Congress will be needed if the original compact received such consent.

When the states of New Jersey and New York sought an amendment to the Port Authority of New York and New Jersey Compact, congressional approval was delayed in 1976 by U.S. Representative Elizabeth Holtzman of New York who complained the Authority should not be allowed to engage in a new activity— industrial development—when the Authority had failed to solve the transportation problems which led to the creation of the Authority. She agreed to withdraw her objection to the granting of consent to the compact amendment provided the Authority would conduct a study of the economic feasibility of constructing a rail tunnel under the Hudson River.

Section 10 of Article I of the U.S. Constitution expressly authorizes Congress to revise state laws relative to import and export duties, but there is no similar provision in the same section relating to interstate compacts. By statute, Congress effectively withdrew its consent to a Kentucky–Pennsylvania compact providing that the Ohio River would be kept free of obstructions, and the U.S. Supreme Court upheld the statute in 1855 in *Pennsylvania v. Wheeling and Belmont Bridge Company* under the supremacy of the laws clause.[36] The court ruled that compacts do not restrict the power of Congress to regulate interstate commerce.

Compacts may contain a provision that they can be terminated only by unanimous agreement of party states as illustrated by Article X of the Colorado River Compact.[37] Other compacts contain a provision for termination, provided a stipulated notice, such as sixty days, is given by a state desiring to terminate the compact. Boundary compacts, however, cannot be terminated. Still other compacts provide for the withdrawal of a member.

Florida has withdrawn from and rejoined the Atlantic States Marine Fisheries Compact on several occasions and the Virginia General Assembly in 1995 voted to withdraw from the compact because the assembly was convinced the Virginia fishing quotas, Striped Bass in particular, were too low.[38]

Is a congressional statute terminating a compact subject to the Fifth Amendment's Due Process of Law guarantee? The answer apparently is no since the guarantee extends only to persons.

Can states agree to terminate a compact if citizens whose rights would be affected object? The U.S. Supreme Court in *Georgetown v. Alexander Canal Company* in 1831 opined that citizens of a state are not parties to the compact.[39] This ruling comports with international law which does not make provision for citizens of signatory nations to be involved in the termination of a treaty.

NUMBER AND TYPES OF COMPACTS

Compacts can be bilateral, multilateral, sectional, or national in terms of membership. Individual states participate in eleven to thirty-four compacts with six states' members of more than thirty compacts.[40]

Congress approved only seventeen compacts prior to 1900. The thirty-six compacts established between 1789 and 1920 dealt with state boundaries with the exception of the Virginia–West Virginia Compact of 1862 providing for the separation of West Virginia from Virginia.

States entered into approximately 125 compacts between 1920 and 1969. Patricia S. Florestano identified nineteen new compacts in the period 1970–79 and twenty-two new compacts between 1980 and 1992.[41] With respect to types of compacts, Florestano also reported that border compacts have been replaced in number by regional compacts, the majority of compacts since 1970 created commissions or agencies, and the nature of compacts has changed dramatically with a sharp decline in boundary compacts and a sharp increase in river waters and management compacts, and environmental and transportation compacts.[42] A small number of compacts have been designed to facilitate interlocal governmental cooperation in a bistate area as illustrated by compacts creating interstate school districts. There has been a decline in the number of compacts entered into in recent years as the result of Congress utilizing its preemption powers with more frequency.[43] In addition, a relatively large number of compacts have become inactive, in part because of congressional preemption.

Until the Port of New York Compact was entered into by New Jersey and New York in 1921, all compacts had been administered by departments of the member states. This compact broke new ground by establishing an authority governed by commissioners, appointed by the governors of New York and New Jersey with consent of the respective senates, to implement the compact.[44]

Types

Compacts entered into by states may be placed in twenty-two categories:

Advisory compacts create an interstate commission lacking regulatory and implementation powers. The Potomac River Compact illustrates this type as its commission is authorized only to study and develop recommendations for water pollution abatement.

There is one *agriculture compact*: Compact on Agricultural Grain Marketing. Maine and Vermont have joined the Northeast Interstate Dairy Compact which becomes effective when joined by a third state.

Boundary compacts establish, with consent of Congress, the official borders of the concerned states and avoid the need for the U.S. Supreme Court to exercise its original jurisdiction to resolve an interstate dispute. Congress in 1990, for example, approved the South Dakota–Nebraska Boundary Compact which settled a dispute generated by the Missouri River changing its course.[45]

Civil defense compacts originated in the cold war period after World War II when the Soviet Union was perceived to be a threat to world peace.

Crime control and corrections compacts date to 1910 when Congress granted its consent in advance to Illinois, Indiana, Michigan, and Wisconsin to enter into an agreement relative to the exercise of jurisdiction "over offenses arising out of the violation of the laws ..." of these states on Lake Michigan waters.[46]

Education compacts originated with the southern states which decided to pool their resources via the Southern Regional Education Compact. The Western Regional Education Compact, for example, obviates the need for each state to finance an expensive professional school. Only three schools of veterinary science service a fifteen-state region under the compact and students from states lacking a veterinary science school may attend these three schools. A similar higher education compact exists in New England, and two interstate school districts, bridging New Hampshire and Vermont, were created by interstate compacts with congressional approval in 1963 and 1969.[47]

The only *energy compact* in effect is the one designed to conserve oil and gas which dates to 1935. Only Iowa has joined the Compact on Energy which becomes effective when joined by five states.

Facilities compacts are entered into by states to facilitate the joint construction and operation of infrastructure facilities such as bridges and tunnels. The Port Authority of New York and New Jersey operates the Holland and Lincoln Tunnels, George Washington Bridge, three jetports, and marine facilities. Similarly, Maine and New Hampshire entered into a 1937 compact, with congressional approval, establishing a bridge authority.[48]

Two compacts relate to *health*: Interstate Compact on Mental Health and New England Compact on Radiological Health Protection.

Maine, New Hampshire, and Vermont have entered into the only operating *lottery compact* although Kansas has joined a proposed multistate lottery agreement.

Low Level radioactive waste compacts, promoted by the Low Level Radioactive Waste Policy Act of 1980, provide a regional solution for the storage of such wastes instead of development of individual storage sites in each state.[49] Forty-five states have entered into a total of nine such compacts with renewable five-year congressional consent (see Figure 1).[50]

LOW-LEVEL RADIOACTIVE WASTE COMPACT STATUS
JULY 1995

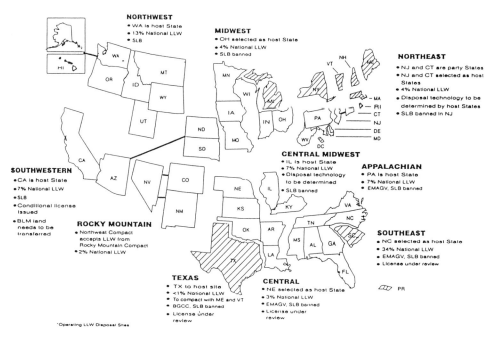

NORTHWEST
- WA is host State
- 13% National LLW
- SLB

MIDWEST
- OH selected as host State
- 4% National LLW
- SLB banned

NORTHEAST
- NJ and CT are party States
- NJ and CT selected as host States
- 4% National LLW
- Disposal technology to be determined by host States
- SLB banned in NJ

SOUTHWESTERN
- CA is host State
- 7% National LLW
- SLB
- Conditional license issued
- BLM land needs to be transferred

ROCKY MOUNTAIN
- Northwest Compact accepts LLW from Rocky Mountain Compact
- 2% National LLW

CENTRAL MIDWEST
- IL is host State
- 7% National LLW
- Disposal technology to be determined
- SLB banned

APPALACHIAN
- PA is host State
- 7% National LLW
- EMAGV, SLB banned

SOUTHEAST
- NC selected as host State
- 34% National LLW
- EMAGV, SLB banned
- License under review

TEXAS
- TX to host site
- <1% National LLW
- To compact with ME and VT
- BGCC, SLB banned
- License under review

CENTRAL
- NE selected as host State
- 3% National LLW
- EMAGV, SLB banned
- License under review

PR

*Operating LLW Disposal Sites

UNAFFILIATED STATES
- 20% National LLW (11 States)
- SC has site - 6% National LLW - SLB
- NY to host site - 10% National LLW - SLB banned
- MA to host site - 2% National LLW - SLB banned
- ME to compact with TX - <1% National LLW
- VT to compact with TX - <1% National LLW
- NH, RI, DC, PR each less than 1% National LLW
- MI

Note: National LLW volume for 1994 = 0.9 million cubic feet disposed
   SLB = shallow land burial
   EMAGV = Earth mounded above grade vault
   BGCC = below ground concrete canisters

Source: U.S. Nuclear Regulatory Commission, 1995.

Figure 3.1

There are several types of *marketing and development compacts*, including the Agricultural Grain Marketing Compact; Midwest Nuclear Compact, promoting use of nuclear energy; Mississippi River Parkway Compact; Illinois-Missouri Compact, establishing a bridge commission; and Illinois–Indiana compact, creating a bridge commission.

Metropolitan problems compacts seek to resolve problems in an interstate region. The renamed Port Authority of New York and New Jersey is the first compact of this type and established an Authority currently responsible for a commuter railroad, highway bridges and tunnels, jetports, marine facilities, World Trade Center, and industrial development programs. The Quad Cities Interstate Metropolitan Authority Compact, entered into in 1990 by Illinois and Iowa, seeks to promote conservation, recreation, commerce on the Mississippi River, solid waste disposal, and transportation. The Washington Metropolitan Area Transit Regulation Compact of 1960—entered into by the District of Columbia, Maryland, and Virginia—is an unusual one in that the District is under the jurisdiction of Congress.

Currently, there are twelve *motor vehicles compacts*, including ones on driver licenses, nonresident violators, equipment safety, and uniform vehicle registration prorogation.

Mutual aid compacts provide that each state will assist another signatory state in an emergency situation such as a forest fire. This type of compact is a standby one administered by regular state agencies.

Natural resources compacts, such as the Connecticut River Atlantic Salmon Compact, seek to promote the conservation and development of resources, including flood control. A Massachusetts–New Hampshire compact established the Merrimack Valley Flood Control Commission which constructs flood control projects in New Hampshire, with Massachusetts compensating New Hampshire for loss of tax revenues.[51] Maryland and Virginia established the Potomac River Fisheries Commission in 1963 to settle a dispute dating to the colonial period when a royal charter made the river a part of Maryland and whose oyster fishermen resented Virginia oyster fishermen intruding on Maryland's waters.[52]

There are five *parks and recreation compacts*, including the Columbia River Gorge Compact and the Palisades Interstate Park Compact.

The *Interstate Compact on Pest Control* established an insurance fund to provide financial support for control of agricultural and forest insects.

Regulatory compacts often are promoted by economic interest groups seeking to deter Congress from preempting the regulatory authority of the states relative to an interstate problem. Existence of such compacts, such as the Interstate Compact to Conserve Oil and Gas, is used as evidence that there is no need for national government regulation since the states are solving the problem through formal cooperative regulatory action.[53]

The Atlantic States Marine Fisheries Compact is an example of a compact which lacks direct enforcement powers. Congress in 1986, however, amended the Atlantic Striped Bass Conservation Act to require individual states to comply with the management plan developed by the Atlantic States Marine Fisheries

Commission or be subject to a Striped Bass fishing moratorium imposed by the U.S. Fish and Wildlife Service in the coastal waters of a noncomplying state.[54]

A different type of regulatory compact is illustrated by the Interstate Sanitation Compact, entered into by New Jersey and New York in 1935 and by Connecticut in 1941, to abate and prevent water pollution in tidal waters of the New York City metropolitan area. The compact later was amended to permit the Compact Commission to monitor, but not regulate, air quality. The commission possesses concurrent regulatory authority with the environmental departments of the three member states. In 1986, the commission commenced to enforce its regulations more aggressively and engendered conflicts with the departments. One result has been the commission and the New York State Department of Environmental Conservation both monitoring discharges from municipal sewage treatment plants and reducing monitoring of discharges from industrial plants.[55]

The proposed Northeast Interstate Dairy Compact, enacted by each New England State Legislature, is a regulatory compact which would authorize an interstate commission to fix the price of fluid or drinking milk above the minimum prices set by the New England federal milk marketing order. The compact was opposed by representatives of other states whose farmers also were suffering from low milk prices, and Congress failed to act on the compact in 1994.

River basin compacts are designed to conserve and make the most efficient use of the basin's resources, particularly water. Such compacts, exemplified by the Colorado River Compact of 1922, typically provide for the apportionment of river water among the party states.

Service compacts are designed to solve social problems by committing each signatory state to provide services to legal residents of other member states. If there are too few families willing to adopt children in a state, the Interstate Compact on the Placement of Children in Interstate Adoption facilitates the adoption of these children by qualified foster parents in other states. Forty-nine states and the Virgin Islands have joined this compact.

With more than 300,000 persons on parole or probation in states other than the ones in which the crimes were committed, it is important that these persons be supervised properly. Congress in 1934 enacted the Crime Control Consent Act consenting to states entering into crime control compacts.[56] Based on this consent, all states, Puerto Rico, and the Virgin Islands have joined the Interstate Compact for Supervision of Parolees and Probationers. This Compact is the first one to be joined by all fifty states.

Similarly, the Juvenile Delinquency Compact and the Corrections Compact provide for the return of delinquents and convicts, respectively, to their states of domicile to serve their sentences. These compacts are premised on the belief that the rehabilitation of delinquents and convicts will be facilitated if they are incarcerated in close proximity to their families.

The 1970 Interstate Agreement on Detainers (writs authorizing confinement of an individual) facilitates speedy and proper disposition of detainers based on trial indictments, information, or complaints from party states. This agreement generated a major political controversy in New York in 1993 when convicted murderer Thomas Grasso, sentenced to death in Oklahoma, was returned to New York to serve a sentence in a state prison for a murder in New York which does not have the death penalty, and with a change in governors he was returned to Oklahoma. This case is analyzed in more detail in Chapter 6.

Tax compacts have become more common with the increase in interstate commerce and the number of states levying sales and income taxes. A tax compact, such as the one between New Jersey and New York, may provide only for exchange of information on in-state vendors relative to purchases by residents of the other state. The Great Lakes Interstate Sales Compact is the first multistate compact focusing on the enforcement of state sales and use taxes.

The Multistate Tax Compact has been entered into by twenty states and seeks to avoid duplicate taxation of individuals and business firms. Thirteen other states are considered to be associate members because they participate in and provide financing for one or more commission programs. The compact was established in 1966 in response to the U.S. Supreme Court's decision in *Northwestern States Portland Cement Company v. Minnesota* holding that a state may tax the net income of a foreign corporation (one chartered in another state) provided the tax is nondiscriminatory and is apportioned fairly on the basis of the corporation's activities with a nexus to the state.[57]

Federal–interstate compacts were foreshadowed when Frankfurter and Landis wrote in 1925 that "the combined legislative powers of Congress and of the several states permit a wide range of permutations and combinations for governmental action. Until very recently these potentialities have been left largely unexplored. ... Creativeness is called for to devise a great variety of legal alternatives to cope with the diverse forms of interstate interests."[58] They cited as examples uniform and reciprocal laws.

Frankfurter and Landis' call for creativeness ultimately was answered in 1961 with the emergence of a new type of compact—the federal–interstate compact— with the enactment of the Delaware River Basin Compact by four states and Congress. Until 1961, Congress either granted or withheld its consent relative to compacts submitted to it. This compact is distinguished by the fact that Congress enacted the compact into federal law, and the United States became a member of the compact which has a national cochairman and a state cochairman, and other members from the national and party state governments. The concerned states were convinced that the serious nature of the water shortage in the Delaware River Basin, accentuated by drought, required the participation of the national government in the development and implementation of a solution. Specifically, the compact is designed to integrate the activities of national and state agencies instead of displacing them.[59]

A second federal–interstate compact, modeled on the Delaware one, became effective in 1971 with the enactment of the Susquehanna River Basin Compact by Congress and the Maryland, New York, and Pennsylvania State Legislatures. There was strong opposition to the proposed compact in the Pennsylvania State

Legislature where several influential members argued the compact would infringe upon the sovereignty of member states. The compact authorizes the Compact Commission to create advisory committees composed of representatives of federal, state, and local governments, water resource and using agencies, labor, and agriculture, and the New York enabling statute stipulates that the mayor of New York City or his designee shall serve as an advisor.[60]

Congress and states also have entered into federal–interstate compacts to promote development in large regions. The Appalachian Regional Commission was established in 1965 by Congress and thirteen states, and has a state cochairman appointed by the governors and a federal cochairman appointed by the president with the advice and consent of the U.S. Senate.[61]

The origin of the commission is traceable to a 1960 meeting of governors and other representatives of ten states convened to develop long-range solutions for problems of Appalachia. The report of the study group was used to persuade President John F. Kennedy to appoint in 1963 a special task force, the President's Appalachian Regional Commission, which published a report in 1964 that served as the basis for the 1965 congressional act.

The commission is distinguished by (*i*) a comprehensive approach to problem solving, (*ii*) roles of the state government, (*iii*) relatively large amount of federal funds, (*iv*) grant administration method, and (*v*) breadth of mission. With respect to grant administration, the commission operates solely out of its Washington, D.C., office and transfers most of its congressional appropriations to federal departments and agencies to administer in the region.

The Interstate Agreement on Detainers is a federal–interstate compact that does not create a compact agency.[62] A detainer notifies a prisoner that he/she is wanted for criminal prosecution in another state. This compact is designed to facilitate interstate rendition, but can create a major controversy as described in Chapter 6.

A different type of federal–state "compact" is the product of a 1980 act of Congress granting its consent to an agreement entered into by the Bonneville Power Administration, a federal agency, with Idaho, Montana, Oregon, and Washington.[63] The enabling statute does not contain the term interstate compact, and the agreement was not negotiated by the concerned states. The Pacific Northwest Electric Power and Conservation Planning Council drafted the "compact" and transmitted it to the states. If the latter did not enact the "compact," a federal council would have been formed by the secretary of the interior to perform the functions of the proposed federal–interstate council.

This type of federal–state agreement also is distinctive because a federal executive agency instead of the U.S. Government is a party to the interstate agreement which established the council as an advisory body to prepare a regional conservation and electric power plan and a program to protect fish and wildlife.[64]

The Northern Forest Lands Council, created by Congress in 1990, was similar to the Pacific Northwest Council, but differed because the Forest Lands Council was a temporary body which disbanded in 1994.[65] The governor of each of four states— Maine, New Hampshire, New York, and Vermont—appointed four members of the council, which was charged with developing ways of maintaining the "traditional patterns of land ownership and use" of the northern forest.

The newest type of compact is the *Indian Tribe–State Gaming Compact* authorized by the Indian Gaming Regulatory Act of 1988.[66] The act was generated by a 1987 U.S. Supreme Court decision in *Cabazon Band of Mission Indians v. California* holding that a state cannot restrict unduly gaming on Indian lands.[67] This decision resulted in an upsurge of gaming on Indian lands, and Congress concluded that tribal governments and their constituents were not benefiting from the gaming and feared organized crime might acquire a stake in such gaming.

The act places gaming in three classes. Class I, limited chiefly to social gaming for small prizes, is subject to complete regulation by Indian tribes. Class II gaming—bingo and bingo-type games, and nonbanking card games—is regulated by the tribes subject to a degree of oversight by the National Indian Gaming Commission. All other types of gaming are in Class III and are prohibited unless a tribe and a concerned state enter into a tribal-state compact which is required to be submitted to the secretary of the interior who is directed to approve or reject the compact within forty-five days and publish a notice in the *Federal Register*. Failure of the Secretary to act within forty-five days of receipt of a compact is deemed an approval of the compact.[68]

These compacts typically are signed by the governor of the state and the chairman of the Indian tribe. On January 16, 1992, the chairman of the Kickapoo tribe and Governor Joan Finney of Kansas signed a compact which was forwarded to Assistant Secretary of the Interior Eddie Brown for approval. The following day, Kansas Attorney General Robert T. Stephan posted a letter to Secretary of the Interior Manuel Lujan maintaining that Governor Finney lacked authority under Kansas laws to enter into the compact. The governor rejected this opinion in a letter to the secretary on January 31.

On February 5, 1992, Attorney General Stephan filed a suit in the Kansas Supreme Court requesting a determination, and on February 28 the assistant secretary of the interior returned the proposed compact because it violated a provision of the act. The tribe and the governor amended the compact and returned it to the assistant secretary on March 2 who received it on March 5. In a March 8 letter, the assistant secretary notified the tribe and the governor that the department was prepared to approve the compact but could not decide the issue of whether the governor possessed authority to bind the state. On July 10, the Kansas Supreme Court in *Kansas v. Finney* opined the governor has authority to negotiate but not sign a compact.[69] Based on this decision, the assistant secretary of the interior returned the compact unapproved.

The tribe on May 19, 1992, brought suit against the secretary of the interior in the U.S. District Court for the District of Columbia seeking a declaratory judgment that the compact was approved since forty-five days had passed since the compact had been submitted to the Department of the Interior. The court in *Kickapoo Tribe of Indians v. Babbitt* on July 13, 1993, entered summary judgment for the defendant because the governor lacked authority to enter into the compact.[70]

OTHER REGIONAL AGENCIES

Congress has recognized the distinctive characteristics of various regions of the United States by establishing regional offices of departments and agencies. This type of administrative regionalism, however, does not involve a regional body with important powers. The first body of this nature was established by an 1879 act of Congress creating the Mississippi River Commission.[71] Its original members were three officers of the U.S. Army Corps of Engineers, one member of the U.S. Coast and Geodetic Survey, and three civilians, two of whom were civil engineers. The president nominated the members subject to the advice and consent of the Senate. The commission was charged with deepening channels, improving navigation safety, preventing destructive floods, and promoting and facilitating commerce, the postal service, and trade.

The 1879 act was amended in 1906, 1916, 1917, 1922, and 1928. The latter amendment made the commission an advisory body reporting to the chief of engineers of the Corps of Engineers, but the composition of its membership has remained unchanged. Three other river basin commissions—Upper Mississippi, Great Lakes, and Ohio River—have been created by the president under authority of the Water Resources Planning Act at the request of the concerned governors.[72]

The Tennessee Valley Authority (TVA) Act of 1933 established a regional body which appeared during the great depression to be a precursor of other nationally controlled regional authorities.[73] Creation of the authority generated considerable controversy and no other national body of its nature has been created.

TVA was not the product of regional pressure on Congress and has been attributed in origin primarily to the efforts of Senator George Norris of Nebraska, a populist, who led a campaign against electric utilities.[74] The cost of TVA-generated electric power was touted by its advocates as a yardstick by which the electric rates of private power companies could be measured.

In contrast to regional offices of federal departments and agencies located throughout the United States, the authority operates in an area of approximately 80,000 square miles in parts of Alabama, Georgia, Kentucky, Mississippi, North Carolina, Tennessee, and Virginia. TVA prides itself on its grass roots programs to involve state and local governments and citizens but has been criticized for seeking to coopt citizens.[75]

The three TVA commissioners, appointed by the president with Senate approval for nine-year terms, possess broad development powers for the river basin, yet have concentrated on dams and channels, production of electricity (128 billion kilowatts in 1993), and fertilizer research. Martha Derthick concluded that "the simplest explanation for TVA's failure to take on a wide range of functions and to perform them more aggressively is that a majority of the original board did not believe it should.[76] In her judgment, "the distinctive virtue of TVA as coordinator is that it incorporates functions that have usually been performed by more than one federal agency."[77]

Donald Davidson in 1940 commented that "the conception of TVA, while proposing to remedy regional disadvantages, ignores the great underlying causes of these regional disadvantages."[78] He concluded that TVA

... is not an agent of a region which of its own will and out of its own resources has won a degree of autonomy or semi-autonomy. It is not a new unit of government, standing in a clearly defined middle ground between the states and the federal government. It is an agent of the federal government ...[79]

Nevertheless, he concluded that TVA is beneficial as a flood control, river management, and land and forest conservation agency.[80]

ADMINISTRATIVE AGREEMENTS

Numerous formal and informal agreements between heads of particular functional departments in two or more states play an important role in solving multistate problems. The agreements may be formal written ones signed, for example, by commissioners of Motor Vehicles and designed to improve highway safety by providing for the suspension or revocation of the motorist's operating license by his/her home state for reckless operation of a motor vehicle in another state(s). Regional associations of state commissioners often promote interstate administrative agreements.

The formal agreement may be based on a general statute granting broad regulatory authority to commissioners—particularly commissioners of Motor Vehicles and Public Health—or a statute implementing a specific interstate compact. An example of the latter is a 1968 New York law authorizing the governor or commissioner of Motor Vehicles to sign administrative agreements with their respective counterparts in other states to implement an interstate compact, such as the Drivers License Compact, and reciprocal recognition of motor vehicle registrations.[81]

Informal agreements typically pertain to emergency situations and are based upon an understanding that one state will assist another state if specific emergencies —civil disorders, forest fires, hurricanes, tornados—occur. These agreements are standby and mutual assistance ones. Many mutual assistance agreements have been formalized by written agreements detailing procedures.

Whereas citizens can access interstate compacts without great difficulty by consulting the consolidated laws of their respective states or the United States statutes at-large if a compact received congressional consent, obtaining copies of interstate administrative agreements is a difficult task since there is no central repository for such agreements. Furthermore, citizens generally are unaware of the existence of these agreements although they may be aware of interstate compacts.

AN ASSESSMENT

An interstate concordat has the potential to effect cooperative actions and settle disputes. In particular, a compact preserves the authority of the concerned states and obviates or reduces the need for congressional preemption to solve a regional problem. Compacts also can eliminate a potential disadvantage—lack of uniformity—in a federal system since a uniform system of law can be established by compacts in two to fifty states. A great advantage of this interstate cooperative device is its ability to formulate a common policy within a region with distinct interests and problems or a multistate agency to build and operate facilities or provide services. In other words, political power can be centralized at the regional level where desirable.

Frankfurter and Landis' conclusions in 1925 remain valid:

With all our unifying processes nothing is clearer than that in the United States there are being built up regional interests, regional cultures, and regional interdependencies. They produce regional problems calling for regional solutions. Control by the nation would be ill-conceived and intrusive. A gratuitous burden would thereby be placed upon Congress and the national administration, both of which need to husband their energies for the discharge of unequivocally national responsibilities. As to these regional problems, Congress could not legislate effectively. Regional interests, regional wisdom, and regional pride must be looked to for solutions.[82]

Granting the validity of their conclusions, one must acknowledge that the device has limitations. Harold J. Laski, a British observer, concluded in 1948 "that the compact clause requires something like geological time to achieve results that are desirable."[83] Furthermore, critics maintain that changing conditions may necessitate a compact amendment, and the process of enacting the amendment by member states and obtaining congressional consent, if the compact is a political one, may be extremely time consuming even if the effort is successful.

Similarly, it is difficult to disagree with Vincent V. Thursby's conclusion that a compact "has certain characteristics which render it ill-adapted to service others" and "is not considered to be a substitute for national action."[84] His conclusion relative to the need for national action has been validated by the sharp increase in congressional preemption statutes, commencing in 1965, which reduce the functional areas subject to regulation by commissions created by compacts. In addition, a number of compacts have been superseded totally or partially by congressional preemption statutes. The 1960 Drivers License Compact has been superseded by a provision of the Commercial Drivers License Act of 1986 which makes it a federal crime for a driver to have more than one license which must have recorded on it all highway violations.[85]

A common criticism of public authorities created by interstate compacts is that they are responsible to no one, and the legislatures of the party states exercise little control over the activities of the authorities. Donald Axelrod explored both intrastate and interstate public authorities throughout the United States and emphasized "two governments working side by side: the visible general government and the shadow government of public authorities. Freed of control and surveillance, and insulated from the voters, many public authorities are quagmires of political patronage, corruption, and mismanagement."[86] Axelrod's criticisms were directed at both intrastate and interstate public authorities, the latter of which included the Port Authority of New York and New Jersey.

As noted, the Port of New York and New Jersey Compact blunts this criticism by authorizing the governors of the two states to veto actions taken by the Authority's Board of Directors. Governor Brendon Byrne of New Jersey in 1977, for example, vetoed on two occasions all decisions of the Port Authority's Board.[87] He also demanded that the increase in bridge and tunnel tolls from $1.00 to $1.50 be repealed until a detailed public transit-aid program was prepared. Similarly, Governor Hugh L. Carey of New York in 1982 vetoed the Authority's budget for its Port Authority Trans-Hudson (PATH) system on the ground the budget "continued the policy of inordinate subsidization of PATH."[88]

The U.S. Advisory Commission on Intergovernmental Relations in 1972 released a report concluding "that the geographic requirements of functional regions defy the rigidities of the single set of jurisdictional lines delineating the territorial extent of a general purpose governmental unit, even if its boundaries have been drawn with consummate skill."[89] The commission also concluded that a number of compact agencies were relatively new and lacked sufficient experience to permit an evaluation of their effectiveness in achieving stated goals.[90] This conclusion has considerably less validity in the late 1990s.

Systematic evaluation of interstate compacts by state legislatures is rare. New York had a Joint Legislative Committee on Interstate Cooperation, created in 1935, which promoted the formation of a number of compacts and monitored compacts and compact agencies.[91] With its dissolution, no similar joint legislative committee exists. The New York State Senate, however, created a Select Committee on Interstate Cooperation which reports on interstate activities and issues, but does not evaluate compacts.[92]

The New York State Legislative Commission on Expenditure Review, a program audit joint committee, in 1990 released a report of its study of the Interstate Sanitation Commission as noted in a preceding section. This evaluation report is the only one of its nature conducted by a New York State legislative committee.

Patricia S. Florestano reported in 1994 that three states—Maryland, Nebraska, and Oklahoma—evaluated interstate compacts.[93] The 1972 Maryland State Legislature created a Commission on Intergovernmental Cooperation, a joint legislative committee, which conducted studies of compacts that the state legislature enacted into law. In the early 1980s, the legislature renamed the commission the Joint Committee on Federal Legislation. Florestano reported in 1994 that "the majority of compacts evaluated gained approval" and added the committee recommended changes in several compacts and withdrawal from membership in the Bus Taxation Proration Compact and the National Guard Compact on the ground they were not needed."[94] The State Legislature accepted the recommendation that the state withdrew from the two compacts.

Marian E. Ridgeway studied compacts which included Illinois as a member. With respect to three compacts, she concluded in 1971 that "they appear merely to provide complexities in administrative organization and practice, and to erect new power centers, often ineffective in accomplishing public ends but generally obstructive while officially establishing particularized vested interests in state-protected positions of individual advantage."[95] She also noted the proliferation of compacts and maintained they were drafted and considered inadequately by state legislatures, are not subject to objective evaluation, and "are to some degree undemocratic and unrepresentative."[96]

Many public authorities created by interstate compacts are exempt from audit by the state auditor or state comptroller of the concerned states because state legislatures were convinced that such authorities can be more effective and efficient if they are not subject to standard state controls and restrictions.

The New York state comptroller, however, conducts audits of the Port Authority of New York and New Jersey. The state comptroller in 1977 uncovered the existence of widespread padding of expense accounts by high-level management officers, reported his findings to the Authority's board, and issued three reports on the subject.[97] The board took disciplinary action against a number of officers and adopted tighter control and reporting requirements for business trips by its employees, including limiting reimbursement to economy-class fares and establishing stringent conditions for reimbursing a spouse's travel costs.

Martha Derthick was convinced in 1974 that the Delaware River Basin Commission had not fully exercised its powers and "has done less than its proponents hoped and its opponents feared."[98] She concluded that the TVA's organizational structure made it an effective body in terms of goal achievement in contrast to the Delaware River Basin Commission which "has been seriously inhibited by its dependent multipartite character."[99] Earlier, Harvey C. Mansfield wrote that TVA "remains the conspicuously successful example of unified basin development and the one with the most cordial relations with the states in its area."[100]

Establishment of the Appalachian Regional Commission generated enthusiasm that this type of federal–state development compact has great prospects for solving multistate problems and led to the creation of similar compacts. A 1979 evaluation report by the U.S. General Accounting Office identified the following seven problems and raised the question whether the commission should serve as a model for the nation.

- The commission's planning policy allows individual states to omit from their plans common regional problems which originally justified the program.

- Inadequate written guidelines for state and district planners permit state plan deficiencies to continue.

- Unquantified program goals and objectives at all planning levels (multistate, state, substate) are not sufficient to measure progress and determine successful achievement.

- Allocation procedures may have underfunded some states while overfunding others.

- Serious grant administration problems have resulted from inadequate internal procedures and lack of federal agency cooperation.

- Commission policy does not adequately address declining state financial share of commission's nonhighway programs and increasing use of supplemental funds to replace other unavailable federal funds.

- Improved project and program evaluation efforts are not geared toward existing commission evaluation policy and planning.[101]

Senator John H. Chafee of Rhode Island in 1990 pointed out that conditions had changed and there were "counties scattered all over the country which are experiencing economic distress similar to, or worse than, the Appalachian counties. At the same time, there are regions in the Appalachia area which are doing very well and have strong economies."[102]

The Reagan Administration's hostility toward federal–state regional developmental commissions led to their demise with the exception of the Appalachian Regional Commission.

CONCLUSIONS

Enactment of an interstate compact by two or more state legislatures can be beneficial for the concerned states, U.S. Supreme Court, and Congress. It is clearly preferable for states, relying upon their Tenth Amendment powers, to solve their problems and disputes directly without outside intervention. A boundary compact, for example, reduces the Supreme Court's docket by eliminating the need for an original jurisdiction suit to solve a dispute.

Employment of the compact device similarly may obviate the need for the fashioning of a solution to a regional problem by Congress which lacks regional expertise. Congress recognizes the value of compacts by granting its consent and by encouraging states to form specific compacts through its consent-in-advance. Furthermore, it must be remembered that Congress is a limited government and cannot provide services that are reserved to the states. Hence, the compact is an attractive device for providing a service on a regional basis.

It is easier to form a compact if it is confined to administrative matters, such as driver license suspension and revocation, and development projects such as construction and operation of self-financing bridges and tunnels. In contrast, it is difficult to form a compact if it is designed to address a contentious issue such as equitable allocation of river water in a dry region. Even if a compact is enacted by the concerned state legislatures, it may not solve the problem.

A compact can link governments horizontally and vertically. Participation by the U.S. government as a compact partner has made relatively little difference in terms of compact effectiveness with the exception of the additional funds appropriated by Congress for the Appalachian Regional Commission.

Compacts are not the only mechanisms for cooperative interstate action. States have three alternatives to compacts—parallel statutes, uniform statutes, and reciprocity statutes and agreements—which are examined in Chapter 10. An important provision of the U.S. Constitution—the Full Faith and Credit Clause—is examined in Chapter 4 in terms of promoting interstate cooperation and protecting the rights of citizens in one state relative to the exterritorial application of their state's statutes, records, and judicial proceedings.

NOTES

1. Felix Frankfurter and James Landis, "The Commerce Clause of the Constitution—A Study in Interstate Adjustments," *Yale Law Journal*, May 1925, pp. 692–3.

2. *Ibid.*, p. 691.

3. *U.S. Constitution*, Art. I, §10. See also *Green v. Biddle*, 8 Wheaton 1 (1823), which is the first Supreme Court decision relating to the contractual nature of a compact.

4. *Pennover v. Neff*, 95 U.S. 714 (1877).

5. Frederick L. Zimmermann and Mitchell Wendell, *The Interstate Compact Since 1925* (Chicago: The Council of State Governments, 1951), p. ix.

6. *Low Level Radioactive Waste Policy Act of 1980*, 94 Stat. 3347, 42 U.S.C.A. §2021d (1994).

7. Calvin Sims, "Port Authority Seeks $1 Rise in Bridge Tolls," *The New York Times*, November 21, 1990, pp. B1 and B6.

8. *New York Laws of 1921*, Ch. 154, Art. XXII, §2. The New Jersey Law contains a similar provision. *New Jersey Laws of 1921*, Ch. 151. Art. XXII, §2.

9. Wallace R. Vawter, "Interstate Compact—The Federal Interest" in Task Force on Water Resources and Power, *Report on Water Resources and Power* (Washington, D.C.: U.S. Commission on Organization of the Executive Branch of the Government, 1955), Vol. III, p. 1702.

10. Frederick L. Zimmermann and Mitchell Wendell, *The Law and Use of Interstate Compacts* (Lexington, KY: The Council of State Governments, 1976), p. 54.

11. *Weeks Act of 1911*, 36 Stat. 69.

12. 73 Stat. 333.

13. *Green v. Biddle*, 21 U.S. 1 (1821).

14. *Florida v. Georgia*, 55 U.S. 478 (1854).

15. *Virginia v. Tennessee*, 148 U.S. 503 at 520 (1893).

16. *Ibid.* at 518.

17. *U.S. Steel Corporation v. Multistate Tax Commission*, 434 U.S. 452 at 473 (1978).

18. *Northeastern Interstate Forest Fire Protection Compact*, 63 Stat. 272 (1949).

19. *Interstate Oil and Gas Compact of 1935*, 49 Stat. 939, and *Atlantic States Marine Fisheries Compact of 1942*, 56 Stat. 270.

20. *Low Level Radioactive Waste Policy Act of 1980*, 94 Stat. 3347, 42 U.S.C.A. §2021d (1994).

21. *James v. Dravo Contracting Company*, 302 U.S. 134 at 148 (1937).

22. *Boulder Canyon Project Act of 1928*, 45 Stat. 1057.

23. *Wabash Valley Compact*, 73 Stat. 694 (1959), and *Washington Metropolitan Area Transit Regulation Compact*, 74 Stat. 1031 (1960).

24. *Tobin v. U.S.*, 306 F.2d 270 at 272–72 (1962), and *Tobin v. U.S.*, 371 U.S. 902 (1962).

25. Zimmermann and Wendell, *The Law and Use of Interstate Compacts*, p. 24.

26. *Congressional Record*, August 5, 1939, p. 11175.

27. The veto message is printed in the 1942 *Congressional Record*, pp. 3285–6.

28. *Hinderlider v. La Plata River and Cherry Creek Ditch Company*, 204 U.S. 92 (1938).

29. *Delaware River Joint Toll Bridge Commission v. Colburn*, 310 U.S. 419 (1940).

30. *Hess v. Port Authority Trans-Hudson Corporation*, 115 S.Ct. 394 (1994).

31. *Cuyler v. Adams*, 449 U.S. 433 (1981).

32. *Murdock v. City of Memphis*, 87 U.S. 590 (1874).

33. See *Ex Parte Young*, 209 U.S. 123 (1908).

34. *Removal of Causes Act of 1920*, 41 Stat. 554, 28 U.S.C.A. §1441 (1994), and Vincent V. Thursby, *Interstate Cooperation: A Study of the Interstate Compact* (Washington, D.C.: Public Affairs Press, 1953), p. 55.

35. *Kansas v. Colorado*, 115 S.Ct. 1733 (1995).

36. *Pennsylvania v. Wheeling and Belmont Bridge Company*, 50 U.S. 647 (1855).

37. *Colorado River Compact*, 45 Stat. 1057.

38. "Virginia General Assembly Takes Steps to Leave ASMFC," *Bay Journal*, March 1995, p. 13.

39. *Georgetown v. Alexander Canal Company*, 37 U.S. 91 at 95–6 (1838).

40. Patricia S. Florestano, "Past and Present Utilization of Interstate Compacts in the U.S.," *Publius*, Fall 1994, p. 23.

41. *Ibid.*, p. 19.

42. *Ibid.*, pp. 21–2. For a listing of all compacts, see William K. Voit, *Interstate Compacts & Agencies* (Lexington, KY: The Council of State Governments, 1995).

43. Joseph F. Zimmerman, *Federal Preemption: The Silent Revolution* (Ames: Iowa State University Press, 1991).

44. *New York Laws of 1921*, Ch. 154, and *New York Unconsolidated Laws*, §§7192 *et seq.* (McKinney 1979).

45. 103 Stat. 1328.

46. 36 Stat. 882.

47. 77 Stat. 332, and 83 Stat. 14.

48. 50 Stat. 536.

49. *Low Level Radioactive Waste Policy Act of 1980*, 94 Stat., 42 U.S.C.A. §2021d (1994).

50. See Carol S. Weissert and Jeffrey S. Hill, "The Low-Level Radioactive Waste Compacts: Lessons Learned from Theory and Practice," *Publius*, Fall 1994, pp. 27–43.

51. "Massachusetts Reimburses New Hampshire," *Worcester (Massachusetts) Telegram*, December 5, 1959, p. 5.

52. "States Act to End Long Oyster War," *The New York Times*, June 14, 1964, p. 55.

53. For information on events leading to the Interstate Compact to Conserve Oil & Gas, see Blakely M. Murphy, ed., *Conservation of Oil & Gas: A Legal History, 1948* (Chicago: Section on Mineral Law, American Bar Association, 1949), pp. 454–5.

54. *Atlantic Striped Bass Conservation Act Amendments of 1986*, 100 Stat. 989, 16 U.S.C.A. §1851 note (1995 Supp.).

55. *Memorandum Report to the Legislature: Interstate Sanitation Commission* (Albany: New York State Legislative Commission on Expenditure Review, 1990).

56. *Crime Control Consent Act of 1934*, 48 Stat. 909, 4 U.S.C.A. §112 (1995).

57. *Northwestern States Portland Cement Company v. Minnesota*, 358 U.S. 450 (1966).

58. Frankfurter and Landis, "The Compact Clause of the Constitution," p. 688.

59. Brevard Crihfield and H. Clyde Reeves, "Intergovernmental Relations: A View from the States," *The Annals*, November 1974, p. 101.

60. *New York Environmental Conservation Law*, §§21-071 and 21-0705 (McKinney 1984).

61. *Appalachian Regional Development Act of 1966*, 79 Stat. 5, 40 U.S.C.A. app. §1 (1986).

62. *Interstate Agreement on Detainers*, 84 Stat. 1397, 18 U.S.C.A. app. §2 (1995 Supp.).

63. *Pacific Northwest Electric Power and Conservation Planning Act of 1980*, 94 Stat. 2697, 16 U.S.C.A. §839b (1985 and 1995 Supp.).

64. See Darryll Olsen and Walter R. Butcher, "The Regional Power Act: A Model for the Nation?" *Washington Public Policy Notes*, Winter 1984, pp. 1–6, and Kevin J. Heron, "The Interstate Compact in Transition: From Cooperative State Action to Congressionally Coerced Agreements," *St. John's Law Review*, Fall 1985, pp. 1–25.

65. *Northern Forest Lands Council Act of 1990*, 104 Stat. 3359, 16 U.S.C.A. §2101 (1991 Supp.).

66. *Indian Gaming Regulatory Act of 1988*, 108 Stat. 2467, 25 U.S.C.A. §2701 (1995 Supp.).

67. *Cabazon Band of Mission Indians v. California*, 480 U.S. 202 (1987).

68. For additional details, see *Implementation of Indian Gaming Regulatory Act: Hearing before the Select Committee on Indian Affairs, U.S. Senate, February 5, March 18, and May 6, 1992* (Washington, D.C.: U.S. Government Printing Office, 1992).

69. *Kansas v. Finney*, 251 Kan. 559 (1992).

70. *Kickapoo Tribe of Indians v. Babbitt*, 827 F. Supp. 37 (1993).

71. 21 Stat. 37.

72. 79 Stat. 244.

73. *Tennessee Valley Authority Act of 1933*, 48 Stat. 58, 16 U.S.C.A. §831 (1985 and 1995 Supp.).

74. Donald Davidson, "Political Regionalism and Administrative Regionalism," *The Annals*, January 1940, p. 141.

75. Philip Selznick, *TVA and the Grass Roots* (Berkeley: The University of California Press, 1949).

76. Martha Derthick, *Between State and Nation: Regional Organizations of the U.S.* (Washington, D.C.: The Brookings Institution, 1974), p. 24.

77. *Ibid.*, p. 28.

78. Davidson, "Political Regionalism and Administrative Regionalism," p. 142.

79. *Ibid.*, pp. 142–3.

80. *Ibid.*, p. 143.

81. *New York Laws of 1968*, Ch. 45, §2, and *New York Vehicle and Traffic Law*, §219 (McKinney 1986).

82. Frankfurter and Landis, "The Compact Clause of the Constitution," pp. 707–8.

83. Harold J. Laski, *The American Democracy* (New York: The Viking Press, 1948), p. 156.

84. Vincent V. Thursby, *Interstate Cooperation: A Study of the Interstate Compact* (Washington, D.C.: Public Affairs Press, 1953), p. 143.

85. *Commercial Drivers License Act of 1986*, 100 Stat. 3207, 49 U.S.C.A. §2701 (1995 Supp.).

86. Donald Axelrod, *Shadow Government: The Hidden World of Public Authorities— And How They Control Over $1 Trillion of your Money* (New York: John Wiley & Sons, Inc., 1992), p. iii.

87. Ralph Blumenthal, "Byrne Again Opposes Port Unit:" Vetoes Its Plan for Bus Projects, *The New York Times*, June 22, 1977, pp. 1 and 36.

88. Ari L. Goldman, "Low Fares Cited as Carey Vetoes PATH's Budget," *The New York Times*, February 11, 1982, p. 1.

89. *Multistate Regionalism* (Washington, D.C.: U.S. Advisory Commission on Intergovernmental Relations, 1972), p. 163.

90. *Ibid.*

91. See, for example, *Report of the Joint Legislative Committee on Interstate Cooperation to the 1966 Legislature* (Albany: New York State Legislature, 1966).

92. See the *1992 Annual Report* (Albany: New York State Senate Select Committee on Interstate Cooperation, 1994).

93. Florestano, "Past and Present Utilization of Interstate Compacts in the U.S.," p. 23.

94. *Ibid.*, p. 24.

95. Marian E. Ridgeway, *Interstate Compacts: A Question of Federalism* (Carbondale: Southern Illinois University Press, 1971), p. 292.

96. *Ibid.*, pp. 295–6.

97. *Review and Evaluation of Port Authority of New York and New Jersey (PA) Actions Relative to Expense Account Irregularities* (Albany: New York State Department of Audit and Control, 1978).

98. Derthick, *Between State and Nation*, p. 57.

99. *Ibid.*, p. 182.

100. Harvey C. Mansfield, "Intergovernmental Relations" in James W. Fesler, ed., *The 50 States and Their Local Governments* (New York: Alfred A. Knopf, Incorporated, 1967), p. 176.

101. *Should the Appalachian Regional Commission Be Used as a Model for the Nation?* (Washington, D.C.: U.S. General Accounting Office, 1979), pp. i–ii.

102. *Oversight and Reauthorization of the Appalachian Regional Commission and the Economic Development Administration: Hearing Before the Subcommittee on Water Resources, Transportation, and Infrastructure, U.S. Senate* (Washington, D.C.: U.S. Government Printing Office, 1990), p. 11.

4

Full Faith and Credit

Sovereign states in a confederation and semisovereign states in a federation, unless mandated by a constitutional provision, are confronted with the question of whether they should recognize the judicial proceedings, records, and statutes of other member states. Nation states commonly extend such recognition on the basis of comity or reciprocity. The Continental Congress, which prosecuted the Revolutionary War, adopted a resolution providing that "full faith and credit shall be given in each of these states to the records, acts, and judicial proceedings of the courts and magistrates of every other state." This resolution was included as Article IV in the Articles of Confederation and Perpetual Union effective in 1781.

Section 1 of Article IV of the U.S. Constitution contains nearly identical language: "Full faith and credit shall be given in each state to the public acts, records, and judicial proceedings of every other state." Suggesting that the comity command (*comitas jurisdictionum*) is not self-executing, the section authorizes Congress "by general law" to "prescribe the manner in which such acts, records, and proceedings shall be proved and the effect thereof." In contrast to the voluntary cooperation that occurs when states enter into interstate compacts to jointly provide services or build and operate facilities, the Full Faith and Credit Clause appears to mandate interstate reciprocity relative to civil matters. Nevertheless, the conflict of laws of various states in the federal system necessitates that a court decide in a given case whether the laws of state A or the laws of state B apply.

The clause establishes a rule of law of states which has been labeled private international law that binds both federal and state courts. Public acts are civil statutes enacted by state legislatures and records are official state documents such as a deed, mortgage, or will. Procedural statutes are not granted full faith and credit. With respect to judicial proceedings, the clause prevents relitigation of a final judgment in a court of a sister state.

A court can recognize a foreign (other state) statutory right, yet deny a remedy by rendering a judgment against the party invoking the statute of a sister state. A court also can shorten the time period during which a foreign judgment can be enforced and can apply its state's statute of limitations if its application does not result in undue discrimination as explained in subsequent sections.

The statutes, records, and judicial proceedings of foreign governments are not protected by the clause, which is restricted to interstate cases, but each state is free to recognize such foreign government ácts, records, and judicial proceedings.[1]

The Full Faith and Credit Clause must be read in conjunction with Section 2 of Article III of the U.S. Constitution which grants diversity of citizenship jurisdiction to federal courts. In cases involving conflict of laws between two states (mutual legislative jurisdiction), a state or federal court is commanded by a literal reading of the Full Faith and Credit Clause to displace the law of one state with the law of another state. If a state statute is applied *extra territorium* in a sister state in a federal system, the sovereignty of the sister state is infringed.

Judge Benjamin Cardozo of the New York Court of Appeals in 1928 described conflict of laws as "one of the most baffling subjects of legal science."[2] Robert H. Jackson labeled the clause "the lawyers' clause" and pointed out it is concerned "with the techniques of the law, and serves to co-ordinate the administration of justice among the several independent legal systems which exist in our federal arrangements."[3]

ORIGIN OF FULL FAITH AND CREDIT

Letters of credence, based upon full faith and credit, were employed in diplomatic practice during the Middle Ages. Kurt H. Nadelmann researched the use of full faith and credit during the colonial period and discovered (*i*) a 1659 Connecticut act providing for full faith and credit if other colonies extended reciprocity, (*ii*) a 1715 Maryland statute according full faith and credit to judgments on debts rendered by courts is sister colonies, (*iii*) a 1731 South Carolina act granting full faith and credit to bonds, deeds, and records of "any of his majesty's plantations in America," and (*iv*) a 1774 Massachusetts act granting full faith and credit to debt judgments of courts in sister colonies.[4]

Delegates to the Philadelphia Constitutional Convention of 1787 were men of wealth and property. Suggestions have been advanced that the Full Faith and Credit Clause was added to the constitution to protect creditors against debtors who move to other states. James Madison in *The Federalist Number 42* argued that the clause would be "a very convenient instrument of justice, and be particularly beneficial on the borders of contiguous states, where the effects liable to justice may be suddenly and secretly transformed in any stage of the process, within a foreign jurisdiction."[5] This comment is preceded by a paragraph on the delegation of the power to regulate bankruptcies to Congress, thereby suggesting a linkage between debt and full faith and credit. Article VI of the constitution, providing for assumption by the new government of debts contracted prior to the constitution, suggests the delegates were concerned with protection of creditors.

Henry J. Friendly in 1928 uncovered evidence from several sources—debates at the Constitutional Convention, state ratification conventions, and newspaper reports—that the grant of diversity of citizenship jurisdiction to federal courts was designed to protect creditors in one state "against legislation favorable to debtors" in another state.[6] He examined Connecticut records during the confederacy involving nine diversity-of-citizenship cases and reported "the record of the court is highly creditable. In only two of them was the domestic party victorious, and these cases could not well have gone the other way."[7] Acknowledging that court records of other states were not complete, he concluded that none of the records indicated "undue prejudice on the part of the local tribunal."[8]

Fear was expressed at the Constitutional Convention that if Congress was not granted power to prescribe the manner of proving the acts, records, and proceedings, "the provision would amount to nothing more than what now takes place among all independent nations."[9] Madison wrote in *The Federalist Number 42* that authorizing Congress to prescribe by general law the manner of proving public acts, records, and judicial proceedings "is an evident and valuable improvement on the clause relating to this subject in the Articles of Confederation."[10]

Others suggested that the grant of diversity of citizenship jurisdiction to federal courts could be employed to subsume the states' judiciary into the federal judiciary. Hamilton in *The Federalist Number 82* rejected this "alienation of state power by implication" argument by pointing out state courts would retain concurrent jurisdiction with the exception of where federal courts were granted exclusive jurisdiction.[11]

In framing the Full Faith and Credit Clause, the delegates took special care not to expand the powers of Congress while establishing a national legal principle which would federalize separate state legal systems through reciprocity, thereby preventing provincialism in jurisprudence. The U.S. Supreme Court in 1983 opined that the "full faith and credit clause like the commerce clause ... has become a nationally unifying force."[12]

CONGRESSIONAL CLARIFICATION

The constitution grants Congress power to supplement and enforce the guaranty of full faith and credit. In 1790 and 1804, Congress enacted statutes prescribing the method of authenticating public acts and records, thereby determining their extrastate effect. The former statute directs that "records and judicial proceedings authenticated shall have such faith and credit given to them in every court within the United States, as they have by law or usage in the courts of the states from where the said records are or shall be taken."[13] The 1804 statute extended full faith and credit to public acts and created an additional method of exemplification of nonjudicial records by prescribing their effect in terms similar to those of the 1790 statute.[14]

Congress took no additional action relative to this constitutional guarantee until 1994 when it enacted a statute establishing standards which state courts must follow in determining their jurisdiction to issue a child support order and the effect which must be given to such orders by the courts of sister states.[15] These standards are examined in a subsequent section.

Congress has taken no other action to clarify the full faith and credit constitutional provision and its extraterritorial effect. State legislatures are free to enact statutes containing less stringent standards for the authentication of judicial proceedings than the standards provided by the congressional statutes. The failure of Congress to provide additional clarification has resulted in the U.S. Supreme Court "legislating" on the subject.

A state legislature is powerless to deny its courts jurisdiction over cases involving duties and rights created under the laws of a sister state. Nor can a court deny to enforce such a duty or right because the court disagrees with the reasoning of a court in a sister state. The clause prohibits a state inquiry into the merits or consistency of a decision by a court in another state. A civil judgment has automatic validity in another state. A court, however, legitimately may inquire whether a sister state court had jurisdiction to render the decision. If a court lacks jurisdiction over the parties or *res* (thing), or a ruling was obtained by fraud, the court' rulings are not entitled to full faith and credit. Furthermore, a court in one state does not have jurisdiction over property located in another state.

The law of the state where a contract or deed is executed (*lex loci contractus*) is binding in other states. State A may require only one witness for a contract whereas State B requires two witnesses. Hence, a contract or deed properly executed in State A must be accorded full faith and credit in State B. If a state does not recognize debts arising from gambling, the state still must accord full faith and credit to a judgment of a court on a gambling debt in another state.

SUPREME COURT CLARIFICATION

The early full faith and credit decisions of the U.S. Supreme Court mandated recognition of judgments of courts of sister states, yet did not refer to an obligation of a state to recognize the statutes of sister states. *In Mills v. Duryee*, the court in 1813 opined that judgments from foreign states had conclusive effect and added: "It is manifest ... that the constitution contemplated a power in Congress to give a conclusive effect to such judgments."[16]

Between 1866 and 1935, the court often invalidated choice of law decisions as unconstitutional. In 1866, for example, the court struck down New York's application of its law in determining the effect to be given to a judgment of an Illinois court.[17] The court in 1877 for the first time explicitly opined that the Full Faith and Credit Clause limits choice of law.[18]

In 1897, the court ruled that a Louisiana statute could not be applied to an insurance contract between a New York insurance company and a Louisiana citizen, since the contract was made in New York even though the insured property was located in Louisiana.[19] An almost identical decision was rendered in 1925 by the court when it held that the law of the state where a fraternal benefit society was organized determined the rights and obligations of the society.[20] James R. Pielemeir explained that these rulings "evidence a perception that the law of the state where the selected event took place metaphysically attached itself to any resulting controversy, determining the parties' rights."[21]

By the 1930s the court's rulings were under attack by legal commentators on the ground that more than one state had legitimate claims relative to a multistate event and that strict adherence to the court's rule would result in the infringement of the sovereign powers of the other concerned states. In 1935, the court acknowledged the need for an accommodation of the conflicting interests of two states when the policy of one state expressed in a statute conflicts with the statute of another state.[22] In deciding whether California should be allowed to apply its workmen's compensation statute to employees of a California firm who were injured in Alaska, the court decided to appraise "the governmental interests of each jurisdiction" and base its ruling "according to their weight."[23] The court added that it assumed "*[p]rima facie* every state is entitled to enforce in its own courts its own statutes, lawfully enacted," and the burden of proof was on the challenger to show that, on a rational basis, the conflicting interests of the foreign state are superior to the conflicting interests of the forum state.[24] In this case, the court found that Alaska's interests were not superior to the interests of California.[25]

If the clause were interpreted by the U.S. Supreme Court literally, the courts of a state would be mandated to discard the laws enacted by its state legislature in favor of the statutes enacted by the legislatures of other states in full faith and credit cases. In 1939, the court opined that "the very nature of the federal union, ... precludes resort to the full faith and credit clause as the means for compelling a state to substitute the statutes of other states for its own statutes dealing with a subject matter concerning which it is competent to legislate."[26] Hence, a forum no longer was required to weigh the conflicting interests of another state. A similar decision was reached by the court in 1955.[27] Pielemeir commented that:

... recent years have witnessed a vast expansion of the scope of personal jurisdiction and a noticeably increased tendency by the states, in their application of newly developing choice of law approaches, to apply their own law in conflicts settings. The combination of these developments has dramatically heightened the opportunities for plaintiffs to shop for favorable forums and laws.[28]

The court in 1951 stressed that "the principal purpose of the clause still remains to facilitate enforcement of judgments rendered in another jurisdiction, rather than to give effect to statutes enacted in other states."[29]

Although the Full Faith and Credit Clause applies only to civil matters, the clause occasionally is invoked in a criminal case. Ronald Gillis, for example, was indicted, tried, and acquitted of murder in Delaware. Subsequently, he was indicted, tried, and found guilty of the same murder in Maryland. The Court of Appeals of Maryland in 1993 held that the dual sovereignty rationale is applicable to the Full Faith and Credit Clause.[30] Gillis argued that the second murder prosecution violated full faith and credit by failing to recognize his acquittal in Delaware. However, the U.S. Supreme Court in 1985 opined that the dual sovereignty doctrine permitted separate prosecutions for the same murder by both Alabama and Georgia.[31]

Divorce proceedings and interstate child support illustrate the complexities of the full faith and credit guarantee. The former involves complex legal questions relative to the validity of a divorce proceeding and the latter illustrates the problems of collecting child support payments from an obligator residing in another state which cooperates with the state where the custodial parent resides by according full faith and credit to the state's child support orders.

DIVORCE PROCEEDINGS

The physical presence of the two concerned parties in a state allows a court to exercise jurisdiction over a suit for divorce. Such a suit may create difficult problems of jurisdiction since one spouse may migrate to another state to seek a divorce. Domicile, a legal concept, determines the jurisdiction of a court, and the residency requirement for establishment of domicile varies from state to state. The U.S. Supreme Court in *Sosna v. Iowa* in 1975 ruled constitutional Iowa's one-year residency requirement prior to the filing of a divorce petition in its courts.[32] The plaintiff maintained that the residency requirement violated the Equal Protection of the Laws and the Due Process of Law Clauses of the Fourteenth Amendment to the U.S. Constitution. Earlier, the court invalidated durational residency requirements if they were imposed by state legislatures as a qualification for medical care, voting, or welfare benefits.[33] The court in rendering these decisions did not imply that a state legislature could never impose such a requirement and expressly disclaimed such an implication.[34]

The *Sosna* court declared:

... Iowa's divorce residency requirement is of a different stripe. Appellant was not irretrievably foreclosed from obtaining some part of what she sought, as was the case with the welfare recipients in Shapiro, the voters in Dunn, or the indigent patient in Maricopa County. She would eventually qualify for the same sort of adjudication which she demanded virtually upon her arrival in the State.[35]

The court continued that Iowa had decided it did not want to become a divorce-mill state, and the residency requirement "furthers the State's parallel interests in both avoiding officious intermeddling in matters in which another state has a paramount interest, and in minimizing the susceptibility of its own divorce laws to collateral attack."[36]

The court's upholding of relatively long-durational residency requirements encourages one or both parties seeking a divorce to travel to states with a short-durational residency requirement and relatively lax requirements for a divorce.

As noted, full faith and credit applies only to *final* court judgments. If, for example, an alimony judgment is modified by the court establishing it, a forum court in a sister state "has at least as much leeway to disregard the judgment, to qualify it, or to depart from it as does the state where it was rendered."[37] Furthermore, a court is not required to give greater effect to a divorce decree of a sister state than to the court's own decrees.

A divorce affects not only the parties to the divorce proceedings, but also affects children, future heirs, and property rights. The failure of a state to extend full faith and credit to a marriage dissolution can result in illegitimate children, annulment of subsequent marriages entered into by the parties, and property distribution problems upon the death of one of the parties to the divorce.

The Domicile Problem

Jurisdiction over the parties involved in a divorce proceeding is an essential requirement for the granting of a divorce. To prevent one party from frustrating a divorce proceeding by moving to another state, a process known as "constructive process" was developed as a method allowing a court to secure jurisdiction over the party who moved to another state. The process involves the posting of a notice of the suit to the absent spouse or advertising a notice in the public press. This process, however, allows a spouse to move to another state and sue for divorce in the hope that his/her spouse would not receive the posted notice or read the advertisement. To prevent this abuse of process, jurisdiction was made dependent upon domicile. Unfortunately, standards for determining domicile vary between the states.

Migratory divorce refers to married persons seeking to circumvent the strict divorce law in their state of residence by establishing domicile in a state with lax requirements, filing for a divorce, and upon receiving the divorce decree, returning to their original state of residence. The key question is whether the original state must accord full faith and credit to the divorce decrees of a court in a sister state.

Domicile in place (*lex domicilii*) refers to the intent of an individual to establish a *bona fide* residence in a state as opposed to the establishment of a residence for the purpose of securing a divorce. In a free society, an individual obviously has the right to change his/her mind relative to place of residence, and courts may be called upon to determine whether residence was fraudulently established for the purpose of obtaining a divorce. Although a number of states do not have an explicit requirement for domicile to become eligible to seek a divorce, these states establish a durational residence requirement which is construed to mean domicile.

If due process—notice, hearing, and appeal—has not been provided in a divorce proceeding, a state does not have to extend full faith and credit to a divorce decree of a sister state court which is the product of such a proceeding. Furthermore, if the decreeing court lacks jurisdiction over the parties, the resulting divorce need not be accorded full faith and credit.

The U.S. Supreme Court in 1869 established a standard of jurisdictional requirements necessary to satisfy the Full Faith and Credit Clause. The case involved a woman who left her husband in the District of Columbia, established domicile in Indiana, and subsequently obtained an Indiana divorce in a suit in which her husband appeared. The court held the District of Columbia courts must respect the decree by noting that "when the court granting the decree had personal jurisdiction of both parties and the domicile of one, its decree was entitled to full faith and credit."[38]

In *Atherton v. Atherton* in 1901, the court developed the concept of matrimonial domicile by maintaining that "full faith must be accorded to a decree rendered by the state wherein the spouses last resided as husband and wife, and the plaintiffs were domiciled."[39] The court decided two companion cases in the same year and opined that a divorce obtained by a spouse who had not complied with the residence requirement of the decreeing forum need not be accorded full faith and credit by a sister state.[40]

The court in 1903 upheld the validity of a Massachusetts statute prohibiting "the enforcement of a divorce obtained in another state by a citizen of Massachusetts, while in fraud of the laws of one state, who goes into another state for the purpose of procuring a decree of divorce."[41]

A very controversial decision was rendered in 1906 by the U.S. Supreme Court which continued to apply the decision for thirty-six years. In *Haddock v. Haddock*, the court by a five to four vote employed a "fault concept" of jurisdiction for the first time and ruled that "an *ex parte* divorce decree rendered by one state when the matrimonial domicile was in another, need not be viewed as a legitimate decree."[42] The court specifically upheld a lower New York court decision in favor of the wife that the defendant had wrongfully abandoned his spouse and had not properly established domicile in Connecticut.

This decision immediately raised the question whether all divorces obtained in another state would be entitled to full faith and credit in other states. The court decided it was more important to protect the resident spouse than to establish national uniformity in divorce litigations. The court in effect provided a new ground for impeachment of the jurisdiction of a court granting a divorce—fault in the marital relationship. Typically, a divorce suit is an action in *res*; that is, the action is directed against the status of the parties and not the individual parties.

The doctrine of estoppel is applied in certain divorce litigation cases. It precludes an individual from subsequently denying the truth of his statements or facts which he led others to believe to be true. Hence, a respondent in a foreign *ex parte* divorce can be estopped by a subsequent marriage to collaterally attack the decree. He cannot accept the benefits of the decree and maintain it is void. The New York State Supreme Court, a general trial court, in 1917 opined that "a second spouse of a libellent to a void divorce will be estopped from denying the validity of that divorce in an annulment proceeding where he himself aided in its procurement."[43]

Full faith and credit also is subject to *res judicata*; that is, a thing adjudicated must be accepted as the truth. Hence, a judicial decision by a competent tribunal unless reversed is conclusive and cannot be raised again by the parties to the suit.

The landmark decisions on the subject of migratory divorce were rendered by the U.S. Supreme Court in 1942 and 1945 and involved the same parties.

In the 1942 decision (*Williams I*), the court overturned the Haddock decision which held that a matrimonial domicile state did not have to recognize an *ex parte* divorce decree granted by a court in another state.[44] A married man and a married woman domiciled in North Carolina traveled to Nevada, established domicile, and each obtained a Nevada divorce. They married each other immediately after receiving their respective divorce decrees and returned to North Carolina. They were charged, tried, and convicted of bigamous cohabitation. The North Carolina trial court, which was upheld by the North Carolina Supreme Court, did not contest whether domicile in Nevada had been established, but found the couple guilty. The convictions were reversed on appeal by the U.S. Supreme Court which opined "that domicile of the plaintiff's spouse in a state is sufficient to entitle a divorce decree by a court of that state to full faith and credit."[45] This decision eliminated the concepts of marital domicile and fault.

The parties in *Williams I* subsequently were tried again on the charge of bigamous cohabitation and, in common with the first trial, were convicted by the trial court which found that the parties were not domiciled in Nevada when the divorce decrees were rendered. The conviction was upheld by the North Carolina Supreme Court. The U.S. Supreme Court was impressed by the timing of the arrival of the two persons in Nevada for divorce purposes, their quick remarriage, and immediate departure for North Carolina. The court affirmed the convictions by ruling "that North Carolina could inquire into the jurisdiction of the Nevada court to render the judgment, and in divorce cases domicile of one of the parties is essential to jurisdiction."[46] Writing for the majority, Justice Felix Frankfurter explained:

The decree of divorce is a conclusive adjudication of everything except the jurisdictional facts upon which it is founded, and domicile is a jurisdictional fact. To permit the necessary finding of domicile by one State to foreclose all States in the protection of their social institutions would be intolerable.[47]

The validity of migratory divorces was raised in question again by this decision, but the court reduced the uncertainty by holding that the party challenging a divorce has the burden of proof. Nevertheless, it is possible that a divorced man and a divorced woman who marry each other may be viewed as married in one state and guilty of bigamous cohabitation in another state.

The court in 1948 retreated slightly from the effect of its *Williams II* ruling by holding in *Sherrer v. Sherrer* that "full faith and credit bars a litigant who has previously appeared in an action from contesting the jurisdictional issues."[48] In the same year, the court in *Coe v. Coe* held that the Full Faith and Credit Clause will prevent the redetermination of the jurisdictional basis of a divorce decree (*i*) when there has been participation by the defendant in the divorce proceedings, (*ii*) when the defendant has been accorded full opportunity to contest the jurisdictional issue, and (*iii*) when the decree is not susceptible to such collateral attack in the courts of the State which initially rendered the decision.[49]

These two decisions mark the emergence of the personal appearance doctrine holding that a personal appearance or the opportunity for one was the factor mandating the application of full faith and credit to a divorce decree. In other words, a court in one state cannot examine the question of domicile relative to a divorce granted by a court in a sister state if the proceedings were adversarial.

In another 1948 divorce case, Justice William O. Douglas developed the concept of the "divisible divorce." He wrote:

The result in this situation is to make divorce divisible—to give effect to the Nevada decree insofar as it effects marital status and to make it ineffective on the issue of alimony. It accommodates the interests of both Nevada and New York in this broken marriage by restricting each state to the matters of her dominant concern.[50]

This case involved a husband who was granted a separation and ordered by a New York court to pay support for his wife and children, and who subsequently obtained a divorce in Nevada and used the divorce as justification for stopping alimony payments. Justice Frankfurter in 1951 asserted that "the expression 'divisible divorce' is a misnomer" because only the judicial proceedings are divided between the divorce and a property settlement.[51]

Collection of interstate child support by a custodial parent is based upon extention of full faith and credit to support orders of a court in a sister state. Although full faith and credit almost always is extended, the custodial parent typically experiences difficulties in collecting child support.

INTERSTATE CHILD SUPPORT

Enforcement of child support orders has become a major problem because of the conjunction of the sharp increase in the number of out-of-wedlock births, legal separations, and divorces with the great mobility of the population. Many custodial parents and their children live in poverty because of parents' inability to collect child support. Although the economic and social ramifications of the failure to collect child support are important, such ramifications are outside the scope of this chapter.

The U.S. Office of Child Support Enforcement (the Office) reported in 1994 that states collected $7.96 billion in child support payments in federal fiscal year 1992 or only 33 percent of the $23.91 billion owed for that year and all previous years.[52] Interstate collections reached a record $626 million in the same year, an increase of 83.6 percent compared to 1987.[53] Nevertheless, the amount is only 7.9 percent of total collections, whereas interstate cases are approximately 30 percent of the total caseload. Furthermore, enforcement of child support in cases with an interstate dimension takes three to six months compared to three to nine weeks for intrastate cases.[54] Mothers living in the same state as the fathers reported receiving on average 70 percent of the anticipated support compared to 60 percent if the fathers lived in other states.[55]

Key U.S. Constitutional Provisions

Of the five interstate relations provisions in the U.S. Constitution, three have direct relevance to the collection of interstate child support. States may enter into interstate compacts for the collection of child support, and interstate rendition may be employed in certain cases if a noncustodial parent fled the state while in child support arrears in violation of a state criminal law. The most important provision that relates to child support is full faith and credit.

Judicial proceedings, including final child support orders, are civil court judgments subject to the clause. Administrative child support orders also are entitled to full faith and credit if they are considered to be "final" by the state in which the issuing administrative agency operates. A limitation of the Full Faith and Credit Clause is that it does not extend to future child support payments since they are not considered to be final. However, a state is free to extend full faith and credit to a modifiable judgment of a court in another state on the basis of comity.

Relative to child support, the final orders of a state to be enforced under full faith and credit are accrued arrearages. Assisting in collection of such arrearages is the Uniform Enforcement of Foreign Judgments Act (UEFJA), drafted by the National Conference of Commissioners on Uniform State Laws (the Conference), which establishes a procedure for judgment creditors to enforce a judgment in another state provided it has enacted the act.[56] Thirty-six state legislatures have enacted one or the other of two versions of the act. The act does not require that the state originally entering the judgment must have enacted the act before the judgment will be enforced in another state. Once a "foreign" judgment is filed in a court, it is treated in the same manner as a domestic judgment, and the respondent is entitled to due process of law.

Although Congress granted exclusive jurisdiction to the U.S. District Court if the amount in controversy between residents of different states is $50,000 or more, Congress exempted interstate child support cases from the $50,000 threshold.[57] Nevertheless, no state had utilized the federal courts to enforce child support orders against an obligor in another state.[58]

Child Support and Interstate Cooperation

Laws in individual states historically made parents responsible for the support of their children but did not address the question of establishing and/or enforcing interstate child support. If the noncustodial parent moved to another state, only interstate rendition was available, and its effectiveness was limited by the difficulty of locating the parent, cumbersome due process procedures, and the availability of rendition only if criminal charges had been filed.

Uniform Reciprocal Enforcement of Support Act. To address the problem, the Conference in 1950 drafted the Uniform Reciprocal Enforcement of Support Act (URESA) which was amended in 1952, 1958, and 1968. The last revision was a substantial one and is referred to as the Revised Uniform Reciprocal Enforcement of Support Act (RURESA). All states, except New York, have enacted one version of the act. Amendments to the New York law in 1981 and 1987 have brought it into nearly total conformity with URESA.[59] URESA is devoted principally to civil procedures but authorizes an enforcement procedure, similar to interstate rendition, for an individual charged with the crime of nonsupport. The act mandates that the prosecuting attorney in the initiating state, if requested by a court or department of welfare, represent the obligee in URESA proceedings and also requires the prosecuting attorney in the responding state to prosecute the case with diligence.[60]

The purpose of each version of the uniform law is to allow the custodial parent an expeditious alternative to appearing in the noncustodial parent's state or to employing "long-arm" jurisdiction. A "long-arm" statute authorizes a court to exercise extraterritorial *in personam* jurisdiction over a nonresident defendant and to treat the interstate case as an intrastate case. "Long arm" statutes are not uniform across the United States and also may be ineffective if they fail to comport with the due process of law requirements of the Fourteenth Amendment to the U.S. Constitution. A key 1978 U.S. Supreme Court decision—*Kulko v. California Superior Court*—held that due process requirements were not satisfied by a California court in applying the Supreme Court's "minimum-contacts" test to the case.[61] The Supreme Court opined:

A father who agrees, in the interest of family harmony and his children's preferences, to allow them to spend more time in California than was required under a separation agreement can hardly be said to have "purposefully availed himself" of the "benefits and protections" of California's law.[62]

The *Kulko* decision extends beyond the involved couple and limits forum shopping (choice of court) by the custodial party who desires to modify the original court order.

Despite URESA's potential contribution to solving the problem of nonsupport, the U.S. Commission on Interstate Child Support (the Commission) in 1992 identified nine major problems with URESA proceedings, including adoption of different versions of the law by various states, subsequent enactment of nonuniform modifications, and divergent judicial interpretations of the law.[63] That led the Conference in 1992 to draft the Uniform Interstate Family Support Act (UIFSA), superseding URESA. The new model law has been enacted by nineteen state legislatures and (*i*) contains a new section on "long-arm" jurisdiction, (*ii*) makes clear that the act may be used to establish an initial support order and to impose a duty to enforce an existing order, (*iii*) utilizes a "one order, one time" approach allowing one state to exercise exclusive jurisdiction over a case on a continuing basis, (*iv*) permits modification of the child support amount only by the original court unless both parties no longer reside in the state or they sign a written agreement that jurisdiction by another state is more appropriate, and (*v*) stipulates that a state requested to enforce an out-of-state court order must accept the decisions of the court and employ its state laws only to enforce remedies. The model law is not a reciprocal one, and a state enacting the model law has an obligation to utilize it regardless of whether the other involved state has enacted the model law.

One UIFSA section resulted from problems with the Child Support Enforcement Amendments of 1984 which require states to expand wage withholding procedures to enforce the support orders of other states.[64] To facilitate child support arrears collection, the American Bar Association and the National Conference of State Legislatures drafted a Model Interstate Wage Withholding Act. Although its major provisions have been enacted into law by eleven state legislatures, the act "is not working well" according to the U.S. General Accounting Office.[65] As a consequence, UIFSA includes a section authorizing direct income withholding; that is, the state sends wage withholding requests directly to out-of-state employers of obligors and bypasses the other state's central registry.[66] A state also may use intrastate income withholding by service of the withholding order on any employer who does business in the state. In each case, wages are withheld and sent to the requesting child support office.

Use of Uniform Laws

States frequently utilize uniform laws in attempts to collect child support from obligors residing in other states. In federal fiscal year 1992, 581,599 requests for assistance in collecting child support payments were sent by various states to other states.[67] More than 50 percent of the cases sent and requests received involved seven states—Florida, Illinois, Michigan, New York, Virginia, Ohio, and Pennsylvania.[68] Several obstacles impede collection efforts. The first obstacle is the difficulty in locating the absent parent. If a noncustodial parent is found in a second state, he/she may flee to a third state before action can be initiated in the second state to enforce the creditor judgment. URESA does not address the question of what actions the first two states should take under these circumstances, and state legislatures have not enacted statutes to address this problem.

A survey of case workers revealed "that 25 to 67 percent of the cases referred to them by other states lacked a correct address, 40 to 78 percent lacked accurate employment information, and 50 to 96 percent lacked wage or income information."[69] Collection of child support payments also may be delayed for a significant period of time if an alleged father denies paternity and seeks to prove in a court of law that he is not the father. Every state provides for paternity establishments, but not every state has a paternity "long-arm" statutory provision. Relative to support payment amounts, many state statutes provide for court hearings which may result in major payment delays because court calendars are crowded.

Collection problems may result from the due process requirements of the U.S. Constitution and the respondent's state constitution. An obligor may challenge collaterally the validity of a judgment rendered by a court in another state on the grounds the court rendering the judgment lacked personal jurisdiction over the defendant or subject matter jurisdiction, there was no due process notice or proper service on the defendant, and there was no opportunity for the defendant to be heard. The defendant also may allege the judgment was obtained by fraud. Service of process is a key due process element, and the organization responsible for serving process may not assign priority to interstate service. A related complication is the lack of uniformity in state statutes of limitations relative to the life of judgments, duration of support, and time for service of process.

Payments may be delayed if there is a dispute involving which court has jurisdiction of an interstate case, as it is possible for courts in more than one state to exert jurisdiction and issue orders that conflict. Resolving such conflicts is time-consuming, expensive, and frustrating for the custodial parent, and also reveals the complex nature of the full faith and credit guarantee. And lack of cooperation by officials in the responding state, including a lower priority assigned to interstate cases, may frustrate efforts to collect child support payments.

The lack of uniformity in state child support statutes and administrative rules also hinders the collection of payments. Furthermore, reliance upon paperwork processes contributes to delays in collecting interstate child support payments, and variations in procedures and forms between counties, which often are responsible for collection, in the same state delay collections. Should the judgment debtor move to another county in the same state, delays in payments may result. The Commission on Interstate Child Support identified another problem: "inadequate training of child support case workers, attorneys, and judges."[70]

National Government Role

Congress limited its role in interstate child support cases for nearly 200 years to its 1790 and 1804 statutes prescribing the method of authenticating public acts, judicial proceedings, and records. Congress initially became interested in interstate child support as a means of reducing Aid to Families with Dependent Children (AFDC) payments to the custodial parent.[71] Subsequently, Congress commenced to pressure the states to enact uniform child support laws and to establish uniform procedures. Congress in 1974 authorized the Internal Revenue Service (IRS) to collect specified child-support arrearages in the same manner as delinquent national taxes are collected.[72]

The following year Congress enacted Title IV-D of the Social Security Act establishing a cooperative national–state program to collect child support payments.[73] To be eligible for federal funds, a state must develop a plan and have it approved by the Department of Health and Human Services. The plan must include procedures for locating an absent parent, establishing paternity and child support payments, enforcing collection of payments, and cooperating with other states seeking to collect payments from an obligor.[74] The Title IV-D program requires each state child support office to provide specified services—such as establishment of paternity and location of a noncustodial parent—free of charge to a custodial parent receiving AFDC. Most funds collected on behalf of AFDC families are utilized to offset AFDC payments.

In 1982 the Federal Income Tax Refund Offset Program was launched to intercept tax refunds to provide funds to pay child support arrearages. The Child Support Enforcement Amendments of 1984 made non-AFDC families eligible to participate in the program, and these families received $174 million in federal tax year 1992, and families receiving public assistance were able to collect $457 million.[75] The amendments also require, among other things, speedy action by states in child support cases and reporting at the request of credit bureaus of child support arrearages exceeding $1,000 in IV-D cases.[76]

A state may request the Office to seek IRS's assistance in intercepting an income tax refund in order to pay child support. Upon receiving verification of a IV-D child-support delinquency certification from the Secretary of Health and Human Services, IRS must treat the child support arrearages as a tax debt and may seize property owned by the obligor for failure to pay the arrearages. The state initiating the request must notify the Office and any other concerned state of the receipt of IRS funds. The Office in 1990 issued regulations requiring the states to submit all eligible non-AFDC child support cases for IRS income tax refund withholding. The states also are required to have a program to intercept state income tax refunds of obligors with arrearages.

Under the 1984 amendments and the Family Support Act of 1988, states must notify the noncustodial parent and that parent's employer in advance that support payments must be withheld from the wages of the parent who becomes one month or more delinquent in court-ordered support payments. The requirement applies to interstate as well as intrastate cases. All states have complied with the act's immediate wage withholding requirement in non-IV-D cases. A 1993 report revealed that small business firms object to immediate wage withholding because of the administrative burden, and noncustodial parents view such withholding as "intrusion into their personal and financial affairs."[77]

The Department of Health and Human Services was authorized by Congress in 1980 to make grants to the states to cover up to 90 percent of their costs of designing, developing, and installing state-wide automated child support systems.[78] The Family Support Act of 1988 requires all states receiving Title IV grants to have such a system meeting national government standards by October 1, 1995.[79]

A 1986 amendment to the Social Security Act prohibits retroactive modification of a support order by stipulating that child support installments are vested judgments as they fall due and are entitled to full faith and credit.[80] The Commission identified an unanticipated consequence of the Amendment:

By virtue of their judgment status, support installments are subject to a state's statute of limitations from the date each installment is due. States have varying statutes of limitations, resulting in uneven ability to enforce arrears in interstate cases.[81]

The Family Support Act of 1988 seeks to improve the financial status of families receiving child support payments by improved enforcement of obligations and the Job Opportunities and Basic Skills (JOBS) Training Program.[82] Specifically, the act places additional emphasis upon (*i*) establishment of paternity, (*ii*) mandatory guidelines for establishing child support orders, (*iii*) review and adjustment of Title IV-D support orders every three years, (*iv*) provision of child support enforcement services by the responsible state agencies within specified time deadlines, and (*v*) immediate wage withholding upon establishment or modification of child support awards unless the concerned parties have signed an agreement for a different arrangement or the concerned court decides not to implement wage withholding for good cause. Under these exceptions, an arrearage exceeding thirty days results in wage withholding. The act also requires that each state install by October 1995 an automated state-wide information system to improve case handling and recordkeeping, and that each parent must provide his/her social security number when a child is born.[83]

The Office of Child Support Enforcement operates the Federal Parent Locator Service, a computerized network, to assist the states in identifying the location of a child support obligor and his/her place of employment to facilitate wage withholding for child support. The service accesses data collected by federal agencies, including the Internal Revenue Service, Social Security Administration, and Department of Defense. The Worldwide Military Locator Service can be employed only by Title IV state offices to locate members of the armed forces who are obligors with child support payment arrearages.

Congress in 1992 amended the Fair Credit Reporting Act to require credit bureaus to record child support delinquencies exceeding $1,000 of the parent failing to make the payments reported by the Office of Child Support Enforcement.[84] A 1994 report reveals that the reports to credit bureaus are "having a positive enforcement impact" and may have a greater effect in the future when creditors deny credit to delinquent obligors.[85]

Congress in 1992 also enacted the Child Support Recovery Act (CSRA) making it a crime for an obligor residing in a state other than the one in which the obligee resides willfully to refuse to pay a past-due support obligation which is defined as one "that has remained unpaid for a period longer than one year, or is greater than $5,000."[86] The act is not designed to be applied generally, but is intended for special cases to act as an impetus encouraging obligors with arrears to make payments.

The act was applied for the first time in Massachusetts on July 14, 1994, when a Michigan surgeon who owed more than $100,000 in child support was charged with a misdemeanor in the U.S. District Court in Boston.[87] Robert Melia, First Deputy Commissioner of the Massachusetts Department of Revenue, described the act as "the nuclear bomb of child support; drop it on the few to deter the many."[88]

The constitutionality of the act, however, is questionable. The U.S. District Court for the District of Arizona in 1995 held the act was unconstitutional on the ground criminalization of the failure to pay child support is not a regulation of interstate commerce.[89] The court based its decision on the U.S. Supreme Court's 1995 ruling that the Federal Gun-Free School Zone Act was unconstitutional.[90] The District Court's decision is under appeal.

In 1994, Congress enacted the Full Faith and Credit for Child Support Orders Act containing national standards which state courts must follow in determining their jurisdiction to issue a child support order and the effect which must be given to such orders by the courts of sister states.[91] The specific purposes of the act are: (*i*) to facilitate the enforcement of child support orders among the states; (*ii*) to discourage continuing interstate controversies over child support in the interest of greater financial stability and secure family relationships for the child; and (*iii*) to avoid jurisdictional competition and conflict among state courts in the establishment of child support orders.[92]

States are required to enforce the terms of a child support order made by a court of a sister state and are forbidden to modify such an order unless the modification is in accordance with the act. A court may modify such an order provided: (*i*) the court has jurisdiction to make such a child support order; and (*ii*) the court of the other state no longer has continuing, exclusive jurisdiction of the child support order because that state no longer is the child's state or the residence of any contestant; or each contestant has filed written consent to that court's making the modification and assuming continuing, exclusive jurisdiction over the order.[93] A court that no longer has jurisdiction, however, may enforce the order relative to nonmodifiable obligations and accrued arrearages prior to the date of the modification of the order.[94]

In interpreting a child support order, a court must apply the law of the state of the court that issued the order. Furthermore, a court in an action to enforce an order must apply the statute of limitation of the forum state or "the state of the court that issued the order, whichever statute provides the longer period of limitation."[95]

Commission Reform Proposals

Upon completing its study of this important problem, the U.S. Commission on Interstate Child Support reached the following conclusions relative to federal government leadership:

The role of the federal government in child support enforcement lacks clarity. On the one hand, the Office of Child Support Enforcement has ... promulgated increasingly stringent regulations governing program operations. OCSE also has begun ... to exact financial penalties from states that fail to satisfy audit criteria. On the other hand, OCSE has become increasingly delinquent in conducting audits. States complain that audits are being conducted on three-year-old performance and that the audit process is unduly long and cumbersome.

At the same time that OCSE is becoming more demanding of state program performance, it is pulling back from its customary role of providing support to state programs through its central and regional offices.[96]

In 1992, the commission recommended that Congress adopt the following.

- Expand the Federal Parent Locate Service into a national one and require states, as a condition-of-aid, to develop and maintain a registry of support orders.

- Mandate a child support obligor to report the amount and recipient of support on a modified W-4 form and require the employer to send a copy to the state employment agency.

- Require each state, as a condition of aid, to enact a law requiring employers to implement an income withholding order transmitted directly from a child support enforcement office in another state.

- Add as a condition-of-aid that each state establish procedures granting the voluntary acknowledgment of parentage the same effect as a judicial determination.

- Amend current law to mandate the health insurance industry to cooperate with custodial parents and the states in providing benefits to children under a health insurance plan.

- Establish minimal staffing standards for state child support agencies and a training program for all personnel involved in the child support process, utilizing a core curriculum developed by the Office.

- Define child support enforcement agencies as law enforcement agencies and require the states to report warrants (child support) issued to state law enforcement agencies.[97]

In addition, the commission urged that other states follow the lead of Arizona, California, and Vermont and deny the issuance or renewal of an occupational license to an obligor who has child support arrearages.[98] Similarly, each state motor vehicle agency should be authorized to deny an application for the issuance or renewal of an operator's license or vehicle registration if there is an outstanding failure to appear warrant in a child support case.[99] Nineteen states in 1995 were denying driver license renewals if the applicants had child support arrearages.

Finally, the commission urged the states lacking criminal nonsupport statutes to enact such statutes, yet indicated "that criminal enforcement is a last resort enforcement device."[100] Two state Supreme Court decisions relative to such statutes are in conflict. The Nevada Supreme Court in 1991 opined that a nonresident criminal nonsupport defendant could be tried in the state even if the offense occurred while he was a resident of another state.[101] Earlier, the California Supreme Court struck down the state's criminal nonsupport statute as violative of the Equal Protection of the Law Clauses of the United States and California Constitutions because nonsupport by an in-state obligor was a misdemeanor whereas nonsupport by a defendant resident in another state for thirty days was a felony.[102]

An Alternative

In its present form, despite new federal policies, child support enforcement is a nearly exclusive state government responsibility with the national government providing financial and other assistance to make state enforcement more effective and by making it a federal crime for an interstate obligor to have arrears for more than one year or greater than $5,000.

An alternative arrangement would be an exclusive national government system with IRS or the Social Security Administration responsible for modifying and enforcing child support orders and collecting payments for disbursement to the custodial parent. This approach, according to its proponents, would produce a uniform law with a nation-wide jurisdictional reach and administrative economies and efficiencies, including access to various national government data bases and improved collection of payments if child support is treated in the same manner as taxes.[103]

The commission rejected such unitary approaches in part because "the relatively short history of the Title IV-D scheme did not allow for a fair review of its success."[104] Other commission concerns were loss of state agency innovation, expense of a national system duplicating the existing system, establishment of a dual family law system with many issues remaining with state courts, inability of the national judicial system to give priority to child support cases, relative inaccessibility of national courts compared to state courts, danger that greater emphasis would be placed on AFDC cases, neglecting establishment of parentage and non-AFDC cases, and a more depersonalized provision of services.[105]

Professor William L. Reynolds of the University of Maryland at Baltimore School of Law recommended a more limited reform proposal: "The federal government should solve interstate problems, especially when the states have shown themselves incapable of doing so effectively. Moreover, if the federal courts limit themselves to questions of enforcement, and do not address modification, emancipation, etc., they will be handling the 'federal' (e.g., inter-state) issues. The state courts can then address the 'state' issues such as modification."[106] The commission did not favor the type of approach suggested by Reynolds because it saw the following problems:

(i) inherent coordination difficulties between the state courts and agencies that set and modify orders and the new federal child support enforcement agency;

(ii) the loss of local knowledge of the appropriate enforcement remedy tailored to the local economy;

(iii) the lack of priority historically given support enforcement by federal agencies such as the IRS;

(iv) the shifting of resources to favor recoupment of AFDC at the expense of non-AFDC case enforcement; and

(v) greater difficulty in tracking down the correct obligee for disbursement of payments if identifying information is inadequate.[107]

The commission reported in 1992, however, that "some scholars believe Congress may extend the reach of a state's 'long-arm' statute based on a fifth amendment analysis, through delegation of its own national reach to state courts and agencies. If so, then a state potentially would have the reach of the national government."[108] As noted, the United States Supreme Court in 1978 held that the presence of children with a parent in a state does not confer jurisdiction over the noncustodial parent who had "minimum contacts" with the state. The commission acknowledged that extending the reach of the national government through the Fifth Amendment would have to be based upon a delegated power and cited "the general welfare clause, the commerce clause, and the full faith and credit clause."[109]

Can Congress override the *Kulko* "minimum-contacts" requirement and extend the reach of the "long-arm" statutes of the states? The Supreme Court might well rule the extension violative of due process of law and a state must have *in personam* jurisdiction over an obligor prior to rendering a binding child support order. If the statute were upheld as constitutional, the custodial parent could use his/her state as a forum to establish or modify a child support order, and the delays and required papers associated with a uniform law would be avoided.

The commission specifically recommended that "Congress make a finding that it is appropriate to allow a state where the child resides, and with which the noncustodial parent has not had contact, to assert jurisdiction over the noncustodial parent in parentage and child support cases" and urged inclusion of a provision in the statute for an expedited appeal to the U.S. Supreme Court.[110] If the statute were to be upheld as constitutional, the commission urged the Congress to mandate that the states extend their "long-arm" statutes in accordance with the national statute.

Congress may lack the power to establish such a system and may fail to provide adequate resources in the event it possesses the power.[111] Congress, part of a limited government, may exercise only delegated powers. Whereas one can argue that certain delegated powers could serve as the basis for a national statute providing for total or partial preemption of the child support powers of the states, it also can be argued that Congress cannot exercise these powers in all cases because such an exercise of power would violate the due process of law guarantee of the Fifth Amendment. Hence, it is reasonable to conclude Congress may be unable to preempt state child support laws. However, Congress could attempt to justify its statute on the basis of the (*i*) general welfare clause as authority to restrict social security grants to states according broad jurisdiction to the "home state" in child support cases, (*ii*) Interstate Commerce Clause, (*iii*) Full Faith and Credit Clause, and (*iv*) Fourteenth Amendment. The Interstate Commerce Clause has been cited as authority for Congress to enact a jurisdictional statute, and references have been made to *Wickard v. Filburn*, holding that the Congress may impose marketing quotas on the intrastate sale of wheat, and Heart of *Atlanta Motel v. United States* upholding Congress' prohibition of racial discrimination in places of public accommodation.[112]

The U.S. Supreme Court gave an extended reach to the interstate commerce power in *Garcia v. San Antonio Metropolitan Transit Authority* by allowing Congress to regulate states as polities.[113] This decision might lead one to conclude that the Interstate Commerce Clause could be employed to preempt the states relative to interstate child support. However, the reach of the Commerce Clause is narrower when individuals are involved because of the due process of law guarantee of the Fifth Amendment. Congress can employ the Interstate Commerce Clause to preempt completely the regulatory powers of the states relative to air pollution abatement, for example, but it is questionable if the power can be employed without limit to preempt the states in cases involving individual rights.

The Full Faith and Credit Clause was employed by Congress in enacting the Parental Kidnapping Prevention Act (PKPA) and the clause has been cited by

Professor Patrick J. Borchers of Albany Law School as a source of authority for a congressional jurisdictional statute.[114] Professor R. Lea Brilmayer of Yale Law School informed the commission that "it seems likely that, by citing its full faith and credit authority, Congress could require states to apply one another's domestic relations law."[115] Professor Paul M. Kurtz of the University of Georgia Law School, however, stressed that the act "is limited to defining precisely which custody orders are to be given full faith and credit in other states. There is nothing in PKPA which requires any state to actually exercise any particular type of jurisdiction."[116] Child custody cases differ from child support cases, and it is possible, according to Kurtz, that "the PKPA itself may be found to be unconstitutional at least in some applications."[117] Reynolds, in a somewhat similar comment, observed "the law has long treated status determinations differently from questions concerning an obligation to pay money."[118] While conceding that the Full Faith and Credit Clause may authorize Congress to extend the jurisdiction of a state court in child support cases beyond its territorial limits, Kurtz noted that an obligor might claim that his/her Fifth Amendment due process of law rights have been violated in the absence of "minimum contacts" with the state exercising extraterritorial jurisdiction.[119]

Professor Brilmayer believes that Section 5 of the Fourteenth Amendment, which authorizes Congress to enforce the guarantees included in the amendment, also may give Congress "the authority to alter the due process limitations on state courts. This rationale is quite controversial, however, and has rarely been tested in court."[120] Kurtz pointed out that the use of Section 5 powers by Congress "to restrict court-recognized due process rights is an open one" and added "the Supreme Court never has squarely dealt with the issue, but has provided dicta suggesting that such Congressional action 'diluting' previously established due process rights would be authorized under the 14th Amendment."[121] Nevertheless, use of Section 5 may be held by the court to violate the Fifth Amendment's due process of law restraint upon the exercise of powers by Congress.

Due process of law is designed to protect the rights of individuals from arbitrary government actions and not to resolve interstate disputes. Assuming Congress possesses the authority to enact a jurisdictional statute, a question may be raised relative to the fairness of a congressional statute assigning jurisdiction to the "home" state of the child. Under such a statute, the custodial parent would have the unilateral right to move to another state, possibly for forum shopping purposes, and the obligor would have no recourse.

Our analysis suggests that Congress lacks the constitutional authority to establish a federal child support system. The powers of Congress are limited, and it must rely principally on conditional grants-in-aid, cross-over sanctions, and tax sanctions to persuade states to implement national policies, including enforcement of child support orders by the IRS or other federal agency.[122]

These observations lead to the conclusion that the Child Support Recovery Act of 1992, if enforced, would be a positive approach to solving the problem by making it a criminal offense for an interstate obligor to have arrearages. This act does not raise questions relative to the constitutional authority of Congress and should not place an inordinate burden on the U.S. District Court. Unfortunately, the U.S. Department of Justice "does not intend to use CSRA as a mere mechanism to collect child support," but will prosecute "egregious cases" and publicize such cases.[123] The Department has prosecuted only a handful of cases and refers nearly all inquiring obligees to their respective state agencies which have been unable to collect the arrears.[124]

SUMMARY AND CONCLUSIONS

Reciprocity underlies the full faith and credit guarantee of the U.S. Constitution relative to the extraterritorial validity of civil acts, records, and judicial proceedings of each state. The clause containing the constitutional command that each state extend full faith and credit employs general language and also authorizes the Congress by general laws "to prescribe the manner in which such acts, records, and proceedings shall be proved, and the effect thereof."

The failure of Congress, except in child support cases, to employ its power to mandate in other than general terms the effect of the Full Faith and Credit Clause has led the U.S. Supreme Court to construct a new common law and legislate relative to one of Congress' constitutional responsibilities. Many important political problems flow from the lack of uniformity in the policies of the states. A most significant federalism problem is the conflict of laws necessitating whether a statute of one state should be superseded by a statute of a sister state.

Section 4 of Article IV of the constitution guarantees "to every State in this Union a republican form of government" which, of course, is a representative form of government. A conflict occurs between this guarantee and the Full Faith and Credit Clause's command that the public acts of states be extended *extraterritorium* in certain cases since the policy of state A can be displaced by the policy of state B. Voters in state A do not participate in the selection of state B legislators and are unable to vote out of office legislators who enacted a policy the voters disagree with. However, a counter-balance to this conflict is that, although Congress can use its delegated powers to displace state powers, states and their voters can utilize the political process to influence congressional decisions.

The full faith and credit problems associated with interstate divorce and alimony proceedings have been resolved to a considerable extent by the *Williams II* decision and the subsequent development of the personal appearance doctrine and the concept of the "divisible divorce." Unfortunately, the problems of interstate child support have not been resolved, and available evidence suggests that interstate collection of child support payments will continue to be a serious problem in the foreseeable future because Congress lacks the constitutional authority to establish a national child support system, and interstate cooperation is inadequate to guarantee that all obligors will make full and timely child support payments.

Chapter 5 examines another nationalizing provision of the U.S. Constitution by focusing upon attempts by states to deny certain privileges and immunities to residents of other states.

NOTES

1. Carol S. Bruch, "The 1989 Inter-American Convention on Support Obligations," *The American Journal of Comparative Law*, Vol. XL, 1992, pp. 201–40.

2. Benjamin Cardozo, *The Paradoxes of Legal Science* (Cambridge: Harvard University Press, 1928), p. 67.

3. Robert H. Jackson, *Full Faith and Credit: The Lawyers' Clause of the Constitution* (New York: Columbia University Press, 1945), p. 5.

4. Kurt H. Nadelmann, "Full Faith and Credit to Judgments and Public Acts," *Michigan Law Review*, Vol. 56, 1957–8, pp. 37–41.

5. *The Federalist Papers* (New York: The New American Library, Inc., 1961), p. 271.

6. Henry J. Friendly, "The Historic Basis of Diversity Jurisdiction," *Harvard Law Review*, March 1928, pp. 496–7.

7. *Ibid.*, p. 493.

8. *Ibid.*, p. 494.

9. Max Farrand, ed., *The Records of the Federal Convention of 1787* (New Haven: Yale University Press, 1966), Vol. III, p. 489.

10. *The Federalist Papers*, p. 271.

11. *Ibid.*, p. 492.

12. *Magnolia Petroleum Company v. Hunt*, 320 U.S. 430 at 439 (1943).

13. 1 Stat. 122.

14. 2 Stat. 298. The two acts are codified as 28 U.S.C.A. §1738 (1988).

15. *Full Faith and Credit for Child Support Orders Act of 1994*, 108 Stat. 4063, 28 U.S.C.A. §1738B (1995 Supp.).

16. *Mills v. Duryee*, 7 Cranch (11 U.S.) 481 at 485 (1813). See also *Bank of Augusta v. Earle*, 38 U.S. 519 (1839).

17. *Green v. Van Buskirk*, 72 U.S. 307 (1866).

18. *Chicago and Alton Rail Road v. Wiggins Ferry Company*, 119 U.S. 615 at 622 (1877).

19. *Allgeyer v. Louisiana*, 165 U.S. 578 (1897).

20. *Modern Woodmen of America v. Mixer*, 267 U.S. 542 (1925).

21. James R. Pielemeir, "Why We Should Worry About Full Faith and Credit to Laws?" *Southern California Law Review*, Vol. 60, Nos. 4–5, 1987, pp. 1304–5.

22. *Alaska Packers Association v. Industrial Accident Commission*, 294 U.S. 532 (1935).

23. *Ibid.*, at 547.

24. *Ibid.*, at 547–8.

25. *Ibid.*, at 549–50.

26. *Pacific Employers Insurance Company v. Industrial Accident Commission*, 206 U.S. 493 at 501 (1939).

27. *Carroll v. Lanza*, 349 U.S. 408 (1955).

28. Pielemeir, "Why We Should Worry About Full Faith and Credit to Laws?" pp. 1307–8.

29. *Hughes v. Fetter*, 341 U.S. 609 (1951).

30. *Gillis v. State*, 333 MD 69, 633 A2d 888 (1993).

31. *Heath v. Alabama*, 474 U.S. 82 (1985).

32. *Sosna v. Iowa*, 419 U.S. 393 (1975).

33. *Memorial Hospital v. Maricopa County*, 415 U.S. 250 (1974); *Dunn v. Blumstein*, 405 U.S. 330 (1972); and *Shapiro v. Thompson*, 394 U.S. 618 (1969).

34. See *Shapiro v. Thompson*, 394 U.S. 618 at 638 (1969).

35. *Sosna v. Iowa*, 419 U.S. 393 at 408 (1975).

36. *Ibid.*

37. *People ex rel. Halvey v. Halvey*, 330 U.S. 610 at 615 (1947).

38. *Cheever v. Wilson*, 76 U.S. 108 at 110 (1869).

39. *Atherton v. Atherton*, 181 U.S. 155 at 156 (1901).

40. *Bell v. Bell*, 181 U.S. 175 (1901), and *Streitwolf v. Streitwolf*, 181 U.S. 179 (1901).

41. *Andrews v. Andrews*, 188 U.S. 14 at 15 (1903).

42. *Haddock v. Haddock*, 201 U.S. 561 at 566 (1906).

43. *Kaufman v. Kaufman*, 163 N.Y.S. 566 (1917).

44. *Williams v. North Carolina*, 317 U.S. 287 (1942).

45. *Ibid.* at 288.

46. *Williams v. North Carolina*, 325 U.S. 226 at 228 (1945).

47. *Ibid.* at 229.

48. *Sherrer v. Sherrer*, 334 U.S. 367 (1948).

49. *Coe v. Coe*, 334 U.S. 378 at 384 (1948).

50. *Estin v. Estin*, 334 U.S. 541 at 549 (1948).

51. *Vanderbilt v. Vanderbilt*, 354 U.S. 416 at 417 and 420 (1951).

52. Office of Child Support Enforcement, *Child Support Enforcement: Seventeenth Annual Report to Congress for the Period Ending September 30, 1992* (Washington, D.C.: U.S. Government Printing Office, 1994), pp. 19 and 70 [hereinafter cited as *1992 Child Support Enforcement*].

53. *Ibid.*, p. 55.

54. Bill Bradley, "Interstate Child Support Enforcement Act," *Congressional Record*, October 1, 1992, p. S16144.

55. U.S. Commission on Interstate Child Support, "*Supporting Our Children: A Blueprint for Reform*" (Washington, D.C.: U.S. Government Printing Office, 1992), p. 4. See also *Interstate Child Support: Mothers Report Receiving Less Support from Out-of-State Fathers* (Washington, D.C.: U.S. General Accounting Office, 1992).

56. A foreign judgment is issued by a court in another state.

57. *Justice Improvement Act of 1988*, 102 Stat. 4646, 28 U.S.C.A. §1332 (1995 Supp.), and *Deficit Reduction Act of 1984*, 98 Stat. 1170, 42 U.S.C.A. §660 (1991).

58. Office of Child Support Enforcement, *Child Support Enforcement: Fifteenth Annual Report to the Congress for the Period Ending September 30, 1990* (Washington, D.C.: U.S. Government Printing Office, 1992), p. 17.

59. *New York Laws of 1958*, Ch. 146, and *New York Domestic Relations Law*, §§30–43 (1988 and 1995 Supp.). See also *New York Laws of 1981*, Ch. 763, and *New York Laws of 1987*, Ch. 815.

60. *Uniform Reciprocal Enforcement of Support Act*, §§12 and 18.

61. *Kulko v. California Superior Court*, 436 U.S. 84 (1978). This case was not a forum shopping one. For an extensive examination of *in personam* jurisdiction, see Patrick J. Borchers, "The Death of the Constitutional Law of Personal Jurisdiction: From *Pennoyer* to Burnham and Back Again," *U.C. Davis Law Review*, Fall 1990, pp. 19–105.

62. *Kulko v. California Supreme Court*, 436 U.S. 84 at 94 (1978). For additional details on "minimum contacts," see *World-Wide Volkswagen Corporation et al. v. Woodson*, 444 U.S. 286 (1980).

63. *Supporting Our Children*," p. 21.

64. *Child Support Enforcement Amendments of 1984*, 98 Stat. 1305, 42 U.S.C.A. §1305 note (1991).

65. *Interstate Child Support: Wage Withholding Not Fulfilling Expectations* (Washington, D.C.: U.S. General Accounting Office, 1992), p. 3.

66. *Ibid.*, p. 4.

67. *1992 Child Support Enforcement*, p. 147.

68. *Interstate Child Support: Case Data Limitations, Enforcement, Problems, Views on Improvements Needed* (Washington, D.C.: U.S. General Accounting Office, 1989), p. 13. There were 18,522 filings in the New York Family Court under the Uniform Support of Dependents Law in calendar year 1992. See the *Fifteenth Annual Report of the Chief Administrator of the Courts* (New York: 1993), p. 36.

69. *Interstate Child Support: Better Information Needed on Absent Parents for Case Pursuit* (Washington, D.C.: U.S. General Accounting Office, 1990), p. 15.

70. "*Supporting our Children*," p. vii.

71. For details, see Linda H. Elrod, "The Federalization of Child Support Guidelines," *Journal of the American Academy of Matrimonial Lawyers*, Vol. 6, No. 1, 1990, pp. 103–11.

72. *Social Services Amendments of 1974*, 88 Stat. 2358, 26 U.S.C.A. §6305 (1982).

73. *Social Security Act Amendments of 1975*, 89 Stat. 1051, 42 U.S.C.A. §1395u (1991).

74. For an analysis of the shift from assistance to regulation, see *Regulatory Federalism: Policy, Process, Impact, and Reform* (Washington, D.C.: U.S. Advisory Commission on Intergovernmental Relations, 1984).

75. *Child Support Enforcement Amendments of 1984*, 98 Stat. 1305, 42 U.S.C.A. §1305 note (1991), and *1992 Child Support Enforcement*, p. 20.

76. *Child Support Enforcement Amendments of 1984*, 98 Stat. 1305, 42 U.S.C.A. §1305 note (1991).

77. *Child Support Enforcement: States Proceed with Immediate Wage Withholding: More HHS Action Needed* (Washington, D.C.: U.S. General Accounting Office, June 1993), p. 2.

78. *Social Security Disability Amendments Act of 1980*, 94 Stat. 463, 42 U.S.C.A. §654 (1991).

79. *Family Support Act of 1988*, 102 Stat. 2343, 42 U.S.C.A. §1305 (1991).

80. *Omnibus Budget Reconciliation Act of 1986*, 100 Stat. 1973, 42 U.S.C.A. §666(a)(9) (1991).

81. "*Supporting Our Children*," p. 27.

82. *Family Support Act of 1988*, 102 Stat. 2343, 42 U.S.C.A. §1305 (1991).

83. For the final rule on the required computerized-support enforcement systems, see the *Federal Register*, October 14, 1992, pp. 46988–7005. The rule is codified as 45 CFR 205, 250, 302, 304, and 307.

84. *Ted Weiss Child Support Enforcement Act of 1992*, 106 Stat. 3531, 15 U.S.C.A. §1681s-1 (1993 Supp.).

85. *Child Support Enforcement: Credit Bureau Reporting Shows Promise* (Washington, D.C.: U.S. General Accounting Office, 1994), pp. 6–7.

86. *Child Support Recovery Act of 1992*, 106 Stat. 3403, 18 U.S.C.A. §228(a)(d)(1)(A) (1995 Supp.).

87. Judy Rakowsky, "Michigan Doctor Sued in US Court for Child Support," *The Boston Globe*, July 15, 1994, pp. 19 and 22.

88. *Ibid.*, p. 22.

89. *U.S. v. Schroeder*, CR 95-010 PHX-PGR (1995).

90. *U.S. v. Lopez*, 115 S.Ct. 1624 (1995).

91. *Full Faith and Credit for Child Support Orders Act of 1994*, 108 Stat. 4063, 28 U.S.C.A. §1 note (1995 Supp.).

92. *Ibid.*, 108 Stat. 4064, 28 U.S.C.A. §1738B note.

93. *Ibid.*, 108 Stat. 4065, 28 U.S.C.A. §1738B(e).

94. *Ibid.*, 108 Stat. 4065–6, 28 U.S.C.A. §1738B(f).

95. *Ibid.*, 108 Stat. 5066, 28 U.S.C.A. §1738B(g)(1–3).

96. "*Supporting Our Children*," p. 28.

97. *Ibid.*, pp. 34–5, 37–9, 65–73, 171–3, and 178.

98. *Ibid.*, p. 171.

99. *Ibid.*, pp. 172–3.

100. *Ibid.*, p. 178.

101. *Epp v. State*, 107 Nev. 510, 814 P.2d 1011 (1991).

102. *In re King*, 3 Cal.3d 225, 474 P.2d 983 (1970).

103. *Supporting Our Children*, p. 81.

104. *Ibid.*

105. *Ibid.*, pp. 81–2.

106. William L. Reynolds, "Conflicts and Child Support: A Working Paper" (Baltimore: University of Maryland at Baltimore School of Law, November 29, 1990), pp. 12–3.

107. *Supporting Our Children*, p. 82.

108. *Ibid.*, p. 83.

109. *Ibid.* This recommendation is incorporated in S. 689—Interstate Child Support Enforcement Act—introduced by Senator Bill Bradley of New Jersey on April 1, 1993.

110. *Supporting Our Children*, p. 86.

111. For an analysis of the expansion of the powers of the Congress, see Joseph F. Zimmerman, *Federal Preemption: The Silent Revolution* (Ames: Iowa State University Press, 1991).

112. Memorandum to Deputy Executive Director–Counsel Jeff Ball of the U.S. Commission on Interstate Child Support from Patrick J. Borchers of Albany Law School, dated September 4, 1991, p. 1. See also *Wickard v. Filburn*, 217 U.S. 111 (1942), and *Heart of Atlanta Motel v. United States*, 279 U.S. 241 (1964).

113. *Garcia v. San Antonio Metropolitan Transit Authority*, 469 U.S. 528 (1985).

114. Borchers' Memorandum, p. 2.

115. "Memorandum to the Commission on Interstate Child Support" from Professor R. Lea Brilmayer of Yale Law School, dated November 29, 1990, p. 8.

116. "Memorandum to the Commission on Interstate Child Support" from Professor Paul M. Kurtz of the University of Georgia Law School, dated November 29, 1990, p. 3.

117. *Ibid.*

118. Reynolds, "Conflicts and Child Support," p. 4.

119. Kurtz, "Memorandum to the Commission," pp. 7–8.

120. Brilmayer, "Memorandum to the Commission," p. 3.

121. Kurtz, "Memorandum to the Commission," p. 5.

122. Joseph F. Zimmerman, *Contemporary American Federalism: The Growth of National Power* (Leicester: Leicester University Press, 1992).

123. Letter to U.S. Senator Richard C. Shelby from Assistant Attorney General Sheila F. Anthony, dated April 25, 1994, *Congressional Record*, July 21, 1994, p. S 9426.

124. *Congressional Record*, July 21, 1994, p. S 9425.

5

Privileges and Immunities

The privileges and immunities guaranteed by Section 2 of Article IV of the U.S. Constitution are similar to the full faith and credit guarantee in promoting inter-state citizenship and decreasing the quasi-sovereign powers of states. The section stipulates that "the citizens of each state shall be entitled to all privileges and immunities of citizens in the several states." A parallel guarantee is contained in Section 1 of the Fourteenth Amendment which provides that "no state shall make or enforce any law which shall abridge the privileges or immunities of citizens of the United States." The Article IV guarantee is designed to protect sojourners whereas the Fourteenth Amendment guarantee protects citizens of a state against discrimination in terms of privileges and immunities by the state government. The protected privileges and immunities are those possessed by citizens of the United States and cannot be defined by a state.

In common with many other provisions of the U.S. Constitution, general phrase-ology is employed, and no definitions of the terms privileges and immunities are provided. The guarantee, however, suggests equal privileges and immunities. Fur-thermore, the guarantee does not name who is forbidden to deny privileges and immunities to visitors from other states but is assumed that it is the state which may not deny the privileges and immunities.

The privileges and immunities guarantee involves a conflict of laws similar to that encountered by the full faith and credit guarantee. Each state is free to define privileges and immunities, provided they do not diminish the ones protected by the Fourteenth Amendment. A sojourner cannot demand that a state extend to him/her all the privileges and immunities extended by the sojourner's state of residence. However, a visitor can challenge discrimination by mounting a due process of law, equal protection of the laws, or interstate commerce challenge. Brainerd Currie and Herma H. Schreter pointed out that "a state may without offense to the privileges and immunities clause decline to apply its law for the benefit of a citizen of another state if to do so would violate the full faith and credit clause or the due process clause."[1]

If the Privileges and Immunities Clause is interpreted literally, nonresidents automatically are entitled to the privileges and immunities of residents of the state. In effect, the clause would establish a type of national citizenship, yet nonresident citizens of a state would not be state taxpayers and would contribute little to the state. A better understanding of the nature of the clause can be obtained by examining the origin of the clause and its interpretation by the courts.

ORIGIN OF THE GUARANTEE

The royal charter granted to the Virginia Company in 1606 guaranteed the colonists "all liberties, franchises, and immunities within any of our dominions to all intents and purposes as if they had been abiding and born within this our realm of England." Similarly, Article IV of the Articles of Confederation and Perpetual Union sought to promote interstate comity and intercourse by stipulating "the free inhabitants of each of these states, paupers, vagabonds and fugitives from justice excepted, shall be entitled to all the privileges and immunities of free citizens in the several states; and the people of each state shall, in every other, enjoy all the privileges of trade and commerce, ..." The drafters thereby sought to ensure that the citizens of one state would not be aliens when visiting another state.

James Madison in *The Federalist Number 42* was highly critical of the confused language contained in the article:

Why the term free inhabitants are used in one part of the article, free citizens in another, and people in another; or what was meant by superadding to "all privileges and immunities of free citizens," "all the privileges of trade and commerce," cannot easily be determined. It seems to be a construction scarcely avoidable, however, that those who come under the denomination of free inhabitants of a state, although not citizens of such state, are entitled in every other state, to all the privileges of free citizens of the latter; that is, to greater privileges than they may be entitled to in their own state: so that it may be in the power of a particular state, or rather every state is laid under a necessity not only to confer the rights of citizenship in other states upon any whom it may admit to such rights within itself, but upon any whom it may allow to become inhabitants within its jurisdiction.[2]

Madison in particular was critical of the wording of the article because it would allow a state to naturalize "aliens in every other state. In one state, residence for a short term confirms all the rights of citizenship: in another, qualifications of greater importance are required. An alien, therefore, legally incapacitated for certain rights in the latter, may, by previous residence only in the former, elude his incapacity; and thus the law of one state be preposterously rendered paramount to the law of another, within the jurisdiction of the other."[3] He stressed that the proposed U.S. Constitution would prevent this problem by granting the Congress authority to enact a uniform law on naturalization.

Alexander Hamilton in *The Federalist Number 80* justified the need for a national judiciary and specifically referred to the role of the proposed national judiciary in enforcing the privileges and immunities guarantee:

And if it be a just principle that every government ought to possess the means of executing its own provisions by its own authority it will follow that in order to the inviolable maintenance of the equality of privileges and immunities to which the citizens of the Union will be entitled, the national judiciary ought to preside in all cases in which one state or its citizens are opposed to another state or its citizens. To secure the full effect of so fundamental a provision against all evasion and subterfuge, it is necessary that its construction should be committed to that tribunal which, having no local attachments, will be likely to be impartial between the different states and their citizens and which, owing its official existence to the Union, will never be likely to feel any bias inauspicious to the principles on which it is founded.[4]

Brutus, in a letter dated February 14, 1788, presented a most interesting interpretation of the privileges and immunities clause:

... the constitution expressly declares, that "the citizens of each state shall be entitled to all the privileges and immunities of citizens in the several states." It will therefore be no fiction, for a citizen of one state to set forth, in a suit, that he is a citizen of another; for he that is entitled to all the privileges and immunities of a country, is a citizen of that country. And in truth, the citizen of one state will, under this constitution, be a citizen of every state.[5]

Although Congress has not clarified the Privileges and Immunities Clause as Congress partially did for the Full Faith and Credit Clause, Professor Chester J. Antieau of Georgetown University Law Center in 1967 wrote that the former clause can be read in conjunction with the Necessary and Proper Clause as granting Congress power to protect United States citizens relative to their privileges and immunities from infringement by states.[6]

JUDICIAL CLARIFICATION OF THE GUARANTEE

The privileges and immunities clause of Article IV does not specify who is prohibited to deny nonresidents privileges and immunities, but the U.S. Supreme Court opined that an action is required by a state before the clause can be violated.[7] Although distinctions have been made between "citizen" and "residents," the court has held that "for the purposes of analyzing a taxing scheme under the privileges and immunities clause the terms 'citizen' and 'resident' are essentially interchangeable."[8] In addition to challenging a state action on Article IV privileges and immunities grounds, a plaintiff also may have grounds for a challenge based upon the state's alleged violation of the Interstate Commerce Clause and the Due Process of Law, Equal Protection of the Laws, and Privileges and Immunities Clauses of the Fourteenth Amendment.

Chief Justice Fred M. Vinson of the U.S. Supreme Court in 1948 opined:

Like many other constitutional provisions, the privileges and immunities clause is not an absolute. It does bar discrimination against citizens of other states where there is no substantial reason for the discrimination beyond the mere fact that they are citizens of other states. But it does not preclude disparity of treatment in the many situations where there are perfectly valid independent reasons for it. Thus the inquiry in each case must be concerned with whether such reasons do exist and whether the degree of discrimination bears a close relation to them. The inquiry must also, of course, be conducted with due regard for the principle that the states should have considerable leeway in analyzing local evils and in prescribing appropriate cures.[9]

The first federal court interpretation of the Article IV clause was made by Justice Bushrod Washington of the U.S. Supreme Court, who was presiding in the case in the Circuit Court for the Eastern District of Pennsylvania in 1823, whose emphasis on fundamental privileges and immunities has been echoed by other courts. Conceding that it would "be more tedious than difficult to enumerate" the fundamental privileges and immunities, he wrote:

They may, however, be all comprehended under the following general heads: protection by the government; the enjoyment of life and liberty, with the right to acquire and possess property of every kind, and to pursue and obtain happiness and safety; subject nevertheless to such restraints as the government may justly prescribe for the general good of the whole. The right of a citizen to pass through, or to reside in any other state, for purposes of trade, agriculture, professional pursuits, or otherwise; to claim the benefit of the writ of *habeas corpus*; to institute and maintain actions of any kind in the courts of the state; to take, hold, and dispose of property, either real or personal; and an exemption from higher taxes of impositions than are paid by the other citizens of the state; may be mentioned as some of the particular privileges and immunities of citizens which are clearly embraced by the general description of privileges deemed to be fundamental: to which may be added the elective franchise, as regulated and established by the laws or constitution of the state in which it is to be exercised. . . .

But we cannot accede to the proposition . . . that, under this provision of the constitution, the citizens of the several states are permitted to participate in all the rights which belong exclusively to the citizens of any other particular state, merely upon the ground that they are enjoyed by those citizens; much less, that in regulating the use of the common property of the citizens of such state, the legislature is bound to extend to the citizens of all the other states the same advantages as are secured to their own citizens.[10]

Justice Washington's emphasis upon the fundamental character of the Article IV privileges and immunities of United States citizens was undercut by the Supreme Court's 1868 decision in *Paul v. Virginia* holding that nonresidents possessed only the privileges and immunities possessed by citizens of the state of sojourn.[11] In other words, sojourners could be denied a fundamental privilege or immunity provided the right also was denied to the state's citizens. Justice Stephen J. Field, writing for the court, in this case stressed:

It was undoubtedly the object of the clause in question to place the citizens of each state upon the same footing with citizens of other states, so far as the advantages resulting from citizenship in those states are concerned. It relieves them from the disabilities of alienage in other states; it inhibits discriminating legislation against them by other states, it gives them the right of free ingress into other states, and egress from them; it insures to them in other states the same freedom possessed by the citizens of those other states in the acquisition and enjoyment of property and in the pursuit of happiness; and it secures to them in other states the equal protection of their laws. It has been justly said that no provision in the constitution has tended so strongly to constitute the citizens of the United States one people as this.[12]

Chester J. Antieau in 1967 published a highly critical article on the *Paul v. Virginia* decision stressing that the clause protects fundamental rights and attributing Justice Field's decision to his apparent belief that the Privileges and Immunities clause of the newly ratified Fourteenth Amendment would provide adequate protection for the fundamental rights hithertofore protected by the Article IV clause.[13] The Slaughter House cases, however, proved this assumption to be an invalid one.[14] The issue was whether the granting by the Louisiana State Legislature of an exclusive privilege to a company to erect and maintain slaughterhouses and stock landings in New Orleans abridged the privileges and immunities of citizens of the United States protected by the Fourteenth Amendment.

Justice Samuel F. Miller delivered the majority opinion of the court, which was divided five to four, opining the Fourteenth Amendment is not violated "and cannot be successfully controverted that it is both the right and duty of the legislative body, the supreme power of the state or municipality, to prescribe and determine the localities where the business of slaughtering for a great city may be conducted."[15] He added that the statute is based upon "the police power, which is and must, from its very nature, be incapable of any very exact definition or limitation."[16]

The majority opinion specifically ruled that the purpose of the Privileges and Immunities Clause of the Fourteenth Amendment is "to declare to the several states that whatever rights, as you grant or establish them to your citizens, or as you limit or qualify, or impose restrictions on their exercise, the same, neither more nor less, shall be the measure of the rights of citizens of other states within your jurisdiction."[17]

Relative to whether a state legislature may grant an exclusive privilege to a city or a corporation, the majority opinion held:

It may be safely affirmed that the parliament of Great Britain, representing the people in their legislative functions, and the legislative bodies of this country have, from time immemorial to the present day, continued to grant to persons and corporations exclusive privileges, privileges denied to other citizens, privileges which come within any definition of the word monopoly as much as those now under consideration; and that the power to do this has never been questioned or denied.[18]

In effect, the court emasculated the Privileges and Immunities Clause of the Fourteenth Amendment as the court had done to the Privileges and Immunities Clause of Article IV in *Paul v. Virginia*. The nature of the protection offered by the Article IV guarantee can be understood better by examining the exclusions from the guarantee as reflected in court decisions.

Special Position of Corporations

The Privileges and Immunities Clause of Article IV of the U.S. Constitution is very similar to Article IV of the Articles of Confederation and Perpetual Union but significantly does not contain a provision protecting "all the privileges of trade and commerce" which was included in the articles.

In Bank of *Augusta v. Earle*, the U.S. Supreme Court ruled that a corporation "must dwell in the place of its creation, and can not migrate to another sovereignty."[19] Since it cannot sojourn in another state, the corporation is not entitled to privileges and immunities. The Supreme Court also has ruled that associations are not entitled to the privileges and immunities guaranteed to citizens.[20]

Corporations, as legal entities, possess many of the legal characteristics of natural persons, yet are not considered to be citizens. In consequence, states generally are free to discriminate against foreign corporations (ones chartered in another state) and alien corporations (chartered in another nation) by imposing higher license fees and by levying heavier taxes on them than on domestic corporations. A state legislature also might prohibit an alien or foreign corporation from conducting business in the state without violating the Privileges and Immunities Clause. Such action by a state legislature, however, would invite retaliation by other states and nations.

The New York Business Corporation Law, for example, stipulates the following.

(*i*) A foreign corporation shall not do business in this state until it has been authorized to do so as provided in this article. A foreign corporation may be authorized to do in this state any business which may be done lawfully in this state by a domestic corporation, to the extent that it is authorized to do such business in the jurisdiction of its incorporation, but no other business.

(*ii*) Without excluding other activities which may not constitute doing business in this state, a foreign corporation shall not be considered to be doing business in this state, for the purposes of this chapter, by reason of carrying on in this state any one or more of the following activities:

  (*a*) maintaining or defending any action or proceeding, whether judicial, administrative, arbitrative, or otherwise, or effecting settlement thereof or the settlement of claims or disputes;

  (*b*) holding meetings of its directors or its shareholders;

  (*c*) maintaining bank accounts;

  (*d*) maintaining offices or agencies only for the transfer, exchange and registration of its securities, or appointing and maintaining trustees or dispositaries with relation to its securities.[21]

Foreign and alien corporations are not without constitutional protection against discrimination by a state if the action violates the Interstate Commerce Clause by imposing an undue burden on interstate commerce or denies the corporation due process of law or equal protection of the laws.[22] In 1985, for example, the U.S. Supreme Court invalidated on an equal protection of the laws ground an Alabama law which imposed a substantially lower gross premium tax rate on domestic insurance companies than the rate imposed on foreign insurance companies.[23] The law was not invalidated as violative of the Interstate Commerce Clause because Congress enacted the McCarron-Ferguson Act of 1945 exempting insurance companies from regulation by Congress under the Interstate Commerce Clause.[24]

Taxation and Privileges and Immunities

The U.S. Supreme Court has been particularly sensitive since 1870 to the tax burdens placed on nonresidents who have no influence in the state legislature which imposes the tax. *In Ward v. Maryland*, the court in 1870 invalidated a Maryland statute requiring nonresidents to pay a $300 a year license fee for the privileges of trading in goods not manufactured in Maryland.[25] Maryland traders, depending on their inventory, paid a fee ranging from $15 to $150. Violators of the statute were subject to a fine of not less than $400 for each offense.

Justice Nathan Clifford wrote the opinion and stressed:

... the clause plainly and unmistakably secures and protects the rights of a citizen of one state to pass into any other state of the union for the purpose of engaging in lawful commerce, trade or business, without molestation; to acquire personal property; to take and hold real estate; to maintain actions in the courts of the state; and to be exempt from any higher taxes or excises than are imposed by the state upon its own citizens.... Inasmuch as the constitution provides that the citizens of each state shall be entitled to all privileges and immunities of citizens in the several states, it follows that the defendant might lawfully sell, or offer, or expose for sale within the district described in the indictment, any goods which the permanent residents of the state might sell, or offer, or expose for sale in that district without being subjected to any higher tax or excise than that exacted by law of such permanent residents.[26]

Thirty-two years later in *Travellers' Insurance Company v. Connecticut*, the court examined a Connecticut tax levied on the value of stock in local insurance corporations.[27] The nonresident stockholders' shares were assessed at market value whereas shares of residents were assessed at market value minus the proportionate value of all real estate owned by the corporation which had paid a local government property tax. In view of the fact nonresident stockholders did not pay local government property taxes, and resident stockholders paid such taxes at approximately the rate of the tax imposed by the state on nonresidents' stock, the court ruled the tax was constitutional because there was a reasonable distribution of tax burdens between the two types of stockholders.

In 1920, the court examined in *Shaffer v. Carter* an Oklahoma tax levied on income derived by a nonresident from local property or business and reached a conclusion similar to the above one; that is, the burden placed on a nonresident was no more onerous than the burden placed on a resident.[28]

The court in the same year in *Travis v. Yale and Towne Manufacturing Company* struck down a New York State nonresident income tax because each resident taxpayer was granted a personal exemption for himself/herself and each dependent, but the nonresident taxpayer was denied such exemptions.[29] Specifically the court opined:

They (nonresidents) pursue their several occupations side by side with residents of the State of New York—in effect competing with them as to wages, salaries, and other terms of employment. Whether they must pay a tax upon the first $1,000 or $2,000 of income, while their associates and competitors who reside in New York do not, makes a substantial difference.... This is not a case of occasional or accidental inequality due to circumstances personal to the taxpayer ... but a general rule, operating to the disadvantage of all nonresidents ... and favoring all residents.[30]

In 1948, the court struck down a state statute imposing a license fee of $2,500 on each shrimp boat owned by a nonresident and a license fee of $25 on each boat owned by a resident and stressed that the Privileges and Immunities Clause guarantees that citizens of one state have the right to conduct business in another state "on terms of substantial equality with the citizens of that state."[31]

A most interesting suit—*Austin v. New Hampshire*—involving a privilege and immunities challenge and a equal protection of the law challenge was decided by the U.S. Supreme Court in 1975.[32] The New Hampshire General Court (state legislature) enacted a commuters income tax statute providing:

A tax is hereby imposed upon every taxable nonresident, which shall be levied, collected and paid annually at the rate of four percent of their New Hampshire derived income ... less an exemption of two thousand dollars; provided, however, that if the tax hereby imposed exceeds the tax which would be imposed upon such income by the state of residence, if such income were earned in such state, the tax hereby imposed shall be reduced to equal the tax which would be imposed by such other state.[33]

Employers withheld the 4-percent tax on the income of nonresidents even if their home states levied a lower tax. If a nonresident paid an excess tax, the excess is refunded upon the filing of a New Hampshire tax return subsequent to the close of the tax year.

A 4-percent tax also was imposed on residents by the commuter income tax, but residents were exempt from the tax "provided ... such income shall be subject to a tax in the state in which it is derived ..." or "such income is exempt from taxation because of statutory or constitutional provisions in the state in which it is derived, or ... the state in which it is derived does not impose an income tax on such income...."[34]

These exemptions resulted in no New Hampshire income tax being levied on residents' earned domestic and foreign income. New Hampshire defended the tax by arguing that an onerous burden is not placed upon Maine residents who work in New Hampshire since Maine grants a tax credit to its residents for income taxes paid to other states. In effect, the commuter income tax diverted revenues to New Hampshire that otherwise would be received by Maine which could repeal the tax credit. The court rejected the New Hampshire argument by opining "we do not think the possibility that Maine could shield its residents from New Hampshire' tax cures the constitutional defect of the discrimination in that tax. In fact, it compounds it. For New Hampshire in effect invites appellants to induce their representatives, if they can, to retaliate against it."[35] Having found that the tax abridges the privileges and immunities of citizens of another state, the court did not address the question whether the tax violated the Equal Protection of the Laws Clause of the Fourteenth Amendment.

Justice Harry A. Blackmun dissented and declared "this is a noncase. I would dismiss the appeal for want of a substantial federal question. We have far more urgent demands upon our limited time than this kind of litigation."[36] He added:

The reason these appellants ... pay a New Hampshire tax is because the Maine Legislature ... has given New Hampshire the option to divert this increment of tax (on a Maine resident's income earned in New Hampshire) from Maine to New Hampshire, and New Hampshire willingly has picked up that option. All that New Hampshire has done is what Maine specifically permits and, indeed, invites it to do.[37]

Beneficial Services

The U.S. Supreme Court has ruled that the guarantee of privileges and immunities does not apply to beneficial services, that is, institutions and resources in which the state has property rights. The court affirmed summarily two lower-court rulings which held valid durational residence requirements for students seeking to pay the lower in-state tuition at state universities and colleges.[38] The rationale for significantly higher tuition for nonresidents is that they have not contributed to the state through payment of taxes prior to entering the university, and taxes they pay as students do not amount to the differential between resident and nonresident tuition which typically is substantial. If the nonresident tuition exceeds the cost of educating these students, a privileges and immunities challenge of the nonresident tuition probably would be successful.[39]

A state in its *parens patriae* (father of its people) capacity also may limit the use of state property by nonresidents or exclude them entirely. Nonresident hunting and fishing license fees typically are substantially higher than fees for residents. The nonresident fees, however, must be uniform for residents of all of the other states. Similarly, a state may not exclude the residents of one state from hunting big game unless the state excludes the residents of all of the other states.

As noted in an earlier section, Justice Bushrod Washington in *Corfield v. Coryell* ruled that nonresident citizens do not have all the rights of resident citizens of a state. In particular, he declared in this case that fisheries on public lands of the state were "common property" of the citizens of New Jersey. In *McCready v. Commonwealth*, the U.S. Supreme Court in 1876 examined a Virginia statute which forbade the planting of oysters in the waters of the Commonwealth by nonresidents. McCready was convicted and appealed the decision to the Virginia Court of Appeals which upheld the constitutionality of the act. He appealed to the U.S. Supreme Court which, speaking through Justice Morrison R. Waite, opined, "we think we may safely hold that the citizens of one state are not invested by this clause of the constitution with any interest in the common property of the citizens of another state. . . . The planting of oysters in the soil covered by water owned in common by the people of the state is not different in principle from that of planting corn upon dry land held in the same way. Both are for the purposes of cultivation and profit; and if the state, in the regulation of its public domain, can grant to its own citizens the exclusive use of dry lands, we can see no reason why it may not do the same thing in respect to such as are covered by water."[40]

In *Baldwin v. Montana Fish & Game Commission*, the U.S. Supreme Court in 1978 ruled that nonresidents do not have a fundamental right to a hunting license and that it was constitutional for a state to charge a nonresident a higher license fee for hunting elk because such hunting is "recreation" and not a means of "livelihood."[41]

Political and Other Privileges

The blanket wording of the Privileges and Immunities Clause suggests nonresidents should possess all the privileges and immunities of residents, including the right to vote and to hold public office. Such a suggestion, however, conflicts with the residency requirements established for U.S. Representatives and Senators by the U.S. Constitution.[42] If nonresidents possessed the political privileges of residents, states would cease to be quasi-sovereign politics. The U.S. Supreme Court in *Dunn v. Blumstein* in 1972 upheld the right of a state to restrict the voting privilege to its citizens and in *Baldwin v. Montana Fish & Game Commission* in 1978 rendered a similar ruling relative to the right to hold elective public office.[43]

States have established durational residency requirements as conditions of eligibility for various privileges and immunities. Iowa was a dry state in the 1880s which allowed a person holding a state license to sell intoxicating liquors for medicinal and other legal purposes but restricted the issuance of such a license to Iowa citizens. In *Kohn v. Melcher*, the plaintiff was an Illinois citizen who sold spiritous liquors to the defendant in Atlantic, Iowa.[44] Kohn sued Melcher to recover the price of the spirits sold to the defendant and maintained the Iowa statute was invalid because it abridged his privileges and immunities. Judge Oliver P. Shiras of the U.S. Circuit Court for the Western Division of the Southern District of Iowa noted the purpose of the statute was to prevent the evasive sale of intoxicating liquors to citizens and upheld the constitutionality of the statute by concluding:

An impartial examination of the several sections of the statute of Iowa ... shows that the restrictions complained of were adopted not for the purpose of securing an undue advantage to the citizens of the state, but for the purpose of preventing violations of the prohibitory law of the state, and although, in effect, the citizens of other states, as well as the larger part of the citizens of Iowa, are debarred from selling in Iowa, liquors to be resold for legal purposes, and in that sense commerce between the states may be affected, yet this is but an incidental result; and as the intent and purpose of the restrictions, *i.e.*, preventing violations of the prohibitory laws, are within the police power of the state, it cannot be held that the sections of the statute under consideration violate any of the provisions of the federal constitution.[45]

Extended durational citizenship in a state is required for quasi-political rights to practice certain professions, such as medicine, dentistry, and law. Although plaintiffs have alleged that such a requirement for the issuance of a license to practice medicine violates the Article IV guarantee of privileges and immunities, the courts generally have held that states possess the police power to regulate the practice of medicine and hence such a practice is not a privilege of citizenship of the concerned state or of the United States.[46] Courts have rendered similar decisions in cases involving the practice of dentistry.[47]

The U.S. Supreme Court in *Bradwell v. Illinois* in 1873 rendered a most interesting decision relative to the admission of a citizen to the bar of a state.[48] The plaintiff was a citizen of Illinois who possessed the requisite qualifications prescribed by state statute for admission to the bar, but her application for admission was rejected because she was a married woman. She sought relief in a writ of error to the U.S. Supreme Court maintaining that the refusal to admit her to the bar denied her one of her privileges as a citizen of the United States. Justice Samuel F. Miller rejected her contention because the record revealed she was a citizen of Illinois, the state against whom she complained.[49] Justice Joseph P. Bradley in a concurring opinion pointed out "it is the prerogative of the legislator to prescribe regulations founded in nature, reason, and experience for the due admission of qualified persons to professions and callings demanding special skill and confidence. This fairly belongs to the police power of the state."[50]

In 1985, the U.S. Supreme Court in *Supreme Court of New Hampshire v. Piper* declared that "the practice of law is important to the national economy" and "the legal profession has a noncommercial role and duty that reinforce the view that the practice of law falls within the ambit of the Privileges and Immunities Clause."[51] The court specifically referred to a situation where only a nonresident lawyer would champion an unpopular cause. The case involved a Vermont citizen, residing within 400 yards of New Hampshire, who met all requirements for admission to the New Hampshire bar, including a good moral character and passing the state bar examination, but whose application for admission to the bar would be denied until she established a home address in New Hampshire.

She filed an action in the U.S. District Court which granted her motion for summary judgment by declaring the practice of law to be a fundamental right and finding that the plaintiff had been denied this right without a "substantial reason."[52] The U.S. Court of Appeals for the First Circuit, sitting *en banc* and evenly divided, affirmed the District Court's judgment.[53]

The New Hampshire Supreme Court advanced four justifications for its action in refusing to admit a nonresident to the bar, including the possibility the nonresident would be less likely: (*i*) to become, and remain familiar with local rules and procedures; (*ii*) to behave ethically; (*iii*) to be available for court proceedings; and (*iv*) to do *pro bono* and other volunteer work in the state.[54]

The U.S. Supreme Court found that these justifications did not meet "the test of 'substantiality,' and the means chosen do not bear the necessary relationship to the state's objectives."[55]

The U.S. Supreme Court has upheld residency requirements for the holding of elective office, but generally strikes down such requirements for appointive positions. In *Hicklin v. Orbech*, the court in 1978 ruled unconstitutional an Alaskan statute requiring all contracts in connection with the construction of oil and gas pipelines to exploit the state's resources must give preference in hiring to Alaskan residents.[56] In 1984, the court opined that "the pursuit of a common calling is one of the most fundamental of those privileges protected by the clause."[57] In the same decision, the court declared that the Privileges and Immunities Clause applies to municipal residency requirements as well as to state ones.[58]

In 1978, however, the court upheld a section of the New York Executive Law providing that the state may restrict appointment of members of the state police to U.S. citizens and maintained "it would be as anomalous to conclude that citizens may be subjected to the broad discretionary powers of non-citizen police officers as it would be to say that judicial officers and jurors with power to judge citizens can be aliens."[59] The court issued a similar ruling in 1979 relative to public school teachers because they exercise discretion in what they teach.[60]

SUMMARY AND CONCLUSIONS

A federal system of government not only involves a division of political powers between the national government and the states, resulting in the loss of complete state sovereignty over specified matters, but also necessitates provisions to guarantee interstate comity and eliminate the disabilities of alienage of sojourners in a state. The Interstate Commerce Clause and the Privileges and Immunities Clause in particular seek to prevent the erection or the elimination of barriers to interstate commerce, thereby fostering an economic union of the states.

In addition to the loss of powers resulting from the delegation of powers to Congress, invocation of the Full Faith and Credit Clause, examined in Chapter 4, or the Privileges and Immunities Clause forces a state to surrender part of its remaining sovereignty. The latter clause seeks to eliminate the disabilities of alienage by protecting the private rights of sojourners.

Federalism necessitates a careful balancing of national powers, state powers, and individual rights. The balance needs to be finely tuned on a continuing basis as the economy and society change. The employment of ambiguous terms, such as privileges and immunities, in the constitution makes the document a flexible one, capable through judicial interpretation of adjusting the balance as needed.

Employment of reasonableness as a standard of review by the Supreme Court permits it to sanction discrimination against nonresidents to protect state autonomy provided the discrimination is reasonable when measured in terms of a valid state goal such as conservation of natural resources and solution of health and safety problems.

Strong state governments capable of responding to the problems of their citizens are essential components of a federal system, and court interpretations of restraints on the powers of the states should not be overly restrictive. On the other hand, discrimination by a state legislature against nonresidents may be invidious and violate principles of fair government such as no taxation without representation. The Supreme Court generally has invalidated statutes taxing nonresidents if the statutes do not accord the same privileges and immunities as are accorded to residents.

A strong case can be made for the use of the Privileges and Immunities Clause to eliminate durational residency requirements which are longer than simple residency requirements, for the practice of several professions, such as dentistry, medicine, and ophthalmology, by individuals who demonstrate their scientific competence through testing. These requirements simply add a monopolistic element to each profession and protect resident practitioners.

Whereas the Full Faith and Credit Clause and Privileges and Immunities Clause protect the rights of individuals, the Interstate Rendition Clause of the U.S. Constitution seeks to ensure that persons charged with crimes do not escape justice by fleeing to another state. Chapter 6 examines the origin of the clause and its interpretation by the U.S. Supreme Court.

NOTES

1. Brainerd Currie and Herma H. Schreter, "Unconstitutional Discrimination in the Conflict of Laws: Privileges and Immunities," *Yale Law Journal*, Vol. 69, 1969, p. 1390.

2. *The Federalist Papers* (New York: New American Library, 1961), pp. 269–70.

3. *Ibid.*, p. 270.

4. *Ibid.*, p. 478.

5. Ralph Ketcham, ed., *The Anti-Federalist Papers and the Constitutional Convention Debates* (New York: New American Library, 1986), p. 303.

6. Chester J. Antieu, "Paul's Perverted Privileges or the True Meaning of the Privileges and Immunities Clause of Article Four," *William and Mary Law Review*, Fall 1967, pp. 1–2.

7. *United States v. Harris*, 106 U.S. 629 at 643 (1882).

8. *Austin v. New Hampshire*, 420 U.S. 656 at 662, n. 8 (1975).

9. *Toomer v. Witsell*, 344 U.S. 385 at 396 (1948).

10. *Corfield v. Coryell*, 6 F.Cas. 546 at 551–2 (CC ED Pa., 1823).

11. *Paul v. Virginia*, 75 U.S. 168 (1868).

12. *Ibid.* at 180.

13. Antieau, "Paul's Perverted Privileges or the True Meaning of the Privileges and Immunities Clause of Article Four," p. 25.

14. *Butchers' Benevolent Association v. Crescent City Live-Stock and Slaughter House Company*, 83 U.S. 36 (1873).

15. *Ibid.* at 61.

16. *Ibid.* at 62.

17. *Ibid.* at 77.

18. *Ibid.* at 66.

19. *Bank of Augusta v. Earle*, 38 U.S. 519 (1839). The court rendered a similar decision relative to the Privileges and Immunities Clause of the Fourteenth Amendment in *Orient Insurance Company v. Daggs*, 172 U.S. 561 (1899).

20. *Hemphill v. Orloff*, 277 U.S. 537 (1928).

21. *New York Business Corporation Law*, §1301 (McKinney 1986).

22. *Bibb v. Navajo Freight Lines, Incorporated*, 359 U.S. 520 (1959). See also *Fulton Market Cold Storage Company v. Cullerton*, 582 F.2d 1071 (C.A. Ill., 1978), certiorari denied, 439 U.S. 1211 (1978).

23. *Metropolitan Life Insurance Company v. Ward*, 470 U.S. 869 (1985).

24. *McCarron–Ferguson Act of 1945*, 59 Stat. 33, 15 U.S.C.A. §1011 (1976).

25. *Ward v. Maryland*, 79 U.S. 418 (1870).

26. *Ibid.* at 430.

27. *Travellers' Insurance Company v. Connecticut*, 185 U.S. 364 (1902).

28. *Shaffer v. Carter*, 252 U.S. 37 (1920).

29. *Travis v. Yale and Town Manufacturing Company*, 252 U.S. 60 (1920).

30. *Ibid.* at 80–1.

31. *Toomer v. Witsell*, 334 U.S. 385 at 396 (1948).

32. *Austin v. New Hampshire*, 420 U.S. 656 (1975).

33. *New Hampshire Revised Statutes Annotated*, §77–B:2(II) (1970).

34. *Ibid.*, §77–B:2(I) (1970).

35. *Austin v. New Hampshire*, 420 U.S. 656 at 666–7 (1975).

36. *Ibid.* at 668.

37. *Ibid.*

38. *Sturgis v. Washington*, 414 U.S. 1057 (1973), and *Starns v. Malkerson*, 401 U.S. 985 (1971).

39. Gary J. Simson, "Discrimination Against Nonresidents and the Privileges and Immunities Clause of Article IV," *University of Pennsylvania Law Review*, Vol. 128, 1979, p. 395.

40. *McCready v. Commonwealth*, 94 U.S. 391 at 395–6 (1876).

41. *Baldwin v. Montana Fish & Game Commission*, 436 U.S. 371 at 388 (1978).

42. *United States Constitution*, Art. I, §§2–3.

43. *Dunn v. Blumstein*, 405 U.S. 330 at 343–4 (1972), and *Baldwin v. Montana Fish & Game Commission*, 436 U.S. 371 at 383 (1978).

44. *Kohn v. Melcher*, 29 Fed. Rep. 433 (1887).

45. *Ibid.* at 437 (1887).

46. See, for example, *Ex parte Spinney*, 10 Nev. 232 (1875), and *State v. Randolph*, 23 Ore. 74 (1892).

47. Examples include *Wilkins v. State*, 113 Ind. 514 (1887), and *State v. Creditor*, 44 Kan. 565 (1890).

48. *Bradwell v. Illinois*, 83 U.S. 130 (1873).

49. *Ibid.* at 138.

50. *Ibid.* at 142.

51. *Supreme Court of New Hampshire v. Piper*, 470 U.S. 274 (1985).

52. *Piper v. Supreme Court of New Hampshire*, 539 F.Supp. 1064 (1982).

53. *Piper v. Supreme Court of New Hampshire*, 723 F.2d 110 (1983).

54. *Supreme Court of New Hampshire v. Piper*, 470 U.S. 274 at 285 (1985).

55. *Ibid.*

56. *Hicklin v. Orbech*, 437 U.S. 518 (1978).

57. *United Building & Construction Trades Council v. Mayor & Council of Camden*, 465 U.S. 208 (1984).

58. *Ibid.* at 215–8.

59. *Foley v. Connelie*, 435 U.S. 291 at 299–300 (1978).

60. *Ambach v. Norwick*, 441 U.S. 68 (1979).

6

Rendition of Fugitives from Justice

The terms extradition and rendition frequently are employed interchangeably by the media. The former properly describes the process, established by a treaty, for the return of a fugitive from justice by one nation to the nation from which the fugitive fled. Extradition treaties entered into by the United States with foreign nations limit extraditable crimes to those listed in a treaty and a returned fugitive cannot be tried for any other crime. A governor of a state in the United States has no authority to extradite a fugitive from justice to a foreign country since states are forbidden by the U.S. Constitution to enter into treaties with foreign governments.[1]

The term interstate rendition properly is employed to describe the process, established by the U.S. Constitution and a congressional statute, for the return of a fugitive from justice by one state to the state from which the fugitive fled. The governor of each concerned state plays a key role in the rendition process. In contrast to international law, a returned fugitive can be tried for the offense with which he/she was charged in the rendition documents and any other offense he/she may have committed in the demanding state.

Rendition is essential in a confederation or a federation to prevent criminals and persons charged with crimes from fleeing to another state to seek sanctuary and immunity from punishment or prosecution. The process was employed during the colonial period, particularly among the colonies of the New England Confederation established in 1643.[2] Hence, it was not surprising that the drafters of the Articles of Confederation and Perpetual Union decided to include Article IV which stipulates:

If any person guilty of, or charged with treason, felony, or other high misdemeanor in any state shall flee from justice, and be found in any of the United States, he shall upon the demand of the Governor or executive power, of the state from which he fled, be delivered up and removed to the state having jurisdiction of his offense.

The drafters of the U.S. Constitution included several provisions in the document to promote interstate harmony. They recognized that the failure of a state to return a fugitive from justice to the requesting state could cause friction between the two states which might be extended to other areas of interstate intercourse. Hence, they included the following paragraphs in the U.S. Constitution:

A person charged in any state with treason, felony, or other crime, who shall flee from justice, and be found in another state, shall on demand of the executive authority of the state from which he fled, be delivered up, to be removed to the state having jurisdiction of the crime.

No person held to service of labour in one state, under the laws thereof, escaping into another, shall, in consequence of any law or regulation therein, be discharged from such service or labour, but shall be delivered upon on claim of the party to whom such service or labour may be due.[3]

The second paragraph of the rendition provision, referred to as the "runaway slave" paragraph, was repealed by ratification of the Thirteenth Amendment in 1865.

In contrast to the full faith and credit provision, the constitution does not specifically grant Congress power to prescribe in greater detail the manner in which a fugitive would be rendered to the demanding state. Nevertheless, Congress utilized the Rendition and Full Faith and Credit Clauses to enact the Rendition Act of 1793 which was prompted by a dispute over rendition procedures between the governors of Pennsylvania and Virginia. To settle this dispute and prevent future disputes regarding procedures, President George Washington suggested that Congress enact a statute to clarify the procedures.[4] Congressional debates over the bill did not express concern for the need to protect the rights of alleged fugitives from justice. The act provides:

Whenever the executive authority of any state or territory demands any person as a fugitive from justice, of the executive authority of any state, district, or territory to which such person has fled, and produces a copy of the indictment found or an affidavit made before a magistrate of any state or territory, charging the person demanded with having committed treason, felony, or other crime, certified as authentic by the Governor or Chief Magistrate of the state or territory from whence the person so charged has fled, the executive authority of the state, district, or territory to which such person has fled shall cause him to be arrested and secured, and notify the executive authority making such demand, or the agent of such authority appointed to receive the fugitive, and shall cause the fugitive to be delivered to such agent when he shall appear. If no such agent appears within thirty days from the time of the arrest, the prisoner may be discharged.[5]

Although the constitutional clause only refers to a state, Congress included district and territory in the 1793 act. The clause and the act also do not provide for the enforcement of an interstate rendition demand even though the act recognizes that the clause may not be self-executing by imposing what appears to be a mandatory duty on the governor of the asylum state. The act stipulates that all expenses incurred in the arrest, incarceration, and transportation of a fugitive from justice must be paid by the demanding state.

To assist states to regain custody of fugitives from justice, Congress employed its interstate commerce power in 1934 to enact the Fugitive Felon and Witness Act which makes it a federal crime for an individual to travel in foreign or interstate commerce with the intent to avoid confinement after conviction or prosecution for specified crimes or to avoid giving testimony in a criminal proceeding where the commission of an offense punishable by imprisonment in a state prison is charged.[6]

State Statutes

State legislatures are free to enact statutes relative to the arrest and detention of fugitives from justice provided they do not conflict with the constitutional clause or the Rendition Act.[7] A fugitive from justice whose mandatory return is demanded under the clause and act is held in custody under the color of the asylum state law.

There clearly is a need for state statutes to govern the rendition of fugitives from justice who were not in the demanding state at the time of the occurrence of a crime. For example, a Mr. Hall, while standing in North Carolina, shot across the state boundary line and killed a Mr. Bryson who was in Tennessee. Hall was indicted, tried, and convicted in a North Carolina court for murder. He appealed his conviction to the Supreme Court of North Carolina which reversed the conviction on the ground that the crime occurred in Tennessee where Hall's bullet entered Bryson's body.

The governor of Tennessee subsequently demanded that the governor of North Carolina arrest and render Hall to Tennessee to stand trial for murder. The governor of North Carolina honored the demand, but Hall appealed the rendition warrant to the judiciary. In 1894, the North Carolina Supreme Court ruled that Hall was not subject to rendition because he had not been in Tennessee at the time of the crime and hence could not be rendered to Tennessee.[8]

A person similarly can commit an "affect" crime, such as nonsupport of a child, against the laws of one state while present in a second state. The "affect" crime under the Uniform Criminal Extradition Act or a uniform law or interstate compact is considered to be a statutory equivalent of the rendition clause's required presence of the person in the state at the time of the commission of the crime. A governor may employ discretion in deciding whether to honor the request of the governor of a sister state for the rendition of a person accused of an "affect" crime, and the uniform act authorizes the governor to make the surrender of the person conditional upon the agreement of the governor of the demanding state that the person surrendered will not be held to answer a criminal charge(s) other than the one set forth in the rendition request.

If an asylum state governor mistakenly considers his/her hands to be tied by the mandatory constitutional clause and act, and issues a warrant for a person's return to the requesting state for an "affect" crime, the warrant can be invalidated by a court.[9]

Forty-one states and the District of Columbia have enacted the Uniform Close Pursuit Act which negates the need for interstate rendition in certain cases by authorizing police from other states to pursue criminals and fugitives from justice across state boundaries provided the police are closely pursuing the criminals and fugitives. The New York statute, for example, authorizes police in neighboring states in hot pursuit of a criminal or fugitive to enter New York and "to arrest and hold in custody such person on the ground that he has committed a crime in another state which is a crime under the laws of the State of New York. . . ."[10]

All states have enacted the Uniform Law to Secure the Attendance of Witnesses from Within and Without a State in Criminal Proceedings which was drafted by the National Conference of Commissioners on Uniform Laws.[11] This law authorizes the courts of a state to deliver a witness to an officer of the requesting state after receiving a certificate signed by a judge of the requesting state explaining the necessity of the witness's appearance in a criminal prosecution or a grand jury investigation. In effect, this law establishes a witness rendition process.

The U.S. Supreme Court in 1959 upheld the validity of the Florida Uniform Law for Securing the Attendance of Witnesses. Writing for the court, Justice Felix Frankfurter held that the statute did not (i) discriminate against the privileges and immunities of citizens of other states, (ii) violate a citizen's right to travel because the statute involved only a temporary interference with the right to travel, and (iii) violate due process of law.[12] Furthermore, the court ruled that the forwarding state had immediate personal jurisdiction over the witness which was sufficient jurisdiction to order an act which would be performed extraterritorially, and the constitution did not prevent states from enacting cooperative statutes to increase interstate comity relative to a matter not delegated to Congress.

In his dissent, Justice William O. Douglas stressed the constitutional rendition provision only relates to a fugitive from justice, and there is no authorization in the constitution to expand the rendition power.[13]

The Uniform Criminal Extradition Act, drafted by the National Conference of Commissioners on Uniform Laws in 1926 and revised in 1935, has been enacted into law by all states except Mississippi.[14] The act was drafted because state statutes and judicial decisions in the 1920s lacked uniformity which made cooperation among states difficult in rendering fugitives from justice. The act spells out in detail the form of demanding and requisition documents, arrest and detention, bail, *habeas corpus* proceedings, sufficiency of the criminal charge, and similar matters. It also stresses the exclusively ministerial (nondiscretionary) nature of the governor's duties relative to interstate rendition.

Under the Uniform Act, a person who leaves a demanding state to serve a sentence in another state is not considered to be a fugitive from justice, and the return of such a person is governed by the Interstate Agreement on Detainers which is examined in a subsequent section. The act also provides that the governor of a state can return a person to a demanding state even though the person was not present during the commission of a crime in the demanding state if (i) the person committed an act which intentionally resulted in a crime in the demanding state, and (ii) the act for which rendition is sought is punishable by the laws of the asylum state.[15] In granting a request, the asylum state governor can make the rendition conditional upon the demanding state governor's agreement that the person to be rendered will be prosecuted only for the crime for which such rendition was granted.[16]

In 1990, Governor Mario M. Cuomo rejected the rendition demand of Governor Guy Hunt of Alabama that four officials of the Home Dish Satellite Networks be sent to his state because they had been indicted for violating the Alabama obscenity statute. Governor Cuomo based his rejection on the fact that the officials had not been in Alabama at the time of the commission of the crime and added "the statute allegedly violated does not require, and the indictment does not allege, that the material in question is obscene under New York's statewide community standard, which is an integral part of New York's obscenity statute as construed by our highest court."[17]

The Interstate Compact for Out-of-State Parolee and Probationer Supervision— enacted by all states, the District of Columbia, and Puerto Rico—authorizes a state party to the Compact to permit any person convicted of an offense within the state and placed on probation or released on parole to reside in any other state party to the Compact.[18] It also provides that "all legal requirements to obtain extradition of fugitives from justice are hereby expressed waived on the part of states party hereto, as to such persons."[19] Hence, a parolee or probationer may be returned to the sending state without a preliminary hearing.

With respect to a state where nonpayment of child support is a crime, the state can demand that an obligor residing in another state be returned as a fugitive from justice under provisions of the constitutional clause and congressional statute. Such a state, however, has an alternative to rendition in the Uniform Reciprocal Enforcement of Support Act, enacted by all states except New York, which has enacted a parallel statute.[20] The uniform law, examined in Chapter 4, establishes procedures for the interstate enforcement of familial support obligations.

SUPREME COURT CLARIFICATION

The U.S. Supreme Court in 1861 delivered its first interpretation of the Interstate Rendition Clause of the constitution and the Rendition Act of 1793 in *Kentucky v. Dennison* which involved an action, under the court's original jurisdiction, for issuance of a writ of *mandamus* against the governor of Ohio for the rendition of Dennison, a freed slave, charged with the crime of assisting the escape of a slave.[21] Dennison obtained an opinion from the attorney general of Ohio to the effect the Rendition Clause of the constitution covered only acts which would be crimes under the laws of Ohio.[22] The court rejected this opinion and wrote "under such a vague and indefinite construction the article would not be a bond of peace and union, but a constant source of controversy and irritating discussion."[23] The court added:

Looking, therefore, to the words of the constitution—to the obvious policy and neces- sity of this provision to preserve harmony between states, and order and law within their respective borders ... —the conclusion is irresistible that this compact engrafted in the constitution included, and was intended to include, every offence made punishable by the law of the state in which it was committed, and that it gives the right to the Executive Authority of the state to demand the fugitive from the Executive Authority of the state in which he is found; that the right given to "demand" implies that it is an absolute right; and it follows that there must be a correlative obligation to deliver, without any reference to the character of the crime charged, or to the policy or laws of the state to which the fugitive has fled.[24]

The court examined the 1793 act and also found that there was an absolute right for the governor of a state to demand the return of a fugitive from justice and stressed that the duty of the governor of the asylum state is "merely ministerial— that is, to cause the party to be arrested and delivered to the agent or authority of the state where the crime was committed."[25] Nevertheless, the court determined that directive words in the clause "were not used as mandatory and compulsory, but as declaratory of the moral duty" imposed on the governor of the asylum state by the constitution.[26] The court added:

The act does not provide any means to compel the execution of this duty, nor inflict any punishment for neglect or refusal on the part of the Executive of the state; nor is there any clause or provision in the constitution which arms the Government of the United States with this power. Indeed, such a power would place every state under the dominion of the General Government, even in the administration of its internal concerns and reserved rights. And we think it clear, that the Federal Government, under the constitution, has no power to impose on a state officer, as such, any duty whatever and compel him to perform it.[27]

In effect, the court declared the duty imposed by the constitution on the governor of the asylum state is a mandatory one, yet U.S. courts lack authority to issue a writ of *mandamus* to compel performance of this ministerial duty.

The refusal of a governor to return a fugitive to a demanding state has led to bad relations between the states and in several instances to retaliation. In 1932, for example, Governor A. Harry Moore of New Jersey refused to return Robert E. Burns, a fugitive from a chain gang, to Georgia and explained that the governor of Georgia had refused earlier to return a fugitive to New Jersey.[28] Governor Charles F. Hurley of Massachusetts refused to return a fugitive from a chain gang to Georgia in 1937 and Georgia Governor Eurith D. Rivers retaliated by paroling a prisoner subject to the condition that he travel to Massachusetts.[29] The following year, Governor Rivers refused the request of Governor Hurley for the return of a Boston man charged with nonsupport of his wife and children in retaliation for Governor Hurley's refusal to return a fugitive.[30]

In 1885, the Supreme Court opined that a person arrested and held in an asylum state as a fugitive from justice is entitled to challenge the legality of his incarceration by seeking issuance of a writ of *habeas corpus* in the U.S. District Court.[31] Three years later, the U.S. Supreme Court held that the Rendition Clause and the 1793 act do not contain a mechanism for the return of a person abducted from one state to a sister state.[32]

The court in 1893 ruled that a fugitive rendered to stand trial for the offense listed in the requisition documents can be tried upon return to the demanding state for all crimes committed in the state.[33] The fugitive subsequently can be rendered to other states to stand trial for crimes committed in those states. A decade later, the court opined that a demanding state can correct errors in dates or time periods in the original requisition documents by providing accurate information.[34] In 1905, the court held that a fugitive from justice does not have a right to a hearing in the asylum state, but most governors will hold a hearing upon receiving a timely demand from the fugitive from justice.[35]

The court acknowledged in 1905 that its broad interpretation of the rendition clause and statute might result in a person being detained wrongly in the asylum state and thus wrongly rendered to a distant state to stand trial.[36] In 1917, the court elaborated on this point by explaining that the fugitive is not being sent "for trial to an alien jurisdiction, with laws which our standards might condemn," but is simply being returned to be tried under the protection of the U.S. Constitution.[37]

In 1906, the court held that the Rendition Clause and the Rendition Act do not provide for the return to the asylum state of a fugitive who has been returned to the demanding state by fraud, perjury, or violence.[38] The court in the same year held:

A person charged by indictment or by affidavit before a magistrate with the commission within a state of a crime covered by its laws, and who, after the date of the commission of such crime leaves the state—no matter for what purpose or with what motive, or under what belief—becomes, from the time of such leaving, and within the meaning of the constitution and the laws of the United States a fugitive from justice.[39]

The court in *Illinois ex rel. McNichols v. Pease* in 1907 spelled out the following seven fundamental principles underlying the rendition process.

1. A person charged with a crime who flees from justice to another state "may be brought back to the state in which he stands charged with a crime...."

2. The governor of an asylum state has the duty to arrest and surrender a fugitive to an agent of the demanding state when it forwards an "indictment or affidavit certified as authentic and made before a magistrate charging" the fugitive with a crime in the demanding state.

3. The governor of the asylum state may decline to issue a rendition warrant unless it is proven "that the accused is substantially charged with a crime against the laws of the demanding state and is, in fact, a fugitive from justice."

4. The governor of the asylum state may determine whether the alleged criminal is a fugitive from justice in a way "he deems satisfactory." He is not obligated to demand additional proof from the demanding state.

5. If the governor of the asylum state determines the person is a fugitive from justice "and if a warrant of arrest is issued, ... the warrant will be regarded as making a *prima facie* case in favor of the demanding state" and mandating rendition of the fugitive.

6. A *habeas corpus* proceeding "is appropriate for determining whether the accused is subject" to being rendered to the demanding state.

7. A person arrested as a fugitive from justice is entitled in a *habeas corpus* proceeding "to question the lawfulness of his arrest and imprisonment" by offering proof that he/she is not a fugitive from justice.[40]

The issue in *Charlton v. Kelly* in 1912 was whether a fugitive from justice would be allowed to use insanity as a reason to avoid being returned to the demanding state. The Supreme Court answered in the negative and opined that insanity can be raised only in the court with jurisdiction over the crime.[41] Four years later, the court ruled that the constitutional clause and rendition act do not mandate that a fugitive must be confronted by witnesses against him/her prior to the fugitive's rendition to the demanding state.[42]

The court in *Biddinger v. Commissioners* in 1917 emphasized that the constitutional clause sought to eradicate territorial boundaries between states to facilitate bringing to a speedy trial a person accused of violating the criminal laws of a state and added:

... the proceeding is a summary one, to be kept within narrow bounds, not less for the protection of the liberty of the citizen than in the public interest; that when the extradition papers required by the statute are in proper form the only evidence sanctioned by this court as admissible on such a hearing is such as tends to prove that the accused was not in the demanding state at the time the crime is alleged to have been committed; and, frequently and emphatically, that defenses cannot be entertained on such a hearing, but must be referred to investigation to the trial of the case in the courts of the demanding state.[43]

The Supreme Court in 1952 made clear that U.S. courts will not consider issuing a writ of *habeas corpus* directing the release of an escaped prisoner, held for rendition to the demanding state, who maintains he suffered in the demanding state cruel and unusual punishment in violation of the Eighth Amendment to the U.S. Constitution until after the prisoner has exhausted remedies in the courts of that state.[44]

In 1980, the court invalidated a writ of *habeas corpus* issued by the Supreme Court of California directing the Superior Court to conduct hearings to determine if the operation of the prison in which Arkansas planned to confine the fugitive violated Eighth Amendment's prohibition of cruel and unusual punishment, and held that such claims should be heard in the courts of Arkansas.[45]

The U.S. Supreme Court in *Miranda v. Arizona* in 1966 ruled that arresting officers immediately must warn an arrestee of the right to be silent and the right to be represented by an attorney who will be provided by the government in the event the arrestee cannot afford one.[46] Does a fugitive from justice have Miranda rights? The U.S. Court of Appeals for the Second Circuit in 1967 answered the question in the negative and explained that the evidence used in a rendition proceeding is not being used to convict the fugitive.[47]

Reversal

The U.S. Supreme Court's 1987 decision in *Puerto Rico v. Branstad* reversed the court's first interpretation of the Interstate Rendition Clause and Rendition Act in its 1861 decision in *Kentucky v. Dennison* relative to the role of the governor of the asylum state in an interstate rendition proceeding.[48] The court's opinion supporting the reversal makes it surprising that the *Kentucky v. Dennison* decision was the law of the land for 126 years, as the court cited cases as early as 1876 in which it held that a person suffering personal injury as the result of the refusal of a state officer to perform a ministerial duty could seek a writ of *mandamus* in a federal court against a state officer to compel performance of the duty.[49] The court also cited more recent cases, including *Brown v. Board of Education*, in which the court imposed a duty on state officers to obey its interpretation of the U.S. Constitution.[50] The court supported its decision by opining:

Considered *de novo*, there is no justification for distinguishing the duty to deliver fugitives from the many other species of constitutional duty enforceable in the federal courts.... That this is a ministerial duty precludes conflict with essentially discretionary elements of state governance, and eliminates the need for continuing federal supervision of state functions. The explicit and long-settled nature of the command ... eliminates the possibility that state officers will be subjected to inconsistent direction. Because the duty is directly imposed upon the states by the constitution itself, there can be no need to weigh the performance of the federal obligation against the powers reserved to the states under the Tenth Amendment.[51]

The court specifically rejected the contention "that an 'executive common law' of extradition had developed through the efforts of Governors to employ the discretion accorded to them under *Dennison*" which is superior to the constitutional command.[52] Not all legal commentators agree with the court on this point. Jay P. Dinan, for example, maintains "denying asylum state governors the ability to use discretion by threat of *mandamus* can possibly result in inequitable outcomes in certain individual cases" because equitable claims that the fugitive has been rehabilitated or has paid his debt to society by serving a long prison sentence for a minor crime would be denied.[53]

Respondents in *Branstad* also maintained that the petitioner could not benefit from the court's reversal of its *Dennison* decision because Puerto Rico is not a state and hence lacks authority to demand rendition of fugitives from justice under the constitutional rendition clause. The court dismissed this contention by basing its ruling in the case on the Rendition Act of 1793 which specifically refers to territories.[54]

What are the federalism implications of the *Branstad* decision? Is the decision additional evidence that the Tenth Amendment is a nullity and offers no protection to the rights of states? Although the decision deprives the governor of a discretionary power sanctioned by the *Dennison* decision, the court's opinion conforms with the intent of the framers of the constitution who employed mandatory language in the constitution requiring an asylum state to return a fugitive from justice to the demanding state.[55]

INTERSTATE AGREEMENT ON DETAINERS

Prisoners in a federal system charged with crimes in one or more states and confined in prison in one state may be deprived of their rights to a speedy trial on outstanding charges unless special arrangements are made for their return from the state of confinement to the state(s) with charges against the person. Recognizing the need for a solution to this problem, the Council of State Governments in 1956 proposed the Interstate Agreement on Detainers to remedy the problem.[56] Several states quickly enacted the proposed agreement into law and forty-seven states and the District of Columbia currently have enacted the agreement.[57]

If there is an untried indictment, information, or complaint against a person entering a term of imprisonment in a penal facility of a state, the prisoner must be notified and be brought to trial within 180 days after providing the prosecuting officer with written notice of his place of imprisonment and his request for a final disposition of the indictment, information, or complaint. The appropriate prosecuting officer is entitled to have a prisoner against whom a detainer has been lodged made available in the receiving state upon submission of a written request for temporary custody of the prisoner to the appropriate officer in the state where the prisoner is confined. In response to the request, the appropriate officer in the state of the prisoner's custody must offer to deliver the prisoner for temporary custody by the receiving state. The prisoner must be returned to the sending state at the earliest practicable time after the termination of the trial.

The agreement became an issue in the 1994 gubernatorial election campaign in New York. Thomas Grasso was convicted of murder in New York in 1992 and sentenced to twenty years to life in prison. Subsequently, he was returned under the agreement to Oklahoma to stand trial for a 1990 murder. He pleaded guilty and expressed a wish to die which was supported by his mother. Oklahoma in 1993 refused to return Grasso to New York, as required by the agreement, to serve his New York sentence and prepared to execute him.[58] Oklahoma Attorney General Susan B. Loving wrote to New York Correction Commissioner Thomas A. Coughlin, III that "the state of Oklahoma has a legitimate and strong interest in insuring that this valid judgment and sentence be carried out expeditiously."[59] The commissioner rejected the view of the attorney general and demanded the return of Grasso.

Seeking enforcement of the agreement, New York brought an action in the U.S. District Court in Muskogee, Oklahoma. Judge Frank Sealy on October 8, 1993, ruled that Oklahoma was obligated by the agreement to return Grasso to New York.[60] The Judge indicated that the two states could enter into a cooperative custodial agreement under which Grasso could serve his New York prison sentence in Oklahoma and be executed by the state upon the expiration of the New York prison sentence. Commissioner Coughlin rejected the suggestion and indicated that a prisoner could apply to the sentencing judge for a modification of sentence.[61]

On October 11, 1993, Governor Mario M. Cuomo of New York wrote to Governor David Walters of Oklahoma that "I'm sure that in adopting the Compact on the Interstate Agreement on Detainers my Legislature did not intend that I or my appointees could negate a New York sentence and choose another state's because we liked it more.... Only a New York Court could change the New York sentence."[62]

New York State Supreme Court Justice Charles Kuffner, who sentenced Grasso, rejected Governor Cuomo's suggestion that the justice could change Grasso's sentence and added "the only way the case can go away is if the Governor either exercises clemency or pardon as part of his prerogative under the executive branch of government. He is the only one who has that power."[63]

In his October 8, 1993, ruling, Judge Sealy did not enjoin the carrying out of Grasso's execution scheduled for October 19, 1993. Twelve hours before the scheduled hour, Judge Sealy prohibited the execution and ruled that New York could force Grasso to serve his New York sentence.[64]

Governor Cuomo also was criticized for rendering fugitive James Harris to Alabama to complete a prison sentence and rendering Shawn Williams to South Carolina to stand trial in the shooting death of one man and the wounding of another. Williams could be sentenced to death if convicted. Governor Cuomo issued a statement on December 28, 1993, maintaining "the law required me to sign the orders returning Harris to Alabama and Williams to South Carolina, and I obeyed the law, notwithstanding Williams may have to face a death penalty.... At the same time, the law required me to return Thomas Grasso, a man convicted of murder in New York to Oklahoma to stand trial there for another murder.... The law *also* required that Grasso be returned to New York to complete his prison sentence here before being sent to Oklahoma to receive the death sentence. Once again, I had no choice but to obey the law."[65] Prison officials in New York estimated it would cost the state more than one-half million dollars to incarcerate Grasso until 2011, and critics maintained that spending that sum would be a waste of funds since Oklahoma would execute Grasso in 2011 and should be allowed to execute him in 1993.[66]

George E. Pataki, New York Republican gubernatorial candidate in 1994, pledged he would return Grasso to Oklahoma for execution upon election as governor. Pataki kept his promise, and Grasso was returned to Oklahoma where he was executed on March 20, 1995.

SUMMARY AND CONCLUSIONS

A sound interstate rendition procedure is essential in a federal system of governance to ensure that criminals and accused persons do not escape justice by finding a haven in another state. The constitutional clause and congressional statute do not preempt totally the power of state legislatures to enact statutes governing the process of interstate rendition. These statutes facilitate the process and also authorize the rendition of persons who were not in a demanding state at the time a crime was committed.

The role of the governor of an asylum state has been limited since 1987 by the U.S. Supreme Court which deprived the governor of the discretionary authority to refuse to honor a rendition demand by another state made in accordance with the constitutional clause and congressional act. A governor, however, retains discretion relative to the rendition of a person accused of a crime who was not in a demanding state when a crime was committed. A governor's ability to respond to a demanding state's request for a return of a fugitive who fled the demanding state also is limited in certain cases by the Interstate Agreement on Detainers.

States have three alternatives to pursuing the rendition of a person who commits a crime in a state and subsequently flees to another state. The Uniform Close Pursuit Act authorizes police to cross state boundary lines to apprehend fugitives, and the Uniform Criminal Extradition Act authorizes a procedure similar to the constitutional rendition procedure. A state also may employ the Uniform Reciprocal Enforcement of Support Act in lieu of seeking the rendition of an obligator.

The Articles of Confederation and Perpetual Union quickly demonstrated their inadequacy in coping with the mercantilist policies of states. The U.S. Constitution specifically delegated power to the Congress to enable it to establish a national free trade system by regulating interstate commerce. Nevertheless, states continue to erect trade barriers which cause interstate disharmony. Chapter 7 examines interstate trade barriers and competition for industry and tourists.

NOTES

1. *United States Constitution*, Art. I, §10.

2. See James A. Scott, *The Law of Interstate Rendition Erroneously Referred to as Interstate Extradition*: A Treatise (Chicago: Sherman Hight, Publisher, 1917), pp. 180–1.

3. *United States Constitution*, Art. IV, §2.

4. Scott, *The Law of Interstate Rendition*, pp. 5–7.

5. *Rendition Act of 1793*, 1 Stat. 302, 18 U.S.C.A. §3182 (1985). The constitutionality of the act was upheld in *Prigg v. Pennsylvania*, 41 U.S. 536 (1842).

6. *Fugitive Felon and Witness Act of 1934*, 48 Stat. 782, 18 U.S.C.A. §1073 (1976 and 1994 Supp.).

7. *Prigg v. Pennsylvania*, 41 U.S. 536 (1842), and *Moore v. Illinois*, 55 U.S. 13 (1852).

8. *Hall v. State*, 114 N.C. 900, 19 S.E. 602 (1894).

9. *People ex rel. Bernheim, v. Warden*, 94 Misc.2d 577 (Supreme Court, N.Y. County, 1978).

10. *New York Criminal Procedure Law*, §140.55 (McKinney 1992).

11. See, for example, *California Penal Code*, §§1334–1334.6 (West 1982 and 1994 Supp.).

12. *New York v. O'Neill*, 359 U.S. 1 (1959).

13. *Ibid.*

14. See, for example, *California Penal Code*, §§1547–56.2 (West 1992 and 1994 Supp.).

15. See, for example, *New York Criminal Procedure Law*, §570.16 (McKinney 1984).

16. *Ibid.*, §570.18.

17. Sam H. Berhovek, "Cuomo Turns Down Request to Extradite Cable Officials," *The New York Times*, June 21, 1990, p. B4. See also the 1988 congressional statute relative to the distribution of obscene materials by cable or subscription television, 102 Stat. 4502, 18 U.S.C.A. §1468 (1994 Supp.).

18. *New York Executive Law*, §259-m(1).

19. *Ibid.*, §259-m(3).

20. For examples, see *Massachusetts General Laws*, Ch. 273A, §§1–17 (1990 and 1994 Supp.), and *New York Domestic Relations Law*, §§30–43 (McKinney 1988 and 1995 Supp.).

21. *Kentucky v. Dennison*, 24 How. 66 (1861).

22. *Ibid.* at 69.

23. *Ibid.* at 102.

24. *Ibid.* at 103.

25. *Ibid.* at 106.

26. *Ibid.* at 107.

27. *Ibid.*

28. "Burns Extradition Refused by Moore," *The New York Times*, December 22, 1932, pp. 1 and 3.

29. "Hurley Frees Fugitive," *The New York Times*, July 28, 1937, p. 9.

30. "Renew Extradition Row," *The New York Times*, May 28, 1938, p. 3.

31. *Roberts v. Reilly*, 116 U.S. 80 at 94 (1885).

32. *Mahon v. Justice*, 127 U.S. 700 (1888).

33. *Lascelles v. Georgia*, 184 U.S. 537 (1893).

34. *Hyatt v. New York*, 188 U.S. 691 (1903).

35. *Murray v. Clough*, 196 U.S. 364 (1905).

36. In re Strauss, 197 U.S. 324 (1905).

37. *Biddinger v. Commissioner*, 245 U.S. 128 at 133 (1917).

38. *Pettibone v. Nichols*, 203 U.S. 192 (1906).

39. *Appleyard v. Massachusetts*, 203 U.S. 227 (1906).

40. *Illinois ex rel. McNichols v. Pease*, 307 U.S. 100 at 108–10 (1907).

41. *Charlton v. Kelly*, 299 U.S. 447 (1912).

42. *Bingham v. Bradley*, 241 U.S. 511 (1916).

43. *Biddinger v. Commissioners*, 245 U.S. 128 at 134–5 (1917).

44. *Sweeney v. Woodall*, 344 U.S. 86 (1952).

45. *Pacileo v. Walker*, 449 U.S. 86 (1980).

46. *Miranda v. Arizona*, 384 U.S. 436 (1966).

47. *United States v. Flood*, 374 F.2d 554 (2d Cir. 1967).

48. *Puerto Rico v. Branstad*, 489 U.S. 219 (1987).

49. *Board of Liquidation v. McComb*, 92 U.S. 531 at 541 (1876).

50. *Brown v. Board of Education*, 349 U.S. 294 (1955).

51. *Puerto Rico v. Branstad*, 489 U.S. 219 at 227 (1987).

52. *Ibid.*

53. Jay P. Dinan, "*Puerto Rico vs. Branstad*: The End of Gubernatorial Discretion in Extradition Proceedings," *Toledo Law Review*, Spring 1988, pp. 671–4.

54. *Puerto Rico v. Branstad*, 489 U.S. 219 at 231 (1987).

55. See Kenyon Bunch and Richard J. Hardy, "Continuity or Change in Interstate Extradition? Assessing *Puerto Rico v. Branstad*," *Publius*, Winter 1991, pp. 51–67.

56. *Suggested State Legislation Program for 1957* (Chicago: The Council of State Governments, 1956), pp. 178–85.

57. See, for example, *New York Criminal Procedure Law*, §§580.10–.20 (1984). See also *Interstate Agreement on Detainers*, 84 Stat. 1397, 18 U.S.C.A. app. §1 (1994 Supp.).

58. Sarah Lyall, "New York Battles Oklahoma Over Custody of a Murderer," *The New York Times*, May 6, 1993, p. 1.

59. *Ibid.*, p. B10.

60. *Coughlin et al. v. Poe, et al.*, No. 93-558-S, 1993.

61. News release issued by New York Commissioner of Corrections Thomas A. Coughlin, III, dated October 11, 1993.

62. News release issued by Governor Mario M. Cuomo of New York, October 11, 1993.

63. Marc Humbert, "Governor Says Cuomo Letting Personal Bias Drive Grasso Case," *Times Union* (Albany, N.Y.), October 13, 1993, p. B–2.

64. Doug Ferguson, "Federal Judge Rules Killer Must Serve New York Sentence," *Times Union* (Albany, N.Y.), October 19, 1993, p. 1.

65. News release issued by Governor Mario M. Cuomo of New York, December 28, 1993.

66. Lyall, "New York Battles Oklahoma Over Custody of a Murderer," p. B10.

7

Interstate Economic Protectionism

The start of the Revolutionary War in 1776 coincided with a revolution in economic thought initiated by publication of Adam Smith's *Wealth of Nations* which demonstrated that the mercantilistic practice of nations erecting trade barriers against goods produced in other nations hindered the growth of the wealth of a nation, whereas free trade among nations would produce specialization of production in nations with the greatest comparative cost advantage, thereby increasing the wealth of all nations.[1]

The thirteen independent states, which acted as a coalition during the Revolutionary War, formed a confederation in 1781 when Maryland, the thirteenth state, ratified the Articles of Confederation and Perpetual Union. The newly created unicameral Congress, however, was granted few powers and lacked the power to regulate commerce among the states.

Trade barriers soon thereafter were erected by several states. In 1784, tariffs were imposed by the New England states and most of the Middle Atlantic states on imported goods. Massachusetts goods, for example, were subject to discriminatory duties in Connecticut, and Delaware goods were subject to similar duties in Pennsylvania. New York imposed clearance fees on coastal ships visiting its ports, and also imposed fees on boats carrying vegetables that were rowed across the Hudson River. Discriminatory duties almost immediately invited retaliation by other states in the form of imposition of similar duties. Chief Justice John Marshall of the U.S. Supreme Court in 1827 made reference to "the oppressed and degraded state of commerce, previous to the adoption of the constitution...."[2]

Alexander Hamilton in *The Federalist No. 6* referred to "the rivalships and competitions of commerce between commercial nations" which led to wars between Greek city states, Rome and Carthage, and Great Britain and Spain.[3] Based upon this history of commercial rivalries leading to wars, Hamilton asked whether there was any evidence "which would seduce us into expectation of peace and cordiality between the members of the present confederacy, in a state of separation."[4] In the absence of the proposed U.S. Constitution, he maintained that each state would adopt a commercial policy that "would occasion distinctions, preferences, and exclusions, which would beget discontent . . ." and "the infractions of these regulations, on one side, the efforts to prevent and repel them, on the other, would naturally lead to outrages and these to reprisals and wars."[5]

James Madison in *The Federalist No. 42* stressed the need for "a superintending authority over the reciprocal trade of confederated states" because a seaport state importing goods from abroad could impose duties on goods which would pass through the state to other states and similarly could impose duties on products from a sister state to be exported to other nations.[6] Referring to Connecticut, New Jersey, and New York, Hamilton wrote that New York would impose import duties and "a great part of these duties must be paid by the inhabitants of the two other states in the capacity of consumers of what we import."[7]

To prevent the imposition of barriers by states against goods from foreign nations and other states, five specific provisions designed to ensure free trade were included in the constitution.

1. A state may not levy an import or export duty without the consent of Congress which may revise or abolish the duty, and the duty can be levied only to raise revenue to finance the state's inspection laws with any surplus revenue dedicated to the U.S. Treasury.[8]

2. A state is forbidden to deny any of its privileges and immunities to citizens of other states, a subject examined in Chapter 5.[9]

3. Congress is granted the power to regulate commerce with foreign nations, the Indian tribes, and among the states.[10]

4. Congress is forbidden to levy export duties.[11]

5. Congress may not give preference to the ports of one state over the ports of any other state.[12]

In establishing a federal system, the drafters of the U.S. Constitution were aware that there would be clashes between the delegated powers of Congress and the reserved powers of states, and included the Supremacy of the Laws Clause in the constitution to resolve such clashes in favor of Congress.[13] The need for the clause is indicated by the fact that states have employed four types of reserved powers to create interstate trade barriers.

INTERSTATE TRADE BARRIERS

States use their police, proprietary, license, and tax powers for legitimate purposes, but individual states on occasion purposely utilize one or more of these powers to create interstate trade barriers to protect their industries and merchants. Courts, including the U.S. Supreme Court, recognize that these powers may be employed to impose a burden on interstate commerce, yet the courts will uphold the constitutionality of such statutes based on these powers under certain circumstances as explained in subsequent sections.

Potential barriers may be created by other subtle means. The Vermont Department of Agriculture, for example, established a "seal of quality" program. Farms producing products that meet the state's standards are allowed to affix the state's seal of quality to their products which may result in additional sales and higher prices for Vermont products in interstate commerce.

Interest groups play major roles in determining the policies of a state. If one interest group is a dominant one or exercises considerable influence, its policies typically are reflected in state statutes. Farmers historically have been an effective political force in many states and have worked for the enactment of statutes and promulgation of rules and regulations protecting their products from competition from farmers in other states.

Police Power Barriers

The importance of the police power of the states cannot be overemphasized since it serves as the basis for a vast amount of social and economic regulation. The police power, as broadly interpreted by the U.S. Supreme Court, enables states to limit personal and property rights in order to protect and promote public safety, health, morals, convenience, and welfare. The almost undefinable scope of the police power was emphasized by Justice Oliver Wendell Holmes of the U.S. Supreme Court who wrote "the police power extends to all great public needs. It may be put forth in aid of what is sanctioned by usage, or held by the prevailing morality or strong and preponderant opinion to be greatly and immediately necessary to the public welfare."[14]

The police power may be exercised by the enactment and enforcement of a law or it may be wielded summarily by public officials to cope with emergencies such as epidemics and fires. Local governments exercise the police power as instrumentalities of the state.

The police power has been employed to discriminate against persons and goods from sister states, but its use in many instances is legitimate. In 1981, five southern states—Alabama, Florida, Mississippi, South Carolina, and Texas—imposed quarantines on all products from California in an effort to stop the spread of the Mediterranean fruit fly.[15] Similarly, New York in 1983 imposed a quarantine on the importation of poultry products from four Pennsylvania counties because of the presence of a virus, avian influenza, on ninety poultry farms which subsequently led to the killing of approximately three million chickens by federal and Pennsylvania officials.[16]

There is agreement that states must use the police power to inspect food to prevent adulteration and fraud, and on occasion must impose quarantines to prevent the spread of insect pests and animal diseases. However, the relatively widespread erection of trade barriers erected by states against farm products, particularly dairy products, of other states became a serious problem during the Great Depression of the 1930s when farm states attempted to protect the income of their farmers.[17] A more recent illustration of the illegitimate use of the police power by states was a 1959 Florida requirement that eggs imported from other states had to be labeled "Imported" and egg shippers had to purchase and apply "Imported" labels.[18]

New Jersey during the same time period allowed only eggs laid within the state to qualify under its consumer labeling system.[19]

Similarly, states have enacted statutes prohibiting the sale of fresh meat unless it was inspected twenty-four hours prior to slaughter, requiring inspection of meats slaughtered more than 100 miles from where the meats are offered for sale, and prohibiting the sale of milk not produced within a specified milkshed for the ostensible purpose of ensuring the milk is fresh. Kindred statutes allowing only eggs produced within the state to be labeled "fresh eggs" at one time were enacted by Arizona, Florida, and Georgia. More recently, the 1973 Kansas State Legislature enacted a bill requiring all beef and other red meats sold in the state to be labeled "Imported" unless the meat was produced in the state. Fortunately, the governor vetoed the bill. California's quarantine and motor vehicle regulations during the Great Depression were employed as subterfuges to prevent the immigration of impoverished persons. And North Carolina in the 1970s had a statute forbidding the labeling of apples by other than federal grading systems. This statute had the effect of preventing apple producers in the state of Washington from using a grading system that they had publicized through national advertising, a subject examined in a subsequent section.

New York in 1994 temporarily forbade the sale of milk by the Vermont Milk Producers, Incorporated, which advertises its milk as free of synthetic hormones, on the ground the labels on the cartons violated the federal Food and Drug Administration's (FDA) recommendations for milk produced without the synthetic hormone recominant bovine somatropin.[20] New York contended the FDA considers the hormone safe and the milk labels of the Vermont Milk Producers, Incorporated, suggest that milk other than their milk was inferior.[21] New York officials conferred with FDA officials and lifted its ban on the milk.

The 1984 New York State Legislature, citing its authority under the Twenty-First Amendment to the U.S. Constitution, enacted a statute allowing grocery stores to sell a diluted wine provided it was made from grapes grown in the state. U.S. District Court Judge Charles L. Brieant in 1985 invalidated the statute on the ground it "is plain and simple economic protectionism of New York-grown grapes, at the expense of out-of-state grapes, and a violation of the Commerce Clause of the most simple kind."[22]

Local governments also have employed the police power to erect interstate trade barriers. The city of Madison, Wisconsin, enacted an ordinance forbidding the sale of milk unless it was pasteurized within five miles of the center of the city. This ordinance discriminated against many Wisconsin producers as well as ones in other states, and is examined in greater detail in a subsequent section.

Congress cooperates with the states relative to state exercise of the police power as illustrated by the following examples: A 1796 congressional statute prohibits shipment of goods in interstate commerce in violation of state health and quarantine laws.[23] The Contagious Disease Act of 1903 authorizes the secretary of agriculture to cooperate with states to suppress dangerous livestock diseases but also provides that states may not hamper interstate shipment of animals if a federal inspector certifies they are free of a disease and have not been exposed to a disease.[24]

Proprietary Powers Barriers

States in their sovereign capacity are the proprietors of the public domain and in their corporate capacity hire employees and expend public funds to execute their reserved powers. Although the U.S. Constitution forbids a state to deny privileges and immunities to citizens of other states as described in Chapter 6, states as proprietors are allowed by courts to enact citizen preference statutes discriminating against nonresidents and foreign corporations. However, these types of statutes may be invalidated on other grounds even if upheld on interstate commerce grounds.

Proprietary powers were utilized by New York in 1889 to make aliens ineligible for employment by the state, by California in 1897 to give preference to building materials and institutional supplies produced in the state, by New Hampshire in 1901 to favor printing firms owned by residents, and by Maine in 1909 to give preference to Maine contractors.[25]

States commonly restrict public employment, with a few exceptions, to state residents, and local governments similarly often restrict most public service positions to their residents. Similarly, preference in building materials, construction contracts, and public school textbooks typically is given to in-state firms. Currently, eleven states grant preference to in-state bidders in purchasing products; fourteen states give preference to products, including coal and building stone, extracted in their respective state; and thirteen states favor in-state firms with preference in printing contracts. Twenty-two states with preference laws, however, seek to break down proprietary powers barriers by providing for the waiver of such barriers on the basis of reciprocity.

Licensing and Taxing Powers Barriers

State legislatures have enacted statutes requiring itinerant vendors to obtain state licenses, imposing discriminatory license fees and taxes on foreign corporations, and subjecting chain stores to special taxes frequently based on the number of units in the chain. The U.S. Supreme Court in 1931 upheld the constitutionality of an Indiana graduated license taxes levied on chain stores.[26]

Dairy states at one time levied high taxes on colored oleomargarine in efforts to protect their farmers. Tax discrimination favoring state-produced beers and wines has been common. The Florida State Legislature enacted a statute imposing a $295 "impact fee" on motor vehicles purchased or titled in other states that subsequently are registered in Florida as a means of recovering the cost of highway construction and maintenance. The Florida Supreme Court in 1994, however, invalidated the fee on the ground it violates the Interstate Commerce Clause of the U.S. Constitution.[27]

The most common barrier to interstate trade is a tax barrier. Numerous state taxes have been enacted which facially violate the Interstate Commerce Clause, yet a number of these taxes have not been invalidated by the U.S. Supreme Court as explained in a subsequent section.

Commenting on trade barriers in 1940, Professor F. Eugene Melder wrote:

It would be a mistake to give the reader the impression that the growth of trade barriers between the states necessarily represents deliberate attempts of state legislators to wall off their respective states from the rest of the Union. Many times lawmakers enact such laws in almost complete innocence of their consequences.[28]

REMOVAL OF TRADE BARRIERS

Interstate trade barriers have been removed by reciprocal state statutes, congressional preemption statutes, and judicial decisions. The U.S. Supreme Court has given the Interstate Commerce Clause an exceptionally broad interpretation and allows Congress nearly complete freedom to regulate such commerce. In the absence of a congressional statute on the subject, the court employs its dormant commerce clause doctrine to invalidate state statutes and regulations imposing an undue burden on interstate commerce. And states, of course, are free to enact reciprocity statutes providing for the removal of barriers to interstate trade.

Reciprocity

In contrast to congressional preemption statutes and judicial decisions based upon such statutes and/or the U.S. Constitution, reciprocity is based upon comity and has the advantage of preventing the erection of trade barriers. Reciprocity statutes and administrative agreements extend privileges and/or relax restraints provided other states extend the same privileges and/or relax the same restraints. Income tax statutes typically incorporate reciprocal provisions to ensure that citizens of a state are not subject to double taxation by one or more sister states.

Since reciprocity is noncontractual in nature, congressional consent is not required for agreements based on reciprocity to become effective. Writing for the U.S. Supreme Court in 1939, Chief Justice Charles E. Hughes opined relative to the Massachusetts and Missouri reciprocity acts:

Each state has the unfettered right at any time to repeal its legislation. Each state is competent to construe and apply its legislation in cases that arise within its jurisdiction. If it be assumed that the statutes of the two states have been enacted with a view to reciprocity in operation, nothing is shown which can be taken to alter their essential character as mere legislation and to create an obligation which either state is entitled to enforce as against the other in a court of justice.[29]

The court held that the reciprocity clause of the Missouri Death Tax Act did not give rise to a controversy between the two states which conferred original jurisdiction on the court.

The movement for reciprocity was promoted by the development of the motor vehicle in the early decades of the twentieth century. A reciprocity Conference on

Motor Vehicles was held in French Lick, Indiana, in 1931 to promote reciprocity.[30] Similarly, an Interstate Bus and Truck Conference was held in 1933 in Harrisburg and in Salt Lake City in 1934 to promote reciprocity of bus and truck registrations.[31] And a National Conference on Interstate Trade Barriers was held in Chicago in 1939 under the sponsorship of the Council of State Governments and State Commission on Interstate Cooperation.[32]

Based upon comity, each state and each Canadian province recognize the registration of vehicles by other states and provinces. With certain exceptions involving age, each state and each Canadian province recognize driver licenses issued by other states and provinces. Typically, the registration reciprocity agreements provide that a vehicle may be driven in another state or province for a specified period of time without the owner being required to register the vehicle in the other state or province.

The New York Vehicle and Traffic Law, for example, contains two provisions relative to vehicle registration reciprocity. The governor or the commissioner of Motor Vehicles is authorized to enter into an interstate compact providing for the reciprocal recognition of vehicle registrations and the commissioner is authorized to enter into reciprocal agreements with other states to become a member of the international registration plan.[33]

The New York law also authorizes a nonresident of age sixteen years or older licensed by another state to operate a motor vehicle or motorcycle in New York.[34] In addition, motor vehicle violations are subject to reciprocity agreements under which a motorist convicted of a motor vehicle violation in a sister state may have his/her license suspended or revoked by the home state because of the convictions in another state. Thirty-six states and the District of Columbia treat out-of-state convictions in the same manner as in-state convictions, and fourteen states do not.[35] Several foreign nations also notify states of their drivers whose licenses have been suspended or repealed.[36]

Reciprocity agreements also are common relative to certain occupations and professions. Only Connecticut, Florida, Massachusetts, and Rhode Island did not have medical license reciprocity agreements by 1930.[37] Reciprocity agreements also relate to the professions of dentistry, embalming, pharmacy, architecture, engineering, and law. States also have entered into reciprocity agreements relative to milk, interstate transportation of dependent and indigent persons, and interstate transportation of patients with tuberculosis.[38]

Interstate compacts, examined in Chapter 3, have the potential for removing interstate trade barriers, but have not been employed for this purpose to date.

Preemption Statutes

Acting under its delegated power to regulate interstate commerce and the complementary Supremacy of the Laws Clause of the U.S. Constitution, Congress enacted statutes designed to ensure the nation is a free trade area unhindered by burdensome state restrictions and taxes.[39] Congress, however, does not always exercise its delegated powers fully and in a number of instances did not exercise certain delegated powers for decades.

The constitution grants Congress power to regulate bankruptcies, but Congress only enacted minor acts in 1800, 1843, and 1867 which later were repealed.[40] By 1898, however, the divergent provisions of state bankruptcy laws were creating serious problems for interstate commerce, and Congress decided to preempt state regulatory authority with the exception of homestead exclusions from bankruptcy proceedings.[41] Similarly, Congress enacted statutes to provide for uniform safety regulation of railroads.[42]

More recently, Congress enacted the Wool Products Labeling Act of 1940 and the Fur Products Labeling Act of 1951 to establish national labeling systems.[43] The Automotive Information Disclosure Act of 1958, the Egg Products Inspection Act of 1970, and the Nutrition Labeling and Education Act of 1990 are other examples of preemption acts providing for national uniformity, thereby eliminating trade barriers between states.[44]

Concern with the lack of uniformity in the labeling of grains led Congress to enact the Grain Standards Act of 1968 forbidding states and their local governments to "require the inspection or description in accordance with any standards of kind, class, equality, condition, or other characteristics of grain as a condition of shipment, or sale, of such grain in interstate or foreign commerce, or require any license for, or impose any other restrictions upon, the performance of any official inspection function under this act by official inspection personnel."[45]

Congress in the late 1970s and early 1980s decided there should be no state economic regulation of the airline, trucking, and bus industries, and enacted the Airline Deregulation Act of 1978, Motor Carrier Act of 1980, and Bus Regulatory Reform Act of 1982.[46]

The competitive advantage of the motor trucking industry in servicing many markets led to a major diversion to it of freight from railroads in the twentieth century. Railroad companies exerted great influence in many state legislatures until mid-century and encouraged the imposition of weight and size restrictions on motor trucks for the ostensible purpose of protecting the public's investment in highways. The trucking industry complained that the differences in truck weight and size limits in the various states resulted in higher operating costs that were passed on to consumers. In particular, operators of tandem trucks and "triple rigs" maintained that they had to decouple one or two trailers before they could enter or pass through certain states.

Congress responded to these complaints by enacting the Surface Transportation Assistance Act of 1982 totally preempting state truck size and weight limits relative to trucks operating on interstate highways and on sections of the national-aid highway system as determined by the secretary of transportation.[47] The reader should recognize that state officials do not always oppose total preemption statutes and occasionally memorialize Congress to enact a preemption statute. For example, the National Governors' Association's policy position for 1980–81 expressed its concern with the increased costs imposed on truckers by nonuniform weight and size dimensions and urged "that Congress immediately enact legislation establishing national standards for weight (80,000 gross; 20,000 per single axle, 34,000 for tandem) and length (60 ft.)."[48]

The act eliminated the patchwork quilt of conflicting state truck size and weight limits on the covered highways, but also created safety problems in states where the highways were not designed to accommodate large trucks. Congress responded to the safety concerns of states by enacting the Tandem Truck Safety Act of 1984 and the Motor Carrier Safety Act of 1984 clarifying the authority of state and local governments to impose reasonable safety restrictions on the operation of truck tractor–semitrailer combinations and directing the secretary of transportation to issue regulations containing minimum safety standards for commercial motor vehicles.[49]

Trucking companies continued to pressure Congress to remove two interstate trade barriers—state requirements that trucks must be registered in more than one state because statutes in various states required trucks operating on a regular basis within a state to be registered in that state and state fuel tax reporting requirements.

Congress responded by enacting the Surface Transportation Efficiency Act of 1991 whose Title IV is labeled the Motor Carrier Act of 1991. The latter act in effect forces all states to participate in the International Registration Plan.[50] Failure to participate strips a state of authority to establish and enforce any other commercial registration plan.

Similarly, the Motor Carrier Act of 1991 forces all states to participate in the International Fuel Agreement since a state may not enact a statute or promulgate a regulation requiring payment of a fuel tax "unless such law or regulation is in conformity with the International Fuel Agreement with respect to collection of such a tax by a single base state and proportional sharing of such taxes charged among the states where a commercial vehicle is operated."[51]

The United States has a long history of decentralized banking arising from the fear of concentrated economic power. In 1924, the U.S. Supreme Court ruled that national chartered banks could not establish branches, but state chartered banks were free to do so if allowed by state law.[52] Congress in 1927 enacted the McFadden Act authorizing national banks to establish branches with the approval of the comptroller of the currency provided state law allowed branches.[53]

A bank desiring to establish branches in its home state and/or other states could do so by establishing a bank holding company which would control separate banks that were not legally branches. Congress in 1956 decided to provide for federal regulation of bank holding companies by authorizing such companies to acquire other banks only if the board of governors of the Federal Reserve System approved.[54] The act, however, contained a savings provision allowing states to continue to exercise their powers to regulate banks and bank holding companies and their subsidiaries.[55]

Commencing with a 1982 New York statute, all states except Hawaii by 1994 enacted statutes authorizing bank holding companies incorporated in sister states to acquire a bank, provided reciprocity applied. The southeastern and New England states, however, each adopted a regional approach based upon reciprocity by sister states within a defined region, which resulted in the creation of so-called "super-regional" banks and the exclusion of the large California and New York banks. This regional trade barrier approach was upheld as constitutional by the U.S. Supreme Court in 1985.[56]

The use of the holding company device impedes interstate commerce by increasing the cost of bank operations and restricts the potential benefits to consumers of branch banking services. Persons who are customers of a branch bank in Connecticut, for example, generally could not make a deposit at the bank's New York branches.

To eliminate the remaining restraints on branch banking, Congress enacted the Interstate Banking and Branching Efficiency Act of 1994.[57] The act, however, apparently will lead to state law conflicts, as state usury laws are not uniform. The U.S. Supreme Court in 1978 opined, relative to an interstate loan, that the laws of the state where the bank headquarters is located, and not the laws of the borrower's state, determine the rate of interest that may be charged.[58] Hence, a bank could circumvent strict usury laws by locating its home office in a state with less restrictive statutes. Under the 1994 act, a bank may be located officially in more than one state relative to state usury laws. A key question is whether a Delaware bank that purchases branches in Pennsylvania, for example, will be able to collect Delaware loan charges in Pennsylvania. In other words, will a bank be able to export interest rates from its home state to sister states where the bank has branches?

It is important for the reader to recognize that Congress can authorize states to regulate interstate commerce. The McCarran–Ferguson Act of 1945 delegates the power to regulate the insurance industry to the states, and several states enacted statutes favoring domestic insurance companies.[59] In addition, Congress has enacted statutes to assist states in the enforcement of their police power. Examples include the 1796 and 1797 statutes forbidding the interstate shipment of goods in violation of the health or quarantine laws of a state and the Plant Quarantine Act of 1912 authorizing states to establish a quarantine against the shipment of diseased or infested plants not subject to a federal quarantine.[60]

Judicial Decisions

The most frequent and significant means for removing interstate trade barriers has been judicial decisions. Alleged barriers have been challenged on the grounds that they violate one or more of the following provisions of the U.S. Constitution: Interstate Commerce Clause, Privileges and Immunities Clause (examined in Ch. 5), and Equal Protection of the Law.

The Early Decisions. Ratification of the U.S. Constitution as a replacement for the Articles of Confederation highlighted a general consensus that a free-trade zone had been created and state legislatures should not enact statutes based upon economic provincialism. Delegation of the power to Congress to regulate interstate commerce suggested to the states that erection of trade barriers would be fruitless since Congress could invalidate them. Congress was slow to enact statutes regulating such commerce, and the U.S. Supreme Court's interpretation of the dormant commerce clause as a negative command came to be relied upon by plaintiffs to invalidate state statutes creating interstate trade barriers.

The court was first called upon to strike down an interstate trade barrier in *Gibbons v. Ogden* in 1824.[61] Writing for the court, Chief Justice Marshall developed the doctrine of the continuous journey which held that Congress possessed the power to regulate a steamship that traveled only in New York State because some of the merchandise and passengers carried on the ship will continue their journey after disembarking the state and will continue to be transported to other states. The New York State Legislature had enacted a statute granting a monopoly on the operation of steamboats in the state to Robert Fulton and Robert R. Livingston. Thomas Gibbons challenged the monopoly on the basis of the Interstate Commerce Clause and a coasting license issued under provisions of a 1793 act of Congress. In effect, Marshall developed the dormant commerce clause doctrine which holds the clause, without benefit of an act of Congress, limits the powers of states, and the court would determine what the limits are.

In 1827, Marshall rendered an opinion building upon *Gibbons v. Ogden*. He held invalid a Maryland law imposing a discriminatory tax of fifty dollars on importers on the ground the license tax interfered with foreign commerce in the same manner as "a tax directly on imports."[62] Although the case dealt with foreign commerce, the majority indicated "the principles laid down in this case ... apply equally to importations from a sister state."[63] Professor William B. Munro wrote that Marshall "found the organic law, the constitution, full of silences which had to be made articulate. And his initial task was to assert the right of the Supreme Court to the exercise of this function."[64]

Roger B. Taney, Marshall's successor as chief justice, held sharply different views on interpretations of the constitution. In the license cases, he acknowledged in 1847 that Congress possesses plenary power to regulate interstate and foreign commerce but added "the State may nevertheless, for the safety or convenience of trade, or for the protection of the health of its citizens, make regulations of commerce for its own ports and harbors, and for its own territory; and such regulations are valid unless they come in conflict with a law of Congress.[65]

In 1851, the Taney Court in *Cooley v. The Board of Wardens* ruled that there were details of commerce that could be regulated by states until the regulations are supplanted by an act of Congress.[66] This ruling led to other rulings holding that states could regulate interstate commerce provided the regulations were not an undue burden on such commerce or have an impermissible indirect effect on such commerce. This case involved a Pennsylvania requirement that all ships coming into a harbor must take on a pilot paid at a fixed rate to ensure the safe entrance of the ships into the harbor. Congress still allows states to regulate harbor pilots and also to regulate anchorage rules, harbor buoys and lights, and erection of docks, piers, and wharves. In addition, states may construct bridges and dams over navigable waters.

A facially discriminatory Alabama tax of fifty cents per gallon imposed on dealers importing liquors into the state was upheld in 1869 by the U.S. Supreme Court which developed the doctrine of complementary exaction holding, in this case, that other sections of Alabama law imposed the identical fifty-cent tax on brandy and whiskey produced in the state.[67]

The court does not always uphold a facially discriminatory tax under the doctrine of complementary exaction. In 1886, the court invalidated a Michigan statute imposing a $300 fee on persons selling or soliciting for the sale of liquors to be shipped into the state.[68] Michigan maintained it also imposed a $400 annual tax upon firms manufacturing and selling liquors in the state, which was a more burdensome tax. The court rejected this argument and noted that the two taxes affected different classes of parties since one tax was on the principal party and the other tax was on the agents of the principal who sold or were soliciting orders for the principal. In the court's opinion, the different nature of the taxes gave "an immense advantage to the product manufactured in Michigan, and to the manufacturers and dealers of that state...."[69]

Justice John M. Harlan of the U.S. Supreme Court in 1890 opined that animal inspection laws designed to ensure that meat is fit for human consumption were valid exercises of the police power, but were invalid if the laws were designed to prevent the importation of meats of animals slaughtered in other states.[70]

Twentieth Century Decisions. Courts typically start with the presumptive validity of state statutes allegedly burdening the free flow of commerce across state lines. Robert H. Jackson, solicitor general of the United States in 1940, wrote relative to state and local government regulations that:

The menace consists in its perversion. The purpose to discriminate may not appear on the face of the most burdensome measure. It often appears only in its administration and application, and this is usually not susceptible of proof. The question before the court in most instances is not whether state regulation is preferable to federal regulation, but whether state control is better than no control at all. Unable to solve the problems in any practicable manner, the Supreme Court must be slow to condemn laws which do not clearly discriminate against interstate commerce.[71]

Writing as a Justice of the U.S. Supreme Court in 1949, he explained "this court consistently has rebuffed attempts of states to advance their own commercial interests by curtailing the movement of articles of commerce ... while generally supporting their right to impose even burdensome regulations in the interest of local health and safety."[72] Similarly, Justice Harlan F. Stone wrote the function of the court "is only to determine whether it is possible to say that the legislative decision is without rational basis."[73]

In 1926, the U.S. Supreme Court upheld the constitutionality of a facially discriminatory Louisiana tax of twenty-five mills on the railroad rolling stock of foreign corporations lacking a domicile in the state.[74] The Louisiana Constitution of 1921 exempted payers of this tax from local taxes, and there was only a four-mill difference between the state tax and the average local tax which the court concluded did not amount to substantial discrimination in light of the lack of evidence that the state tax was designed to discriminate against nonresidents.[75]

The court in 1932 upheld the constitutionality of a South Carolina six-cents-per-gallon license tax imposed on individuals importing petroleum products for consumption in the state on the ground the tax was a complementary one since other state laws imposed a similar six-cents-per-gallon license tax on petroleum product dealers who sold such products in the state.[76] The court specifically held "there is no demand in the constitution that the state shall put its requirements in any one statute. It may distribute them as it sees fit, if the result, taken in its totality, is within the state's constitutional power."[77]

The Supreme Court in 1933 upheld an animal quarantine order of the New York State Commissioner of Agriculture and Markets forbidding the shipment into the state of cattle unless they were from herds certified as free of Bang's disease after three tests during the preceding year.[78] The order, issued during the Great Depression, was designed to prevent the importation of cattle into New York in order to protect domestic farmers and was successful in preventing the importation of cattle.

In 1935, the court in *Baldwin v. G.A.F. Seelig, Incorporated*, invalidated New York's Milk Control Act because the court concluded the act was designed to inflate the price of milk in order to protect New York milk producers from competition of milk producers in another state.[79] The act was a classic example of economic provincialism. Professor Michael E. Smith of the University of California, Berkeley, commented that this decision "was a major step in the movement away from the older, special doctrines based on subject matter toward the present pervasive distinction between discriminatory and nondiscriminatory regulations. The decision also initiated the abandonment of other older doctrines, such as the conceptual distinction between interstate and intrastate commerce and between direct and indirect impacts on interstate commerce."[80]

In *South Carolina State Highway Department v. Barnwell Brothers*, Justice Harlan F. Stone delivered a unanimous opinion holding that states retain authority to regulate the weight and width of trucks provided there was a rational basis for the regulations in the absence of congressional regulation.[81] Stressing that the states had the power to initiate action to conserve highways and improve traffic safety, he opined "the fact that many states have adopted a different standard is not persuasive. The conditions under which highways must be built in the several states, their construction, and the demands made upon them are not uniform."[82] However, as noted in an earlier section, the Surface Transportation Assistance Act of 1982 preempts totally the authority of states to regulate the weight and width of commercial vehicles operating on interstate highways and sections of the national-aid highway system as determined by the secretary of transportation.

In 1938, Justice Stone wrote "it was not the purpose of the commerce clause to relieve those engaged in interstate commerce from their just share of state tax burdens even though it increases the costs of doing the business ... and the bare fact that one is carrying on interstate commerce does not relieve him from many forms of state taxation which add to the cost of his business."[83]

In 1946, the U.S. Supreme Court upheld against a commerce clause challenge that a South Carolina gross receipts tax levied on out-of-state insurance companies by interpreting the McCarren–Ferguson Act, which delegates authority to the states to regulate the insurance industry, as validating the tax.[84] In 1985, however, the court ruled the act does not shield a state tax discrimination against a foreign insurance company from an equal protection of the laws challenge and invalidated an Alabama law levying a substantially higher gross premiums tax rate on foreign insurance companies compared to the rate levied on domestic insurance companies.[85]

The court in 1951 invalidated a City of Madison, Wisconsin, ordinance forbidding the sale of milk not pasteurized within five miles of the center of the city.[86] The city attempted to justify the ordinance on the ground it protects the health of the public, but the court responded that the city could send its inspectors beyond five miles to inspect pasteurization plants and levy an inspection fee on the pasteurizes.

In 1961, the court invalidated an Alaskan 4-percent license tax on freezer ships and floating cold storage units based on the value of the raw fish caught in the state's waters.[87] Arctic Maid alleged the tax discriminated against interstate commerce because the tax did not apply to fish caught and frozen in Alaska prior to canning in Alaska. The court accepted the state's argument that the tax was a complementary one since Alaskan canneries paid a 6-percent tax on the value of salmon they obtained for canning.[88]

Similarly, the court in 1969 upheld an Alabama business license tax of five dollars per week levied on traveling photographers for each local government in which they operated.[89] The court noted that the state imposed a twenty-five dollar annual tax on fixed-location photographers and added:

... there is no basis for concluding that the $5 per week tax on transient out-of-state photographers is so disproportionate to the tax imposed on photographers with a fixed location as to bear unfairly on the former. In none of the cities for which appellant's complaint gives the details of its activities would the transient tax imposed on it have exceeded that which a fixed location photographer would have had to pay to operate in the city.[90]

Professor Smith noted that the Supreme Court "has distinguished state regulation of the private economic market, which is subject to the commerce clause, from state participation in the market, which is not."[91] In 1976, the court upheld, against a commerce clause challenge, a Maryland law granting subsidies to in-state derelict motor vehicle firms in order to promote the proper disposal of the vehicles.[92] The following year, the court invalidated a North Carolina statute prohibiting the labeling of apples by other than the federal grading system.[93] All North Carolina growers used the federal grading system, and hence the statute discriminated against Washington state apples whose growers advertised nationally their apples which are graded by Washington state standards. Although North Carolina emphasized it was employing the police power to protect consumers from being misled by various labeling systems, the court pointed out the statute was restricted to closed cartons in apples which consumers typically do not see.

In 1980, the court ruled that South Dakota could give preference to resident purchase of cement produced by a state-owned factory.[94] In 1983, the court upheld a City of Boston ordinance granting preference to city residents relative to employment in city-funded construction projects.[95] The following year, however, the court opined that such discrimination in city construction projects in Camden, New Jersey, is subject to a challenge under the Privileges and Immunities Clause of Article IV of the constitution, a subject examined in Chapter 5.[96]

In *Maryland v. Louisiana*, the court in 1981 rejected Louisiana's claim that its "First Use" tax within the state of gas not subject to a severance tax levied by Louisiana or another state was valid as a complementary tax.[97] The facts in the case made clear that the tax targeted natural gas from the outer continental shelf (OCS). The court specifically held the tax was not similar to a use tax that complements a sales tax and opined:

... Louisiana claims that the First-Use Tax compensates for the effect of the state's severance tax on local production of natural gas ... Louisiana has an interest in protecting its natural resources, and, like most other states, has chosen to impose a severance tax on the privilege of severing resources from its soil. But the First-Use Tax is not designed to meet these same ends since Louisiana has no sovereign interest in being compensated for the severance of resources from the federally owned OCS land.[98]

The court in 1984 examined a West Virginia business and occupation tax levied upon the privilege of engaging in business with the amount of the tax determined by a firm's gross receipts. Each type of business activity, including manufacturing and wholesaling, was subject to the tax, and a single firm engaged in more than one activity would be taxed more than once. The tax statute, however, provided that a firm engaged in manufacturing is exempt from the tax if the firm is also engaged in wholesaling. The court opined:

... manufacturing and wholesaling are not "substantially equivalent events" such that the heavy tax on in-state manufacturers can be said to compensate for the admittedly lighter burden placed on wholesalers from out of state. Manufacturing frequently entails selling in the state, but we cannot say which portion of the manufacturing tax is attributable to manufacturing, and which portion to sales. The fact that the manufacturing tax is not reduced when part of the manufacturing takes place out of state, makes clear that the manufacturing tax is just that, and not in part a proxy for the gross receipts tax imposed on Armco and other sellers in other states.[99]

Justice John Paul Stevens, in delivering an opinion of the U.S. Supreme Court in 1987, noted the variation in the court's decisions relative to state taxes and the commerce clause and emphasized "the difficulties of reconciling unrestricted access to the national market with each state's authority to collect its fair share of revenues from interstate commercial activity."[100] The court invalidated a Pennsylvania axle tax and registration marker fee because these flat taxes failed the "internal consistency" test which holds that a permissible tax is one that would not result in interference with free trade if levied by every jurisdiction. The flat taxes discriminate against out-of-state truckers since on average they travel only one-fifth as many miles per year in the state as state truckers travel.

The Twenty-First Amendment to the U.S. Constitution repealed the prohibition (Eighteenth) amendment and stipulates in Section 2 "the transportation or importation into any state, territory, or possession of the United States for delivery or use therein of intoxicating liquors, in violation of the laws thereof, is hereby prohibited." This broad statement appears to grant states complete control over intoxicating liquors. State action based on this amendment, however, can conflict with the Interstate Commerce Clause.

In *Bacchus Imports Limited v. Dias*, the U.S. Supreme Court in 1984 invalidated, as a violation of the dormant commerce clause, a Hawaii 20-percent excise tax on the sale of wholesale liquor, except Hawaiian-produced alcoholic beverages.[101]

In 1986, the U.S. Supreme Court invalidated a section of the New York Alcoholic Beverage Control Law stipulating that a distiller licensed to conduct business in New York may not sell its beverages to wholesalers except in accordance with a monthly price schedule previously filed with the authority and an affirmation that the schedule prices are not higher than the lowest prices the distiller charges wholesalers in other states during the month.[102]

To prevent the loss of sales of alcoholic beverages to neighboring states with lower prices and to ensure that residents could purchase such beverages at prices not exceeding those in other states, the Connecticut State Legislature enacted a statute similar to New York's but differing in that out-of-state shippers could change their prices after the posting of the price schedule and affirmation. The court struck down the statute on the ground it has an impermissible extraterritorial effect, and "the commerce clause dictates that no state may force an out-of-state merchant to seek regulatory approval in one state before undertaking a transaction in another."[103] Chief Justice William H. Rehnquist dissented because Connecticut has no local brewers who would benefit from the statute and "does not seek to erect any sort of tariff barrier to exclude out-of-state beer; its residents will drink out-of-state beer if they drink beer at all, ..."[104]

The court in 1990 struck down a Florida excise tax, preferentially treating beverages made from Florida agricultural crops and cited the commerce clause.[105] Interestingly, the court did not order a retroactive refund of all taxes paid, but devised a "meaningful backward-looking relief" by holding that the remedy need only cure the discriminatory aspect of the tax and noted:

Florida may reformulate and enforce the liquor tax during the contested period in any way that treats petitioner and its competitors in a manner consistent with the dictates of the commerce clause ... More specifically, the state may cure the invalidity of the liquor tax by refunding to petitioner the difference between the tax it paid and the tax it would have been assessed were it extended the same rate reductions that its competitors actually received.[106]

As noted, a state may require its residents to pay a compensating use tax, at the same rate as the retail sales tax, on items purchased outside the state for use within the state. The Interstate Commerce Clause and the Due Process of Law Clause of the Fourteenth Amendment, however, impose limits on the taxing powers of a state. A particularly vexing problem for state tax collectors is created by the mail-order firm located in other states. In *National Bellas Hess, Incorporated v. Department of Revenue of Illinois*, the U.S. Supreme Court in 1967 ruled invalid an Illinois tax law requiring an out-of-state mail-order firm, which had neither sales representatives nor offices in the state, to collect a use tax on goods purchased for use in Illinois on the ground the law placed an undue burden on interstate commerce and violated the Due Process of Law Clause of the Fourteenth Amendment.[107] The court opined a "seller whose only connection with customers in the state is by common carrier or the United States mail" lacks the required minimum contacts with the state under the Due Process of Law Clause.[108]

The court rendered a decision in a similar case in 1992 relative to a mail-order firm directing its marketing activities at residents of North Dakota, although lacking offices and sales representatives in the state. The court specifically held in *Quill Corporation v. North Dakota* that "to the extent that our decisions have indicated that the due process clause requires physical presence in a state for the imposition of duty to collect a use tax, we overrule those holdings as superseded by developments in the law of due process."[109]

The court drew a distinction between the "minimum contacts" with a state required by the Due Process of Law Clause and the "substantial nexus" with the state required by the commerce clause, and ruled that requiring Quill Corporation to collect the use tax placed an impermissible burden on interstate commerce since Quill Corporation lacked a "substantial nexus" (physical presence) in the state required by the commerce clause.[110] The court added "that the underlying issue is not only one that Congress may be better qualified to resolve, but also one that Congress has the ultimate power to resolve."[111]

The interstate shipment of wastes, particularly hazardous wastes, has become a contentious issue in recent decades as the amount of such wastes has increased dramatically. Several states have sought to insulate themselves against becoming depositories for wastes by enacting statutes prohibiting the entry of wastes. In 1978, the U.S. Supreme Court invalidated a New Jersey statute prohibiting importation of most liquid or solid wastes originating in other states as a protective trade barrier violating the dormant Interstate Commerce Clause.[112] The court added in a note that its ruling did not address the question whether a state could restrict the use of its facilities to its residents under the "market participant exception" to the clause which pertains when a state is a market participant and not a market regulator.

The court in 1992 held that Michigan could not evade the dormant commerce clause's ban on interstate trade barriers by authorizing its counties to exercise their discretion relative to private landfill operators in their respective counties to prohibit them accepting wastes generated outside their respective counties.[113] The court in the same year also struck down as facially discriminatory an Alabama special fee on the disposal of hazardous wastes generated in sister states as violating the dormant commerce clause.[114] The court left open the question whether a differential surcharge would be valid if based on the cost of disposing of wastes from other states.

In 1994, the court ruled unconstitutional an Oregon $2.50 per ton surcharge on the disposal of wastes generated in sister states in view of a surcharge of only $0.85 per ton on the disposal of in-state generated waste.[115] Oregon did not claim that the disposal of waste from sister states imposed higher costs on Oregon compared to in-state generated wastes, but maintained the surcharge is a "compensatory tax" to force shippers of wastes from other states to pay their equitable share of the costs imposed on the state by the disposal of their wastes. The court opined:

Although it is often no mean feat to determine whether a challenged tax is a compensatory one, we have little difficulty concluding that the Oregon surcharge is not such a tax. Oregon does not impose a specific charge of at least $2.25 per ton on shippers of waste generated in Oregon for which the out-of-state surcharge might be considered compensatory. In fact, the only analogous charge on the disposal of Oregon waste is $0.85 per ton.[116]

The court pointed out its reluctance "to recognize new categories of compensatory taxes" and, referring to its *Armco* decision, opined "earning income and disposing of waste at Oregon landfills are even less equivalent than manufacturing and wholesaling."[117] Chief Justice Rehnquist in a strong dissent criticized the majority for invalidating fees based on costs and tying "the hands of the states in addressing the vexing national problem of solid waste disposal."[118]

The court in 1994 also invalidated a town ordinance in New York State mandating that solid wastes processed or handled within the town be processed or handled at the town's transfer station.[119] The town entered into a contract with a private firm authorizing it to construct a solid waste station for separating recyclable items from nonhazardous wastes and operate it for a period of five years. The town guaranteed the firm a minimum flow of waste, thereby enabling the firm to levy a tipping fee exceeding the disposal cost of unsorted waste on the private market. Other recycling firms could receive and sort wastes at their facilities, but they were required to bring the nonrecyclable wastes to the transfer station, thereby preventing them from shipping the wastes directly to disposal sites. The court wrote " . . . the flow control ordinance drives up the cost of out-of-state interests to disposal of their solid waste. Furthermore, the ordinance prevents anyone except the favored local operator from performing the initial processing step."[120]

A Missouri 1.5-percent use tax on the privilege of consuming, storing, or using within the state articles of personal property purchased in sister states met with the court's displeasure when it held in 1994 the tax to be impermissibly discriminatory in those local governments where the use tax exceeded the sales tax.[121] The court reemphasized that the commerce clause "embodies a negative command forbidding the states to discriminate against interstate trade."[122]

The Interstate Horseracing Act of 1978 is another example of a congressional statute delegating powers to states.[123] This act grants states limited powers to preempt the federal prohibition of interstate off-track wagering. Under the act, interstate simulcasts of horse races require the consent of state agencies and a horsemen's association. In 1994, the U.S. Court of Appeals for the Sixth Circuit overturned a District Court ruling that the act was invalid because it restricts commercial free speech protected by the First Amendment to the U.S. Constitution.[124]

In closing this section on judicial decisions, it is important to note that state courts also invalidate state statutes that create interstate trade barriers. In 1986, for example, the Supreme Court of New Hampshire ruled that a statute imposing taxes on foreign registered motor carriers facially discriminated against interstate commerce.[125] Similarly, the Maine Supreme Judicial Court in the same year struck down a statute imposing a reciprocal tax on motor vehicles registered in states imposing a tax or fee on the same class of motor vehicles registered in Maine.[126] The statute was held to discriminate against only motor vehicles registered in the thirteen states imposing a tax on Maine vehicles since the statute levied a tax that was not imposed on Maine registered trucks.

CONCLUSIONS

Interstate free trade is a basic premise of the United States federal system, yet states employ their reserved powers to erect trade barriers in response to pressure from interest groups or in retaliation against barriers raised by sister states. During an earlier period, many barriers were based upon the police power, and states maintained that their statutes and regulations, which interfered with the free flow of commerce among the states, were designed to protect the health, safety, welfare, and morals of their respective citizens. More recently, states have employed their proprietary powers to favor their business firms and citizens. The oldest and most common form of trade barrier, however, is based upon the power of taxation.

Reciprocity has been an effective method of removing certain obstacles to free trade, particularly motor vehicle registration and operators' licenses. Congress always possessed the power to remove barriers by preempting state statutes and regulations establishing barriers, but it was not until the 1970s that the Congress enacted such preemption acts on a regular basis to facilitate interstate commerce.

The judiciary has been the principal body in terms of removing interstate trade barriers since the early decades of the nineteenth century. By developing the doctrine of the dormant commerce clause, the Supreme Court took upon itself authority, in the absence of a congressional statute, to determine whether state statutes and regulations placed an impermissible burden on interstate commerce. Periodically, the U.S. Supreme Court admits it is not the best equipped body to render decisions involving interstate trade controversies. In 1992, the court opined that the issue in *Quill Corporation v. North Dakota* "is not only one that Congress may be better qualified to resolve, but also one that Congress has the ultimate power to resolve."[127] Congress did not accept the court's invitation to determine whether states should be allowed to require interstate mail-order firms to collect the state use tax on items sold to state residents.

It is not surprising that Congress fails to accept the court's recommendation that a problem be resolved by statute. If a bill is introduced to resolve a major interstate problem, Congress will be under great pressure from several competing interest groups whose political action committees make contributions to the campaign funds of many members of Congress. Furthermore, Congress operates under severe time restraints which make impossible the fashioning of a resolution for each of several interstate commerce problems. In consequence, Congress typically defers to the courts unless a consensus develops in Congress for a particular course of action.

Protectionism is only one form of interstate economic competition. States actively compete for tourists and for industry. Chapter 8 examines in particular the incentives that several states offer to induce business firms to locate, expand, and/or remain in the state.

NOTES

1. Adam Smith, *An Inquiry into the Nature and Causes of the Wealth of Nations* (New York: The Modern Library, 1937).

2. *Brown v. Maryland*, 12 Wheaton 419 at 445 (1827).

3. *The Federalist Papers* (New York: New American Library, 1961), pp. 54–8.

4. *Ibid.*, p. 59.

5. *Ibid.*, pp. 62–3.

6. *Ibid.*, pp. 267–8.

7. *Ibid.*, p. 63.

8. *United States Constitution*, Art. I, §10.

9. *Ibid.*, Art. IV, §2.

10. *Ibid.*, Art. I, §8.

11. *Ibid.*, Art. I, §9.

12. *Ibid.*

13. *Ibid.*, Art. VI.

14. *Noble State Bank v. Haskell*, 219 U.S. 104 at 111 (1911).

15. "States Impose Quarantines on California Produce," *The Keene (N.H.) Sentinel*, July 10, 1981, p. 5.

16. "Sick Chickens Force Quarantine in PA," *Knickerbocker News* (Albany, N.Y.), November 5, 1983, p. 2A, and William Robbins, "3 Million Chickens Destroyed in Bid to Halt Spread of Virus," *The New York Times*, November 28, 1983, pp. 1 and B11.

17. George R. Taylor, Edgar L. Burtis, and Frederick V. Waugh, *Barriers to Internal Trade in Farm Products* (Washington, D.C.: U.S. Government Printing Office, 1939).

18. Lester R. Johnson, "No Maine Potatoes in Idaho?" *Congressional Record*, June 15, 1959, p. A5127.

19. *Ibid.*

20. Bill Eager, "Vermont Milk Legal in New York," *Times Union* (Albany, N.Y.), June 11, 1994, p. B-2.

21. *Ibid.*

22. "Act Aiding Sale of State Wines is Struck Down," *The New York Times*, January 31, 1985, p. B 3.

23. 1 Stat. 474.

24. *Contagious Disease Act of 1903*, 32 Stat. 791.

25. Frederick E. Melder, *State and Local Barriers to Interstate Commerce in the United States* (Orono, Maine: University Press, 1937), p. 14.

26. *State Board of Tax Commissioners v. Jackson*, 283 U.S. 527 (1931).

27. *Department of Revenue v. Kuhnlein*, 646 So.2d 717 (1994).

28. F. Eugene Melder, "Trade Barriers Between States," *The Annals*, January 1940, p. 58.

29. *Massachusetts v. Missouri*, 308 U.S. 1 at 16–7 (1939).

30. W. Brooke Graves, *Uniform State Action: A Possible Substitution for Centralization* (Chapel Hill: The University of North Carolina Press, 1934), pp. 192–3.

31. *Ibid.*, pp. 195–7.

32. Hubert R. Gallagher, "Work of the Commission on Interstate Co-Operation," *The Annals*, January 1940, pp. 105–6.

33. *New York Vehicle and Traffic Law*, §§219 and 405 (McKinney 1986 and 1995 Supp.).

34. *Ibid.*, §250 (1995 Supp.).

35. *State and Provincial Licensing Systems* (Washington, D.C.: National Traffic Safety Administration, 1990), p. 123.

36. *Ibid.*, p. 108.

37. Graves, *Uniform State Action*, p. 229.

38. See *New York Agriculture and Markets Law*, §258-n (McKinney 1991); *New York Social Services Law*, §32 (McKinney 1992); and *New York Public Health Law*, §2205 (McKinney 1993).

39. Joseph F. Zimmerman, *Federal Preemption: The Silent Revolution* (Ames: Iowa State University Press, 1991).

40. *Bankruptcy Act of 1800*, 2 Stat. 19; *Bankruptcy Act of 1843*, 5 Stat. 440; and *Bankruptcy Act of 1867*, 14 Stat. 517.

41. *Bankruptcy Act of 1898*, 30 Stat. 544, 11 U.S.C.A. §1 (1993).

42. *Hours of Service Act of 1907*, 34 Stat. 1415, 45 U.S.C.A. §22 (1986 and 1995 Supp.), and *Boiler Inspection Act of 1911*, 36 Stat. 913, 45 U.S.C.A. §22 (1986 and 1995 Supp.).

43. *Wool Products Labeling Act of 1940*, 54 Stat. 1128, 15 U.S.C.A. §68 (1995 Supp.), and *Fur Products Labeling Act of 1951*, 65 Stat. 175, 15 U.S.C.A. §69 (1995 Supp.).

44. *Automotive Information Disclosure Act of 1958*, 72 Stat. 325, 15 U.S.C.A. §1231 (1982); *Egg Products Inspection Act of 1970*, 84 Stat. 1623, 21 U.S.C.A. §301 (1972); and *Nutrition Labeling and Education Act of 1990*, 104 Stat. 2353, 21 U.S.C.A. §301 note

(1995 Supp.).

45. *United States Grain Standards Act of 1968*, 82 Stat. 769, 7 U.S.C.A. §71 (1980).

46. *Airline Deregulation Act of 1978*, 92 Stat. 1708, 49 U.S.C.A. App. §§1305 and 1371 (1994); *Motor Carrier Act of 1980*, 94 Stat. 793, 49 U.S.C.A. §1101 (1995 Supp.); and *Bus Regulatory Reform Act of 1982*, 96 Stat. 1104, 49 U.S.C.A. §10521 (1994 Supp.).

47. *Surface Transportation Assistance Act of 1982*, 96 Stat. 2097, 23 U.S.C.A. §101 (1990 and 1995 Supp.). For a detailed analysis, see Seung-Ho Lee, *Federal Preemption of State Truck Size and Weight Laws: New York State's Reaction and Preemption Relief* (Albany: Unpublished Ph. D. Dissertation, State University of New York at Albany, 1994).

48. *Policy Positions: 1980–81* (Washington, D.C.: National Governors' Association, 1980).

49. *Tandem Truck Safety Act of 1984*, 98 Stat. 2829–30, 42 U.S.C.A. §2301 (1994 Supp.), and *Motor Carrier Safety Act of 1984*, 98 Stat. 2832, 42 U.S.C.A. §2501 (1994 Supp.).

50. *Motor Carrier Safety Act of 1991*, 105 Stat. 2140, 49 U.S.C.A. App. §2302(b)(1) (1995 Supp.).

51. *Ibid.*

52. *St. Louis v. Missouri*, 263 U.S. 640 (1924).

53. *McFadden Act of 1927*, 44 Stat. 1224, 12 U.S.C.A. §§36 and 332 (1989).

54. *Bank Holding Company Act of 1956*, 70 Stat. 133, 12 U.S.C.A. §1841 (1989).

55. *Ibid.*, 70 Stat. 135, 12 U.S.C.A. §1849(a).

56. *Northeast Bankcorp. v. Board of Governors of the Federal Reserve System*, 472 U.S. 159 (1985).

57. *Interstate Banking and Branching Efficiency Act of 1994*, 108 Stat. 2339, 12 U.S.C.A. §159 (1985). See also Susan McLaughlin, "The Impact of Interstate Banking and Branching Reform: Evidence from the States," *Current Issues in Economics and Finance*, May 1995, pp. 1–5.

58. *Marquette National Bank v. First of Omaha Corporation*, 439 U.S. 299 (1978).

59. *McCarran-Ferguson Act of 1945*, 59 Stat. 33, 15 U.S.C.A. §1011 (1976).

60. 1 Stat. 474 and 619, and *Plant Quarantine Act of 1912*, 37 Stat. 315, 7 U.S.C.A. §151 (1980).

61. *Gibbons v. Ogden*, 9 Wheaton 1 (1824).

62. *Brown v. Maryland*, 12 Wheaton 419 at 420 (1827).

63. *Ibid.* at 449.

64. William B. Munro, *The Government of the United States*, 4th ed. (New York: The Macmillan Company, 1937), p. 55.

65. *Thurlow v. The Commonwealth of Massachusetts* (The License Cases), 5 Howard 504 at 572 (1847).

66. *Cooley v. The Board of Wardens of the Part of Philadelphia*, 53 U.S. 299 (1851).

67. *Hinson v. Lott*, 75 U.S. 148 (1869).

68. *Walling v. Michigan*, 116 U.S. 446 (1886).

69. *Ibid.* at 459.

70. *Minnesota v. Barber*, 135 U.S. 313 (1890).

71. Robert H. Jackson, "The Supreme Court and Interstate Barriers," *The Annals*, January 1940, pp. 75–6.

72. *H.P. Hood & Sons v. Du Mond*, 336 U.S. 525 at 535 (1949).

73. *Clark v. Paul Gray, Incorporated*, 306 U.S. 583 at 594 (1939).

74. *General American Tank Car Corporation v. Day*, 270 U.S. 367 (1926).

75. *Ibid.* at 373. See also *Louisiana Constitution of 1921*, Art. X, §16.

76. *Gregg Dyeing Company v. Query*, 286 U.S. 472 (1932).

77. *Ibid.* at 480.

78. Mintz *et al. v.* Baldwin, 289 U.S. 346 (1933).

79. *Baldwin v. G.A.F. Seelig, Incorporated*, 294 U.S. 511 (1935).

80. Michael E. Smith, "State Discriminations Against Interstate Commerce," *California Law Review*, Vol. 74, 1986, pp. 1205–6.

81. *South Carolina State Highway Department v. Barnwell Brothers*, 303 U.S. 177 (1937).

82. *Ibid.* at 195.

83. *Western Live Stock v. Bureau of Revenue*, 303 U.S. 250 at 254 (1938).

84. *Prudential Insurance Co. v. Benjamin*, 328 U.S. 408 (1946).

85. *Metropolitan Life Insurance Company v. Ward*, 470 U.S. 869 (1985).

86. *Dean Milk Company v. City of Madison*, 340 U.S. 349 (1951).

87. *Alaska v. Arctic Maid*, 366 U.S. 199 (1961).

88. *Ibid.* at 204.

89. *Stanley Studios, Incorporated v. Alabama*, 393 U.S. 537 (1969).

90. *Ibid.* at 542.

91. Smith, "State Discriminations Against Interstate Commerce," p. 1222.

92. *Hughes v. Alexandria Scrap Corporation*, 426 U.S. 794 at 808–9 (1976).

93. *Hunt v. Washington Apple Advertising Commission*, 432 U.S. 333 (1977).

94. *Reeves Incorporated v. State*, 447 U.S. 429 at 436–7 (1980).

95. *White v. Massachusetts Council of Construction Employees*, 460 U.S. 204 (1983).

96. *United Building & Construction Trades Council v. Camden*, 465 U.S. 208 (1984).

97. *Maryland v. Louisiana*, 451 U.S. 725 (1981).

98. *Ibid.* at 758–9.

99. *Armco, Incorporated v. Hardesty*, 467 U.S. 638 (1984).

100. *American Trucking Association v. Scheiner*, 483 U.S. 266 at 269 (1987).

101. *Bacchus Imports Limited v. Dias*, 468 U.S. 263 (1984).

102. *Brown–Forman Distillers v. New York State Liquor Authority*, 476 U.S. 573 (1986).

103. *Healy et al. v. Beer Institute, Incorporated*, 491 U.S. 324 at 337 (1989).

104. *Ibid.* at 347.

105. *McKesson Corporation v. Division of Alcoholic Beverages & Tobacco*, 496 U.S. 18 (1990).

106. *Ibid.* at 39–40.

107. *National Bellas Hess, Incorporated v. Department of Revenue of Illinois*, 386 U.S. 753 (1967).

108. *Ibid.* at 758.

109. *Quill Corporation v. North Dakota*, 112 S.Ct. 1904 at 1911 (1992).

110. *Ibid.* at 1911–3.

111. *Ibid.* at 1916.

112. *Philadelphia v. New Jersey*, 437 U.S. 617 (1978).

113. *Fort Gratiot Sanitary Landfill, Incorporated v. Michigan Department of Natural Resources*, 112 S.Ct. 2019 (1992).

114. *Chemical Waste Management, Incorporated v. Hunt*, 112 S.Ct. 2009 (1992).

115. *Oregon Waste Systems, Incorporated v. Department of Environmental Quality*, 114 S.Ct. 1345 (1994).

116. *Ibid.* at 1352.

117. *Ibid.* at 1353.

118. *Ibid.* at 1355–6.

119. *C & A Carbone, Incorporated v. Town of Clarkstown, New York*, 114 S.Ct. 1677 (1994).

120. *Ibid.* at 1681.

121. *Associated Industries of Missouri v. Lohman*, 114 S.Ct. 1815 (1994).

122. *Ibid.* at 1820.

123. *Interstate Horseracing Act of 1978*, 92 Stat. 1811, 15 U.S.C.A. §3004 (1982).

124. *Kentucky Division, Horsemen's Benevolent & Protective Association, Incorporated v. Turfway Park Racing Association*, 20 F.3d 1406 (6th Cir. 1994).

125. *Private Truck Council of America, Incorporated v. State of New Hampshire*, 517 A.2d 1150 (N.H. 1986).

126. *Private Truck Council of America, Incorporated v. Secretary of State*, 503 A.2d 214 (Me. 1986).

127. *Quill Corporation v. North Dakota*, 112 S.Ct. 1904 at 1916 (1992).

8

Interstate Competition for Tourists, Sports Franchises, and Business Firms

There typically is competition among states in a federal system for a greater share of national revenues and the location of national government facilities, including research laboratories and regional offices of national agencies. In addition, states engage in interstate economic competition by advertising to attract tourists and gamblers and by tax and other incentives to attract business firms, retain firms considering relocation to another state or nation, and encourage firms to expand in the state. Among these firms are those holding major and minor league sports franchises which provide jobs for residents and income for a variety of businesses, including hotels and restaurants.

Relatively little criticism has been directed at state tourist advertising, but serious questions have been raised about the desirability of interstate competition for business firms. Critics contend that tax and other incentives distort locational decisions, do not always produce net benefits for a state, little or no accountability exists relative to the governmental incentives, and such competition is a zero sum game with respect to firms which have decided to relocate or to construct a new factory. Kentucky's attraction of a Canadian steel firm in 1993 by a tax incentive of approximately $350,000 per new job for a 400-employee plant convinced several observers that interstate competition for industry is out of control and should be curtailed by Congress.[1]

What had been primarily interstate competition for industry in the 1950s and 1960s became international competition in the 1970s as many nations offered incentives to foreign business firms. Other nations with low-wage rates, such as China, have been able to attract certain types of labor-intensive foreign firms without offering other economic incentives. States can do little to offset this competition.

This chapter briefly examines the competition for tourists, gamblers, and sports franchises and focuses its attention primarily upon interstate competition for industry. In particular, the importance of taxes and regulatory policies of states in influencing the location or expansion of plants is analyzed.

COMPETITION FOR TOURISTS AND GAMBLERS

States recognize that tourists are a major asset since taxes can be levied on hotels, motels, and meals with a significant proportion of the tax burden falling upon residents of sister states and foreign nations. Tourist spending also generates jobs and income for state residents and domestic business firms.

Advertising is essential if large numbers of tourists are to be attracted to a state. In 1994, states spent in excess of $110 million to attract tourists, with Illinois spending more than $24 million whereas Delaware, ranked fiftieth in spending, had an advertising budget of $739,000.[2] States employ Madison Avenue firms to develop sophisticated print, radio, and television advertisements. Special attention is paid to developing a catchy slogan since New York in the 1970s launched its popular "I Love New York" campaign and logo. Several states decided that a slogan placed on the license plates for residents' vehicles, such as Maine's "Vacationland," is an effective method of advertising. Neighboring New Hampshire, also a tourist state, uses a revolutionary war slogan—"Live Free or Die"—on the motor vehicle plates it issues instead of a tourist slogan. New Hampshire, however, gains free national advertising by holding the first presidential primary election in the nation.

The success of slogans varies considerably, and several states have decided to abandon a slogan. The "Escape to Wisconsin" slogan, for example, was discontinued after state officials discovered "some residents were removing the word 'to' from the bumper sticker so that it read 'Escape Wisconsin.' "[3] Charles Mahtesian pointed out in 1994 that "Florida's latest slogan ... could be read in Spanish as 'Florida is Two-Faced.' "[4]

States employ professional advertising firms to test market slogans, logos, and radio and television advertisements. Utilizing detailed information from the U.S. Bureau of the Census, the firms prepare specific marketing programs for targeted audiences. Each state seeks to present the most desirable image in general and specific images for segments of the tourist market. Each state also attempts to avoid any suggestion of a negative image. The marketing program must be adjusted periodically as public tastes and interest change.

Local governments heavily dependent upon tourists often link their tourist advertising to the state's advertising. If a local government gains a bad reputation, such as New Orleans' reputation as a murder capital of the United States, the city and the state have the difficult task of attracting tourists who are concerned about personal safety.

A number of states and cities also seek to attract gamblers. Las Vegas, Nevada, and Atlantic City, New Jersey, are the prime examples of cities highly dependent upon gamblers for tax revenues.

The growth of independent movie producers and the relative decline of the Hollywood studio system have generated campaigns by local governments to attract movie and television producers. A major film production on location in a municipality provides a significant infusion of spending and temporary jobs for residents. New York City benefits from the spending of approximately three billion dollars annually by movie and television firms shooting films in the city.[5] In contrast to Los Angeles which charges film companies for police to maintain law and order, New York City provides police free of charge.[6]

Competition for sports franchises often generates bidding wars among states and threats of retaliation. The New York Giants and New York Jets of the National Football League moved from New York City to New Jersey. Fearing that the New York Yankees baseball team would be enticed to move from the Bronx to New Jersey by an offer of a new stadium, Governor Mario M. Cuomo of New York in 1993 indicated that he would seek an amendment to the New York State Constitution to legalize casino gambling if New Jersey lured the Yankees to leave the Bronx.[7] Legalized casino gambling in New York State would have a severe negative economic impact upon casino gambling in Atlantic City, New Jersey.

While the Yankees remain in New York, the Albany–Colonie Class AA baseball team left the state in 1995 for Norwich, Connecticut, where a new stadium will be constructed with the assistance of a $6.5 million state appropriation and a Norwich contribution of $1.4 million.[8] Similarly, the Albany Firebirds of the Arena Football League relocated from Albany to Bennington, Vermont, in 1994 in order to save approximately $200,000 in workmen's compensation premiums.[9] The team will continue to play its six "home" games in Albany.

Competition for tourists, gamblers, and sports franchises, in terms of direct and indirect state spending, is relatively insignificant when compared to state grants, loans, and tax expenditures—tax abatements and exemptions—offered to industrial firms to locate in a state.

COMPETITION FOR INDUSTRY

States during the 1820s to the 1840s promoted industrial development by financing in part the expansion of canals and railroad lines. Reckless state financing of railroad and canal companies created serious fiscal problems in several states including New York which necessitated the levying of a special New York state property tax to raise revenue. Taxpayer reaction to the New York tax took the form of pressure upon the state legislature to propose constitutional amendments, which subsequently were ratified by the voters, restricting the power of the state legislature to incur indebtedness.[10] These restrictions, for example, are contained in the current New York Constitution which also forbids the state legislature to give or loan money to assist any private corporation.[11] Not surprisingly, state legislatures have discovered a method for evading the constitutional prohibitions and restrictions—the state-controlled public authority which is exempt from the constitutional provisions.

Organized campaigns to attract manufacturing and processing industries date to the nineteenth century when railroads and public utility companies sought to encourage business firms to locate factories in the service areas of the railroads and the utilities. Today, promoters of industrial firm location and expansion work closely with state economic development agencies.

The Federal Reserve Bank of Boston in 1963 published a lead article in its review, entitled "New War Between the States," which highlighted the use of special subsidy techniques by individual states to lure manufacturing companies to locate plants in their respective states.[12] The article described "Blue's" weapons— privately financed Business Development Corporations (BDCs) and state financing of industrial buildings by means of direct loans or insurance—used by northern states and "Grey's" weapons—exemption of new industrial firms from state and/or local taxation and issuance of municipal bonds for private industrial financing— used principally by southern states.[13] Twenty-eight states authorized the use of one or more of these weapons between 1960 and 1963.

The first BDC was chartered by Maine in 1949 and authorized to issue stock to raise funds to permit it to borrow additional funds from commercial lending institutions for economic development purposes. The charter exempts commercial banks from state-lending standards when money is loaned to a BDC, which typically makes loans to small growing firms unable to obtain long-term financing from other sources. Not surprisingly, BDCs have a significantly higher ratio of losses to outstanding loans than the ratio of a commercial bank's loans to its regular business customers.

State Industrial Building Authorities are loan insurance programs for industrial buildings with the authorities typically insuring loans from commercial lenders for up to 90 percent of the value of the land and buildings of an industrial firm. The cost of the insurance is paid by the borrower in the form of a charge of 0.5 to 1 percent on the outstanding loan balance. Several states provide direct loans in place of loan insurance. As noted, the New York Constitution prohibits such direct loans.

A majority of the states authorize municipalities to borrow funds for industrial development by issuing bonds which are financed by revenues generated by the industrial facilities. Critics maintain that a firm may have been attracted to the municipality without this form of subsidy, and the issuance of tax exempt municipal bonds constitutes the equivalent of a federal tax subsidy to a private firm. In most states, industrial properties developed with the aid of municipal industrial development bonds are exempt from property taxes.

Tax exemptions are the most common ingredient employed in the competition for industry by states. However, the U.S. Advisory Commission on Intergovernmental Relations has pointed out that such competition involves more than the offer of tax benefits. Specifically, the commission identified "competition in the areas of education, public welfare, and public works infrastructure ... and right-to-work laws and laws regulating workers' compensation insurance."[14]

Commencing in the early 1960s, many state legislatures amended their tax laws to provide for free ports, that is, property tax exemption for products produced for interstate shipment. These free ports attracted major distribution centers, often to the disadvantage of neighboring states which are forced to establish similar free ports.

Real property tax reductions and exemptions are limited typically to a period of three to ten years. If used extensively, these reductions and exemptions lead to a major reduction of property tax base and the shifting of the tax burden to other taxpayers. The use of such reductions and exemptions obviously discriminates against existing industrial firms.

Keon S. Chi of the Council of State Governments reported that forty-four states in 1993 "offered tax breaks to businesses for equipment and machinery, goods in transition, manufacturers' inventories, raw materials in manufacturing, and job creation."[15] He specifically noted that the number of states utilizing tax incentives to create jobs increased from twenty-seven to forty-four between 1984 and 1993 with most of the activity concentrated in the south. In recognition of the number of women with children in the work force, several states offer tax credits for the cost of day care.

Table 8.1 lists fifteen state tax incentives for business firms, ranging from corporate income tax exemption to tax incentive for creation of jobs, tax credits for use of specified state products, and accelerated depreciation of industrial equipment. Table 8.2 lists sixteen state financial incentives for business firms, ranging from state-sponsored industrial development authorities to state loans for building construction, state aid for plant expansion, and incentives for establishing an industrial plant in an area of high unemployment.

A newer development is the use of industrial development incentives customized to meet the needs and wishes of a firm being recruited. Chi reported that such incentives "have been offered ... the service industry (Sears, Roebuck & Company, $240 million, in Illinois; Chase Manhattan in New York City, $235 million; NBC, $150 million, New York City); manufacturing companies (Canada's Dofasco and Co-Steel, $140 million to Gallatin County, Ky.); aviation (Northwestern Airlines Maintenance facility, $350 million, to Duluth, Minn.); and domestic and foreign automobile companies (General Motors, $70 million, to Spring Hill, Tenn.; Toyota, $147 million, to Georgetown, Ky.)."[16]

Chi advises state government officials considering the offer of customized incentives to an industrial firm to:

- seek additional information when offering customized incentives packages and refrain from offering such incentives packages to lure businesses from other states;
- require more thorough analyses to evaluate information on the economic impact of a customized incentive package, and examine policy alternatives;
- establish clear and consistent policies on business incentives, with enforceable contract provisions applicable to recipient firms as a condition of the customized incentive award;
- be aware of the potential ethical problems that can be associated with recruiting large business from other states.[17]

State's Business Climate

Business firms' perceptions of whether a state's policies are friendly, neutral, or hostile influence decisions on plant locations, expansions, and closings. In general, firms prefer low taxes that do not impact their profits negatively and regulations

Table 8.1
State Tax Incentives for Business: Changes Between 1984–93, 1989–93

Types of Tax Incentives	Year										Changes between 1984–93	Changes between 1989–93
	1984	1985	1986	1987	1988	1989	1990	1991	1992	1993		
					Number of States							
Corporate Income Tax Exemption	28	31	33	33	31	32	34	35	35	36	+8	+4
Personal Income Tax Exemption	22	24	26	27	28	32	32	32	32	32	+10	0
Excise Tax Exemption	16	16	18	19	19	21	22	22	22	23	+7	+2
Tax Exemption or Moratorium on Land, Capital Improvements	32	34	33	34	35	35	35	36	36	36	+4	+1
Tax Exemption or Moratorium on Equipment, Machinery	32	34	35	35	39	41	41	41	41	41	+9	0
Inventory Tax Exemption on Goods in Transit	46	47	47	48	48	48	49	49	49	49	+3	+1
Tax Exemption on Manufacturers Inventories	43	43	44	44	44	45	45	46	46	46	+3	+1
Sales/Use Tax Exemption on New Equipment	38	42	42	44	44	45	46	47	47	47	+9	+2
Tax Exemption on Raw Materials Used in Manufacturing	44	45	45	45	45	47	48	48	49	49	+5	+2
Tax Incentive for Creation of Jobs	27	30	31	32	35	39	40	43	44	44	+17	+5
Tax Incentive for Industrial Investment	24	29	29	30	32	33	35	36	37	37	+13	+4
Tax Credits for Use of Specified State Products	6	5	4	6	7	5	4	4	4	4	−2	−1
Tax Stabilization Agreements for Specified Industries	5	5	5	5	5	6	6	7	7	7	+2	+1
Tax Exemption to Encourage Research and Development	19	22	24	25	25	27	28	31	31	34	+15	+7
Accelerated Depreciation of Industrial Equipment	36	34	34	35	35	36	39	39	39	40	+4	+4

Source: Keon S. Chi, "State Business Incentives: Options for the Future," *State Trends Forecasts*, June 1994, p. 4.

Table 8.2
State Financial Incentives for Business: Changes Between 1984–93, 1989–93

Types of Financial Incentives	Year										Changes between 1984–93	Changes between 1989–93
	1984	1985	1986	1987	1988	1989	1990	1991	1992	1993		
						Number of States						
State Sponsored Industrial Development Authority	37	38	38	38	38	38	40	40	40	40	+3	+2
Privately Sponsored Development Credit Corporation	38	37	36	37	37	37	36	38	38	39	+1	+2
State Authority or Agency Revenue Bond Financing	37	41	42	44	44	44	44	43	44	44	+7	0
State Authority or Agency General Obligation Bond Financing	12	13	12	14	15	15	18	19	20	20	+8	+5
City and/or County Revenue Bond Financing	50	49	49	49	49	49	49	49	49	49	−1	0
City and/or County General Obligation Bond Financing	30	31	33	33	33	34	37	36	37	37	+7	+3
State Loans for Building Construction	30	34	35	36	38	40	40	41	40	40	+10	0
State Loans for Equipment, Machinery	27	33	34	35	37	39	42	42	41	42	+15	+3
City and/or County Loans for Building Construction	21	26	29	32	34	37	39	41	44	45	+24	+8
City and/or County Loans for Equipment, Machinery	22	26	27	29	32	35	38	41	44	45	+23	+10
State Loan Guarantees for Building Construction	20	26	22	22	25	25	28	25	26	28	+8	+3
State Loan Guarantees for Equipment, Machinery	21	21	23	23	26	25	29	28	28	31	+10	+6
State Financing Aid for Existing Plant Expansion	37	39	38	41	42	43	44	44	44	44	+7	+1
State Matching Funds for City and/or County Industrial Financing Programs	12	15	18	20	20	21	22	22	25	26	+14	+5
State Incentive for Establishing Industrial Plants in Areas of High Unemployment	24	25	27	31	31	33	36	40	41	41	+17	+8
City and/or County Incentive for Establishing Industrial Plants in Areas of High Unemployment	28	30	29	31	30	30	32	33	35	35	+7	+5

Source: Keon S. Chi, "State Business Incentives: Options for the Future," *State Trends Forecasts*, June 1994, p. 4.

that are not overburdensome. Studies generally reveal that the level of taxation is not a major factor considered by business firms in deciding upon the region of the United States in which to locate a new plant.[18] Tax differentials become more important once a firm has decided upon the region in which to locate a plant. Attention is focused by the firms on the tax differentials between neighboring states which possess key location advantages.

In viewing the tax climate of a state, a business firm typically is concerned with the total tax burden. If state taxes are relatively low, but local government taxes are burdensome, a firm seeking a plant location may shift its attention to a neighboring state with low, combined state and local government taxes. States considered to be tax friendly to businesses tend to rely heavily upon sales and excise taxes for revenue. High corporate and personal income tax rates produce a negative business perception of a state which must rely upon other factors— such as a skilled labor force, good transportation facilities, and a central market location—to attract industrial firms or offer new firms various financial incentives for locating a plant in the state. Taxes that minimize the compliance costs imposed upon firms also improve a state's image as does deregulation or regulatory reforms reducing compliance costs.

The U.S. Advisory Commission on Intergovernmental Relations in 1967 concluded that once a state or local government becomes identified as a high tax government "it is difficult to erase the image" and that "for many firms the particular state and/or local levy which appears to have the greatest influence on managerial decisions is the general property tax. In jurisdictions where this tax is levied upon business inventories it is possible to discern a clear interrelationship between the property tax costs and decisions made by management."[19] The commission noted that a textile firm with plants in North Carolina and South Carolina could minimize taxes by keeping inventories in the latter state where most inventories are tax exempt.[20] Burroughs Corporation had been paying a $6,615 inventory tax on each $150,000 computer stored in California but avoided this tax commencing in 1964 by storing all warehouse merchandise for California in Reno, Nevada, where there is no inventory tax.[21]

A second study of plant location was conducted by the commission in 1981 which reinforced many of the conclusions reached in its 1967 study. The 1981 report revealed that labor costs for the typical manufacturer are many times larger than combined state and local government taxes and hence a slight differential in wages is more important than a slight tax differential to the firm.[22] The commission found that interstate and interregional movements of large manufacturing firms are relatively uncommon. However, the Great Lakes and Mideast regions experienced the loss of more firms to another region, the Southeast, than to sister states in their own region.[23] The commission added:

It is noteworthy that several high-tax states and several low-tax states do not show the level of manufacturing firm births that might be expected if the association between taxes and firm births were causal. The high-tax states are Massachusetts, Arizona, Wyoming, California, and Hawaii. Wyoming can be dismissed as an aberration because (1) it is remote; (2) it is relatively sparsely settled; and (3) its high taxes originate in natural resource exploitation where the burden is passed on to the users of the resources, only a few of whom reside in Wyoming. Aside from Wyoming, the experience in other high-tax states cannot be explained easily. Despite above-average taxes per $1,000 of personal income, four states show above-average birthrates of single establishment manufacturing firms.[24]

Massachusetts, a high tax state, experienced a greater growth in new manufacturing firms between 1969 and 1976 than its 1969 percentage of major manufacturing firms in New England.[25] Nevertheless, Massachusetts' high tax image undoubtedly discouraged the location of a number of new firms in the Commonwealth. To improve its business climate, Massachusetts in 1993 increased its investment tax credit on its corporation income tax from 1 to 3 percent.[26] A high-tax state seeking to improve its tax policy image and avoid significant revenue loss for its treasury, typically will restrict its tax incentives to new firms.

Regardless of the magnitude of the impact of state–local income taxes on the decision of a domestic company to relocate a factory or construct a new factory in a given state, taxes will have no impact on the decision of certain foreign corporations to locate factories in the United States because their respective nations grant the corporations tax credits against their tax liability for corporation income taxes paid in the United States.[27]

A firm rationally seeking to maximize profits will locate a factory where its production costs will be the lowest. The optimal location varies by industry. If a factory, such as an aluminum factory, consumes large quantities of electrical energy, it is probable that energy costs will be a key locational determinant. A firm needing highly skilled employees will seek a location where these individuals reside. There have been a number of instances where a firm was unable to attract a sufficient supply of skilled labor to its existing plants and decided to construct a plant in relative close proximity to the Massachusetts Institute of Technology to recruit its graduates and take advantage of its professors who serve as consultants. The availability of a large parcel of land at a reasonable cost; proximity to excellent air, ground, and water transportation facilities; raw materials; and total state and local government taxes, and regulatory climate are other important locational factors.

Relative to the regulatory climate, most states limit the interest charges on credit card debt to protect residents. If a state legislature decreases the allowable maximum interest rate charge on credit card debt, banks will move their credit card operations to another state, such as Delaware and South Dakota, which have deregulated such interest rates. Furthermore, banks will threaten to move their credit card operations to sister states if the state legislature decides to end deregulation of such interest rates.[28]

ASSESSING TAX AND OTHER INCENTIVES

Proponents of tax and other fiscal incentives to attract business firms to a state cite five principal advantages of such incentives. First, the cost of conducting a business in a state can be reduced immediately and significantly for a new firm. Second, large tax and fiscal incentives can help to negate to an extent adverse locational factors such as transportation costs. Third, incentives can be the deciding factor when a company is preparing to make a final decision relative to a short list of sites in two or three states. Fourth, fiscal inducements can be employed to encourage existing business firms to expand within the state. Fifth, the incentives improve the image of the business climate of the state.

Critics of incentives identify five disadvantages. First, the incentives typically are restricted to new plants and consequently discriminate against existing firms. Second, the incentives result in revenue losses that could have been utilized for other policy objectives, including improving taxpayer equity. Questions, for example, have been raised about Alabama's 1993 incentives of approximately $300 million to attract a Mercedes–Benz plant when the state has been mandated by a court to spend hundreds of millions of additional dollars to upgrade its public school system.[29] Third, the incentives often are insufficient to negate other adverse locational factors and do not achieve their objectives. Fourth, deductibility of state and local government taxes allowed under the federal corporation income tax reduces the value of tax incentives to the point they have little effect. Fifth, incentives may result in firms relocating to sister states without increasing total regional production and employment. Economist Dick Netzer concluded that "the empirical evidence on what works in economic development is thin or unpersuasive."[30]

Border Wars

Competition between states in a region to entice firms to move to neighboring states generates bad interstate relations which may make interstate cooperation on other matters of regional importance difficult to achieve. Recognizing that interstate competition for business firms was undesirable, New York City, Connecticut, and New Jersey in 1991 reached an agreement that they would not compete for each other's firms through advertisements or aggressive recruiting. However, New Jersey broke the agreement within a few months and created a recruitment fund with revenues from income of the World Trade Center which is owned by the Port Authority of New York and New Jersey, and was established by an interstate compact entered into by New York and New Jersey.[31]

The intense competition for industry between New Jersey and New York was illustrated in 1995 when Governor George E. Pataki of New York rejected a proposed contract providing for the state-owned New York Power Authority to supply low-cost power to New Jersey Transit.[32] Governor Pataki explained "the Power Authority made a deal to provide low cost economic development power to the State of New Jersey. We took a look at that and said 'My God, what is going on?' "[33] The governor failed to explain that the power would be supplied to New Jersey Transit only for use by its trains after they entered New York City carrying commuters and tourists.

Moreover, Connecticut in 1994 induced Swiss Bank to move from New York City by offering tax incentives of $120 million over the next decade.[34] Mayor

Rudolph W. Giuliani of New York City was furious and arranged for the city to purchase advertisements in Connecticut newspapers maintaining a bidding competition will hurt both Connecticut and New York and "Connecticut taxpayers will pay $60,000 for each job, an unbelievable amount."[35] Connecticut officials maintained that New York City broke the 1991 agreement and that they had been approached by Swiss Bank which was seeking a new location. The officials estimate that Swiss Bank will generate in excess of $300 million in tax revenues, and tax inducements of $120 million are reasonable in the light of new tax revenues and employment brought to the state.[36]

The National Governors' Association recognizes the undesirability of border wars and interstate competition for industry and in 1993 development guidelines designed to reduce the tax and other incentives employed by states to attract industry.[37] Specifically, the association's guidelines for state subsidies to business firms call for:

- using individual state development objectives, identified criteria, and a calculated rate of return to offer public subsidies that will be available to and benefit all businesses;

- assisting projects that otherwise would not occur, rather than just influencing site location;

- encouraging joint ventures between government and businesses;

- investing in people and in communities as foundations of a healthy economic environment, instead of concentrating resources in the fortunes of one company or project;

- providing special assistance to encourage investment in distressed areas or to bring jobs to populations experiencing high unemployment; and

- developing provisions to recoup subsidies if the business community fails to deliver promised benefits in return for state subsidies.[38]

The association is convinced "the use of development subsidies to foster and sustain economic growth remains much more an 'art' than a science" and called for the use of cost–benefit analysis by decisionmakers prior to offering tax and fiscal incentives to a business firm.[39] Stressing that permanent economic growth is not based upon "one-time investments," the association recommends that states calculate the rate of return on development subsidies to determine their ability to generate resources that can be invested in the future.[40]

CONGRESSIONAL REGULATION OF INTERSTATE INDUSTRIAL COMPETITION

The U.S. Constitution grants plenary power to Congress to regulate interstate and foreign commerce, but Congress has not used this power to limit or regulate interstate industrial competition which has been fueled in part by congressional tax policy.

The question of intergovernmental tax immunity was first raised in *McCulloch v. Maryland* when the Supreme Court addressed in 1819 the question whether a state could tax a federal instrumentality—the Bank of the United States.[41] The court replied in the negative. Intergovernmental tax immunity was made reciprocal fifty-two years later when the court in *Collector v. Day* opined that the salary of a state official could not be taxed by the national government.[42]

The court in *Pollock v. Farmers Loan & Trust Company* in 1895 invalidated a federal income tax because it was not apportioned on the basis of population among the states and made the interest on state and local bonds taxable.[43] This decision was reversed by ratification of the Sixteenth Amendment by the states authorizing Congress "to lay and collect taxes on incomes, from whatever source derived, without apportionment among the several states, and without regard to any census or enumeration." The "from whatever source derived" clause indicates that Congress, if it so decides, can tax the interest received on municipal bonds issued by state and local governments.

The Internal Revenue Act of 1913 exempted interest income from municipal bonds, issued by state and local governments from the new federal income tax.[44] In this regard, Justice William Brennan wrote from a constitutional standpoint in *South Carolina v. Baker* in 1988:

We see no constitutional reason for treating persons who receive interest on government bonds differently than persons who receive income from other types of contracts with the government, and no tenable rationale for distinguishing the costs imposed on states by a tax on state bond interest from the costs imposed by a tax on the income from any other state contract.[45]

Justice Brennan specifically stressed that "states must find their protection from congressional regulation through the national political process, not through judicially defined spheres of unregulable state activity."[46] In effect, he echoed, relative to Congress' power to tax, Justice Harry A. Blackmun's 1985 opinion in *Garcia v. San Antonio Metropolitan Transit Authority* that "the principal and basic limits on the federal commerce power are inherent in all state participation in federal government action."[47]

The Tax Reform Act of 1986 requires state and local governments that reinvested borrowed funds in private securities resulting in an arbitrage profit must remit the profit to the U.S. Treasury.[48] The requirement was challenged by South Carolina and the Supreme Court ruled "that subsequent case law has overruled the holding in *Pollock* that state bond interest is immune from a nondiscriminatory federal tax.[49] Hence, Congress at any time could restrict the issuance of municipal bonds for economic development purposes by subjecting the interest received from municipal bonds to the federal income tax.

Congress first limited the use of the proceeds of municipal bond issues in the Revenue and Expenditure Control Act of 1968 by making the interest on industrial development bonds taxable with the exceptions of exempt purposes—residential real property, convention and sports facilities, airports, wharves, public transit facilities, sewage and solid waste disposal facilities, and air and water pollution control facilities.[50] Congress in 1969, 1971, 1978, 1980, 1982, 1984, and 1986 enacted statutes relating to the use of tax exempt bonds.[51] The latter act made major changes in existing law by eliminating the tax eligibility of convention, sports, parking, and private pollution control facilities.[52]

Congress in 1984, concerned with the loss of federal government revenues, decided to establish a volume limit on several types of industrial bonds which first were issued by Mississippi in 1913.[53] The volume cap was a feature of the Tax Reform Act of 1986 which established for each state a dollar volume maximum amount of tax-exempt bonds—$50 per capita or $150 million—that can be used to finance private activities.[54] Table 8.3 classifies by type of activity and year of authority new-issue tax-exempt private-activity bonds and Figure 8.1 ranks by state the volume of tax-exempt private-activity bonds issued in 1989. The table reveals that in excess of $15 billion in such bonds were issued in 1989 and that California utilized completely its volume cap authority in contrast to Rhode Island which utilized only a small percentage of its volume cap authority. Table 8.4 lists the responsible agency for administering the volume cap in each state.[55]

Dennis Zimmerman wrote that "attacking the growth problem with a fairly comprehensive volume limit accomplishes two goals simultaneously. First, it accommodates the diversity with which state and local governments divide responsibility between the public and private sectors. ... Second, it enables the federal government to control its revenue loss."[56] The volume cap has been successful in reducing the issuance of municipal bonds to finance private activities.

Critics, however, are not satisfied with the changes. Netzer found no justification for "small-issue industrial development bonds" and stressed that "they are so widely used that they must largely cancel out the locational effects ..." and result in federal revenue losses that are "large relative to user benefits."[57] A similar conclusion was reached in 1993 by the U.S. General Accounting Office which released a report revealing that the federal government's revenues were decreased by more than two billion dollars as the result of the tax-exempt status of interest on industrial development bonds."[58] The report also concluded that evidence was lacking that projects financed by the bonds created new jobs, assisted start-up firms, aided economically depressed areas, and persuaded firms not to move operations to other nations.[59] Developers clearly benefited from the bonds. Interviews with sixty-six developers in Indiana, New Jersey, and Ohio revealed that 60 percent of the developers would have proceeded with the identical project or a scaled-down project if industrial development bond funds were unavailable.[60]

SUMMARY AND CONCLUSIONS

Individual states in a federal system have a built-in inducement to engage in competition to attract tourists, gamblers, and business firms from other states and nations as they can create jobs and increase the business of existing firms and tax revenues. The position of a state in terms of such competition is analogous to that of a firm in a market characterized by perfect competition. If another firm offers a lower price on an identical product, the first firm is forced to lower its price to

Table 8.3
New-Issue Tax-Exempt Private-Activity Bonds Issued in 1989 Subject to the Volume Cap: By Type of Activity and Year of Authority (in millions)

Activity	Total Volume		1989 Cap		Carry Forward	
	Amount	Percent	Amount	Percent	Amount	Percent
Mortgage Revenue Bonds	$5,606	36.9%	$3,491	35.7%	$2,115	39.1%
Student Loans	1,250	8.2	592	6.1	658	12.2
Small Issues	3,228	21.3	3,228	33.0	0	0.0
Multifamily Housing	1,292	8.5	817	8.4	475	8.8
Qualified Redevelopment	175	1.1	45	0.5	128	2.4
Mass Commuting Vehicles	1	0.0	1	0.0	0	0.0
Furnishing of Water	162	1.1	34	0.3	128	2.4
Local Furnishing of Electricity or Gas	777	5.1	389	4.0	388	7.2
Local Distribution of Heating or Cooling	4	0.0	4	0.0	0	0.0
Hazardous Waste Disposal	85	0.6	81	0.8	3	0.1
Sewage Disposal	422	2.8	250	2.6	173	3.2
Solid Waste Disposal	1,633	10.8	463	4.7	1,170	21.6
Takeover of IOUs	0	0.0	0	0.0	0	0.0
High-Speed Rail	0	0.0	0	0.0	0	0.0
Pollution Control	309	2.0	153	1.6	156	2.9
Private-Use Portion	137	0.9	137	1.4	–	0.0
Other Categories	104	0.7	88	0.9	16	0.3
All Activities	$15,182	100.0%	$9,773	100.0%	$5,409	100.0%

Notes: Columns may not total due to rounding.
Source: The Volume Cap for Tax-Exempt Private-Activity Bonds: State and Local Experience in 1989 (Washington, D.C.: U.S. Advisory Commission on Intergovernmental Relations, 1990), p. 16.

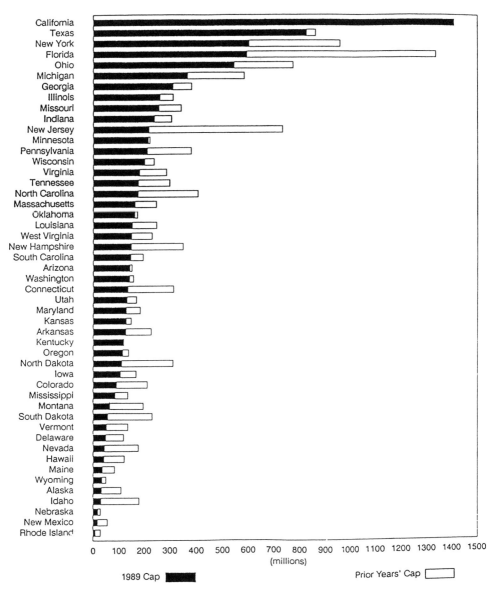

Source: Dennis Zimmerman, *The Volume Cap for Tax-Exempt Private-Activity Bonds: State and Local Experience in 1989* (Washington, D.C.: U.S. Advisory Commission on Intergovernmental Relations, 1990), p. 21.

Figure 8.1
Tax-Exempt Private-Activity Bonds issued in 1989 Using 1989 and Prior Years Volume Cap Authority; Ranked by Volume of Issues Using 1989 Authority

Table 8.4
State Agencies Responsible for Administering the Allocation of Private-Activity Bond Volume Cap, 1989

State	State Administering Agency
Alabama	Industrial Development Authority
Alaska	State Bond Committee
Arizona	Department of Commerce
Arkansas	Development Finance Authority
California	Debt Limit Allocation Committee
Colorado	Department of Local Affairs, Division of Local Government
Connecticut	Private-Activity Bond Commission
Delaware	Department of Finance
Florida	Department of General Services, Division of Bond Finance
Georgia	Department of Community Affairs
Hawaii	Department of Budget and Finance, Finance Division
Idaho	Department of Commerce
Illinois	Office of the Governor
Indiana	Employment Development Commission
Iowa	Iowa Finance Authority
Kansas	Department of Commerce
Kentucky	Private-Activity Bond Allocation Committee and Office of Financial Management and Economic Analysis
Louisiana	State Bond Commission and Office of the Governor
Maine	Finance Authority of Maine
Maryland	Department of Economic and Employment Development
Massachusetts	Executive Office for Administration and Finance
Michigan	Department of Treasury
Minnesota	Department of Finance, Cash and Debt Management Division
Mississippi	Department of Economic Development
Missouri	Department of Economic Development
Montana	Department of Administration, Office of the Director
Nebraska	Investment Finance Authority
Nevada	Department of Commerce
New Hampshire	Housing Finance Authority and Industrial Development Authority
New Jersey	Department of the Treasury
New Mexico	State Board of Finance, Department of Finance and Administration
New York	State Budget Division
North Carolina	Federal Tax Reform Allocation Committee
North Dakota	Office of the Governor
Ohio	Director, Department of Development
Oklahoma	Department of Commerce
Oregon	State Treasury and Private-Activity Bond Committee
Pennsylvania	Department of Commerce, Bureau of Bonds

(continues)

Table 8.4 (*continued*)

State	State Administering Agency
Rhode Island	Public Finance Management Board
South Carolina	State Budget and Control Board
South Dakota	Office of the Governor
Tennessee	Department of Economic and Community Development, Division of Community Development
Texas	Department of Commerce
Utah	Department of Economic and Community Development, Division of Community Development
Vermont	Emergency Board
Virginia	Department of Housing and Community Development
Washington	Department of Community Development
West Virginia	Department of Community and Industrial Development
Wisconsin	Department of Development, Housing and Economic Activity Development Authority, and Building Commission
Wyoming	Office of the Governor

Source: Dennis Zimmerman, *The Volume Cap for Tax-Exempt Private-Activity Bonds: State and Local and Experience in 1989* (Washington, D.C.: U.S. Advisory Commission on Intergovernmental Relations, 1990), p. 9.

match that of its competitor or lose business. If a state lowers its business taxes or exempts new firms from such taxes, other states in a region may lose a number of business firms to the lower tax state or witness the expansion of domestic firms in the foreign state.

There is no denying the fact that a successful industrial development program aimed at firms in other states and nations can produce major benefits in terms of new jobs, extra business for domestic firms, increased tax revenues after expiration of the tax exemptions, improvements in infrastructure as part of the strategy to attract firms, and if the policy is successful, political advantages for a politically ambitious governor or mayor who desires to be elected to a higher office. In addition, the efforts to recruit business firms may divert public attention away from important divisive issues that need to be addressed by the governor and the state legislature.

Somewhat surprisingly, domestic companies which do not receive the tax concessions offered to foreign firms seldom complain about discrimination in tax expenditures. The explanation may lie in the fact that the new business firms will generate business for many existing firms, lower the unemployment rate which may result in a lower state unemployment compensation tax, and reduce tax burdens when the tax exemptions for the new firms expire. Offers of major tax and fiscal incentives to foreign firms, however, may backfire by promoting domestic firms to threaten to cancel expansion plans or leave the state if they are not offered concessions. The ABC, CBS, and NBC television networks are examples of firms that received economic concessions after threatening to leave New York City for New Jersey.

A state's industrial development strategy based upon tax and other fiscal incentives can suffer from major disadvantages. The incentives shift the tax burden to other taxpayers during the tax exemption period; impose opportunity costs by depriving the state of tax revenues essential for solving other state problems, such as educational and environmental ones; are not always successful as illustrated by the closure of the Volkswagen plant in Pennsylvania; and can be described as a zero sum game if new firms are attracted only from sister states in the region. Furthermore, the use of incentives to lure companies from other states can generate bad relations among states.

The National Governors' Association has recognized the problems generated by interstate competition for business firms. The association's guidelines for the use of tax and other incentives by a state to attract business firms are sensible ones, but unfortunately are dependent for success upon voluntary compliance by all states.

Congress could employ its commerce and tax policies to regulate interstate competition for industry but has evidenced little inclination to do so beyond imposing a cap on the volume of tax exempt bonds that may be used to help finance private business activities.

Chapter 9 examines another type of interstate competition—efforts by states to maximize their tax revenues by exporting the burden to individuals and firms in sister states.

NOTES

1. Gary Enos, "Big Breaks Lure Plant to Ky.," *City & State*, June 21, 1993, p. 1.

2. Charles Mahtesian, "How States Get People to Love Them," *Governing*, January 1994, p. 44.

3. *Ibid.*, p. 46.

4. *Ibid.*, p. 47.

5. "N.Y.P.D. Freebie," *Forbes*, April 10, 1995, p. 22.

6. *Ibid.*

7. "Cuomo Warns N.J. to let Yankees Alone," *Times Union* (Albany, N.Y.), October 7, 1993, p. B-2.

8. Pete Dougherty, "The Yanks Are Going—to Norwich," *Times Union* (Albany, N.Y.), March 15, 1994, pp. 1 and A-7.

9. Bob Croce, "Firebirds Moving Home Base to Vermont," *Times Union* (Albany, N.Y.), May 14, 1994, pp. 1 and A-7.

10. See, for example, *Constitution of New York*, Art. VII, §§9–12 (1846).

11. *Constitution of New York*, Art. VII, §8 (1894).

12. "New Wars Between the States," *New England Business Review*, October 1963,

pp. 1–5.

13. *Ibid.*, pp. 1-2.

14. *Interjurisdictional Tax and Policy Competition: Good or Bad for the Federal System?* (Washington, D.C.: U.S. Advisory Commission on Intergovernmental Relations, 1991), p. 4. See also Daphne A. Kenyon and John Kincaid, eds., *Competition Among States and Local Governments* (Washington, D.C.: The Urban Institute, 1991).

15. Keon S. Chi, "State Business Incentives: Options for the Future," *State Trends Forecasts*, June 1994, p. 27.

16. *Ibid.*, p. 11.

17. *Ibid.*, pp. 13 and 15.

18. *State-Local Taxation and Industrial Location* (Washington, D.C.: U.S. Advisory Commission on Intergovernmental Relations, 1967), p. 63.

19. *Ibid.*, pp. 61-2.

20. *Ibid.*, p. 61.

21. Donald Moffitt, "More States Cancel Inventory Tax on Items for Sale Elsewhere," *The Wall Street Journal*, January 25, 1964, p. 1.

22. *Regional Growth: Interstate Tax Competition* (Washington, D.C.: U.S. Advisory Commission on Intergovernmental Relations, 1981), p. 32.

23. *Ibid.*, p. 34.

24. *Ibid.*, p. 37.

25. *Ibid.*, p. 46.

26. Robert Tannenwald, "Massachusetts' Tax Competitiveness," *New England Economic Review*, January/February 1994, p. 31.

27. James B. Hines, Jr., "Altered States: Taxes and the Location of Foreign Direct Investment in America," National Bureau of Economic Research, Incorporated, Working Paper No. 4397, July 1993, p. 1.

28. Alan B. Abbey, "Cuomo Intensifies Bank Reform Effort," *Times Union* (Albany, N.Y.), January 9, 1994, pp. B-1 and B-6.

29. Charles Mahtesian, "Romancing the Smokestack," *Governing*, November 1994, p. 38.

30. Dick Netzer, "An Evaluation of Interjurisdictional Competition Through Economic Development Incentives" in Daphne A. Kenyon and John Kincaid, eds., *Competition Among State and Local Governments* (Washington, D.C.: The Urban Institute Press, 1991), p. 234.

31. Mahtesian, "Romancing the Smokestack," p. 38.

32. "State Won't Become N.J.'s Power Broker," *Times Union* (Albany, N.Y.), July 22, 1995, p. B-2.

33. *Ibid.*

34. Thomas J. Lueck, "New York Buys Ads Charging 'Raid' of Company by Connecticut," *The New York Times*, October 11, 1994, p. B1.

35. *Ibid.*

36. *Ibid.*, p. B5.

37. John E. Petersen, "Interstate Meat Markets: The High Price of Buying Jobs," *Gov-*

erning, October 1993, p. 60.

38. Jay Kayne and Molly Shonka, *Rethinking State Development Policies and Programs* (Washington, D.C.: National Governors' Association, 1994), p. 3.

39. *Ibid.*, p. 14.

40. *Ibid.*

41. *McCulloch v. Maryland*, 17 U.S. 316 at 431 (1819).

42. *Collector v. Day*, 78 U.S. 122 (1871).

43. *Pollock v. Farmers Loan & Trust Company*, 157 U.S. 492 (1895).

44. *Internal Revenue Act of 1913*, 38 Stat. 166.

45. *South Carolina v. Baker*, 485 U.S. 505 at 524–5 (1988).

46. *Ibid.* at 512.

47. *Garcia v. San Antonio Metropolitan Transit Authority*, 469 U.S. 528 at 556 (1985).

48. *Tax Reform Act of 1986*, 98 Stat. 793, 4 U.S.C.A. §§421–6 (1985).

49. *South Carolina v. Baker*, 485 U.S. 505 at 521–3 (1988).

50. *Revenue and Expenditure Control Act of 1968*, 82 Stat. 251.

51. For details, see Dennis Zimmerman, *The Private Use of Tax-Exempt Bonds: Controlling Public Subsidy of Private Activity* (Washington, D.C.: The Urban Institute Press, 1991), pp. 178–351.

52. *Tax Reform Act of 1986*, 98 Stat. 793, 4 U.S.C.A. §§421–6 (1985).

53. *Deficit Reduction Act of 1984*, 98 Stat. 494.

54. *Tax Reform Act of 1986*, 98 Stat. 793, 4 U.S.C.A. §§421–6 (1985).

55. For details on administration of the volume cap, division of the cap between state and local governments, and type of activities financed, see Dennis Zimmerman, *The Volume Cap for Tax-Exempt Private-Activity Bonds: State and Local Experience in 1989* (Washington, D.C.: U.S. Advisory Commission on Intergovernmental Relations, 1990).

56. Zimmerman, *The Private Use of Tax-Exempt Bonds*, p. 219.

57. Netzer, "An Evaluation of Interjurisdictional Competition," p. 237.

58. *Industrial Development Bonds: Achievement of Public Benefits is Unclear* (Washington, D.C.: U.S. General Accounting Office, 1993), p. 10.

59. *Ibid.*, p. 21.

60. *Ibid.*, p. 20.

9

Interstate Tax Revenue Competition

The federal system of the United States encourages state lawmakers to develop innovative taxes that will fall exclusively or more heavily upon taxpayers in other states and nations. By exporting taxes, the lawmakers reduce the tax burden placed upon their constituents, enhance their state revenues, and increase prospects of reelection.

The nature of tax exportation varies considerably among the states. A state may levy heavier taxes upon foreign business firms than on domestic firms. If a state is a tourist state, the state legislature will place special taxes upon hotels and motels, and restaurant food costing more than one dollar.[1] A state legislature also may decide to raise revenue from nonresidents by levying a low excise tax on alcoholic beverages sold exclusively through state-operated stores, thereby encouraging residents of border states to purchase beverages in state stores. Similar price differentials, attributable to excise taxes, enhance the excise tax revenues of the low tax state, and encourage casual and organized crime smuggling of alcoholic beverages, cigarettes, and motor fuel.

However, state excise taxes can be avoided through purchases of products at military post exchanges and on Indian reservations. Furthermore, Congress allows the importation of a limited number of cigarettes and one quart of alcoholic spirits from other nations free of tax. A 1985 report revealed that seven states identified post-exchange abuse as the source of the greatest loss of cigarette tax revenues, and eight states indicated that abuse of Indian reservation sales was their first or second most serious problem relative to cigarette excise tax collection.[2]

The differential in premiums on motor vehicle insurance also encourages motorists in a high insurance cost state to register motor vehicles in a neighboring state with lower premiums by use of a "convenience" address, thereby depriving the state of residence of motor vehicle fees. Massachusetts has had a problem with many of its residents residing near the New Hampshire border registering their vehicles in New Hampshire where insurance rates relatively low and there is no mandatory insurance coverage as in Massachusetts.[3] In 1995, Massachusetts police began to place orange stickers on vehicles with New Hampshire license plates outlining registration requirements. If the vehicle is spotted a second time, it is logged by plate number, location, and time. After thirty days, the owner will be notified to come to the Registry of Motor Vehicles for a hearing which will decide whether the owner is a *bona fide* Massachusetts resident.

The great complexities associated with state taxation in a federal system are illustrated by the problem of taxing professional athletes who play in cities in a number of states. Currently, there is no uniform system for taxing professional athletes who cross state boundaries. In New York State, a visiting athlete is subject to the state income tax based upon the number of days he plays in the state during the year. An athlete who is a resident of New York receives a tax credit for income taxes paid in other states.

Several states do not collect income taxes from visiting athletes, other states follow New York's lead and base the tax upon the number of days the athletes played games in the state, and still other states based their income tax upon the number of games, practice days, and preseason training in the state. According to the New York State Department of Finance and Taxation, the average professional basketball player taxed by the state in 1994 earned $823,000 annually, and the average football player earns $868,000 annually.[4]

Tax exportation is a particular problem in a federal system with several resource-rich states which levy severance taxes on extractive industries and harvest taxes on timber. The incidence of these taxes has a major extraterritorial incidence as the taxes to a large degree are shifted to consumers in other states. The extractive taxes defended on the ground that an irreplaceable state resource is being depleted and the extraction imposes environmental costs upon the state.

To reduce domiciliary taxation and to increase extraterritorial taxation, states often employ conditional tax credits and apportionment formulas which make state taxes exceedingly complex and impose significant compliance costs upon foreign firms. Not surprisingly, such firms often challenge the credits and formulas in court as explained in a subsequent section.

In contrast to the provisions in the U.S. Constitution granting Congress the power to coin money and forbidding states to coin money, Section 8 of Article I authorizes Congress to regulate interstate commerce but Section 9 does not forbid states to regulate such commerce. The Supremacy of the Laws Clause of Article VI, however, provides for the negation of a state statute that conflicts directly with a congressional statute.

Although Congress possesses plenary power to regulate interstate commerce, Congress surprisingly did not enact a statute to regulate state taxation of interstate commerce until 1959 when a narrow statute was enacted in response to a 1959 decision of the U.S. Supreme Court holding that a state could tax the apportioned net income of a firm which engaged only in interstate business within the state.[5] The statute stipulates that a seller may not be subjected to a state income tax if the seller merely solicits orders for the sale of tangible goods but excludes service industries from this exemption. Subsequently, Congress enacted statutes restricting the ability of states to tax transportation industries, national banks, federal savings and loan associations, generation of transmission of electricity, and stock transfers in order to prevent discrimination against out of state firms.[6]

In the absence of congressional statutes prohibiting or restricting the ability of state legislatures to levy discriminatory taxes on interstate commerce, individuals and business firms subject to taxation discrimination turn to the courts. The U.S. Supreme Court did not invalidate a state tax as violating the commerce clause until 1872 when the court struck down a Pennsylvania tax of two cents per ton levied on the transportation of goods.[7] The court noted that the tax was based on tonnage, and the distance the freight moved did not affect the tax and hence it was "not proportioned to the business done in transportation."[8] The court continues to be the primary protector of interstate commerce against discriminatory taxation as explained in subsequent sections.

TAX DIFFERENTIAL PROBLEM

The concurrent power of a state in a federal system to levy excise and sales taxes on various products has led to a wide diversity in retail prices, particularly alcoholic beverages and tobacco products, in various states. The compensating use tax, levied at the same rate as the sales tax on out of state purchases of goods for use in the state, helps a state with a high sales tax to prevent the loss of tax revenue through their residents' purchase of motor vehicles in states with a low or no sales tax. However, despite the compensating use tax, residents residing near the border of a state with a low or no sales tax frequently make purchases out of state to evade their home state's sales tax. A number of states with sales taxes have signed cooperative agreements allowing other states to audit the books of stores which attract business from out-of-state residents, thereby permitting the home state to levy the use tax on purchases made by their residents in other states.

Tax Differential Case Studies

So-called "sin" taxes levied by states' sales of on alcoholic beverages and tobacco products have been important sources of state revenue. When such state excise taxes were low, there was little incentive for individuals to smuggle products from low-excise tax states to their home states, and most smuggling was of the casual type and did not result in significant state revenue loss.

Buttlegging. Cigarette tax evasion is not a recent phenomenon, but did not become a major problem until 1965 when the New York State Legislature increased the state excise tax on cigarettes from five to ten cents per package, and several other states followed New York's lead.

Governor Nelson A. Rockefeller of New York convened a Cigarette Tax Enforcement Conference in New York City in 1967 which was attended by representatives of thirteen states, members of Congress, and Federal Bureau of Investigations officials. Only North Carolina, a tobacco-producing state, did not levy an excise tax on tobacco products at that time, and Malcolm L. Fleisher of the Retail Tobacco Dealers of America estimated that "retailers in New York City have lost 25 percent of their cigarette sales and millions of dollars in other business because of slackened customer traffic."[9]

Addressing the conference, Governor Rockefeller reported that his state would lose approximately forty million dollars in cigarette tax revenues because of evasion and urged conferees to consider:

- stronger laws in our cities and states;
- the strengthening of federal law without impeding legitimate interstate commerce;
- an expanded role for the FBI in the war against violators;
- the possibility of a plan for the collection of taxes at the source to be made by the cigarette manufacturers;
- the possibility or even desirability of centralized collection by the federal government.[10]

The illegal cigarettes typically originate in North Carolina and were transported by automobiles, trucks, private airplanes, and ships. In 1971, the state of New York and New York City inaugurated a twenty-four-hour telephone number—(212) 267-1617—for the receipt of information on buttlegging.[11]

By 1975, the U.S. Advisory Commission on Intergovernmental Relations estimated that states and local governments lost approximately $400 million in cigarette excise tax revenue because of tax evasion.[12] The problem became more acute in the 1990s as states increased the excise tax sharply to raise additional revenues and to persuade smokers to reduce or stop smoking as a health measure. Massachusetts voters in a 1992 referendum increased the state excise tax on a package of cigarettes by twenty-five cents to fifty-one cents, effective January 1, 1993, when the federal excise tax was increased four cents per package. The result of these tax increases was a price of approximately $3.00 per package in Massachusetts compared to approximately $2.10 in neighboring New Hampshire where some outlets charged less than $2.00.[13] New Hampshire tax officials reported they anticipated collecting several additional millions of dollars in cigarette tax revenues annually, and Vermont tax officials also projected a sharp increase in cigarette excise tax revenues as the result of the tax increase in Massachusetts.[14] In contrast, Massachusetts tax officials projected that cigarette excise tax revenues would increase only 25 percent in 1993 even though the tax rate was increased 100 percent.[15] Vermont tax officials in 1993 also projected a sharp increase in cigarette excise tax revenues because of the increase in the New York excise tax from thirty-nine to fifty-six cents in June 1993.[16] In 1995, however, the tax differential was decreased when Vermont raised its cigarette excise tax from twenty to forty-four cents.

Congress has attempted to help state and local governments collect excise taxes on tobacco products by enacting the Jenkins Act of 1949 which prohibits the use of the postal service to evade payments of state and local government excise taxes.[17]

The act does not cover other modes of transportation of cigarettes, and a violation is only a misdemeanor. As a consequence, buttleggers have been prosecuted when possible under the Mail Fraud Act of 1909 since a violation of the act is a felony.[18]

As noted, Governor Rockefeller in 1967 suggested the need for strong national laws to solve the problem. In 1972, he filed a statement with the Judiciary Committee of the U.S. House of Representatives in support of a bill—H.R. 12184—prohibiting the transportation of "contraband cigarettes," which are defined as more than 20,000 cigarettes lacking appropriate state tax stamps in the possession of any person other than manufacturers, licensed distributors, an officer or agent of the U.S. Government, or a common or contract carrier.[19] H.R. 12184 would impose a fine of up to $10,000 and imprisonment for up to two years for anyone found guilty of violating the proposed law.

Governor Rockefeller in 1973 appointed a task force to develop legislative recommendations for the elimination of buttlegging and stated:

Cigarette bootlegging is making the ordinarily honest citizen an unthinking partner of organized crime. The person who buys bootleg cigarettes is unwittingly financing other enterprises of organized crime, including narcotics, the corruption of public officials, extortions, and loan-sharking.

Parents who buy bootleg cigarettes and at the same time worry about their children and drug abuse ought to keep in mind that the profits from the one illicit business go to finance the other.[20]

By 1975, the New York State Commission of Investigation estimated that in excess of 100,000 cartons of contraband cigarettes were sold in the state every day of the year.[21] New York State Senator Roy M. Goodman of New York City reported in 1976 that buttleggers sold more than one-half of the cigarettes in the city and made profits of one million dollars a week.[22] He also sought the suspension of the city's eight-cents-per-cigarette package excise tax in order to reduce the incentive for organized crime to smuggle and sell cigarettes. Appearing with the senator were five black-hooded executives of tobacco companies who reported their companies had been targets of hijacking, and their warehouses and safes containing tax indicia had been burglarized.[23]

New York State Commissioner of Taxation and Finance James H. Tully, Jr. in 1977 urged the repeal of all state excise taxes and an increase in the federal excise tax to produce revenues to reimburse states for revenue losses attributable to their excise tax repeals.[24] He also reported that his state would save more than $100 million annually in administrative and enforcement costs and also would gain approximately $400 million in revenues lost to buttleggers if his proposals were implemented.[25]

By 1977, the disparity between state and local government excise taxes on cigarettes ranged from two cents a package in North Carolina to twenty-three cents in New York City, enabling buttleggers to make a $2.10 profit on a carton sold in the city. The retail price of cigarettes varied from 57.6 cents a package in Connecticut to 35.8 cents in North Carolina, a differential of 21.8 cents.

Reacting to the growing buttlegging problem, Congress enacted the Contraband Cigarette Act of 1978 prohibiting the distribution, possession, purchase, receipt, shipment, or transportation of more than 60,000 cigarettes lacking the tax indicia of the state where the cigarettes are found.[26] This act apparently has had a deterrent effect on cigarette smuggling. However, New York State Department of Taxation and Finance investigators in 1981 seized 44,000 cartons of unstamped cigarettes of the 60,000 cartons that had been hijacked from a tractor-trailer in Virginia.[27] Moreover, the Advisory Commission on Intergovernmental Relations reported in 1985 that "a relatively small percentage of those persons arrested for cigarette smuggling were convicted and very few were sent to jail."[28]

In enacting the act, Congress stressed that states retain primary enforcement responsibility for cigarette excise tax collection, and the national government's role is limited to assisting in enforcement which is beyond the jurisdictional reach of a state. The act stipulates:

Nothing in this chapter shall be construed to inhibit or otherwise affect any coordinated effort by a number of states, through interstate compact or otherwise, to provide for the administration of state cigarette tax laws, to provide for the confiscation of cigarettes and other property seized in violation of such laws and to establish cooperative programs for the administration of such laws.[29]

The Advisory Commission's 1985 report also revealed that "thousands of wholesalers and retailers in the high-tax states have gone out of business" because of buttlegging and that a major problem involves counterfeiting of state cigarette tax indicia which are decals or meter impressions. Buttleggers purchase cigarette packages without tax indicia in low-tax states and pay the state excise taxes but offer the wholesaler a premium price if the cigarettes are supplied without tax indicia. These cigarettes are stamped with counterfeit stamps and, in collusion with retailers, wholesalers, and operators of vending machines, are sold at retail.

State-licensed stamping agents have the opportunity to supply buttleggers with unstamped cigarettes and stamping machines, and stamps "can be stolen," resulting in the sale of illicit cigarettes through legitimate retail channels.[30] The 1985 Advisory Commission report revealed "stamping agent fraud was a problem in seven states...."[31]

In general, states do not devote major resources to cigarette excise tax enforcement. Penalties for violating the tax law range from token—a few hundred dollars —to major fines, and prison sentences in Massachusetts, Pennsylvania, and Texas. The passage of time reveals that buttleggers are becoming more sophisticated. In 1993, the New York State Department of Taxation and Finance arrested three residents of the Tuscarora Indian Reservation in Niagara County in western New York who established marketing territories for their contraband cigarettes on Long Island and provided their purchasers with an 800 telephone number for use in placing orders.[32]

The buttlegging problem could be solved if states levied a uniform cigarette excise tax. A 1984 survey, by the Advisory Commission on Intergovernmental Relations, revealed that state revenue commissioners or cigarette tax administrators generally were opposed to a uniform excise tax—twenty-eight were opposed, fourteen were in favor, and eight did not respond.[33] A uniform tax would remove the incentive for organized smuggling, but casual smuggling would continue because of minor variations in the price of cigarettes in the various states.

Canada and its provinces also have been plagued by cigarette smuggling since Canadian taxes are approximately five times higher than United States and state excise taxes, resulting in a carton costing more than forty-five dollars in Canada compared to a cost of fifteen to twenty dollars in border states. Smugglers typically sell their cigarettes for approximately thirty dollars a carton. The Ontario Flue-Cured Tobacco Growers' Marketing Board estimated in 1994 that one-quarter of the cigarettes sold in Canada are illegal and the Ontario Provincial Police estimated in 1994 that 50,000 cartons of cigarettes are smuggled each day near Cornwall.[34] The city is located across the St. Lawrence River from New York and had been a quiet city. However, conditions changed with increased smuggling, and in 1994 "shootings erupt almost nightly" and "cars have been torched with firebombs, shots have been fired into a civic complex on the waterfront, and a building housing the radio station, and the hallway outside a pool hall has been bombed."[35]

Most of the contraband cigarettes are smuggled through the Akwesasne Reserve which includes both sides of the international border and is the home of approximately 12,000 Mohawk Indians. Under the Jay Treaty of 1794, the British and the U.S. governments granted the Mohawks free passage throughout their territory and the right to conduct commerce across the international boundary line without a duty or tax.

To combat the problem, the Royal Canadian Mounted Police, Ontario Police, and Cornwall Police formed a task force and have seized large amounts of illegal cigarettes. The Mohawk Police, however, refuse to participate in the task force because they are fearful the task force will lead to violent clashes between the officers and the Mohawks.

On February 9, 1994, Canadian Prime Minister Jean Chretien announced that Canada was reducing the current federal excise tax of sixteen dollars a carton to eleven dollars, called upon the provinces to make similar excise tax reductions, and reported that the antismuggling force of the Royal Canadian Mounted Police would be increased by 100 percent to 700 officers, and marine patrols on the St. Lawrence River and the Great Lakes would be increased.[36]

Canada also is faced with the problems of the smuggling of alcoholic beverages, clothing, jewelry, and perfume because of high Canadian taxes. Smugglers also are bringing narcotics, firearms, and illegal immigrants into Canada.[37]

New York state loses approximately $100 million annually in excise tax revenues on the sale of tax-exempt cigarettes and gasoline to non-Indians on Indian reservations. States possess very little regulatory authority over Indian tribes under various treaties between the tribes and the U.S. government. In general, the treaties recognize Indian tribes as sovereign nations, and commerce on the reservations is governed by the federal Indian Trade and Intercourse Act and the Indian Trader Act.[38]

The U.S. Supreme Court in *Moe v. Confederated Slaish and Kootenai Tribes of Flathead Reservations* in 1976 held that a state excise tax could not be levied upon the purchase of cigarettes by an Indian resident of a reservation, but the tax could be imposed on sales to nonresidents.[39] Four years later, the court in *Washington v. Confederated Colville Tribes* ruled that a state could levy its excise tax on purchases of cigarettes on reservations by nonmembers of the Indian tribe and require tribal sellers to purchase and affix state tax stamps on cigarettes sold to nonmembers.[40] The court also opined that the state could seize unstamped cigarettes being shipped from other states to the reservations if the tribes did not assist in the collection of the state tax but did not issue a ruling relative to the state's contention it possesses authority to seize cigarettes on reservations intended for sale to nonmembers.

Seizure of contraband products and their transport are the principal methods of enforcing excise taxes, but this method cannot be used on reservations. In 1989, New York decided to promulgate regulations limiting the number of tax-free cigarettes that wholesalers may sell to retailers on reservations based upon the per capita consumption of cigarettes in the state multiplied by the number of members of a tribe. If the wholesalers sell more than the computed amount, they must pay the fifty-six cents a package excise tax in advance to the state. New York State courts invalidated the regulations, and the decisions were appealed to the U.S. Supreme Court.[41] In 1994, the court reversed the lower court decisions and opined that the Indian Trader Act of 1876 did not preempt state authority to promulgate reasonable regulations to assess and collect a lawful state tax, and the New York tax scheme did not impose an excessive burden on Indian traders.[42]

Alcoholic Beverage Taxation.   Congress prior to national prohibition enacted two statutes exempting state liquor laws from the Interstate Commerce Clause in order to help "dry" states to enforce their prohibition laws. The Wilson Act of 1890 provides that upon introduction to a state, liquor becomes subject to the police power of the state.[43] Judicial interpretation of the act weakened its provisions and enabled a mail order firm to ship liquor to a consignee in a "dry" state for personal consumption. The Webb–Kenyon Act of 1913 responded to this development by making illegal the receipt and resale of alcoholic beverages in contravention of state laws.[44] The provisions of these two acts generally were incorporated into the Twenty-First Amendment repealing national prohibition. Not surprisingly, there are clashes between the amendment and the Interstate Commerce Clause which the courts are called upon to resolve. In *Bacchus Imports Limited v. Dias*, the U.S. Supreme Court in 1984 invalidated a Hawaii excise tax levied on the sale of liquor at wholesale because the tax act exempted several beverages produced in the state.[45]

State excise taxes on alcoholic beverages have produced a relatively wide differential in the retail prices of such beverages in various states with low-tax states gaining sales and excise tax revenues from nonresidents. The repeal of national prohibition with the ratification of the Twenty-First Amendment on December 5, 1933, induced states to establish two systems for the control of the sale of alcoholic beverages.

Eighteen states control directly the wholesale and retail sale of alcoholic beverages and the other states indirectly control such sales through licensing systems.[46] New Hampshire, a control state, maintains low prices and low excise taxes which enables it to attract purchasers from neighboring states and the Province of Quebec. To exploit the out-of-state market, New Hampshire locates many of its state liquor stores near the border of neighboring states and the State Liquor Commission spends eighty percent of its advertising appropriations in other states. New Hampshire sales are also aided by the absence of a bottle deposit law which exists in neighboring states. When Massachusetts imposed a bottle deposit, it had the effect of increasing the price of beer by nearly three dollars per case. Maine estimates that it loses ten million dollars in excise tax revenue to New Hampshire and has only one enforcement officer for each of its sixteen counties.

Border surveillance by high-excise tax states has become common. Massachusetts has been feuding with New Hampshire since it established state operated liquor stores following repeal of national prohibition. Massachusetts Tax Commissioner Henry F. Long during the 1930s stationed enforcement officers near New Hampshire liquor stores prior to major holidays who wrote down the license plate numbers of Massachusetts vehicles.[47] The commissioner would send a tax bill to the owner of each such vehicle for the excise tax on a case of liquor. The Massachusetts "Blue Laws" until 1983 closed all but essential stores on Sundays and hence New Hampshire with open stores had an additional sales advantage.

New York tax officials employed roadblocks in the 1960s in an attempt to halt the smuggling of alcoholic beverages between New Jersey and Staten Island, and between Plattsburgh, New York, and Vermont where alcoholic beverage prices are lower.[48] In 1994, two Canadians were arrested in New York for transporting 397 cases of liquor after their truck and automobile were trailed by officers of two states from a Maryland discount liquor store through Pennsylvania to New York.[49] Interestingly, Vermont agents write down the license plate numbers of all vehicles parked outside New Hampshire liquor stores, and Vermont State Police, stop these vehicles in Vermont. A number of trucks owned by smugglers from upstate New York have been stopped by the Vermont State Police, and their loads of alcoholic beverages seized as contraband because the Vermont state excise tax has not been paid.

Maryland criticized Pennsylvania for having its agents park their marked vehicles near Maryland liquor stores to persuade Pennsylvania residents not to purchase alcoholic beverages in Maryland, which has been having *its* tax agents spy on Maryland vehicles parked near liquor stores in the District of Columbia where prices of alcoholic beverages are lower.[50]

In 1965, the Warren County, New Jersey, prosecutor signed expulsion orders relative to Pennsylvania tax agents who were writing down the registration numbers of Pennsylvania vehicles near liquor stores in Phillipsburg, New Jersey.[51] Similarly, the District of Columbia and a number of cities in Indiana and Kentucky have made it illegal for tax agents from neighboring states to write down registration numbers of vehicles parked near liquor stores.[52]

How effective is border surveillance in reducing alcoholic beverage excise tax evasion? The director of New York's Miscellaneous Tax Bureau stated "that border patrols can't really make a dent in 'liquor runs.' The patrols are sporadic, expensive, and enforcement is almost impossible even after the letters are sent."[53] Nevertheless, he reported that 40 percent of the recipients of the letters paid the tax.[54]

New York in 1993 changed its tax law to curtail smuggling of alcoholic beverages from New Jersey by New York City bars and restaurants.[55] The amendment requires shippers of such beverages to obtain a license from the State Department of Taxation and Finance and to maintain a manifest for each shipment. For the first time, the state legislature imposed a penalty of forfeiture of the seized liquors. Enforcement of this law revealed that large quantities of alcoholic beverages are being shipped from southern states to warehouses in upstate New York prior to being smuggled through Indian reservations into Canada.[56]

EXPORTATION OF TAXES

The opportunities that an individual state has to maximize its tax revenues while protecting its taxpayers by levying taxes that residents of other states will pay vary considerably. Resource-rich states, minerals and timber principally, are in a position to levy severance taxes on industries which export most of their products to other states. In addition, states in levying taxes authorize tax credits which may not be available to foreign firms and utilize apportionment formulas, which place a lighter tax burden on domestic firms. The Interstate Commerce Clause protects commerce and not taxpayers in other states engaged in interstate commerce. Indirectly, the clause protects such taxpayers if a state tax is invalidated by courts on the ground it impedes the free flow of commerce among states.

Severance Taxes

The levying of state severance taxes, at rates of 1 or 2 percent of the value of a resource, has a long history dating to a 1846 Michigan tax, and little controversy was generated by the taxes. By 1981, thirty-three states were levying such taxes, and several increased the tax rate sharply, touching off complaints by Eastern and Midwestern states that the resource-rich states in the West were exploiting their monopolies.[57] The U.S. Supreme Court in 1982 ruled that Indian tribes possess the power to levy mineral severance taxes but did not decide whether the taxes could be imposed on minerals extracted from fee lands owned by non-Indians in a reservation or whether the taxes could be imposed on territory outside a reservation termed "Indian Country."[58]

Nine energy-rich states levy special severance taxes on coal, natural gas, and oil, which are consumed principally in other states. These taxes are a major source of state government revenue. Texas receives approximately one-quarter of its revenue from oil and natural gas severance taxes and has no need to levy a state income tax. The rates of these taxes vary greatly from 4.6 percent on oil in Oklahoma to 12.5 percent in Alaska. The highest tax rate is 30.5 percent levied on coal by Montana.

The resource-rich states maintain they need the tax revenue to develop economically viable local governments after the resource is depleted, repair environmental damage resulting from mining, and cover the societal costs associated with the growing mining communities. They also contend the tax revenues are "used to help provide public services for all the people who are migrating here from the East."[59]

The U.S. Supreme Court issued three resource taxation decisions in the 1920s, collectively referred to as the *Heisler* Trilogy, holding that severance was similar to manufacturing in that both preceded the flow of interstate commerce and hence were local activities exempt from commerce clause scrutiny.[60] The court in *Heisler* expressed fear that a ruling expanding the commerce power to include articles to be exported from a state would nationalize all industries.[61] The local activity doctrine has a corollary holding that a state could levy a tax on "local incidents" of an interstate business activity, that is, generation of electrical power.[62] This corollary was an exception to the general holding that a state could not tax the privilege of conducting interstate business.

In *Pike v. Bruce Church, Incorporated*, the court in 1970 opined:

Where the statute regulates evenhandedly to effectuate a legitimate local public interest, and its effects on interstate commerce are only incidental, it will be upheld unless the burden imposed on such commerce is clearly excessive in relation to putative local benefits ... If a legitimate local purpose is found, then the question becomes one of degree. And the extent of the burden that will be tolerated will of course depend on the nature of the local interest involved, and on whether it could be promoted as well with a lesser impact on interstate activities.[63]

The court abandoned the privilege doctrine and adopted a flexible test in 1977 to determine the constitutionality of a Mississippi privilege tax by adopting "a standard of permissibility of state taxation based upon its effect rather than its legal terminology."[64] In *Complete Auto Transit Incorporated v. Brady*, the court ruled a state tax is valid if it "is applied to an activity with a substantial nexus with the taxing state, is fairly apportioned, does not discriminate against interstate commerce, and is fairly related to the services provided by the state."[65]

Montana and Wyoming have approximately 40 percent of the coal reserves of the United States, including approximately 68 percent of the most desirable low-sulfur coal whose use is encouraged by the federal Clean Air Act. Ninety percent of Montana's mined coal is exported to other states. Montana had levied a minor severance tax on mined coal in 1921, and in 1975 increased the tax to 30.5 percent on coal with a heating value of 7000 British Thermal Units (BTU) per pound.[66] Wyoming in the same year increased it severance tax from 2.0 percent to 17.5 percent.[67] The sharp increases in the severance taxes raised the two issues of whether an undue burden had been placed on interstate commerce and taxation without representation since consumers in sister states are not represented in the state legislatures which raised the severance tax rates. The latter claim was in effect supported by the Montana State Legislature's conference committee which argued in its report that the increased tax would fall primarily upon nonresidents.

In 1978, four Montana coal and eleven utility companies in sister states challenged the constitutionality of the Montana tax on the ground it violates the commerce clause. The Montana Supreme Court in 1980 upheld the decision of the trial court that the tax was constitutional.[68] In 1981, the U.S. Supreme Court, by a five to four vote, affirmed the decision of the Montana Supreme Court.[69] The court specifically ruled that the federal Mineral Lands Leasing Act of 1920 and the Federal Coal Leasing Amendments of 1975 did not preempt the power of the Montana State Legislature to levy a severance tax.[70] The court also abandoned the *Heisler* case local activities exceptions.

The court held that the taxpayers had nexus to the state, apportionment was not an issue since there was no possibility of multiple taxation, the tax was not discriminatory since the same tax rate was applied regardless of where the coal was shipped, and a firm with a nexus to the state was required to support governmental services in general and not simply services related to the firm's activities.

This decision made it clear that severance taxes were constitutional even if the bulk of the taxed products were exported to sister states. The only limitations on such taxes are that they must be designed to raise revenue for the general support of the state government and must not be so arbitrary that the taxes constitute use of a prohibited power such as confiscation.[71]

Supporting this decision, Stephen F. Williams explained:

Thus, Montana's export of ninety percent of its coal by no means shows that it would export ninety percent of the tax. Apart from the long-term contracts, a court could discover what portion of the tax was exported only after complex economic inquiries. The rules as to the incidence of taxes are easy to state, but hard to apply. The difficulties are suggested by the variance in results when economists seek to estimate price elasticities. For example, estimates of the long-term price elasticity of demand for motor gasoline, a much studied matter, range from $-.22$ (very inelastic) to -1.3 (quite elastic).[72]

Walter Hellerstein, an expert on state taxation, also agrees with the court's decision and is convinced "the court is an institutionally incapable and politically inappropriate body for determining the appropriate level of a tax."[73] Bills, such as S. 463 of 1984, have been introduced in Congress which would limit the rate of a state mineral severance tax to the amount of revenue that would enable the state to recover direct costs associated with the extraction of the mineral. Strong opposition to such bills has come from the mineral- and timber-rich states and from other groups which maintain that states in a federal system should be free to determine the nature of their tax systems provided the systems do not violate the U.S. Constitution.

The Supreme Court in 1981 also was called upon to decide whether a Louisiana "first use" tax on natural gas produced on federal offshore land was constitutional. The tax statute exempted gas used to drill oil or gas within the state, but did not provide a similar exemption for gas used to drill for oil or gas in sister states. The court invalidated the tax and opined:

A state tax must be assessed in light of its actual effect considered in conjunction with other provisions of the state's tax scheme ... the Louisiana first-use tax unquestionably discriminates against interstate commerce in favor of local interests as the necessary result of various tax credits and exclusions.[74]

Tax Apportionment

The increase in the number of multistate corporations in the nineteenth century and the more recent increase in multinational corporations have produced the need for a nondiscriminatory tax system by each state. Three methods are employed by states to determine their respective share of a multistate or multinational corporation's income: separate accounting, specific allocation, and formula apportionment. Separate accounting has limited applicability because it is difficult to separate income earned in a state from income earned outside the state. Specific allocation similarly has limited applicability and provides that specified types of income, such as interest, must be allocated to a single state and cannot be divided among states.

Principal reliance is placed by states upon formula apportionment to determine a firm's income earned within a state. A three factor formula—payroll, property, and sales—is employed to determine the ratio between a corporation's income earned in the state relative to its multistate or multinational income. The apportionment formula is not uniform among the states and hence the definition of taxable income varies.

The Supreme Court has issued decisions relative to the apportionment of taxes between states since 1891 when a Pennsylvania tax on nondomiciliary-scheduled railroad rolling stock was upheld because the tax was apportioned based upon track mileage in the state relative to the total track mileage used by the rolling stock.[75] Eight years later the court expanded its 1891 ruling to apply to nondomiciliary railroad cars which did not move over regular routes on a continuous basis since the tax was apportioned on the basis of the average number of such cars in the state during the year.[76] Concerned with the possibility of double taxation, the court in 1905 invalidated as violative of due process of law a Kentucky tax levied on the entire fleet of rolling stock since many cars were located permanently outside Kentucky and could be subjected to taxation by another state.[77]

In 1906, the court upheld a New York tax on the entire rolling stock of a domestic railroad which owned a large number of cars that were not often in the state and opined that due process of law was not denied since the concerned railroad did not show that its rolling stock could be taxed in a nondomiciliary state.[78]

The court's 1906 ruling was extended in 1944 to airlines when a Minnesota personal property tax levied on the entire fleet of a domestic airline corporation was upheld even though the airplanes were flying continuously in interstate commerce except for the time periods when they were loading and unloading passengers and cargo, or were being maintained.[79] Justice Felix Frankfurter opined there was no evidence that "a defined part of the domiciliary corpus ... acquired a permanent location; *i.e.*, a taxing situs elsewhere."[80]

New York's gross receipts tax on transportation services was invalidated by the court in 1948 on the ground the tax receipts were not apportioned on the basis of miles that buses traveled through various states.[81] Nearly one-half of the bus travel involved in this case occurred in New Jersey and Pennsylvania.

In 1949, the court ruled valid an *ad valorem* property tax apportioned by the miles of inland water traversed by vessels owned by foreign corporations.[82] In its earlier decisions, the court opined that vessels could be taxed only by the domiciliary state. In 1954, the court applied its railroad rolling stock decisions by upholding a nondomiciliary apportioned state property tax levied on airplanes owned by an interstate airline which had regularly scheduled stops in the state.[83]

The validity of Iowa's single-factor gross receipts formula, instead of the standard three-factor formula (payroll, property, and sales), for apportioning net income was examined by the Supreme Court in *Moorman Manufacturing Company v. Bair* in 1978. The Illinois plaintiff alleged that the Iowa one-factor formula created the possibility of multiple taxation since most states, including Illinois, used the three-factor formula. Most of the appellant's property and payrolls were located outside Illinois, and employment of the three-factor formula would allocate 12 percent of the firm's 1972 net income to Iowa. The Iowa one-factor sales formula increased the allocation to 18 percent. However, the court in effect ruled that there is no requirement for a nationally uniform apportionment formula and to challenge the Iowa formula successfully the firm would have to prove that its net income allocated to Iowa was generated by activities in other states.[84]

Florida had been prorating on a mileage basis the fuel tax levied on common carriers but in 1983 repealed the prorating tax on fuel sold to airlines and replaced it with a 5-percent tax on a state-determined price of $1.148 a gallon.[85] Airlines purchasing fuel in Florida were required to pay the tax regardless of whether they operated primarily outside Florida.[86] The plaintiff alleged the tax was not consistent with a nonscheduled air service agreement entered into by the United States and Canada in 1974 and also was preempted by the Federal Aviation Act. The U.S. Supreme Court in 1986 rejected these arguments and ruled the tax was not preempted by the act and did not violate the dormant commerce clause.[87]

The following year the court heard a challenge to the constitution of an axle tax and marker fee levied on trucks in Pennsylvania. The plaintiff alleged the flat taxes subjected out-of-state trucking firms to a higher charge per mile traveled in Pennsylvania compared to domestic trucks and did not approximate the cost of the use of the Commonwealth's highways. The court in *American Trucking Associations v. Scheiner* ruled that the flat taxes failed the internal consistency test requiring that a state tax levied by every state would not place an impermissible burden on interstate commerce.[88]

In delivering the decision of the court, Justice John Paul Stevens noted "our task is by no means easy; the uneven course of decisions in this field reflects the difficulties of reconciling unrestricted access to the national market with each state's authority to collect its fair share of revenues from interstate commercial activities."[89] He added that the court's recent decisions rejected a "somewhat metaphysical approach to the commerce clause" that emphasized the character of the privilege and not tax consequences.[90]

Dissenting in this case, Justice Antonin Scalia highlighted the difficulties faced by the court in adjudicating claims that a state tax discriminates against foreign firms:

Legislative action adjusting taxes on interstate and intrastate activities spans a spectrum, ranging from the obviously discriminatory to the manipulative to the ambiguous to the wholly innocent. Courts can avoid arbitrariness in their review only by policing the entire spectrum (which is impossible), by policing none of it, or by adopting rules which subject to scrutiny certain well-defined classes of actions thought likely to come at or near the discriminatory end of the spectrum.[91]

In 1989, the court rendered another significant tax apportionment decision and distinguished it from the *Scheiner* decision. The case involved a 1985 Illinois Act levying a 5-percent tax on interstate telecommunications originating or terminating in Illinois charged to an Illinois service address regardless of whether the call was an interstate or an intrastate one. The act also authorized a tax credit provided the taxpayer offers proof that a tax had been paid in a sister state on the same call.

The court acknowledged that an interstate telephone call could be subject to double taxation but held that this possibility is insufficient to invalidate the tax.[92] Justice Thurgood Marshall noted that the Illinois tax differed from the flat taxes levied on trucks by Pennsylvania because the latter taxes burdened foreign truckers in contrast to the Illinois tax whose burden fell on an Illinois resident "who presumably is able to complain about and change the tax through the Illinois political process."[93] He emphasized the commerce clause is not designed to protect residents of a state from taxes levied by their state legislatures. Marshall also noted that the mileage travel by domestic and foreign trucks on Pennsylvania highways could be determined, whereas the precise path of electronic telephone signals cannot be determined.

Using the unitary tax system, the New Jersey Division of Taxation assessed the Bendix Corporation (now Allied-Signal, Incorporated) for taxes on an income which included a gain resulting from the corporation's sale of stock which it owned in another corporation. The Supreme Court in 1992 upheld the use of the unitary tax system, but ruled that New Jersey must refund the tax on the gain because a state may not tax a nondomicilliary corporation's income derived from an unrelated business activity such as the sale of stock.[94] Justice Anthony M. Kennedy specifically opined:

... the unitary business rule is a recognition of two imperatives: the states' wide authority to devise formulae for an accurate assessment of a corporation's intrastate value or income; and the necessary limit on the states' authority to tax value or income which cannot in fairness be attributed to the taxpayer's activities within the state.[95]

The court in 1995 decided another case involving alleged failure of a state to apportion a tax and, by a 7 to 2 vote, upheld Oklahoma's sales tax on the price of interstate bus tickets sold in the state by opining the tax did not violate the dormant commerce clause.[96] The court distinguished this decision from its 1948 decision striking down New York's gross receipts tax on transportation services, by noting that multiple taxation could occur in the New York case since each state might levy a gross receipts tax on the same transportation services, whereas the Oklahoma sales tax was levied on the purchase of a ticket, and no other state could levy a sales tax on the same ticket.

State Taxation of Multinational Corporations

Taxation of the worldwide operations of multinational corporations by states has generated diplomatic protests by Japanese, United Kingdom, and other foreign governments. The protests have been directed at California's employment of a unitary business–formula apportionment method to determine the amount of its franchise tax. The state determines the total earnings of a corporation, including its California operations, and develops an allocation fraction for the firm by taking an unweighted average of three ratios: California payroll to worldwide payroll, California property value to total property value, and California sales to total sales. The corporation's taxable income allocatable to California is determined by multiplying the firm's allocation fraction by the total income of the unitary business.

Alcan Aluminum Limited, a Canadian firm, and Imperial Chemical Industries PLC, a United Kingdom firm, challenged unsuccessfully the constitutionality of the California unitary tax in the U.S. District Court, but on appeal the U.S. Court of Appeals for the Seventh Circuit reversed the decision, and an appeal was made to the U.S. Supreme Court.[97] In 1990, the court ruled that the two firms had standing to bring suit under Article III of the U.S. Constitution, but suits of this nature were barred by the Tax Injunction Act of 1937.[98]

Barclays Bank, a British corporation, and the Colgate-Palmolive Company, a Delaware corporation, challenged California's unitary tax system on the ground it violated the Interstate Commerce and Due Process Clauses of the U.S. Constitution. Barclays Bank also contended the system places a distinct burden on a foreign-based multinational company and results in double international taxation. Justice Ruth B. Ginsburg, in delivering the court's 1994 opinion, noted there was no evidence that Congress intended to prohibit the unitary system and "the history of Senate action on a United States/United Kingdom tax treaty ... reinforces our conclusion that Congress implicitly has permitted the states to use the worldwide combined reporting method."[99]

Had California lost the case, the state would have had to repay approximately 2,000 multinational corporations in excess of $2.1 billion in tax refunds and abatements of pending assessments.[100]

Tax Credits

States commonly authorize tax credits for a variety of purposes. California, for example, allows a corporation income tax credit of 8 to 12 percent for the cost of research, and a 10-percent credit for the cost of a solar energy system installed in commercial buildings in the state.[101] Illinois grants a tax credit for employment of workers in enterprise zones, and Virginia offers a 10-percent tax credit for the cost of equipment used in the state for processing recycled personal property.[102] Tax incentives also are a powerful tool used by states to encourage firms to locate or expand facilities within their respective states but possess the potential for discriminating against interstate commerce.

New Mexico levied a tax on the generation of electricity at a rate of approximately 2 percent of the retail charge per net kilowatt hour. The U.S. Supreme Court invalidated the tax in 1979 because the authorized tax credit could be used only to offset the gross receipts tax on local sales of electricity, and the credit could not be used by firms selling electricity to sister states.[103] The court specifically noted that the Tax Reform Act of 1976 prohibits discriminatory taxation against consumers in sister states in the generation of electricity.[104]

The New York State Legislature in 1968 enacted amendments to its tax law relative to the transfer tax on securities by providing for a 50-percent lower tax rate for transactions by nonresidents if the sales are made in New York and establishing $350 as the maximum tax imposed on a resident or nonresident taxpayer if the sales occur in New York.[105] In *Boston Stock Exchange v. State Tax Commission*, the Supreme Court invalidated the amendments as "favoring local enterprises at the expense of out-of-state businesses."[106] The court added:

> Our decision today does not prevent the states from structuring their tax systems to encourage the growth and development of intrastate commerce and industry. Nor do we hold that a state may not compete with other states for a share of interstate commerce; such competition lies at the heart of a free trade policy.[107]

New York also imposed a franchise tax on corporations including the income of subsidiaries engaged in the export of goods but provided a partially offsetting credit for income from exports shipped from a New York place of business. Rejecting the state's argument that the credit merely forgave "a portion of the tax that New York had jurisdiction to levy" under a fairly apportioned formula, the court ruled that the tax credit violates the commerce clause because it discriminates against foreign firms in an attempt to persuade them to conduct more business in New York.[108]

The Supreme Court in *Armco Incorporated v. Hardesty* in 1984 was faced with the question of whether a West Virginia 0.27-percent gross receipts tax on the business of selling tangible property at wholesale violated the commerce clause because the tax exempted West Virginia manufacturers from the tax. West Virginia also levied a 0.88-percent tax on the value of products manufactured in the state. Although a West Virginia manufacturer had a larger tax burden, the court invalidated the gross receipts tax because "a state may not tax a transaction or incident more heavily when it crosses state lines than when it occurs entirely within the state."[109]

Alabama enacted a statute levying a substantially lower gross premiums tax rate on Alabama insurance companies compared to the rate levied on foreign insurance companies. The statute allowed foreign insurance corporations to reduce but not eliminate the differential in the tax rate by investing in Alabama assets and securities. The Supreme Court in 1985 struck the tax down and noted the McCarran–Ferguson Act of 1945 exempts the insurance industry from the restrictions of the commerce clause but does not exempt the industry from the Equal Protection of the Laws Clause.[110]

The state of Washington utilized a different tax scheme to discriminate against interstate commerce by providing that a manufacturer who sold products within the state and paid the wholesale tax was not subject to the manufacturing tax. The Supreme Court opined the tax violated the Interstate Commerce Clause and rejected Washington's contention that the imposition of the manufacturing tax on goods manufactured in the state and sold in sister states was valid as a compensating tax because the state failed to identify the burden that would be compensated for by the tax.[111]

The U.S. Court of Appeals for the Second Circuit in 1993 decided a complex case involving the Vermont motor vehicle use tax which also grants a credit against the use tax for any sales tax paid to the state. Most Vermont residents never have to pay the use tax because of the credit. A nonresident who purchases an automobile in another state and moves to Vermont discovers he is not entitled to a tax credit in Vermont or in his former state where he purchased the vehicle. The U.S. District Court held that the tax did not violate the Interstate Commerce Clause and an appeal was made to the Court of Appeals.[112]

The U.S. Supreme Court earlier had examined the tax and struck it down on the grounds it violated the Equal Protection of the Law Clause, but the court did not address the Interstate Commerce Clause issue raised by the plaintiff.[113] The Supreme Court specifically explained that it "again put to one side the question whether a state must in all circumstances credit sales or use taxes paid to another state against its own use tax."[114]

In response to this decision, Vermont promulgated a new rule narrowing the scope of the tax by stipulating the tax credit is not available to a Vermont resident who purchases and registers an automobile in a sister state prior to registering it in Vermont.[115] The Court of Appeals ruled that the modified tax failed to meet the internal consistency test and hence was not apportioned fairly and violates the commerce clause by placing "a greater tax burden on vehicles transported into Vermont from other states than it does on Vermont-based vehicles not so transported."[116]

SUMMARY AND CONCLUSIONS

As explained in this chapter, the nature of extraterritorial taxation varies considerably from state to state and includes taxes levied upon tourists from sister states, discriminatory taxes levied upon foreign corporations, and severance taxes. Other states raise revenue from nonresidents by levying low-excise taxes on alcoholic beverages and cigarettes to increase significantly the volume of sales of these products and maximize excise tax revenues.

Surprisingly, Congress did not enact a statute, based on the power to regulate interstate commerce, restricting the taxing powers of states until 1959 and has enacted only a handful of such statutes, which are limited in their coverage to specific institutions or circumstances, in an effort to prevent discriminatory taxation by a state against interstate commerce.

The court cases presented in this chapter illustrate the ingenuity and complexity of state tax schemes and the use of certain schemes to increase the revenue of a state at the expense of sister states. Business firms with a nexus to a state engaged in interstate commerce can be taxed to cover their fair share of the expenses of a state. The courts, out of necessity, have to balance a state's need for revenue against any burden the state's taxes place on the flow of commerce throughout the nation.

Little controversy was generated by state severance taxes on mineral and timber resources until the late 1970s when several states increased the rate of these taxes significantly, thereby generating friction with states that are major importers of minerals and timber and charges that the taxes were profiteering. Nevertheless, the U.S. Supreme Court has upheld the constitutionality of such taxes.

Multistate and multinational corporations have a heavy tax burden placed on them by certain states, particularly ones employing unitary taxation. Determining the proper method of taxing a nondomiciliary corporation engaged in interstate commerce in a particular state is a difficult task. Controversy also has swirled around the tax apportionment formulas utilized by states to determine the tax liability of nondomiciliary corporations. The unitary tax system employed by California has generated strong protests from foreign governments, yet the system has been upheld as constitutional by the U.S. Supreme Court.

The principal defender of taxpayers against unfair interstate tax revenue competition is the judiciary. The U.S. Supreme Court has noted it acts "as a defense against state taxes, which, whether by design or inadvertence, either give rise to serious concerns of double taxation, or attempt to capture tax revenues that, under the theory of the tax, belong of right to other jurisdictions."[117] The court also declines to assume the responsibility for formulating and mandating a specific system of state taxation of interstate commerce and makes clear that Congress possesses plenary authority to regulate state taxation of interstate commerce.

Evidence reveals that states will continue to design taxes that can be exported in part to business firms and consumers in other states. The invalidation by a court of tax exportation schemes of a state simply encourages the concerned state to seek to develop a new tax that can survive judicial scrutiny.

Whereas interstate tax revenue competition generates friction among many states, they nevertheless cooperate formally and informally on a wide range of activities and programs as explained in Chapter 10. In particular, the Multistate Tax Commission seeks to promote uniformity in the taxation of multistate and multinational corporations, thereby promoting the equitable collection of taxes by each state and easing the compliance burden placed upon the corporation.

NOTES

1. *Revenue Diversification: State and Local Travel Taxes* (Washington, D.C.: U.S. Advisory Commission on Intergovernmental Relations, 1994). See also Ellen Perlman, "Taxing Travelers to the Hilt," *Governing*, December 1994, pp. 20–1.

2. *Cigarette Tax Evasion: A Second Look* (Washington, D.C.: U.S. Advisory Commission on Intergovernmental Relations, 1985), p. 11.

3. Shelly Murphy, "Drive Free and Lie? Not on His Watch," *The Boston Globe*, May 6, 1995, pp. 1 and 6.

4. "State Pioneers Tax Change for Visiting Athletes," *Times Union* (Albany, N.Y.), August 4, 1994, p. B–2.

5. *Northwestern States Portland Cement Company v. Minnesota*, 358 U.S. 490 (1959). See also 71 Stat. 555 and 15 U.S.C.A. §§381–4 (1995 Supp.).

6. See *Railroad Revitalization and Regulatory Reform Act of 1976*, 90 Stat. 31, 49 U.S.C.A. §11503 (1994); *Tax Reform Act of 1976*, 90 Stat. 1914, 15 U.S.C.A. §391 (1995 Supp.); *Airline Deregulation Act of 1978*, 92 Stat. 1708, 49 U.S.C.A. §1513(s) (1994); *Motor Carrier Act of 1980*, 94 Stat. 793, 49 U.S.C.A. §11503(a) (1994); *Tax Reform Act of 1976*, 90 Stat. 31, 49 U.S.C.A. §11503 (1994); *An act to Clarify the Liability of National Banks for Certain Taxes*, 83 Stat. 434, 12 U.S.C.A. §548 (1989 and 1995 Supp.); and *Home Owners Loan Act of 1993 as Amended*, 12 U.S.C.A. §1264(h) (1989 and 1995 Supp.).

7. *Case of the State Freight Tax*, 82 U.S. 232 (1872).

8. *Ibid.* at 273.

9. James K. Batten, "Tax, Law Aides to Map Cigarette Bootleg War," *Knickerbocker News* (Albany, N.Y.), August 30, 1967, p. 3B.

10. "At Cigarette Tax Enforcement Conference, New York City, September 12, 1967." *Public Papers of Nelson A. Rockefeller: 1967* (Albany, N.Y.: Office of the Governor, 1968), p. 1311.

11. John L. Considine, "Cigarette Smuggling Big Business," *Knickerbocker News* (Albany, N.Y.), January 22, 1971, p. 16A.

12. *Cigarette Tax Evasion: A Second Look*, p. 2.

13. "Massachusetts Tax is Good News," *The Keene (N.H.) Sentinel*, January 4, 1993, p. 5.

14. "Whopping Tax Reduces Bay State Cigarette Purchases," *The Union Leader* (Manchester, N.H.), November 19, 1993, p. 22.

15. "Vt. Benefits from NY, Mass. Taxes," *The Union Leader* (Manchester, N.H.), June 22, 1993, p. 7.

16. Craig Brandon, "Butt Smugglers," *Times Union* (Albany, N.Y.), June 24, 1993, p. 1.

17. *Jenkins Act of 1949*, 63 Stat. 884, 15 U.S.C.A. §375 (1976).

18. *Mail Fraud Act of 1909*, 35 Stat. 1088, 18 U.S.C.A. §1341 (1984 and 1995 Supp.).

19. "Governor Supports Bill to Make Interstate Transport of Contraband Cigarettes a Federal Crime." *Public Papers of Nelson A Rockefeller: 1972* (Albany, N.Y.: Office of the Governor, 1973), p. 1099.

20. Press release issued by the Office of Governor Nelson A. Rockefeller, Albany, N.Y., February 11, 1973, p. 1.

21. Diane Henry, "Interstate Police Force Urged to Combat Cigarette Smuggling," *The New York Times*, March 26, 1975, p. 31.

22. Farnsworth Fowle, "Goodman Renews Effort to Life City's Cigarette Tax," *The New York Times*, January 16, 1976, p. 31.

23. *Ibid.*

24. "If the U.S. Collected All Cigarette Taxes," a letter to the editor from James H Tully, Jr., *The New York Times*, May 19, 1977, p. A34.

25. *Ibid.*

26. *Contraband Cigarette Act of 1978*, 53 Stat. 1291, 18 U.S.C.A. §2341 (1993).

27. Ron Kermani, "Smoking Out Counterfeit Cigs: N.Y.'s Biggest Arrest," *Sunday Times Union* (Albany, N.Y.), November 8, 1981, pp. 1 and A-8.

28. *Cigarette Tax Evasion: A Second Look*, p. 23.

29. *Contraband Cigarette Act of 1978*, 53 Stat. 1291, 18 U.S.C.A. §2341 (1993).

30. *Cigarette Tax Evasion: A Second Look*, pp. 2 and 11.

31. *Ibid.*, p. 12.

32. Kenneth C. Crowe, II, "State Stockpiling Contraband Liquor," *Times Union* (Albany, N.Y.), December 9, 1993, pp. B-1 and B-11.

33. *Cigarette Tax Evasion: A Second Look*, p. 31.

34. Clyde H. Farnsworth, "Smuggled Smokes Make Life for Some in Canada a Bit Uneasy," *Times Union* (Albany, N.Y.), January 1, 1994, p. B-12.

35. *Ibid.*

36. Clyde H. Farnsworth, "Canada Cuts Cigarette Taxes to Fight Smuggling," *The New York Times*, February 9, 1994, p. A3.

37. Colin Nickerson, "Smuggling Surge Roils Canada," *The Boston Globe*, February 16, 1994, p. 14.

38. *Indian Trade and Intercourse Act of 1790*, 1 Stat. 135, and *Indian Trader Act of 1876*, 19 Stat. 200, 25 U.S.C.A. §261 (1983). See also Bureau of Indian Affairs Regulations, 25 CFR 140.1–.26 (1993).

39. *Moe v. Confederated Slaish and Kootenai Tribes of Flathead Reservations*, 425 U.S. 463 (1976).

40. *Washington v. Confederated Colville Tribes*, 447 U.S. 134 (1980).

41. *Milhelm Attea & Brothers, Incorporated v. Department of Taxation and Finance*, 164 App. Div.2d 300 (1990), and *Milhelm Attea & Brothers, Incorporated v. Department of Taxation and Finance*, 81 N.Y.2d 417 (1993).

42. *Department of Taxation and Finance v. Milhelm Attae & Brothers, Incorporated*, 114 S.Ct. 2028 (1994).

43. *Wilson Act of 1890*, 26 Stat. 313, 27 U.S.C.A. §121 (1994 Supp.).

44. *Webb–Kenyon Act of 1913*, 37 Stat. 699, 27 U.S.C.A. §122 (1994 Supp.).

45. *Bacchus Imported Limited v. Dias*, 468 U.S. 263 at 275–6 (1984).

46. *Summary of State Laws & Regulations Relating to Distilled Spirits* (Washington, D.C.: Distilled Spirits Council of the United States, Incorporated, 1993).

47. John H. Fenton, "Officials of Massachusetts and New Hampshire to Study Liquor Price War," *The New York Times*, December 14, 1969, p. 73.

48. "Roadblocks Used by State to Shut Off Tax-Free Liquor," *Knickerbocker News* (Albany, N.Y.), February 9, 1966, p. 6A.

49. Kenneth C. Crowe II, "Pair to Answer Liquor-Smuggling Charges Today," *Times Union* (Albany, N.Y.), June 9, 1994, p. B–7.

50. "Two States Clash on Liquor Sales," *The New York Times*, December 14, 1969, p. 73.

51. Homer Bigart, "Jersey Routs Pennsylvania Spies in Border War on Whiskey Prices," *The New York Times*, March 5, 1965, pp. 1 and 26.

52. Stacy MacTaggert, "The Neverending Whiskey Wars," *Governing*, October 1994, p. 32.

53. "The Eyes of Taxers," *Times Union* (Albany, N.Y.), December 26, 1976, p. B-1.

54. *Ibid.*, p. B–10.

55. *New York Laws of 1993*, Ch. 508, and *New York Tax Law*, §421 (McKinney 1995 Supp.).

56. Kenneth C. Crowe II, "State Stockpiling Contraband Liquor," *Times Union* (Albany, N.Y.), December 9, 1993, pp. B-1 and B-11.

57. "Court Holds States Free to Set Resource Taxes," *The New York Times*, July 3, 1981, p. B12, and William K. Stevens, "Taxes by Energy States Causing East–West Split," *The New York Times*, October 15, 1994, p. B12.

58. *Merrion v. Jicarilla Apache Tribe*, 455 U.S. 130 (1982).

59. Stevens, "Taxes by Energy States Causing East–West Split," p. B12.

60. *Hope Natural Gas Company v. Hall*, 274 U.S. 284 (1972); *Oliver Mining Company v. Lord*, 262 U.S. 172 (1923); and *Heisler v. Thomas Colliery Company*, 260 U.S. 245 (1922).

61. *Heisler v. Thomas Colliery Company*, 260 U.S. 245 at 259–60 (1922).

62. *Utah Power & Light Company v. Pfost*, 286 U.S. 165 (1932).

63. *Pike v. Bruce Church, Incorporated*, 397 U.S. 137 at 142 (1970).

64. *Complete Auto Transit Incorporated v. Brady*, 430 U.S. 274 at 281 (1977).

65. *Ibid.* at 279.

66. *Montana Code Annotated*, §15-35-103 (1981).

67. *Wyoming Statutes*, §39-6-303 (Westlaw 1995).

68. *Commonwealth Edison Company v. Montana*, 615 P.2d 847 (1980).

69. *Commonwealth Edison Company v. Montana*, 453 U.S. 609 (1981).

70. *Mineral Lands Leasing Act of 1920*, 41 Stat. 437, 30 U.S.C.A. §181 (1986), and *Federal Coal Leasing Amendments of 1975*, 90 Stat. 1089, 30 U.S.C.A. §181 (1986).

71. *Ibid.* at 621 n. 11 and 627 n. 17.

72. Stephen F. Williams, "Severance Taxes and Federalism: The Role of the Supreme Court in Preserving a National Common Market for Energy Supplies," *University of Colorado Law Review*, Winter 1982, pp. 293–4.

73. Walter Hellerstein, "Commerce Clause Restrains on State Taxation: Purposeful Economic Protectionism and Beyond," *Michigan Law Review*, February 1987, pp. 762–3.

74. *Maryland v. Louisiana*, 451 U.S. 725 at 756 (1981).

75. *Pullman's Palace Car Company v. Pennsylvania*, 141 U.S. 18 (1891).

76. *American Refrigerator Transit Company v. Hall*, 174 U.S. 70 (1899).

77. *Union Refrigerator Transit Company v. Kentucky*, 199 U.S. 194 (1905).

78. *New York ex. rel. New York Central & Harlem River Rail Road v. Miller*, 202 U.S. 584 (1906).

79. *Northwest Airlines, Incorporated v. Minnesota*, 322 U.S. 292 (1944).

80. *Ibid.* at 295.

81. *Central Greyhound Lines, Incorporated v. Mealey*, 334 U.S. 653 (1948).

82. *Ott v. Mississippi Valley Barge Line Company*, 336 U.S. 169 (1949).

83. *Braniff Airways, Incorporated v. Nebraska State Board*, 347 U.S. 590 (1954).

84. *Moorman Manufacturing Company v. Iowa*, 437 U.S. 267 (1978).

85. *WardAir Canada, Incorporated v. Florida*, 477 U.S. 1 (1986).

86. *Florida Statutes*, §212.08(4)(a)(2) (1985).

87. *WardAir Canada, Incorporated v. Florida*, 477 U.S. 1 (1986).

88. *American Trucking Associations v. Scheiner*, 483 U.S. 266 (1987).

89. *Ibid.* at 269.

90. *Ibid.* at 294–5.

91. *Ibid.* at 305.

92. *Goldberg v. Sweet*, 488 U.S. 252 (1989).

93. *Ibid.*

94. *Allied–Signal, Incorporated v. Director, Division of Taxation*, 112 S.Ct. 2251 (1992).

95. *Ibid.* at 2259.

96. *Oklahoma Tax Commission v. Jefferson Lines, Incorporated*, 115 S.Ct. 1331 (1995).

97. *Alcan Aluminum v. Franchise Tax Board of California*, 860 F.2d 688 (1988).

98. *Franchise Tax Board of California v. Alcan Aluminum*, 493 U.S. 331 (1990), and *Tax Injunction Act of 1937*, 50 Stat. 738, 28 U.S.C.A. §1341 (1993).

99. *Barclays Bank v. Franchise Tax Board of California*, 114 S.Ct. 2268 at 2283–4 (1994).

100. Dan Freedman, "High Court Upholds Global Tax Scheme," *Times Union* (Albany, N.Y.), June 21, 1994, p. C-8.

101. *California Revenue and Tax Code*, §§23601.5 and 23609 (1990 and 1991).

102. *Illinois Revised Statutes*, Ch. 120, par. 2-201(G) (1991); *Virginia Laws of 1990*, Ch. 709; and *Virginia Code Annotated*, §58.1-445.1 (1995 Supp.).

103. *Arizona Public Service Company v. Snead*, 441 U.S. 141 at 145 (1979).

104. *Tax Reform Act of 1976*, 90 Stat. 1914, 15 U.S.C.A. §391 (1994 Supp.).

105. *New York Laws of 1968*, Ch. 827, and *New York Tax Law*, §270c (McKinney 1967).

106. *Boston Stock Exchange v. State Tax Commission*, 429 U.S. 318 (1977).

107. *Ibid.* at 336–7.

108. *Westinghouse Electric Corporation v. Tully*, 466 U.S. 388 (1984).

109. *Armco Incorporated v. Hardesty*, 467 U.S. 638 at 642 (1984).

110. *Metropolitan Life Insurance Company v. Ward*, 470 U.S. 869 (1985).

111. *Tyler Pipe Industries v. Washington Department of Revenue*, 483 U.S. 232 at 243–4 (1987).

112. *Barringer v. Griffes*, 801 F.Supp. 1284 (1992).

113. *Williams v. Vermont*, 472 U.S. 14 (1985).

114. *Ibid.* at 28.

115. *Vermont Agency of Transportation, Department of Motor Vehicles*, Rule 86-28-E (July 5, 1985).

116. *Barringer v. Griffes*, 1 F.3d 1331 at 1338–9 (2nd Cir. 1993).

117. *Trinova Corporation v. Michigan Department of Treasury*, 111 S.Ct. 818 at 836 (1991).

10

Formal and Informal Interstate Cooperation

A federal system has several potential advantages and disadvantages.[1] One of the latter—lack of national uniformity in laws, court decisions, and administrative actions–is viewed by supporters of strong states as an advantage allowing each state to tailor policies to its unique conditions, experiment with new programs, and prevent undue concentration of political power in national government. Nevertheless, lack of uniform statutes creates problems for mobile individuals and for business firms operating on a multistate basis.

Chapter 4 explores the conflicts of laws between states, the Full Faith and Credit Provision of Article IV of the U.S. Constitution, constitutional authorization for Congress to prescribe the method by which statutes of each state "shall be proved and the effect thereof," and the role of the U.S. Supreme Court in adjudicating cases involving conflicts in state laws. A literal interpretation of the Full Faith and Credit Clause of Article IV would mandate that laws enacted by a state legislature conflicting with laws of other states be discarded by the state's courts in favor of statutes enacted by the legislatures of sister states in cases raising the issue of full faith and credit.

However, the U.S. Supreme Court in 1939 ruled that the Full Faith and Credit Clause could not be utilized to mandate a state to replace its statutes with the statutes of other states and added in a 1951 decision that the major purpose of the Full Faith and Credit Clause is to facilitate enforcement of judgments rendered in a sister state and not to give effect to the statutes enacted in other states.[2] In consequence, multistate business firms and individuals can be affected adversely by conflicts in the laws of the various states. As explained in Chapter 4, a person legally divorced in one state who remarries lawfully in a second state can be charged by the latter state with bigamy.

The disharmony in the statutes of the various states generally created few problems during the time period when state governments engaged in a very limited number of regulatory activities and provided few services, citizens seldom traveled out of state on a regular basis, and most business firms operated intrastate. The roles of governments changed significantly as population, urbanization, and industrialization increased concomitant with the development of modern means of transportation and communications facilitating citizen mobility and interstate commerce.

The U.S. Supreme Court contributed to the lack of uniformity in state insurance statutes by opining in 1868 that insurance was not commerce, and hence its regulation fell within the domain of the states.[3] The court reversed this decision in 1944. However, Congress in turn overruled this decision by enacting the McCarran–Ferguson Act in 1945 which delegates the power to regulate the insurance industry to the states, thereby allowing state legislatures to enact nonuniform statutes including ones that discriminate against insurance companies chartered by sister states.[4] This discrimination and conflicting provisions in state insurance statutes have generated strong pressures for congressional preemption of state regulation of the insurance industry.[5] Similarly, nonuniform state product liability statutes have pitted manufacturers and others against the trial lawyers relative to the bills in Congress which would preempt state product liability laws.

States have sought to promote greater uniformity in policies and programs by entering into interstate compacts and administrative agreements, and enacting uniform laws. Not all compacts (*i*) are designed to achieve national uniformity, (*ii*) are open to membership to all states, or (*iii*) have been enacted into law by each state legislature. Chapter 3 examines the use of various types of interstate compacts to achieve policy uniformity and other goals, including reciprocity, on a national or regional basis. As noted in Chapter 3, the process of negotiating the typical compact is a long and tedious one which is not always successful. Even if the negotiators reach an agreement on a compact, their state legislatures may reject the proposed compact.

States also cooperate on a formal and informal basis to solve regional and national problems. Such cooperation typically is promoted by regional and national associations of state officials. Uniform state laws enacted by many state legislatures on a given subject are the product of each legislature enacting a bill identical to a statute enacted by another state legislature which proved to be effective in achieving its goals. Staffs of state legislatures, when drafting important bills, typically examine the statutes of other states and bills introduced in the legislatures of sister states.

This chapter examines the role of the National Conference of Commissioners on Uniform State Laws, model state laws drafted by other national associations, *ad hoc* and informal interstate administrative agreements, and the role of Congress in promoting enactment of uniform state laws.

UNIFORM STATE LAWS

The movement for the enactment of uniform statutes by state legislatures after the Civil War was stimulated by the growth of interstate commerce and travel, fear that Congress would exercise its powers of preemption to nullify many concurrent powers of the states, and the inability of the states and the inability of courts to adapt the English common law in each state except Louisiana, which relies upon the Napoleonic Code, to the resolution of problems faced by multistate business firms.[6]

Although Congress had enacted only a handful of total preemption statutes by the end of the Civil War, pressures for congressional action were building and resulted in the enactment of the Interstate Commerce Act in 1887 and the Sherman Anti-Trust Act in 1890.[7] States placed heavy reliance upon the English common law to govern private transactions, but the common law had been amended in part in a nonuniform manner by each state legislature, and the courts in the various states were not consistent in their interpretation of the unamended common law. In response to those problems, various organizations promote enactment of uniform statutes by state legislatures which promise to facilitate the growth of interstate commerce and travel by removal of legal impediments, obviate the need for congressional preemption of certain state-reserved powers, and ensure common judicial interpretation of the common law as amended by uniform state statutes.

Commissioners on Uniform State Laws

The origin of the National Conference of Commissioners on Uniform State Laws is traceable to the encouragement given by the Alabama Bar Association to the enactment of uniform state laws. In 1889, the American Bar Association approved a formal resolution committing the association to work for uniform state laws.[8] The following year, the New York State Legislature enacted a statute authorizing the governor to appoint three commissioners to study laws pertaining to marriage and divorce, notarial certificates, insolvency, and other problems and to determine the best means to ensure the enactment of uniform laws by all state legislatures.[9] The New York statute was endorsed by the American Bar Association.

Seven states sent representatives to the first meeting of the conference held in Saratoga Springs, New York, on August 24, 1892. The commissioners drafted and urged state and territorial legislatures to enact uniform laws relating to acknowl-edgments on written instruments, validating wills lawfully executed without the state, and recognizing as valid wills probated in a sister state. The commissioners also approved a table of weights and measures and noted "it will probably be a sur-prise to most people to learn that legal weights of a bushel ... with the exception of wheat alone, vary in all the states."[10]

The initial proposals were not followed by another proposal until 1896 when the Negotiable Instruments Law was drafted. It was the first uniform law to be enacted by every state and the District of Columbia, and subsequently became the core of Article 3 of the Universal Commercial Code.

Thirty-one states and two territories appointed commissioners by 1900, and by 1910 only Nevada and the Territory of Alaska had failed to appoint commissioners; they appointed commissioners in 1912. There are also Canadian Commissioners on Uniform Provincial Laws. In addition, the Hague Conference (1893) and the Rome Institute (1926) seek to promote uniformity of law among nation states.[11]

Commissioners are appointed by the fifty states, District of Columbia, Puerto Rico, and the U.S. Virgin Islands. The number of commissioners from a state varies, but most states appoint at least three. The governor typically is responsible for appointing the commissioners. The governor of New York, for example, appoints three commissioners who serve at his pleasure.[12] The conference is composed of approximately 300 nonpartisan judges, attorneys, and law professors who serve without compensation. Their roles are two-fold—draft uniform laws and persuade their respective state legislature to enact them. The latter role is a most crucial one and often is time-consuming. Fourteen years, for example, were required to persuade forty-nine states to enact the Uniform Commercial Code which was drafted in 1951, and it was not until 1991 that the final state—Louisiana—enacted most of the code's provisions. The expenses of the conference are financed by the states with the assessment determined by the population of each state.

Most proposed uniform laws are private laws, based upon the common law, governing legal relationships among private individuals. No state department or agency is involved in administering a uniform law. Courts, however, provide remedies, such as injunctive relief and money damages, if there is a breach of a legally enforceable private obligation established by a uniform statute. The contractual relationship between a landlord and a tenant, for example, is governed by the Uniform Residential Landlord and Tenant Act without intervention by a state administrative agency. This private law contrasts with public law whereby the state legislature assigns duties—promulgation and enforcement of rules and regulations—to a state instrumentality.

Draftsmanship. The conference endorsed uniform laws drafted by other organizations until 1914 when it discontinued the practice. Subsequently, the conferences' Scope and Program Committee examines each proposed uniform law and makes a recommendation to the Executive Committee as to whether it would be desirable and feasible to draft such a law. If the Scope and Program Committee's proposal is approved by the Executive Committee, an expert Drafting Committee, composed of commissioners, is appointed. For example, experts on real estate law were appointed to the Drafting Committee for the Uniform Simplification of Land Transfer Act. Other experts were invited to provide guidance to the committee. Those lawyer and nonlawyer experts represented associations of builders, consumers, and other interested organizations.

Each Drafting Committee meets on a regular basis during a given year and does not submit a draft of a uniform act until it has been subjected to extensive review. As preliminary drafts are prepared, they are distributed to the commissioners, advisers, and interested parties for criticisms and suggestions. Subsequently, comments and suggestions received are reviewed, and the final draft uniform law is prepared. Preliminary drafts of uniform state laws have been enacted into law by a number of state legislatures as illustrated by the Florida, Illinois, New York, and Virginia state legislatures enacting into law prudent investor statutes based on drafts of the uniform state law. To be approved, a draft law must be examined section by section by all commissioners, functioning as a committee of the whole, at two annual meetings. On the motion for final approval of a draft uniform law, each state has one vote. The draft cannot be approved as a uniform law unless it receives the votes of a majority of states, provided there is a quorum of twenty states present. Commissioners spend much of their one-week annual meeting considering the draft laws, and "it is a rare draft that leaves an annual meeting in the same form it comes in."[13]

Subsequent to the annual meeting, committees revise uncompleted drafts based upon criticisms and suggestions made by conferees. Because of the great importance of the Uniform Commercial Code, a permanent editorial board continuously reviews the code and develops recommended amendments.[14] Revisions of the Model Administrative Procedure Act required the appointment of a new committee because the act was drafted before the explosion in state rules and regulations in the 1960s and 1970s.

Uniform laws have been drafted on a wide variety of topics, including Fiduciaries (1922), Common Trust Fund (1952), Alcoholism and Intoxication Treatment (1971), Parentage (1973), Rules of Criminal Procedure (1987), Securities (1988), Interstate Family Support (1992), and Victims of Crimes (1992).

The conference drafts model acts, in addition to uniform laws, to provide guidance to state legislatures on subjects where uniformity is desirable but is not essential. The Model Administrative Procedure Act, for example, has been modified and enacted into law by most state legislatures. Twenty-five model acts have been drafted, and they deal with audio–visual deposition, eminent domain, land sales practices, post-mortem examinations, sentencing and corrections, and water use, among other topics.

An Assessment.   The conference's record has been a mixed one in terms of persuading state legislatures to enact its uniform laws. Rodney L. Mott reported in 1940 that only one uniform law—Uniform Negotiable Instrument Act—had been adopted by all states and territories, and one-half of the state and territorial legislatures had enacted only eight other uniform laws.[15] As mentioned, although forty-nine states by 1967 had enacted the Uniform Commercial Code drafted in 1951, Louisiana did not adopt most of its provisions until 1991.

Mott identified legal and political obstacles to the enactment of uniform laws by state legislatures. He noted that "very often the terms used must be changed to conform to the legal phraseology in other statutes of the particular state. Thus, the term 'felony' has a wide variety of meanings in American criminal law, and civil and criminal procedures vary from state to state."[16]

Mott highlighted as political obstacles the facts that most state legislatures meet biennially, often for a short session, and the majority of state legislators serve a single two-year term. The lack of continuity in membership in a state legislature and policies made the enactment of uniform statutes a difficult task. He also found that state legislatures in enacting uniform laws frequently amended them and "that the acts which have been adopted quickly by a large number of states have suffered less mutilation than those which have raised controversial issues."[17]

Enactment of a uniform state law, as Mott discovered, is not a guarantee that there will be a change in state policy since "the doctrine of *stare decisis* is so strongly entrenched in American legal thinking that it is sometimes difficult for the courts to realize that the legislature, in enacting a uniform act, really intended to change the ancient rules which had been enforced in that state. . . ."[18] The different judicial interpretations of a uniform act create implementation problems, and there is no single court that can review the interpretations of an act by the courts of the fifty states and issue an interpretation binding upon the various state courts.

Kim Q. Hill and Patricia A. Hurley in the mid-1980s conducted a study of the enactment of uniform state laws to determine the factors that explain their enactment. They discovered that ten uniform state laws had not been adopted by any state by 1985, and only four such laws—anatomical gift, attendance of out-of-state witnesses, reciprocal enforcement of support, and child custody jurisdiction—had been enacted by all states.[19] Forty-nine state legislatures had enacted the Uniform Commercial Code and forty-eight state legislatures had enacted the Uniform Partnership Law. They also reported that "almost 70 percent have fewer than twenty adoptions, and only 15 percent could be called widely adopted."[20]

Hill and Hurley, not surprisingly, found that the enactment rate of uniform state laws varied greatly, with the Minnesota adoption rate constituting more than three times the Mississippi and Louisiana adoption rate. Although Hill and Hurley do not offer an explanation for the low enactment rate in Louisiana, it is apparent that Louisiana's use of the Napoleonic Code, rather than the English common law, no doubt makes the enactment of a uniform state law more difficult.

In general, midwestern and northwestern states have the highest propensity to adopt uniform state laws, and southern states, reflecting their states' rights position, have the lowest propensity to adopt such laws. Hill and Hurley used four independent variables—industrialization, wealth, professional legislature, and political culture—in their study to explain the adoption rate of uniform state laws by various states. They found that industrialization is correlated negatively with enactment of such laws, wealth has a modest positive correlation, a professional legislature has no correlation, and political culture has the highest correlation.[21] Multiple regression analysis produced the same findings as the bivariate analysis.[22]

Hill and Hurley utilized Daniel J. Elazar's conception of political culture as an independent variable in their analysis. Elazar identified three political cultures— individualistic, moralistic, and traditionalistic. The individualistic culture elevates private concerns and "places a premium on limiting community intervention— whether governmental or nongovernmental—into private activities to the minimum necessary to keep the marketplace in proper working order."[23]

The moralistic political culture seeks to improve society by regulating private interests to promote the greater good for all and is based on the belief that all citizens should participate in the governance process.[24] According to Elazar, the traditionalistic political culture seeks the continuance of the existing governmental and social order, and "political leaders play conservative and custodial rather than initiatory roles unless pressed strongly from the outside."[25]

The only independent variable in Hill and Hurley's study associated positively with the enactment by state legislatures of uniform state laws is the moralistic political culture. They concluded that such a culture is receptive to such laws because it eliminates "impediments of law ... to the exercise of private associations across state lines," and many state laws have a "good government character."[26]

Other Model Acts

Various associations of state and local government officials, interest groups, citizen groups, and the U.S. Advisory Commission on Intergovernmental Relations prepare model state acts to guide state legislatures in enacting or revising statutes. The Council of State Governments has been a major promoter of uniform and model state statutes and in 1995 published the 54th Edition of its *Suggested State Legislation*. The council is composed of twelve affiliated organizations (ranging from the conference of Chief Justices to the National Conference of State Legislatures), thirty-six cooperating organizations (ranging from the Association of State and Interstate Water Pollution Control Administrators to the Parole and Probation Compact Administrators' Associations), and six adjunct organizations (ranging from the Association of Paroling Authorities International to the National Association of State Emergency Medical Services Training Coordinators).[27]

The council publishes annually "Suggested State Legislation" prepared by the Committee on Suggested State Legislation which originated in 1940 when a number of state and federal officials held a meeting to examine state laws on the subject of internal security.[28] This meeting resulted in a publication entitled "A Legislative Program for Defense." Following the entrance of the United States into World War II, the committee met and developed "Suggested State War Legislation." In 1946, the publication was retitled "Suggested State Legislation."

The volume includes model acts suggested by state officials which are reviewed by the subcommittee on scope and agenda and approved by the Committee on Suggested State Legislation at its annual meeting.

The Council of State Governments does not advocate enactment of the suggested acts, but offers them as guides to be employed by state legislatures in drafting new statutes or amendments to statutes. The following criteria are employed to determine the acts to be included in Suggested State Legislation.

- Is the issue a significant one currently facing state governments?
- Does the issue have national or regional significance?
- Are fresh and innovative approaches available to address the issue?
- Is the issue of sufficient complexity that a bill drafter would benefit from having a comprehensive draft available?
- Does the bill represent a practical approach to the problem?
- Does the bill represent a comprehensive approach to the problem, or is it tied to a narrow approach that may have limited relevance for many states?

- Is the structure of the bill logically consistent?
- Does the bill represent a practical approach to the problem?

The National Association of Insurance Commissioners (NAIC) originated as the National Convention of Insurance Commissioners when the New York superintendent of insurance invited his counterparts in thirty-six states to seek the enactment of a uniform insurance law.[29] In 1935, the name of the organization was changed to the National Association of Insurance Commissioners. Ross E. Cheit reported that more than 150 model acts have been drafted by the association as of 1993.[30] Recognizing that conditions vary between states, many model acts are not designed to produce uniform state laws throughout the nation.

The earlier acts focus on financial regulation and preventing the insolvency of insurance companies, whereas many of the more recent acts focus on protection of consumers. The earlier model acts received a better reception in state legislatures than the consumer protection model acts. Cheit found that states with a traditionalist political culture have the greatest tendency to enact the model acts in contrast to Hill and Hurley's finding that states with a moralistic culture have the greatest propensity to enact uniform state laws.[31] He also found that state insurance departments in their rules and regulations are more apt to adopt the model acts than the state legislatures.[32]

The Multistate Tax Commission, formed by an interstate compact, was a direct response to the recommendations of the Willis Committee in 1965 that Congress impose tax jurisdiction standards, apportionment rules, and tax base definitions on the states.[33] Eight states entered into the compact on August 4, 1967, and its current membership is nineteen states and the District of Columbia. Fourteen additional states are associate members of the compact, and five other states participate in various commission projects. Incorporated in the compact is the Uniform Division of Income for Tax Purposes Act. The prime purposes of the compact are the elimination of duplicative taxation by states and facilitation of taxpayer convenience and compliance.

The commission has drafted the Uniform Protest Statute and Uniform Principles Governing State Transactional Taxation of Telecommunications, and a Recommended Formula for the Apportionment and Allocation of Net Income of Financial Institutions.[34] In addition, the commission has drafted model regulations for corporate income tax allocation and apportionment regulations; special industry rules for construction contractors, railroads, airlines, trucking companies, television and radio broadcasting, and publishing; and recordkeeping regulation for sales and use tax purposes.[35]

Model acts also are developed by regional associations. The Coalition of Northeastern State Governors, for example, drafted in 1989 the Model Toxics in Packaging Act which seeks to reduce the amount of heavy metals in packaging and packaging components distributed in the United States.[36] Sixteen states enacted the model act into law by 1994, including nine states which are not members of the coalition.

FORMAL ADMINISTRATIVE AGREEMENTS

States have entered into formal agreements with sister states relative to most functions. These agreements can involve subjects ranging from driver license reciprocity to gun control to the "Powerball Lottery" formed by six states and the District of Columbia. As noted in Chapter 3, many state legislatures have enacted into law mutual aid interstate compacts. Heads of certain departments— particularly state police, fire marshall, and civil defense—also have signed similar interstate administrative agreements with their counterparts in other states providing for mutual assistance in emergencies.

A number of statutes in each state authorize the heads of departments and agencies to enter into cooperative administrative agreements with officials in sister states. Table 10.1 contains details on driver license reciprocity. The New York Vehicle & Traffic Law, for example, stipulates "the Governor or Commissioner of Motor Vehicles may enter into a written agreement or compact with any state authorized to be a party to such compact or affected by such reciprocal provisions...."[37] The law also authorizes the commissioner to execute a reciprocal agreement with the Motor Vehicle Commissioner of another state relative to the appearance of a person licensed in one state to answer a summons or an appearance ticket for a moving traffic violation issued by an officer in the other state.[38] The commissioner is specifically empowered to become a member of the International Registration Plan described in Chapter 7.[39]

Similarly, the New York Highway Law authorizes the commissioner of Transportation to enter into cooperative contracts with an adjoining state for the construction, maintenance, and reconstruction of state highway connections with the adjoining state.[40] The New York commissioner of Agriculture and Markets is empowered by statute to enter into uniform milk control agreements, including sanitary requirements, with other states and the federal government.[41] The New York commissioner of Social Services is delegated authority by statute to enter into reciprocal agreements with counterpart commissioners in other states relative to the interstate transportation of dependent and indigent persons and to arrange for the acceptance, transfer, and support of persons receiving public assistance in other states.[42] Finally, the commissioner of Public Health is authorized by New York law to enter into reciprocity agreements with other states relative to the interstate transportation of persons with tuberculosis, and for their hospital care and treatment.[43]

In addition to administrative reciprocity agreements involving all sister states, individual states also enter into administrative agreements with a small number of states for special purposes. Maryland, West Virginia, and the Interstate Commission on the Potomac River Basin in 1993 signed an agreement establishing a cooperative program to improve water quality and restore biological life to a section of the North Branch Potomac River.[44] In 1994, Governor Mario M. Cuomo of New York and Governor Pedro Sossello of Puerto Rico signed a cooperation agreement to share education, health, law enforcement, and social services resources.[45] More than one million Puerto Ricans reside in New York state.

Table 10.1
Driver License Reciprocity

State	Time Limit to obtain License after Establishing Residence	License from former State		Examination required for persons possessing Current License from former State			
		Surrendered to New State	Must be Returned to State of Issuance	Knowledge	Signs and Signals	Vision	Vehicle Operation
Alabama	30 Days	Yes	4/Yes	x	x	x	–
Alaska	90 Days	Yes	Yes	x	x	x	–
Arizona	Immediately	Yes	Yes	x	x	x	Discretion of examiner
Arkansas	30 Days	Yes	4/No	x	x	x	–
California	10 Days	Yes	4/No	x	x	x	–
Colorado	30 Days	Yes	Yes	x	x	x	May be waived
Connecticut	60 Days	Yes	Yes	May be waived	May be waived	x	May be waived
Delaware	60 Days	Yes	Yes	–	x	x	May be waived
Dist. of Col.	30 Days	Yes	Yes	x	–	x	May be waived
Florida	30 Days	Yes	4/No	May be waived	May be waived	x	May be waived
Georgia	30 Days	Yes	Yes	x	x	x	Waived
Hawaii	(5/)	Yes	Yes	x	x	x	May be waived
Idaho	90 Days	Yes	4/No	x	x	x	7/Waived
Illinois	90 Days	Yes	Yes	x	x	x	Waived
Indiana	60 Days	Yes	Yes	x	x	x	Waived
Iowa	Immediately	Yes	4/Yes	x	x	x	Waived
Kansas	90 Days	Yes	Yes	x	x	x	Waived
Kentucky	Immediately	Yes	4/No	8/x	8/x	8/x	Waived
Louisiana	90 Days	Yes	Yes	–	–	x	May be waived
Maine	30 Days	Yes	Yes	x	If illiterate	x	May be waived
Maryland	30 Days	Yes	4/Yes	May be waived	May be waived	x	May be waived
Massachussetts	Immediately	Yes	Yes	x	–	x	–
Michigan	Immediately	Yes	Yes	x	x	x	Waived
Minnesota	60 Days	Yes	Yes	x	x	x	May be waived
Mississippi	60 Days	Yes	Yes	x	x	x	May be waived
Missouri	Immediately	Yes	Yes	x	x	x	May be waived
Montana	90 Days	Yes	Yes	May be waived	May be waived	x	May be waived
Nebraska	30 Days	Yes	4/No	x	x	x	May be waived
Nevada	45 Days	Yes	Yes	x	x	x	May be waived
New Hampshire	60 Days	Yes	Yes	May be waived			
New Jersey	60 Days	Yes	Yes	x	–	x	Discretionary
New Mexico	30 Days	Yes	Yes	x	–	x	–
New York	30 Days	Yes	Yes	10/x	10/x	10/x	10/Waived
North Carolina	30 Days	Yes	4/No	x	x	x	Discretionary
North Dakota	60 Days	Yes	4/No	x	x	x	May be waived
Ohio	30 Days	Yes	Yes	x	x	x	Discretion of examiner
Oklahoma	Immediately	Yes	Yes	x	x	x	May be waived
Oregon	Immediately	Yes	Yes	x	x	x	May be waived
Pennsylvania	60 Days	Yes	Yes	x	x	x	May be waived
Rhode Island	30 Days	Yes	Yes	x	x	x	–
South Carolina	90 Days	Yes	Yes	–	–	x	May be waived
South Dakota	90 Days	Yes	4/No	x	x	x	May be waived
Tennessee	30 Days	Yes	4/Yes	May be waived	May be waived	x	May be waived
Texas	30 Days	Yes	Yes	x	x	x	May be waived
Utah	60 Days	Yes	Yes	x	x	x	Waived
Vermont	6 months or reciprocal agreement	Yes	Yes	x	x	x	Discretion of examiner
Virginia	30 Days	Yes, if compact State	4/No	May be waived	May be waived	x	Waived
Washington	30 Days	5/yes	4/No	x	x	x	x
West Virginia	Immediately	Yes	Yes	x	x	x	–
Wisconsin	Immediately	Yes	Yes	x	x	x	Discretion of examiner
Wyoming	120 Days/ 30 Days CDL	Yes	4/No	x	x	x	Discretion of examiner
Puerto Rico	120 Days	No	No	x	x	x	May be waived if reciprocal agreement

(Continues)

194

Table 10.1 (*continued*)

Participation in the National Driver register program					Member of		
Driver License Applications checked		*With Drawals Reported for any Reason*		**Signatory to Driver License Services Agreement** *1/*	*National driver License Compact* *2/*	*Nonresident Violator Compact* *3/*	*Other Local Compact*
Original Only	*Original and Renewal*		**Nonresidents may Obtain License**				
–	x	x	No,	No, but State provides service	Yes	Yes	No
x	–	x	Yes	No	Yes	No	No
–	x	x	Yes	No	Yes	No	No
–	x	x	No	No	Yes	Yes	No
x	–	x	Yes 11/	No	Yes	No	No
–	x	x	Yes, visitor, student, military	No	2/Yes	Yes	No
x	–	x	No	Yes	No	Yes	No
–	x	x	No	Yes	Yes	Yes	No
–	x	x	No	No	Yes	Yes	No
	x	x	Yes, noncommercial only	Yes	Yes	Yes	Yes
–	x	x	Yes, to servicemen and students	Yes	No	Yes	No
–	x	x	Yes	No	Yes	Yes	No
–	x	x	No	No	Yes	Yes	No
x	–	x	No	No, but State provides service	Yes	Yes	No
–	x	x	No	Yes	Yes	Yes	No
x	–	x	No	Yes	Yes	Yes	No
x	–	x	No	Yes	Yes	Yes	No
–	x	x	No	No, but State provides service 1/	No	Yes	No
x	–	x	No,10-day temporary licence only	No, but State provides service	Yes	Yes	No
–	x	x	Yes, and surrender foreign license	No, but State provides service	Yes	Yes	Yes
–	x	x	No	Yes	Yes	Yes	No
–	x	x	Yes	No, but State provides services	No	Yes	No
–	x	x	No	Yes	No	No	No
–	x	x	Yes, with Minnesota address	Yes	Yes	Yes	No
x	–	x	No	Yes	Yes	Yes	No
x	–	x	No	Yes	Yes	Yes	No
–	x	x	Yes, surrender all other licenses	Yes	Yes	No	No
x	–	x	No	No	Yes	Yes	No
–	x	x	No	Yes	Yes	Yes	No
–	x	x	No	Yes	Yes	Yes	Yes
x	–	x	No	Yes 9/	Yes	Yes	No
x	–	x	No	No, but State provides service	Yes	Yes	No
x	–	x	No	No	Yes	Yes	Yes
–	x	x	Yes, military	Yes	No	Yes	No
–	x	x	No	No, but State provides service	Yes	Yes	No
–	x	x	No	Yes	Yes	Yes	No
–	x	–	No, but State provides service	No	Yes	Yes	No
–	x	x	Yes 11/	No, but State provides service	Yes	3/No	Yes
x	CDL only	x	Yes, surrender all other licenses	No	No	Yes	No
x	–	x	No	Yes	Yes	Yes	No
–	x	x	No	Yes	Yes	Yes	No
–	x	x	No	Yes	Yes	Yes	No
x	–	x	No	No	Yes	Yes	No
x	–	x	Yes	Yes	No	Yes	No
x	–	x	Yes	Yes	Yes	Yes	No
x	–	x	Yes	No	Yes	Yes	No
–	x	x	Yes	Yes	Yes	Yes	No
–	x	x	No 5/	No, but State provides service	Yes	No	No
x	–	x	Yes,military	Yes	Yes	Yes	No
–	x	x	No	Yes	No	No	Local
–	x	x	No	No	Yes	Yes	No
–	–	–	Yes	No	No	No	No

(*Continues*)

Table 10.1 (*continued*)

1. The agreement for driver license services permits a State licensing agency to conduct tests for nonresidents whose home-State license expires and cannot be renewed without personal appearance and reexamination. KENTUCKY — Can administer test, but does not issue temporary licenses.
2. The National Driver License Compact is an agreement among the States to control problem drivers. It provides for exchange of information to keep unsafe drivers from accumulating violations in many States and escaping control action: It implements the "one license" concept. In COLORADO,there is a law but it is not implemented.
3. The nonresident violator compact allows a driver – violator in a foreign State to proceed to his home State without long delays and posting of bond, his case to be settled without his appearance in court at a later date. OREGON — Legislation passed to become member; scheduled for mid – 1995.
4. The State of issuance is notified that the license was surrendered. IDAHO, MARYLAND — State of issuance notified and NEBRASKA — A list is prepared for distribution to all showing surrender of license from out of State and notification that those drivers are now licensed in Nebraska. TENNESSEE —State license notified monthly of the change and document destroyed. WYOMING — License is invalidated and returned to licensee a surrendered list is of prepared and sent to other States every 2 weeks.
5. OREGON — Appear in person and surrender all other licenses. CALIFORNIA, WASHINGTON — License invalidated and returned to applicant. Residents only may obtain license: non-residents may obtain ID card only.
6. HAWAII — A valid driver license. Class 1, 2, or 3 from any State. U.S. Territory or Possession, or Canadian Province is valid in Hawaii until the expiration date shown on the license if the driver is 18 years or over.
7. IDAHO — Skills test at examiner's discretion: usually waived.
8. KENTUCKY — NO tests required if new resident surrenders an ARKANSAS license that has expired less than 30 days, a CONNECTICUT license expired less than 60 days,or a TENNESSEE license that has not expired. (TENNESSEE applicants are exempt from the written test only; vision test still required.)
9. NEW JERSEY — Reports license withdrawals for all major traffic offenses including DUI, reckless driving, failure to perform duties of a driver involved in an accident, criminal driving while suspended or evoked, fleeing or attempting to elude a police officer and driving after being declared a habitual offender.
10. NEW YORK — Reciprocity is granted for any State, the District of Columbia, any U.S. territory or possession, or any Canadian Province. Reciprocity is not granted for driver licensee of foreign cuntries and all examinations (knowledge, vehicle operation, vision) are required and the application is trated as an "original" request.

Governor Robert P. Casey of Pennsylvania and Governor William D. Schaefer of Maryland in 1993 signed an administrative agreement to build fish ladders at three hydroelectric dams in order to restore migratory fish to the Susquehanna River.[46] In the same year, the governors of Maryland and Virginia and the mayor of the District of Columbia signed an agreement granting the Metropolitan Washington Air Quality Committee authority to develop recommendation for a regional ozone control strategy for the area.[47]

In 1993, New York state officials, frustrated with what they labeled ineffective federal gun control efforts and laws, commenced working with Florida, Georgia, Ohio, Texas, and Virginia—the principal sources of unlicensed guns in New York—to identify and prosecute traffickers in firearms. In addition, New York established a three-member gun-tracing unit to work with police in sister states and federal officials in conducting joint investigations of illegal traffic in firearms.[48]

The states of Connecticut and New York joined with the U.S. Environmental Protection Agency in an agreement in 1994 to protect the ecosystem of the Long Island Sound by renovating sewage-treatment plants, limiting sewage and industrial discharges into the Sound, and reducing nonpoint sources of pollution.[49]

The New York State Department of Agriculture and Markets has a continuing cooperative agreement with Florida, Maine, New Hampshire, and Pennsylvania relative to standardized requirements for interstate movement of bees necessary for crop pollination and also conducts virus testing of twenty-five varieties of strawberries for the Commonwealth of Massachusetts, thereby allowing the foreign shipment of strawberry plants grown in the Commonwealth.[50]

Keon S. Chi of the Council of State Governments reported that thirteen states participate in the Southern Regional Growth Policies Board, ten southern states have established an interstate computerized information system for tracking parents who fail to provide child support, the Northeast Recycling Council promotes recycling to reduce the quantity of solid wastes in need of disposal, the DELMARVA Cooperative purchases products—including motor vehicles and insecticides—for

Delaware, Maryland, and Virginia, and the Treasurers of Arkansas, Louisiana, Mississippi, and Tennessee cooperate with each other to improve financial practices.[51]

AD HOC COOPERATION

Necessity forces administrative cooperation on an *ad hoc* basis. Police in hot pursuit of a fugitive from justice near the state border line radio their counterparts in the neighboring state to apprehend the fugitive. Chapter 9 described the cooperation of Maryland and Pennsylvania police with New York State Police in tracking a vehicle, which was smuggling alcoholic beverages from Maryland to New York. A natural disaster, in the absence of a formal interstate compact or administrative agreement, produces immediate interstate cooperation as illustrated by the response of states to the bombing of the federal office building in Oklahoma City in 1995.

Attorneys general commonly work together on a regional or national basis to combat consumer fraud. In 1993, Keds agreed to a $7.2 million voluntary settlement of lawsuits brought against the firm by the attorneys general of each of the fifty states alleging that consumers were overcharged for certain shoes in retail stores between May 1, 1992, and April 30, 1993.[52]

In the same year, the attorneys general of twenty-three states organized a task force to investigate the marketing practices of large cable television firms, including "negative option" marketing which involves a firm charging a subscriber for a service which has not been requested, and wire insurance.[53] In 1994, Publishers Clearing House agreed to change its methods of promoting its sweepstakes and pay $490,000 in costs to settle a lawsuit brought by the attorneys general of fourteen states alleging the promotions were misleading in that all recipients of the firm's mass mailings were informed they were "tied" as "finalists" in the contests.[54]

Attorneys general, however, were frustrated in their attempts to enforce state deceptive practices statutes relative to airlines' advertising when Justice Antonin Scalia, writing for the majority of the U.S. Supreme Court, held that such statutes were preempted by the Airline Deregulation Act of 1978.[55] Justice John Paul Stevens dissented and wrote "the presumption against preemption of traditional state regulation counsels that we do not interpret Section 105(a) to preempt every traditional state regulation that might have some indirect connection or relationship to airline rates, routes, or services unless there is some indication that Congress intended that result."[56]

The insurance commissioners of forty-nine states in 1994 endorsed a report by Florida's insurance commissioner which maintains the Metropolitan Life Insurance Company failed to take corrective actions based on its internal reports of improper sales practices which violated the statutes of most states.[57] Life insurance policies were sold to individuals who were informed by salesmen that the policies were a retirement or savings plan. The report calls upon the company to pay a $20 million fine with $12.5 million paid to states.

States, cities, and representatives of citizen groups filed a suit against the decision of the secretary of commerce in 1992 not to adjust statistically the results of the 1990 census of population for differential undercounting. The U.S. District Court in 1993 held the secretary's decision was final and was not arbitrary or capricious.[58]

States of necessity negotiate *ad hoc* agreements relative to the location of new trunk highways which cross state boundary lines, and the negotiations may be difficult if one state proposes a location or a relocation of a highway which causes strong citizen opposition in the other state. New Hampshire and Vermont conducted protracted negotiations relative to the location of a new bridge over the Connecticut River near Brattleboro, Vermont. The state boundary is on the western shore of the River and hence New Hampshire is responsible for constructing and maintaining the bridge. Vermont, however, can determine the location of one of its highways that connects with the bridge. In 1993, the Connecticut River Bridges Advisory Commission—composed of state transportation officials, legislators, and residents—reached an agreement to construct the new bridge next to the old bridge.[59]

As noted in Chapter 9, residents of a state may register their motor vehicles in another state which has a lower sales tax, excise tax, and insurance premiums. A significant number of Massachusetts and Maine residents, for example, register their motor vehicles in New Hampshire, which in 1995 agreed to cooperate with its two sister states in solving this problem by revoking vehicle registrations.[60]

The threat that the Portsmouth Naval Shipyard, located between New Hampshire and Maine, will be closed led to the congressional delegations of the two states meeting with Secretary of the Navy John Dalton to convince him that the Shipyard was essential to national security and should not be closed.[61] Three New England states—Maine, New Hampshire, and Vermont—in 1993 reached an agreement to study jointly high technology communications among doctors and between patients and doctors, staffing requirements for hospitals, and health education programs for professionals and citizens.[62]

INTERGOVERNMENTAL RELATIONS COMMISSION

Hubert R. Gallagher reported that the first commission on interstate cooperation was established in 1935 and that by 1940 forty-one states had established commissions based upon the model bill drafted by the Council of State Governments.[63] With a few exceptions, each commission was composed of ten legislators and five administrators. Kansas and Kentucky each designated the Legislative Council to serve as the commission, and New York established a joint legislative committee on interstate cooperation. These commissions convened national and regional conferences to address major problems as illustrated by the National Conference on Interstate Trade Barriers which met in Chicago in 1939.

The federal government played a limited role relative to state and local governments at the time of the formation of the original commissions. By the 1960s, Congress was playing a major role in domestic affairs by making numerous grants-in-aid to state and local governments and by preempting totally or partially the regulatory authority of these governments. Concern with the growing involvement of the national government in traditional areas of state and local government responsibility induced Congress in 1953 to establish the Commission on Intergovernmental Relations, a bipartisan body of twenty-five members, which issued a report in 1955. One of the commission's recommendations was the establishment of a permanent Advisory Commission on Intergovernmental Relations, a recommendation enacted into law by Congress in 1959.[64]

Establishment of the U.S. Advisory Commission on Intergovernmental Relations (ACIR) served as a model for the reorganization of commissions on interstate cooperation in eighteen states which established state ACIRs to study and make recommendations relative to state–local relations. Table 10.2 lists twenty-four active state intergovernmental relations bodies, the basis for each body, approximate budget, number of members, and composition of the governing body. The eighteen state ACIRs follow the model of the U.S. ACIR with a few minor variations. Three legislative committees are composed only of legislators, but the fourth committee has four local government officials and two private citizens who serve as members.

Functions of state intergovernmental relations bodies include conducting research, sponsoring conferences and seminars, providing technical assistance to governments, representing local governments on other commissions, publishing a newsletter, issuing legislative recommendations, and maintaining a data base.[65]

NATIONAL AND REGIONAL ASSOCIATIONS

National and regional associations of state government officials play major roles in solving common problems. Two long-standing national associations are the National Governors' Association (NGA), which grew out of a conference of governors convened by President Theodore R. Roosevelt in 1908, and the Council of State Governments (CSG), which was organized in 1935. NGA, among other activities, cooperated with President George Bush on a "summit" meeting of kindergarten to grade 12 education reform that focused partly on national–state and interstate relations. CSG acts as the secretariat for twenty-four other associations and is affiliated or cooperates with additional associations (see Table 10.3). CSG is a major source of information on intergovernmental relations and includes a chapter on interstate relations in its *Book of the States* which is published biennially.

National associations of state administrative officials also promote interstate cooperation to solve problems in order to fend off congressional preemption of state regulatory powers. Founded in 1871, the National Association of Insurance Commissioners, for example, has initiated action to improve state solvency regulation of property–casualty and life insurance companies by establishing an accreditation program for states.[66]

The International Association of Milk Control Agencies seeks "to promote effective, efficient, and improved administration of economic milk regulations and the general welfare of the dairy industry through cooperation, coordination, research, education, and other activity mutually beneficial to its members."[67] The

Table 10.2

State Intergovernmental Relations Bodies Organizational Type, Legal Basis, and Membership

	Type and Legal Structure			Membership								
State	Type of Organization	Legal Basis	State Legislature	State Executive	County	Municipal Town Township	Regional Special District	School District	Private Citizen	Other-At Large	Total
Colarado	State-Local	J. Resolution	6	3	2	2	2	2			17
Connecticut	State-Local	Statute	4	5		8	1	2	5		25
Florida	State-Local	Statute	8	2	3	3			1	5	22
Illinois	Legislative	Statute	12								12
Indiana	Loc. Advisory Panel	Ex. Order	4	1	12	11					28
Iowa	State-Local	Statute	4		4	4	1	4		4	21
Louisiana	State-Local	Statute	4	4	3	5	1	3			17
Maine	Loc. Advisory Panel	Ex. Order				5	1			6	12
Maryland	Legislative	Statute	16	Ex-Officio		Ex-Officio					16
Massachusetts	State-Local	Statute	6	1		29		4			40
Missouri	State-Local	Ex. Order	4	5	3	7	1	1	10		31
Montana	State-Local	J. Resolution	4	3	4	4			2	3	20
New York	Legislative	Statute	10								10
North Carolina	State-Local	Ex. Order	4	4	3	3				7	21
North Dakota	State-Local	Statute	4	1	2	3	1				11
Ohio	State-Local	Statute	4	1	2	4	1			2	13
Oklahoma	State-Local	Statute	8	3	5	5		1		8	30
South Carolina	State-Local	Statute	8		3	3	2	1			21
Tennessee	State-Local	Statute	11	3	5	4	1	1	4		29
Utah	State-Local	Statute	6	6	4	4			5		21
Virginia	State-Local	Statute	6	3	4	4	1		1		20
Washington	State-Local	Ex. Order	4	5	6	6			2		21
Wisconsin	Loc. Advisory Panel	Statute		3	3	8					14
Total	24		137	53	68	120	11	18	30	35	472

Source: Directory of Intergovernmental Contacts (Washington, D.C.: U.S. Advisory Commission on Intergovernmental Relations, 1994), p. 8.

Table 10.3

The Council of State Governments Associated Organizations 1993

Affiliated Organizations

Conference of Chief Justices
Conference of State Court Administrators
Council on Licensure, Enforcement and
  Regulation*
National Association of Attorneys General
National Association of Secretaries
  of State*
National Association of State Auditors,
  Comptrollers and Treasurers

National Association of State Directors of
  Administration and General Services*
National Association of State Personnel
  Executives*
National Association of State Purchasing
  Officials*
National Association of State Treasurers*
National Conference of Lieutenant
  Governors*
National Conference of State Legislatures

Cooperating Organizations

Adjutants General Association of the
  United States
American Probation and Parole
  Association*
Association of State Correctional
  Administrators
Association of State Dam Safety Officials
Association of State Floodplain Managers,
  Inc.
Association of State and Interstate Water
  Pollution Control Administrators
Chief Officers of State Library Agencies*
Coastal States Organization, Inc.
Council on Governmental Ethics Laws*
Federation of Tax Administrators
Interstate Conference on Water Policy
National Association of Government
  Training and Development Directors*
National Association of Juvenile
  Correctional Agencies
National Association of Regulatory
  Utility Commissioners
National Association of State Agencies
  for Surplus Property
National Association of State Boating
  Law Administrators*
National Association of State
  Controlled Substances Authorities*

National Association of State Foresters
National Association of State
  Information Resource Executives*
National Association of State Juvenile
  Correctional Agencies
National Association of State Land
  Reclamationists
National Association of State Mental
  Health Program Directors
National Association of State
  Telecommunications Directors*
National Association of State Units
  on Aging
National Association of Unclaimed
  Property Administrators
National Child Support Enforcement
  Association
National Conference of Commissioners
  on Uniform State Laws
National Conference of State Fleet
  Administrators*
National Conference of States on
  Building Codes and Standards
National Criminal Justice Association
National Emergency Management
  Association*
National State Printing Association
Ohio River Basin Commission

(Continues)

Table 10.3 (*continued*)

National Association of State
   Departments of Agriculture
National Association of State Facilities
   Administrators*

Parole and Probation Compact
   Administrators' Association*

Adjunct Organizations

Association of Paroling Authorities
   International*
National Association of Government
   Deferred Compensation
   Administrators*
National Association of Governmental
   Labor Officials*

National Association for Public Worksite
   Health Promotion*
National Association of State Election
   Directors*
National Association of State Emergency
   quad Medical Services Training
   Coordinators*

---

* Staffed by the Council of State Governments.
Source: The Book of the States 1994–1995 (Lexington, Kentucky: The Council of State Governments, 1994), pp. 628–29.

Association of State and Interstate Water Pollution Control Administrators, organized in 1961, also promote interstate cooperation by providing technical and management information to its members relative to the clean water program established by Congress.[68]

The Federation of Tax Administrators—composed of representatives of the fifty states, New York City, and the District of Columbia—serves as a clearinghouse for the exchange of tax information.[69] The Federation drafted a Uniform Exchange of Information Agreement, effective on January 30, 1993, which has been signed by the District of Columbia and forty-four states. Prior to this agreement, individual states had entered into bilateral agreements with sister states for the sharing of tax information. The new agreement supersedes the bilateral agreements.

Regional associations of state officials are common. Examples include the Caucus of New England State Legislatures, Coalition of Northeastern Governors, Midwest Governors' Conference, Southern Association of State Departments of Agriculture, and Western States Water Councils. As noted, the Coalition of Northeastern Governors drafted a Model Toxics in Packaging Act which has been enacted into law by sixteen state legislatures. The coalition also studies other common problems, exchanges information, and promotes cooperative activities. The New England Governors also hold an annual conference with the Eastern Canadian Provincial Premiers to explore solutions for economic development, energy, and fishing problems.[70]

The Southeastern Association of Tax Administrators, organized in 1987 by twelve states, exchanges information on sales and uses taxes[71] Similarly, twelve other states and the District of Columbia organized the Northeast States Tax Officials Association for the same purpose. An interesting county level coordinating group—the conference of Southern County Associations—was organized in 1990 by statewide county government associations to address environmental problems on a cooperative basis by sharing information and conducting studies.[72]

FEDERAL PROMOTION OF INTERSTATE COOPERATION AND UNIFORM POLICIES

Congress has initiated several actions designed to promote cooperation by sister states and enactment of uniform state laws. Section 10 of Article I of the U.S. Constitution stipulates that interstate compacts become effective upon their approval by Congress. To encourage states to enter into compacts for forest-fire fighting, supervision of parolees and probationers, and flood control, Congress gave its consent-in-advance for such compacts in 1911, 1934, and 1936, respectively.[73] More recently, Congress enacted the Low-Level Radioactive Waste Policy Act of 1980 declaring that states are responsible for the disposal of such wastes generated within their respective boundaries and encouraging states to enter into interstate compacts for disposal of the wastes.[74] Nine compacts, involving forty-four states, have been formed.

In addition to encouraging interstate cooperation, Congress has initiated actions to facilitate such cooperation as illustrated by the National Driver Register (NDR) which was established by statute in 1960.[75] NDR receives from all states and the District of Columbia information on drivers whose licenses to operate a motor vehicle have been revoked or denied or who have been convicted of major traffic violations. A state motor vehicle department can check electronically with NDR prior to issuing an operator's license to determine whether the applicant has been convicted of motor vehicle violations in other states. If there is a file on a driver, NDR's Problem Driver Pointer System points automatically to the state holding the driver's substantive data and causes the data to be transferred electronically to the state making the request. Similarly, a state in renewing a license or addressing an in-state conviction of a motorist for a traffic violation can contact NDR to determine if the motorist has a violation(s) in another state (see Figure 10.1).

The National Highway Traffic Safety Administration, in a 1993 report to Congress, recommended that responsibility for operating NDR should be transferred from the administration to the American Association of Motor Vehicle Administrators which currently operates the Commercial Driver License Information System on a user fee basis.[76] Such a transfer would allow the association to combine its computer system with NDR's computer system under one timesharing contract that would result in cost savings because of economies of scale. A transfer also would save the federal government approximately $3.5 million annually.

Congress employed a new type of federal preemption—minimum standards preemption—in the Water Quality Act of 1965 and subsequently employed this type of preemption in other regulatory fields.[77] A minimum standards preemption

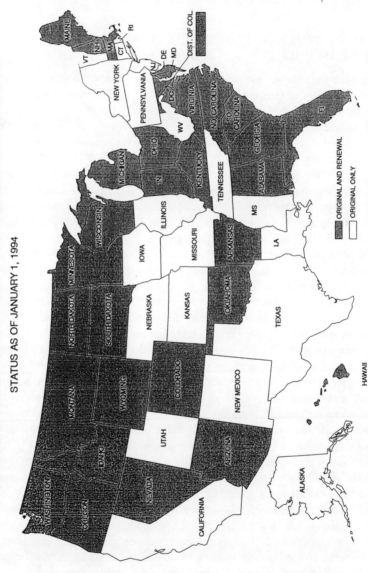

STATES USING NATIONAL DRIVER REGISTER TO CHECK DRIVER LICENSE APPLICATIONS

STATUS AS OF JANUARY 1, 1994

ORIGINAL AND RENEWAL

ORIGINAL ONLY

Source: 1994 Driver License Administration Requirements and Fees (Washington, D.C.: Federal Highway Administration, 1994), p. 6.

Figure 10.1

statute establishes standards and authorizes a federal administrative agency to promulgate other standards applicable to all states which may continue to be solely responsible for regulating the concerned field provided each state established standards as stringent as the national standards and enforces them. States are allowed to have higher standards than the federal ones, and consequently the standards are not uniform throughout the fifty states.

The Clean Air Act Amendments of 1990 established the Ozone Transport Commission composed of twelve northeastern states which share a common smog problem.[78] In 1994, the commission recommended that the U.S. Environmental Protection Agency require the member states and the District of Columbia to adopt the California Low Emission Vehicle Program.[79] Massachusetts and New York have adopted the program, and Connecticut has adopted most of the program.[80] The other states, however, have not adopted the program. On December 19, 1994, the Environmental Protection Agency announced it would permit the northeastern states to adopt the California program.[81] The Ozone Transport Commission in 1994 also agreed to implement a plan to reduce nitrogen oxide emissions from large fossil-fuel burning facilities, mainly electric power-generating plants.[82]

Cross-over sanctions are powerful weapons employed occasionally by Congress to persuade states to enact uniform statutes. A state that fails to enact a uniform statute subject to a cross-over sanction loses federal highway grants-in-aid. Responding to the Arab oil embargo in 1974, Congress employed such a sanction to persuade each state to enact a statute lowering its speed limit to a maximum of fifty-five miles per hour in order to conserve motor fuels.[83] A state failing to enact such a statute would suffer the loss of 10 percent of its highway grants. Congress employed a similar cross-over sanction in 1975 to conserve motor fuels by threatening states with the loss of highway funds if they failed to enact a statute allowing motorists stopped at a red traffic light to make a right turn on red provided no vehicle is approaching the intersection from the left.[84]

The relatively large number of highway accidents involving drivers under the age of twenty-one who had been drinking alcoholic beverages induced Congress in 1984 to enact another cross-over sanction. States which fail to raise the minimum alcoholic beverages purchase age to twenty-one are subject to the loss of highway funds.[85] The constitutionality of the act was upheld by the U.S. Supreme Court in *South Dakota v. Dole* in 1987.[86]

In 1982, Congress for the first time employed a tax sanction when it decided to persuade each state and local government to issue only registered long-term bonds—known as municipal bonds—in place of the traditional bearer bonds. The Tax Equity and Fiscal Responsibility Act of 1982 stipulates that the interest received by holders of bearer bonds would be subject to the federal income tax.[87] Failure to issue registered bonds would necessitate a state or local government to pay a higher rate of interest to attract purchasers for the bonds. The constitutionality of this statute was upheld in 1988 by the U.S. Supreme Court.[88]

Congress also employed a tax sanction in the Tax Reform Act of 1986 which requires state and local governments issuing long-term tax-exempt bonds to return any arbitrage profit to the U.S. Treasury.[89] Subnational governments borrowing funds by the issuance of long-term bonds typically invest the proceeds in U.S. Treasury notes and other safe securities until the funds are needed to pay for various construction projects. The arbitrage profit can be significant if there is a relatively wide interest rate spread between the rate on the municipal bonds and the rate on treasury certificates.

Congress on occasion has been disturbed by lack of a regulatory statute in a given field in several states as well as lack of uniformity of statutes. Concerned by the increase in the number of boating accidents caused by drunk operators, Congress in 1984 directed the U.S. Secretary of Transportation to develop standards to be employed in determining whether the operator of a marine recreational vessel is intoxicated.[90] Complying with the act, the Coast Guard in 1987 promulgated a rule stipulating that a state blood-alcohol-content (BAC) standard, if one exists, is the national standard within that state.[91] In the absence of a state standard, the Coast Guard standard applies. This rule encourages each state lacking a BAC standard to adopt one. Only Iowa, Kentucky, New Mexico, and Oklahoma failed to adopt a BAC standard by 1995.

In 1990, Congress enacted an innovative statute to establish a uniform policy throughout the United States while preserving state sovereignty by mandating states to enact a statute requiring revocation of the operator's license of a motorist convicted of a drug-related crime.[92] The federal law respects state sovereignty by allowing each state to "opt out" of the mandate by means of a state legislative resolution adopted in opposition to the requirement and a letter from the governor to the U.S. secretary of transportation expressing concurrence with the resolution. The approach employed by Congress forces a state legislature to initiate action if it wishes to exclude its state from the requirement in contrast to the usual statute-making process which allows a legislature to ignore a bill mandating driver license revocation for a drug-related conviction.

Congress in the same year took a nonintrusive step to promote uniform fire safety standards in hotels and motels by requiring federal employees to stay only in facilities that comply with the standards contained in the Federal Fire Prevention and Control Act of 1974.[93] To encourage state legislatures to enact the federal standards into state law, Congress stipulated that federal grants to state and local governments may not be used to sponsor or to pay for a conference, convention, meeting, or training seminar in a hotel or motel that does not meet the national fire safety standards.

SUMMARY AND CONCLUSIONS

Major problems are caused by the lack of nationally uniform state statutes, court decisions, and administrative actions. The U.S. Constitution enables the prevention of interstate problems by authorizing employment of interstate compacts by states; providing full faith and credit be given to public acts, records, and judicial proceedings of each state; authorizing Congress to regulate interstate commerce; and empowering the U.S. Supreme Court to adjudicate interstate suits.

The limitations of interstate compacts were analyzed in Chapter 3 and problems associated with full faith and credit were described in Chapter 4. The failure of Congress to exercise in a comprehensive manner its power to regulate interstate commerce to promote uniformity of regulation was highlighted in Chapter 7. Although the judiciary, particularly the U.S. Supreme Court, plays a major role in invalidating discriminatory state legislation of all types, the judiciary may not initiate action.

State legislatures recognize the desirability of uniform national policies, but on occasion enact nonuniform statutes because of pressure from powerful interest groups. Nevertheless, each state participates in the National Conference of Commissioners of Uniform State Laws which has a mixed record of achievement. Model acts are promoted by other organizations, and their record also has been a mixed one.

States also cooperate with each other on the basis of permanent administrative agreements covering a wide range of topics, including vehicle moving violations, cleaning up polluted areas, and provision of personnel and equipment in emergency situations. State administrative officials also cooperate with each other on an *ad hoc* basis as illustrated by attorneys general filing joint suits against alleged perpetrators of consumer fraud.

Twenty-four states have commissions or other organizations concerned with state–local relations which could be restructured to concentrate on interstate relations as well as state–local relations. In addition, national and regional associations promote formal and informal interstate cooperation, including enactment of uniform statutes and model acts.

Congress undoubtedly possesses the most power to promote interstate cooperation and to establish a uniform law on numerous subjects throughout the United States. Although several innovative statutes promoting uniform state laws have been enacted by Congress, these statutes have a relatively limited scope. Chapter 11 assesses the current state of interstate relations and advances recommendations for improving such relations and promoting the enactment of uniform state laws.

NOTES

1. Joseph F. Zimmerman, *Contemporary American Federalism: The Growth of National Power* (Leicester: Leicester University Press, 1992), pp. 6–7.

2. *Pacific Employers Insurance Company v. Industrial Accident Commission*, 206 U.S. 493 at 501 (1939), and *Hughes v. Fetter*, 341 U.S. 609 (1951).

3. *Paul v. Virginia*, 75 U.S. 1 (1868).

4. *United States v. South-Eastern Underwriters Association*, 322 U.S. 533 (1944), and McCarran–Ferguson Act of 1945, 59 Stat. 33, 15 U.S.C.A. §1011 (1976).

5. For details, see Sandra B. McCray, "Federal Preemption of State Regulation of Insurance: End of a 200 Year Era?" *Publius*, Fall 1993, pp. 33–47.

6. For details on preemption, see Joseph F. Zimmerman, *Federal Preemption: The Silent Revolution* (Ames: Iowa State University Press, 1991).

7. *The Act to Regulate Commerce of 1887*, 24 Stat. 379, and *Sherman Anti-Trust Act of 1890*, 26 Stat. 209, 15 U.S.C.A. §1 (1973 and 1995 Supp.).

8. "A 100-Year Tradition of Excellence," unpublished fact sheet issued by the National Conference of Commissioners on Uniform State Laws, no date.

9. *New York Laws of 1890*, Ch. 205, and *New York Executive Law*, §165 (McKinney 1994).

10. "A 100-Year Tradition of Excellence."

11. Allison Dunham, "A History of the National Conference of Commissioners on Uniform State Laws," *Law and Contemporary Problems*, Spring 1965, pp. 234–5.

12. *New York Laws of 1942*, Ch. 597, and *New York Executive Law*, §165 (McKinney 1994).

13. *Ibid.*

14. "Uniform State Laws: What Are They?" Unpublished fact sheet issued by the National Conference on Uniform State Laws, Chicago, IL, no date.

15. Rodney L. Mott, "Uniform Legislation in the United States," *The Annals*, January 1940, p. 84.

16. *Ibid.*

17. *Ibid.*, pp. 85–6.

18. *Ibid.*, p. 87.

19. Kim Q. Hill and Patricia A. Hurley, "Uniform State Law Adoptions in the American States: An Explanatory Analysis," *Publius*, Winter 1988, pp. 120–1.

20. *Ibid.*, p. 121.

21. *Ibid.*, p. 124.

22. *Ibid.*

23. Daniel J. Elazar, *American Federalism: A View from the States*, 3rd ed. (New York: Harper & Row, Incorporated, 1984), p. 115.

24. *Ibid.*, p. 117.

25. *Ibid.*, pp. 118–9.

26. Hill and Hurley, "Uniform State Law Adoptions," pp. 125–6.

27. *The Book of the States: 1994–95* (Lexington, Kentucky: The Council of State Governments, 1994), pp. 628–9.

28. The information in this section is drawn from an unpublished information sheet prepared by the Council of State Governments.

29. Ross E. Cheit, "State Adoption of Model Insurance Codes: An Empirical Analysis," *Publius*, Fall 1993, p. 50.

30. *Ibid.*, p. 51.

31. *Ibid.*, p. 60.

32. *Ibid.*, p. 70.

33. *Model Regulations, Statutes, and Guidelines: Uniformity Recommendations to the States* (Washington, D.C.: Multistate Tax Commission, 1995), pp. iii.

34. *Ibid.*, pp. 72–116.

35. *Ibid.*, pp. 1–70.

36. *Model Toxics in Packing Legislation* (Washington, D.C.: Coalition of Northeastern Governors, 1994).

37. *New York Vehicle & Traffic Law*, §219 (McKinney 1986).

38. *Ibid.*, §517 (McKinney 1986).

39. *Ibid.*, §405 (1995 Supp.).

40. *New York Highway Law*, §10 (McKinney 1979).

41. *New York Agriculture and Markets Law*, §258-n (McKinney 1991).

42. *New York Social Services Law*, §32 (McKinney 1992).

43. *New York Public Health Law*, §20 (McKinney 1993).

44. "Cooperative Agreement on North Branch Potomac Signed," *Potomac Basin Report*, November-December 1993, p. 4.

45. "Cuomo, Puerto Rico Governor Sign Pact," *Times Union* (Albany, N.Y.), August 16, 1994, p. B-2.

46. "Governors Sign Fish Ladder Pact," *Community Affairs* (Pennsylvania Department of Community Affairs), May–June 1993, p. 3.

47. "Air-quality Planners Release List of Potential Emission Control Regulations," a news release issued by the Metropolitan Washington Council of Government, July 1, 1993.

48. James Dao, "States Joining in Combating Illegal Guns," *The New York Times*, April 26, 1993, pp. 1 and B7.

49. "Agreement Reached to Restore Long Island Sound," *EPA Activities Update*, October 3, 1994, p. 1.

50. *Department of Agriculture and Markets Annual Report 1992* (Albany: 1993), p. 34.

51. Keon S. Chi, "Resurgence of Multistate Regionalism," *The Journal of State Government*, July–September 1990, pp. 59–63.

52. "Attention Keds Purchasers," a paid advertisement in the *Times Union* (Albany, N.Y.), November 8, 1993, p. A-5.

53. "State Attorneys General Launch Investigation of Cable Industry," *Times Union* (Albany, N.Y.), November 18, 1993, p. D-8.

54. David Evans, "Contest Offers Mislead Entrants," *Times Union* (Albany, N.Y.), August 25, 1995, p. C-9.

55. *Morales v. Trans World Airlines*, Incorporated, 112 S.Ct. 2031 (1992).

56. *Ibid.* at 2055–6.

57. Michael Quint, "Met Life Asked for $20 Million," *Times Union* (Albany, N.Y.), February 7, 1994, p. B-5.

58. *City of New York v. United States Department of Commerce*, 822 F. Supp. 906 (E.D.N.Y. 1993).

59. Eric Aldrich, "Vt. Officials: There's Progress on Connecticut River Bridge," *The Keene (N. H.) Sentinel*, March 30, 1993, p. 2.

60. "Mass. Starts Crackdown on Illegal NH Plates," *The Union Leader* (Manchester, N.H.), May 9, 1995, p. A10.

61. "Maine and NH Say Shipyard Vital to Defense," *The Union Leader* (Manchester, N.H.), March 18, 1994, p. 7.

62. "NH, Maine, Vt. Joining Forces on Health Care," *The Union Leader* (Manchester, N.H.), November 11, 1993, p. 9.

63. Hubert R. Gallagher, "Work of the Commission on Interstate Cooperation," *The Annals*, January 1940, p. 103.

64. 73 Stat. 703, 42 U.S.C.A. §4271 (1994).

65. *Directory of Intergovernmental Contacts* (Washington, D.C.: U.S. Advisory Commission on Intergovernmental Relations, 1993), p. 5.

66. *State Solvency Regulation of Property-Casualty and Life Insurance Companies* (Washington, D.C.: U.S. Advisory Commission on Intergovernmental Relations, 1992).

67. *Constitution of the International Association of Milk Control Agencies* (Albany, N.Y.: The Association, n.d.), Art. II.

68. *Annual Report 1992–1993* (Washington, D.C.: The Association of State and Interstate Water Pollution Control Administrators, 1994), p. 2.

69. Julie Bennett, "States Look to Share Data, Collect More Taxes," *City & State*, May 24, 1993, p. 13.

70. Jerry Miller, "N.E. Governors, Canadian Leaders Gather," *The Union Leader* (Manchester, N.H.), June 7, 1995, p. A7.

71. Bennett, "States Look to Share Data, Collect More Taxes," p. 13.

72. *Technical Documents and Newsletters* (Atlanta: Conference of Southern County Associations, 1993).

73. *Weeks Act of 1911*, 36 Stat. 961, 16 U.S.C.A. §480 (1985); *Crime Control Consent Act of 1934*, 48 Stat. 909, 18 U.S.C.A. §10 (1969); and *Flood Control Act of 1936*, 49 Stat. 1508, 16 U.S.C.A. §460d (1933).

74. *Low-Level Radioactive Waste Policy Act of 1980*, 94 Stat. 3347, 42 U.S.C.A. §2021d (1994).

75. *National Driver Register Act of 1960* as modified by the *National Driver Register Act of 1982*, 96 Stat. 1740, 23 U.S.C.A. §401 note (1990 and 1995 Supp.). See also 23 CFR 1325 and 1327.

76. *A Report to Congress: NHTSA's Involvement in the National Driver Register* (Washington, D.C.: National Highway Traffic Safety Administration, 1993), p. 43.

77. Joseph F. Zimmerman, *Federal Preemption: The Silent Revolution* (Ames: Iowa State University Press, 1991), pp. 92–7.

78. *Clean Air Act Amendments of 1990*, 104 Stat. 2448, 42 U.S.C.A. §7511c (1995 Supp.).

79. A news release issued by Governor Mario M. Cuomo of New York, dated February 1, 1994.

80. Matthew L. Wald, "E.P.A. Urges Compromise on Auto Pollution Rules," *The New York Times*, September 14, 1994, p. B4.

81. Matthew L. Wald, "California Car Rules Set as Model for the East," *The New York Times*, December 20, 1994, p. A16.

82. "States Agree to NOX Reductions: Benefits to the Bay are Uncertain," *Bay Journal*, November 1994, p. 4.

83. *Emergency Highway Energy Conservation Act of 1974*, 88 Stat. 829.

84. *Energy Policy and Conservation Act of 1975*, 89 Stat. 933, 42 U.S.C.A. §6201 (1983).

85. *National Minimum Drinking Age Amendments of 1984*, 98 Stat. 437, 23 U.S.C.A. §158 (1990 and 1995 Supp.).

86. *South Dakota v. Dole*, 483 U.S. 203 (1987).

87. *Tax Equity and Fiscal Responsibility Act of 1982*, 96 Stat. 324, 26 U.S.C.A. §1 (1988).

88. *South Carolina v. Baker*, 483 U.S. 203 (1988).

89. *Tax Reform Act of 1986*, 100 Stat. 2085, 26 U.S.C.A. §1 (1988).

90. *Coast Guard Authorization Act of 1984*, 98 Stat. 2862.

91. 33 CRF 95.025 (1987).

92. *Department of Transportation Appropriation Act of 1990*, 104 Stat. 2185, 23 U.S.C.A. §105 note (1995 Supp.). See also 57 *Federal Register* 35,986–36,001 (1992).

93. *Hotel and Motel Fire Safety Act of 1990*, 104 Stat. 747, 5 U.S.C.A. §5707(d)(3) (1995 Supp.).

11

Model for Improved Interstate Relations

The preamble to the U.S. Constitution commences with "We the People of the United States, in order to form a more Perfect Union, ..." The constitution has provided a more perfect union than the one provided by the Articles of Confederation and Perpetual Union, yet the union is not a perfect one, as evidenced by interstate disputes and the failure of sister states to cooperate fully with each other on regulatory matters and development projects.

Our findings in Chapters 2–10 permit an assessment of the current state of interstate relations, in terms of cooperation and conflict, as a five on a scale of one to ten, with ten indicating a perfect union. This composite rating, of course, masks major differences in the degree of cooperation and conflict among individual states.

The United States federal system is the product of compromises between states and regional blocks of states relative to their retained powers and powers delegated to Congress. Compromises seldom satisfy completely all parties. As one would anticipate, tensions and disputes among states and between states and Congress are prominent features of the system, which are accentuated by the natural tendency of each state to seek to export taxes, protect state industries from outside competition, and attract industrial firms and various categories of purchasers of merchandise.

Furthermore, the *modus operandi* of most states does not encourage interstate cooperation, coordination, and joint ventures. There is a natural reluctance on the part of states, as semiautonomous entities, to engage in joint ventures, because of the loss of exclusive control that accompanies them.

Global economic competition in the second half of the twentieth century has stimulated interest-group pressure on Congress to exercise more frequently its powers of total and partial preemption of state regulatory authority to lower the cost of production by removing barriers and obstacles to the free flow of commerce among the states.[1] The dramatic increase in the number of preemption statutes since 1965, while promoting interstate commerce, has changed significantly the nature of the federal system by reducing the reserved powers of the states, enlisting states via minimum standards to implement national policies, and regulating states as political entities.[2]

FINDINGS AND CONCLUSIONS

This chapter summarizes findings made in Chapters 2–10 and draws specific conclusions based upon such findings while continuing the theme of interstate cooperation stressed in Chapter 10 by offering a model to improve such cooperation. The previous chapters examined the constitutional provisions pertaining to interstate relations and various interstate disputes, congressional authority to regulate interstate relations and to promote cooperation by sister states, economic protectionism, tax exportation problems, and interstate cooperation. Also examined was the role of the U.S. Supreme Court in adjudicating suits among states and determining whether a state statute or regulation violates the dormant Interstate Commerce Clause or is contrary to a congressional statute based on a delegated power. We begin with findings and conclusions pertaining to the role of the Supreme Court.

The Supreme Court

In view of the fact that the need for a national supreme court was questioned at the Constitutional Convention in 1787, it is surprising that the court plays such a major role in governing interstate relations.

Functioning as an international tribunal, the court wisely decided to exercise its constitutional authority to adjudicate interstate disputes on a discretionary basis and to employ a special master in each such dispute to persuade states to revolve their disputes through negotiations. The findings and recommendations of the special master frequently convince states to settle their disputes out of court on the basis of the master's recommendations. This procedure prevents the court's docket from becoming overburdened by such suits.

Boundary disputes date to 1799 and today typically involve a river changing its course. These disputes do not present the court with the complexities involved in suits involving allocation of river waters, to which the court's doctrine of equitable apportionment, in the absence of an interstate compact, generally has worked satisfactorily. However, the shortage of water in arid states with expanding farming and populations will present the court with greater challenges than Solomon faced and will prevent the court from using its wisdom to satisfy all parties to a dispute. Congress, of course, could help to solve water disputes by employing its power to apportion the waters of major interstate rivers.

In the absence of congressional use of its delegated commerce power to eliminate interstate trade barriers, the court has been forced since 1824 to use its dormant commerce clause jurisprudence to resolve them. Had the court not done so, the lack of congressional action would have encouraged economic Balkanization of the United States. Congress unfortunately has ignored the court's conclusion that

Congress with its delegated powers is better equipped than the court to determine national policies under its delegated powers.

Interstate Compacts

The drafters of the U.S. Constitution wisely recognized that there is a legitimate need for formal interstate compacts, similar to international treaties, and authorized states to enter into compact with the consent of Congress. The device has proven to be very successful in solving particular regional problems such as allocation and apportionment of river waters. The twenty-two types of compacts are a testimony to the adaptability of the device in solving diverse problems.

We do not know how effective each compact has been with respect to whether it achieved its goals in the most economical and efficient manner, because there have been few studies of individual compacts and none in recent years other than the evaluations conducted by committees of the state legislature in Maryland, Nebraska, and Oklahoma.

Although the need for certain types of compacts has been reduced by congressional preemption of the regulatory authority of states in specific cases such as bus regulation, it is apparent that the full potential of the compact device has not been realized because state legislators do not devote a significant amount of time to promoting and monitoring compacts.[3] Our model is designed to increase the number of types of compacts.

The decline of interest in forming interstate compacts during recent decades masks the proliferation of interstate administrative agreements. They are based upon the laws of the party states and generally have the same validity as an interstate compact. A similarity exists between the use of administrative agreements in place of interstate compacts and the use of executive agreements in place of treaties by the president. A parallel also can be drawn between the issuance of executive orders by governors in lieu of the enactment of statutes by the state legislature and employment of administrative agreements in place of compacts.

Full Faith and Credit

Conflict of laws is inevitable in a federal system and the Full Faith and Credit Clause, supplemented by congressional and Supreme Court clarification, has proved to be effective in resolving most conflicts. Interstate child support, however, remains a problem area. The 1994 Full Faith and Credit for Child Support Orders Act and the 1992 Child Support Recovery Act appear to have the potential for facilitating the collection of child support by the custodial parent provided responsible federal administrative agencies vigorously enforce these statutes.[4]

The proposal that Congress establish a national child support system, replacing the state ones, appears to be flawed because the powers delegated to Congress by the U.S. Constitution do not emcompass the power to establish such a system. Whether public support exists for a constitutional amendment authorizing

Congress to establish such a system is questionable. Furthermore, such an amendment would result in a two-tier system with states retaining responsibility for other aspects of child welfare while federal administrators would not have the detailed knowledge possessed by the states in child support cases.

Privileges and Immunities

In common with the Full Faith and Credit Clause, a plaintiff's resort to the Privileges and Immunities Clause may involve a conflict of laws and/or concurrent resort to other constitutional clauses. Not uncommonly, a plaintiff in a privileges and immunities challenge of a state action also will base the challenge on the state's alleged violation of the Interstate Commerce, Due Process of Law, and Equal Protection of the Law Clauses of the U.S. Constitution.

As noted in Chapter 5, the U.S. Supreme Court since 1839 has held that corporations are not entitled to privileges and immunities, and states discriminate against foreign and alien corporations. Such discrimination, however, may be struck down by the courts if an undue burden is placed on interstate commerce.

In contrast with the Full Faith and Credit Clause, the Privileges and Immunities Clause does not authorize Congress by general laws to determine privileges and immunities. The Supreme Court's reasonableness standard, employed in reviewing suits alleging deprivation of privileges and immunities, recognizes that states can have valid reasons, such as natural resources conservation, in discriminating against nonresidents. On the other hand, durational residency requirements longer than simple residency requirements to engage in the practice of various professions are candidates for elimination by the court through its interpretation of the Privileges and Immunities Clause.

Rendition

A procedure for interstate rendition is essential in a federal nation if justice is to be served. The Rendition Act of 1793, as it has come to be interpreted by the Supreme Court, establishes a sound procedure for the return of a fugitive from justice by the asylum state governor to the requesting governor state. Fortunately, the Supreme Court in 1987 reversed its 1861 decision holding that the governor of the asylum state only had a moral obligation to return a fugitive to the requesting state.

However, as explained in Chapter 6, there is a need in each state for a statute governing the rendition of fugitives from justice who were not in the demanding state at the time of the occurrence of the crimes they are charged with such as the "affect" crime of child nonsupport.

Economic Protectionism

Interstate trade barriers have been a continuing problem in the United States since 1781 when the Articles of Confederation and Perpetual Union became effective. Experience reveals that such barriers cannot be eliminated completely either by Congress or the courts because of the ingenuity of state legislatures in devising new barriers. Furthermore, the U.S. Supreme Court in particular has allowed barriers to remain in place provided they do not place an undue burden on interstate commerce.

The police power of the states at one time was the major source of restraints on the free flow of commerce in the United States. In more recent years, tax barriers have become the most common, and courts have had to make decisions relative to the apportionment of tax burdens among states and the extent to which interstate business firms must contribute, through taxes, to help finance services provided by the state to the firms.

The Supreme Court on many occasions has invited Congress to use its delegated powers to resolve the problems flowing from protectionist actions of state legislatures and administrators. Congress generally has ignored the invitations.

Economic Competition

Although states engage in competition to attract tourists, and a few states seek to attract gamblers, state competition is most intense relative to attracting business firms, particularly industrial ones. The latter naturally relocates if costs are substantially lower in another state. The New England states, for example, lost most of their textile and shoe firms after World War II and initiated policies to attract new industries, especially high-technology ones. Today, competition for industrial firms is worldwide and states cannot offer sufficient incentives to discourage firms with labor-intensive operations from moving to low-wage nations.

Studies reveal that industrial location incentives have five major disadvantages and do not necessarily increase production and employment in a given region if firms are attracted to neighboring states in the region. Furthermore, a number of firms attracted to a particular state have moved their operations when the incentives terminated.

The U.S. Internal Revenue Code is responsible to a great extent for interstate competition to attract industrial firms, since the code allows states and local governments to issue bonds paying tax-exempt interest to raise the capital needed to attract the firms. Congress has plenary authority to regulate economic competition by the states, but has been extremely reluctant to exercise such authority.

Tax Revenue Competition

State legislators in many states seek reelection and hence attempt to appeal to their constituents by keeping state taxes as low as possible. One method for achieving this goal is to export the tax burden, to the extent possible, to taxpayers residing in other states. As explained in Chapter 9, legislators have developed clever tax exportation schemes.

The differential in sales taxes and motor vehicle insurance premiums among neighboring states encourages motorists in the high-tax and insurance premium state, particularly if they reside near the state border, to register their vehicles in the state with low rates. This problem, however, is not a major one throughout the United States.

The most serious tax differential problems involve cigarette and alcoholic beverage tax evasion. Congress has attempted to assist states to eliminate these problems by enacting the Jenkins Act in 1949, which makes it illegal to use the postal service to evade state and local government excise taxes on tobacco products, and the Contraband Cigarette Act of 1978 prohibiting distribution, possession, purchase, receipt, shipment, or transportation of more than 60,000 cigarettes lacking the tax indicia of the state where the cigarettes are found.[5]

As noted in Chapter 9, the buttlegging problem would be eliminated if states levied a uniform cigarette excise tax.[6] For a variety of reasons, state legislators generally are opposed to a uniform tax. Congress could help to eliminate this problem and thereby weaken organized crime by employing its power to regulate interstate commerce to establish a policy eliminating excise tax differentials. Similarly, Congress could reduce smuggling of alcoholic beverages across state lines.

The most major tax exportation problem involves severance taxes. If these taxes are levied at a low rate, no particular burden is placed on interstate commerce, and the U.S. Supreme Court will confirm its validity if a suit is brought against it. The court in 1981 even upheld a 30.5-percent Montana severance tax on coal when the bulk of the coal was exported on the grounds there was no possibility of multiple taxation, the tax was nondiscriminatory, and a firm with a nexus to the state was required to support general governmental services.[7] Congress could use its plenary interstate commerce power to place a maximum limit on severance taxes so as to limit states to recoup only their direct costs associated with the extraction of minerals or harvesting of timber.

The rapid development of multistate corporations in the nineteenth century and multinational corporations in the twentieth century created the problem of tax apportionment between the income of a corporation earned in a given state and its national or worldwide income. State tax officials are aware that corporate accounting systems can be adjusted to reduce reported income earned in a given state. As a consequence, states developed three methods of determining their respective share of such a corporation's income. Principal reliance is placed upon a three-factor formula apportionment—payroll, property, and sales—to determine a corporation's income earned in the state. As one would anticipate, corporations challenged the apportionment system utilized by several states, but the U.S. Supreme Court upheld the validity of the apportionment system.[8]

It was not until 1959 that Congress enacted a statute regulating state taxation of interstate commerce, and the statute was a narrow one.[9] The failure of Congress to enact more than a handful of limited statutes regulating state taxation of interstate commerce has resulted in a major burden being placed on general trial and appellate courts which typically have crowded dockets.

Interstate Cooperation

The conflict of laws of the various states can affect individuals and business firms adversely. As explained in Chapter 10, the National Conference of Commissioners on Uniform State Laws has drafted such laws since 1892 and has had mixed success in persuading all or most state legislatures to enact several uniform laws. Other organizations have drafted model acts to guide state legislatures, including the Council of State Governments, U.S. Advisory Commission on Intergovernmental Relations, National Association of Insurance Commissioners, Multistate Tax Commission, and various regional associations.

Unfortunately, nonuniform laws are more common than uniform laws, despite the efforts of the above organizations, and citizen and interest group frustration with the conflict of laws of various states on a given subject leads them to pressure Congress to employ its powers of preemption to replace diverse state laws on a given subject with a uniform congressional statute.

The numerous formal administrative agreements between officials of the fifty states are proof that interstate cooperation is productive and in many instances essential. Similarly, *ad hoc* agreements by administrative officials of two or more states to attack jointly a specific problem are additional evidence of the importance and desirability of such cooperation. National and regional associations of state government officials are major promoters of interstate cooperation to solve problems and thereby negate the need for congressional preemption of state regulatory powers.

There has been a sharp decline in the number of state interstate cooperation commissions since 1940 when forty-one of the forty-eight states had one. These commissions have disappeared or have been downgraded, as in New York where there is only a Senate Select Committee on Interstate Cooperation. Although there are currently twenty-four state advisory commissions on intergovernmental relations, their focus is state–local relations.

Congress has been a significant force encouraging states to cooperate with sister states by (*i*) granting consent-in-advance to interstate compacts, (*ii*) establishing the National Driver Register and the Ozone Transport Commission, (*iii*) employing cross-over sanctions to establish a national uniform maximum speed limit, with the exception of certain rural interstate highways, (*iv*) enacting a tax sanction to pressure state and local governments to issue only registered long-term bonds, and (*v*) enacting an "opt-out" statute to force state legislatures to decide whether a driver convicted of a drug-related crime should be subject to loss of his/her driver's license.

MODEL FOR INTERSTATE RELATIONS

The general neglect of interstate relations by state and national officials has adverse consequences for states and the union. Such relations must be brought out of the twilight zone and onto the center stage in state legislatures and Congress.

A positive approach to improving interstate relations, by decreasing conflict and increasing cooperation, involves greater leadership roles by state legislatures, governors, state departments and agencies, national and regional associations of state administrative officials, Congress, the president, and national departments and agencies. The model specifically calls for:

I. State legislatures to:

(a) create committees, preferably joint ones, and commissions on interstate relations composed of legislators, administrators, and private citizens;

(b) enact uniform state laws or parallel laws;

(c) where appropriate, enact congressional statutes into state law to achieve greater uniformity of laws with respect to concurrent powers;

(d) enter into additional regulatory interstate compacts to solve regional problems, thereby obviating the need for Congress to establish a national uniform policy to solve a specific problem.

II. Governors to:

(a) play a more important leadership role in promoting cooperation with sister states;

(b) establish by executive order an Office of Interstate Relations to conduct research and focus attention on the importance of interstate relations which are overshadowed by national–state relations;

(c) include a section on interstate relations in the annual State of the State Address.

III. Heads of state departments and agencies to:

(a) devote more attention to cooperation with their counterparts in sister states to solve national and regional problems;

(b) review and revise as needed existing interstate administrative agreements and publish such agreements in a readily available form.

IV. Associations of state administrative officials to:

(a) conduct at least one meeting each year devoted to interstate problems and their possible solutions;

(b) sponsor an interstate relations center to conduct research on interstate relations, develop cooperative programming, and propose new policies for enactment by Congress and state legislatures.

V. Congress to:

(a) grant consent-in-advance to states to enter into additional types of interstate compact;

(b) remove trade barriers among states;

(c) curtail state tax competition;

(d) reduce interstate competition for industry;

(e) promote bilateral and multilateral development organizations, such as interstate school districts;

(f) enact additional "opt-out" statutes to force state legislatures to consider enacting uniform laws;

(g) review delegation of regulatory powers to states to determine if the resulting conflict of state laws burdens interstate commerce;

(h) establish a joint committee on interstate relations similar to the Joint Economic Committee.

VI. The president to:

(a) provide strong leadership in solving interstate problems and offering to mediate major regional disputes among states;

(b) direct the White House Intergovernmental Affairs Office to devote more attention to interstate relations;

(c) include a section on interstate relations in the annual State of the Union message emphasizing the theme of a "Union of States."

VII. Heads of national departments and agencies to:

(a) improve coordination with other national departments and agencies with overlapping regulatory responsibilities in order to promote interstate cooperation;

(b) encourage states jointly to attack problems subject to national minimum regulatory standards;

(c) provide leadership in solving regional problems by mobilizing the concerned states;

(d) form joint task forces with their state counterparts to conduct investigations and enforce regulatory standards;

(e) make grants to private organizations to work with groups of states in developing solutions for regional problems.

State Legislatures

As explained in Chapter 10, state legislators generally have lost interest in interstate relations during the past four decades, and commissions on interstate cooperation have disappeared. Unless there is a joint committee or committee in each house focusing on interstate relations, there is no permanent linkage between the legislature and developing and maintaining such relations. The result is a general neglect of such relations and the failure to take advantage of the opportunities to solve regional problems more expeditiously and to provide services in the most economical and efficient manner.

An alternative to such a committee(s) is a commission composed of legislators, administrators, and citizens. Administrators who deal with problems overspilling state boundaries on a daily basis possess the knowledge and expertise to suggest solutions to legislators. Citizens whose businesses or personal affairs are burdened by interstate problems should be able to offer recommendations for alleviating or eliminating the problems.

The need for uniform state laws or parallel laws in the fifty states is great. A joint legislative committee or commission, with staff support, could review all proposed uniform or parallel laws, ensure that bills are introduced in the legislature, and promote their enactment. State legislators generally exercise common sense in considering bills. In most instances, common sense supports enactment of uniform and parallel statutes. Their enactment, however, is stymied if implementing bills are not introduced and reported out of committee to the floor.

Another approach to harmonizing the statutes of the various states is for each state legislature to enact into state law the provisions of a congressional statute on a particular subject. The constitutional provision for concurrent powers allows Congress and the state legislatures to enact statutes dealing with the same matters subject to the Supremacy of the Laws Clause in the event there is a conflict between a congressional statute and a state statute.

The Pure Food and Drug Act, enacted by Congress in 1906, served as the model for a number of state statutes on the same subject.[10] The National Labor Relations Act of 1935 also served as a model for state laws enacted in Massachusetts, New York, Pennsylvania, Utah, and Wisconsin within two years.[11]

Professor J. A. C. Grant of the University of California at Los Angeles observed:

State adoption of national laws is of even greater importance than national adoption of state laws. It has a greater potential field of operation. National adoption of state laws merely unifies a national law with the law of each individual state. State adoption of national law does this and more; it unifies the laws of all cooperating states. It does this to a greater extent than can be accomplished through the National Conference of Commissioners on Uniform State Laws; for the national government, unlike the conference, has a Supreme Court to give definition meaning to its laws. No doubt state courts would be more willing to follow the rulings of the Supreme Court than they are to follow the rulings of the courts of sister states; ... Indeed, in adopting the law of the nation the state would be adopting, not a particular statute, but a complete product, statute, administrative rulings and judicial decisions.[12]

Grant's statement is as valid today as it was in the 1930s.

Professor W. Brooke Graves of Temple University was aware of the problems facing the federal system during the great depression and wrote in 1938 that there were two alternatives relative to improving the functional effectiveness of the system:

One lies in the direction of extreme centralization of power in the hands of the central government, in which case the states must either cease to exist, or be reduced to purely administrative units. The other alternative—more difficult and more desirable—involves the development of cooperation between governmental units to an extent never before attempted. By one method or the other, we must wipe out governmental no-man's-lands and insure the competence of some public authority to deal with whatever problems arise, wherever, and whenever they arise. By one method or the other, we must be able to apply a uniform rule in the control of a given subject, on either a national or a regional basis, as the need may require.[13]

This statement also is as valid in the closing years of the twentieth century as it was in the 1930s.

The continuing failure of state legislatures to take action to solve major regional problems will guarantee that Congress will respond to pressure from interest groups and citizens for the enactment of preemption statutes. The legislatures should enter into additional regulatory interstate compacts to solve regional problems, thereby obviating the need for Congress to establish a national uniform policy to solve each regional problem which may not recognize the need for a different approach because of unique factors in a given region.

Governors

The failure of state legislatures to enact more uniform or parallel statutes and to enter into more interstate compacts is not surprising in view of the fact that their individual constituencies are small and their reelection is dependent heavily upon producing benefits for their constituents whose interests tend to be parochial. The governor, on the other hand, has a statewide constituency. Governors also have a U.S. constitutional duty to return fugitives from justice at the request of a governor of a sister state and appoint individuals to the governing bodies of interstate compact agencies. The governors of New Jersey and New York are authorized by compact to veto actions taken by the commissioners of the Port Authority of New York and New Jersey. In general, governors have not played a major interstate governance leadership role, even though they meet with their fellow governors at annual meetings of their regional and national associations.

If governors are to play a greater leadership role, they must be provided with detailed information. Each governor, by executive order, should establish an Office of Interstate Relations charged with studying problems with other states and the need for uniform state laws.

Each governor also should include a section on interstate relations in the annual State of the State Address to the state legislature and prepare bills on such relations for introduction in the state legislature. On occasion, it may be important for the governor to send a special message on cooperation with sister states to the legislature.

Heads of State Departments and Agencies

State statutes typically grant the heads of departments and agencies broad authority to promulgate rules and regulations and to enter into cooperative agreements with their counterparts in sister states. Chapter 10 noted extensive interstate administrative agreements while also noting the failure to compile these agreements in a single document readily available to officials and the general public.

Heads of departments and agencies should review and revise as needed, in collaboration with their counterparts in other states, existing interstate administrative agreements, and all such agreements should be published by each state in a readily available form.

Numerous agreements between administrators in a state and their counterparts in sister states are *ad hoc* in nature. These officials should review the success of past *ad hoc* agreements and convert, with legislative approval if necessary, the agreements into permanent ones.

Department and agency heads also should notify the state legislature of the desirability of entering into additional interstate administrative agreements in cases where the heads lack statutory authority to enter into such agreements. In addition, the heads are in a position, based upon their experience, to recommend enactment of uniform state laws and model acts, and entrance into new interstate compacts. However, such recommendations probably will not result in the enactment of the recommended laws and compacts unless there is a joint committee on interstate relations or a committee in each house.

State Officials Associations

National and regional associations of state officials hold annual meetings which tend to focus on national–state relations to the general neglect of interstate relations. Multistate problems could be reduced if each association devoted at least one meeting each year to finding solutions and methods of implementing the solutions.

The National Governors' Association, as described in Chapter 8, prepared development guides to reduce state competition for industry. Although these guides have not stopped such competition, they have been helpful. These associations also can be highly successful in preventing interstate conflicts. Jonathan R. Macey and Geoffrey P. Miller concluded, relative to state regulation of the insurance industry, that NAIC has helped to prevent "an internecine regulatory war in attempts to apply their law to as wide a range of practices as possible."[14]

NAIC has a subcommittee which has accredited forty-four state insurance departments, including twelve accredited in 1994, and the other six states and the District of Columbia have enacted laws to facilitate accreditation.[15] NAIC in 1994 helped states to reach a settlement with the Metropolitan Life Insurance Company that provides restitution to individuals misled by the company marketing its life insurance policies as retirement plans and imposes a heavy fine on the company.[16]

Congress

Three interstate roles—inhibitor, facilitator, and initiator—are played by Congress. It inhibits interstate cooperation when it fails to grant its consent to an interstate compact entered into by states, as illustrated by the Mid-Atlantic States Air Pollution Control Compact in 1967. Congress facilitates bilateral and multilateral state cooperation by granting its consent-in-advance to compacts. Congress is also an initiator of solutions to interstate problems by enacting preemption statutes such as the Surface Transportation Assistance Act of 1982 nullifying state size and weight standards for trucks which had created interstate trade barriers.[17]

The U.S. Constitution delegates important powers to Congress to ensure that full faith and credit is given in each state to the statutes, records, and judicial proceedings of sister states and that interstate commerce is facilitated. Congress enacted statutes in 1790 and 1804 prescribing the manner of proving full faith and credit. These statutes generally have been effective.

Congress had relatively little need to enact statutes based upon its power to regulate interstate commerce during the early decades of the federal system since the amount of such commerce was relatively small. It was not until 1887 that Congress utilized its commerce power to regulate railroads, and it failed to use the power to regulate state taxation of multistate business firms until 1959 when a narrow statute was enacted.[18]

The U.S. Supreme Court on a number of occasions has invited Congress to exercise its delegated powers to solve interstate problems. In *Quill Corporation v. North Dakota*, the court in 1992 stressed "that the underlying issue is not only one that Congress may be better qualified to resolve, but also one that Congress has the ultimate power to resolve."[19]

Congress generally exhibits little interest in solving interstate problems other than occasionally using its delegated power to preempt totally or partially the regulatory powers of the states. Individual members of Congress, however, often issue statements if their respective state is engaged in a feud with another state. The failure of Congress to solve interstate problems places a major burden on national courts, particularly the U.S. Supreme Court, to adjudicate suits involving such problems.

The reason why the drafters of the U.S. Constitution made the effectiveness of interstate compacts dependent upon congressional approval is well understood. The U.S. Supreme Court's 1893 doctrine of implied consent has facilitated formation of compacts, but the constitutional requirement no doubt deters states from entering into what are viewed as political compacts.[20] Today, however, there is no danger that two or more states will enter into a compact to secede from the union or initiate actions adverse to the interests of individual sister states not members of the compact.

The question also can be asked why should two neighboring states be barred from entering into a compact to solve a problem unless members of Congress, representing other areas of the nation, grant their consent to the proposed compact. Furthermore, Congress at any time can utilize its delegated commerce power to invalidate any interstate compact or compact provision burdening interstate commerce. As a consequence, Congress should enact a statute granting its consent-in-advance to states to enter into additional types of interstate compact.

Congress has plenary power to remove trade barriers among states but has chosen to rely heavily upon courts to invalidate the barriers. Robert H. Jackson, who later became a U.S. Supreme Court Justice, concluded in 1940 that the court is unable "to eliminate barriers to trade through adjudication of the issue of discrimination, ..."[21]

A court decision is case-specific, and individuals and firms adversely affected by a state trade barrier may be forced to bring suit despite a court's invalidation of a similar barrier in another state. In contrast, a congressional statute would invalidate such barriers without the need for an enforcement suit in most instances. Granted, there is merit to the argument that courts are in a better position than Congress to weigh issues involving the police power of a state and the interstate commerce power of Congress. Nevertheless, a clear need remains for additional congressional statutes invalidating barriers to trade among the several states.

Congress, as explained in Chapter 7, has delegated powers to states which can be employed to create interstate trade barriers. The Interstate Horseracing Act of 1978, for example, grants states limited powers to preempt federal prohibition of interstate off-track wagering. Interstate simulcasts of races, under the act, require the consent of state agencies and a horsemen's association, and the latter may refuse to grant its consent.[22] The U.S. Court of Appeals for the Sixth Circuit in 1994 overturned a U.S. District Court ruling that the act restricted commercial free speech protected by the First Amendment.[23]

The McCarren–Ferguson Act of 1945, by authorizing states to regulate the insurance industry, automatically made possible the erection of interstate trade barriers in the field of insurance.[24] The U.S. Supreme Court has been called upon, as a result of the act, to determine on several occasions whether a state tax on a foreign insurance company violates the Equal Protection of the Laws Clause of the U.S. Constitution.[25]

Our model recommends that Congress should review its delegation of certain regulatory powers to states to determine if resulting conflicts of laws burden interstate commerce and revoke any delegation that is causing major interstate trade barriers.

Because of the numerous and complex issues crowding Congress' agenda, it is unrealistic to expect Congress to remove all such barriers directly. It, however, should enact additional statutes authorizing administrative adjudication of interstate disputes as an alternative to judicial adjudication subject, of course, to appeal to the courts. These statutes would have the beneficial effect of lowering the cost of adjudication, providing speedier decisions, and relieving the workload of the courts.

Currently, the Transportation Safety Act of 1974 authorizes the Material Transportation Bureau of the U.S. Department of Transportation (DOT) to determine whether a state law or rule is preempted.[26] In 1984, DOT introduced consistency rulings of the Materials Transportation Bureau by highlighting:

Despite the dominant role that Congress contemplated for departmental standards, there are certain aspects of hazardous materials transportation that are not amenable to exclusive nationwide regulation. One example is traffic control. Although the federal government can regulate in order to establish certain national standards promoting the safe, smooth flow of highway traffic, maintaining this in the face of short-term disruptions is necessarily a predominantly local responsibility. Another aspect of hazardous materials transportation that is not amenable to nationwide regulation is the problem of safety hazards which are peculiar to a local area.[27]

This statement reveals that DOT weighs the interests of states prior to issuing its consistency rulings. We are convinced that national departments and agencies would weigh state interests carefully in adjudicating cases in which it has been alleged that a state had created barriers to the free flow of commerce among sister states given, among other factors, the potential for appeal and review by the courts.

Congress also possesses plenary power to curtail state tax revenue competition but, unfortunately, has employed the power only to an extremely limited extent. Respecting the nature of the federal union, Congress naturally is reluctant to curtail the revenue-raising capacity of semisovereign states. The lack of congressional action has produced a most undesirable situation relative to the taxation of multistate and multinational corporations by states, since their respective tax-systems are not uniform, thereby placing an undue compliance burden upon the firms and in a number of instances unfairly taxing firms. It would be highly desirable if Congress enacted tax jurisdiction standards, apportionment rules, and tax-base definitions that must be employed by states in order to establish a nationally uniform system of corporate taxation. The failure of states to cooperate fully in taxing interstate commerce, despite the good work of the Multistate Tax Commission, justifies congressional enactment of a comprehensive tax regulatory scheme.

Congress could employ tax credits and cross-over sanctions to promote nationally uniform state business taxes. In 1935, Congress decided that it was essential to have a national unemployment compensation system and included a section in the Social Security Act imposing a national unemployment compensation tax on employers and authorizing a 90-percent tax credit for employers who pay unemployment taxes to a state.[28] This provision encouraged employers to pressure their respective state legislatures to establish an unemployment system based on national standards which would relieve them of 90 percent of the state tax. An alternative approach would be the use of a cross-over sanction threatening a state with the loss of national grants-in-aid if it failed to enact a uniform tax statute.

Interstate competition for industrial firms does not benefit the nation and is costly for many states. Congress has placed a cap on the amount of private activity bonds issued by states, but the cap has not been effective in limiting the issuance of bonds by states to raise funds for industrial development purposes. Congress could reduce such competition by enacting a statute stipulating that the interest on municipal bonds issued for industrial development purposes would be taxable unless the bonds are issued to support the location of industrial firms in central city and rural poverty areas. Such a statute would not solve the problem completely because of the fungibility of funds; that is, bond revenue can be utilized to finance an eligible project, such as sewers, which thereby frees tax revenues planned for sewer projects for industrial development purposes.

The explosion in the number of congressional preemption statutes since 1965 has hindered interstate cooperation to a degree. Chapter 10 explained that state attorneys general have been prevented from cooperatively enforcing state deceptive practices suits against airlines by a 1994 U.S. Supreme Court decision that the Airline Deregulation Act of 1978 preempts state regulation.[29] Congress should review total preemption statutes and amend each statute that prevents states from cooperating with each other to solve a problem provided the barrier is not related directly to the major purpose of the statute.

Pooling of resources by two or more states in their common border areas is a most economical approach to developing public facilities in these areas. There are a number of examples of bridge and tunnel authorities, established by interstate compact, which are highly successful in achieving their respective goals, but there are relatively few examples of other public facilities constructed with bistate or multistate funds. As noted in Chapter 3, New Hampshire and Vermont have established two interstate school districts by compacts.

There are many other border areas in the United States where adequate resources for fully equipped and modern schools are lacking. The sharp drop in the number of school districts since the 1920s is attributable in large measure to the recognition that small schools cannot provide the facilities and range of curricula that can be provided by large schools. To encourage states to pool their resources, Congress could provide block grants to states for the purpose of promoting the development and operation of interstate facilities and programs.

Congress can encourage interstate cooperation by creation of special organizations to facilitate such cooperation. As explained in Chapter 10, Congress in 1960 established the National Driver Register to make the driving records of violators of motor vehicle laws of the fifty states available electronically to each state motor vehicle department.[30] The register has been highly successful in facilitating interstate cooperation by motor vehicle administrators. In 1993, the National Highway Traffic Safety Administration, operator of the register, recommended that Congress transfer responsibility for the register to the American Association of Motor Vehicle Administrators.[31]

The Water Resources Planning Act of 1965 created federal–interstate river basin commissions.[32] The Ohio River Basin Commission was organized in 1971—at the request of the governors of Illinois, Indiana, Kentucky, Maryland, North Carolina, Ohio, Pennsylvania, Virginia, and West Virginia—and charged with developing a comprehensive plan for managing the water and related land resources of the basin. Upon completion of the plan in 1981, the federal government withdrew from the commission, and it was reorganized as an interstate body.

In 1984, Congress established the State Justice Institute and appropriated funds to the institute to be used for grants to improve the administration of justice in state courts.[33] The institute has undertaken numerous projects promoting interstate cooperation, including national conferences on key issues affecting state and national courts, regional judicial education conferences, interstate child support projects, and curriculum adaptation projects to permit a state to adapt and test a model education program developed by another state or a national judicial education provider. The institute also fosters state court coordination and cooperation with the national judiciary which is essential in a federal system where certain types of cases may be heard in either the U.S. District Court or a state court, and these cases can be transferred from a state court to the District Court or vice versa.[34]

The institute, in addition, serves as a clearinghouse and center for dissemination of information on state judicial systems. Currently, the institute is governed by an eleven-member board appointed by the president with the advice and consent of the Senate, and includes six state court judges, a state court administrator, and four members of the public. The success of the institute suggests that it could be transferred to state control.

Chapter 10 analyzed uniform state laws and explained that only a small number of such laws had been enacted by all fifty states. There is no denying the fact that enactment of additional uniform laws, or parallel laws, by all state legislatures would be most helpful in facilitating interstate commerce and benefiting business firms and citizens. An effective method for promoting enactment of such laws, while respecting state sovereignty, would be congressional enactment of an "opt-out" statute relative to uniform laws that fall under the delegated powers of Congress. This action would force each state legislature to consider every uniform state law it has not enacted and probably would result in the enactment of each such law or a parallel statute. If a uniform law is a desirable one, it would be politically difficult for a state legislature to reject the uniform law.

U.S. representatives and senators from various regions historically have worked together to persuade Congress to appropriate funds to benefit their respective regions and encourage states to cooperate with each other. In 1976, the Northeast–Midwest Coalition was formed by 150 representatives and 36 senators formed the Northeast–Midwest Senate Coalition in 1978. Each coalition seeks to inform members of Congress of the impact of federal policies on the region and to promote interstate cooperation. Each coalition also has close ties to the Northeast–Midwest Institute which is a nonprofit policy center working to improve the region's economic vitality and environmental quality by publishing books and reports, developing policies, providing technical assistance, and sponsoring conferences and Capitol Hill briefings. Members of Congress from other regions could form similar coalitions which would help to raise consciousness of interstate relations in Congress.

The President

The president can be a major leader in solving interstate problems and mediating major regional disputes among states. The president also can command media attention at any time and bring the pressure of national public opinion to bear on Congress and/or states if they are failing to address adequately major problems involving interstate relations.

Presidents have been responsible for the establishment of national associations of state officials. The National Governors' Association traces its origin to a 1908 conference of governors convened by President Theodore R. Roosevelt, and the National Committee for Uniform Traffic Laws and Ordinances was created in 1929 at the request of President Herbert C. Hoover.

The proliferation of national grants to state and local governments persuaded recent presidents to establish one or more offices devoted to intergovernmental relations. These offices unfortunately do not focus attention on interstate relations. The president should direct the intergovernmental affairs offices to examine such relations and develop proposals for implementation by Congress, the president, and national departments and agencies.

In common with governors, the president should include a section on the state of interstate relations in the annual State of the Union message proposing actions to make the union of the states a more perfect one as called for in the preamble to the U.S. Constitution. In addition, it would be helpful if the president occasionally sent a special message to Congress dealing with a major interstate problem and containing suggested legislation for solving the problem.

Cabinet Secretaries and Agency Administrators

These officials possess relatively broad discretionary authority to initiate actions to improve interstate relations and solve multistate problems. Conjoint state solutions of certain interstate problems are hindered by the lack of coordination of national departments and agencies having overlapping regulatory responsibilities. Fourteen departments and agencies, for example, are involved with water, which is a particularly acute problem in the arid states of the west. The establishment of additional federal interagency agreements could prove helpful to the states in their joint efforts to solve common problems.

U.S. departments have been successful in promoting interstate cooperation. An example is the role of the U.S. Department of Agriculture in encouraging states to agree on a numbering system for highways. By the early 1920s many major highways were named—Lincoln Highway and Dixie Highway are examples—and markers were erected by numerous trail associations. Each of the latter pressured Congress and state legislatures for funds to improve its highway, and rational long-range planning of highway development by state highway departments was hindered. In 1924, the American Association of State Highway Officials (AASHO) requested the secretary of agriculture, who had jurisdiction over the Bureau of Public Roads, to appoint a joint board to design a numbering and marking system.[35]

The board, composed of twenty-one state highway engineers and three bureau engineers, was appointed by the secretary and developed a numbering system for major highways with even numbers running east to west and odd numbers running north to south. The board also designed highway markers and recommended that AASHO be responsible for implementing the new system. The recommendation was approved and AASHO today retains responsibility for approving all additions or changes to U.S.-numbered highways.

The U.S. Department of Agriculture also has a long history of encouraging states to cooperate in the eradication of insect pests and plant diseases, and the U.S. Fish and Wildlife Service has been an effective promoter of interstate cooperation. Although the service is authorized by the Atlantic Striped Bass Conservation Act Amendments of 1986 to impose a moratorium on striped bass fishing in the coastal waters of any state failing to comply with the management plan developed by the

Atlantic States Marines Fisheries Commission which lacks enforcement powers, the service has not needed to use the moratorium to obtain compliance.[36]

The success of the 1986 act persuaded Congress to enact the Atlantic Coastal Fisheries Management Act of 1993 which applies the 1986 act to other coastal inter-jurisdictional fish—American shad, river herring, summer flounder, and weakfish.[37] The service does not intend "to impose a moratorium, but its threatened use brings the partners to the bargaining table."[38] Assistant Regional Director (Fisheries) James G. Geiger of the service is convinced the 1993 act "will bring the states and the federal agencies together with the same spirit and commitment that has been realized in striped bass management."[39]

In executing its responsibilities under national minimum standards preemption statutes, such as the Clean Air Act as amended, the EPA could encourage states granted regulatory primacy jointly to initiate actions to improve environmental quality.[40] Other national regulatory agencies could take similar action.

National departments and agencies, in a quiet and noncoercive manner, could mobilize concerned states to cooperate in solving regional problems. EPA, for example, in 1995 announced a comprehensive plan it developed, in cooperation with eight Great Lakes states, to restore the health and economy of the lakes.[41] The agency not only mobilized the states, but also involved industry, citizen groups, municipalities, and academia in the six-year program.

National departments and agencies also can form joint task forces with their state counterparts to conduct investigations and research, and enforce regulatory standards. The nature of the work of task forces would differ considerably because of variations in the provisions of national and state laws on each subject. In 1995, for example, the Federal Trade Commission launched a crackdown on funeral homes with state attorneys general to detect homes that fail to give consumers price lists and other information to which they are legally entitled.[42]

Another approach to attacking regional problems is national grants to private organizations to work with groups of states in developing solutions for regional problems. In 1995, EPA made a $200,000 grant to the Chicago Board of Trade which—in partnership with the National Recycling Coalition's Recycling Advisory Council, Washington State's Clean Washington Center, and the New York State Office of Recycling Market Development—will organize an electronic cash exchange for trading recyclable commodities.[43] The exchange will link buyers and sellers of recyclable materials, standardize market information, and provide for price and quality discovery for recyclables.

Federal–Interstate Compact Commissions

Commissions created by interstate compact and by federal interstate compacts play important roles in encouraging cooperation by sister states. The Washington Metropolitan Area Transit Authority was created by an interstate compact entered into in 1967 by the District of Columbia, Maryland, and Virginia.[44] The authority promotes interstate and national government cooperation by lobbying parties to the compact and Congress. The authority is seeking dedicated funding but is aware the source will be different in each state and the District. The authority also is seeking to expand its metro rail system which will require additional state and national government funding.

General Counsel Richard A. Cairo of the Susquehanna River Basin Commission, created by a federal interstate compact, wrote in 1995 that "each time the commission meets, the dialogue among its members is an exercise in cooperation which often heads off possible disputes and identifies areas where the states can work together either on their own initiative or through the commission."[45] He added that the commission serves as an administrative forum to settle any dispute that arises over the waters of the basin, thereby making unnecessary a court suit which would be "more expensive, time consuming, and unpredictable."[46]

Commission encouragement has resulted in Pennsylvania channeling funding to the commission to monitor nutrient levels in the Chesapeake Bay even though the benefits of the project are greater for Maryland. The commission currently is encouraging New York to join the Bay program which involves the District of Columbia, Maryland, Pennsylvania, and Virginia. In addition, the commission and various Maryland, Pennsylvania, and national government agencies intervened in the relicensing proceedings for four lower Susquehanna River hydro-electric projects. The licensees were ordered to undertake a shad restoration program and to construct fish passage facilities. Maryland and Pennsylvania also cooperated by closing the river to shad fishing.

CONCLUDING COMMENTS

A crowded legislative agenda, particularly in states with a constitutional limit on the length of the legislative session, and relatively little legislator interest in interstate relations combine to guarantee the continuation of most current interstate laws and policies unless legislative leaders and governors place interstate relations high on their respective agendas, or Congress initiates actions encouraging states to harmonize conflicting laws and cooperate with each other.

Interstate trade barriers fortunately may be reduced by recent international treaties entered into by the United States. The North American Free Trade Agreement of 1993 (NAFTA) and the General Agreement on Trade and Tariffs of 1994 (GATT) contain broad provisions requiring signatory nations to remove impediments to international trade, including ones created by states employing their police, licensing, and tax powers.[47] The Federation of State Medical Boards of the United States, for example, examined the former treaty in 1993 and concluded that "some state medical boards' requirements concerning citizenship and permanent residency will be affected by NAFTA."[48]

If states fail to exercise their reserved powers in a cooperative manner and to replace the labyrinth of conflicting laws impeding commerce by harmonizing their civil statutes, Congress will continue to preempt on occasion their regulatory authority. Professor Graves' 1938 statement is applicable in the late 1990s: "No student of government can reasonably protest the transfer to the federal government of powers which the states are either unable or unwilling to use effectively."[49]

Congressional action to solve interstate problems will tend to be of the nature of continual tinkering rather than comprehensive reform of interstate relations. The failure of Congress to lead in this area is even more alarming in view of the current drive in Congress to devolve to states more powers which have the potential for creating additional nonuniformity problems. States, for example, currently are raising barriers to the migration of welfare recipients.[50]

If Congress continues to preempt occasionally the regulatory authority of the states over a long period of time, the weakening of the federal nature of the union will deprive the system of a number of its advantages, including the ability of states to respond quickly to solve a state or regional problem and to serve as laboratories of democracies engaged in experimental service delivery and regional and national problem solving programs which can be exported, if successful, to other states and Congress. Furthermore, preemption will reduce opportunities for citizens to play important participatory roles in the governance system.

Can the undesirable consequences of current state policies affecting sister states and congressional preemption be avoided? The answer is yes provided key components of the model presented in this chapter are adopted. Political realities, however, suggest that few model components will be implemented in the near future.

NOTES

1. For details, see Joseph F. Zimmerman, *Federal Preemption: The Silent Revolution* (Ames: Iowa State University Press, 1991).

2. Joseph F. Zimmerman, *Contemporary American Federalism: The Growth of National Power* (Leicester: Leicester University Press, 1992).

3. *Bus Regulatory Reform Act of 1982*, 96 Stat. 1104, 49 U.S.C.A. §10521 (1995).

4. *Full Faith and Credit for Child Support Orders Act of 1994*, 108 Stat. 4063, 28 U.S.C.A. §1 note (1995 Supp.), and *Child Support Recovery Act of 1992*, 106 Stat. 3403, 18 U.S.C.A. §228(a)(d)(1)(A) (1995 Supp.).

5. *Jenkins Act of 1949*, 63 Stat. 884, 15 U.S.C.A. §375 (1976).

6. *Contraband Cigarette Act of 1978*, 53 Stat. 1291, 18 U.S.C.A. §2341 (1993).

7. *Commonwealth Edison Company v. Montana*, 453 U.S. 609 (1981).

8. *Barclays Bank v. Franchise Tax Board of California*, 114 S.Ct. 2268 (1994).

9. 71 Stat. 555, 15 U.S.C.A. §§381–4 (1995 Supp.).

10. *Pure Food and Drug Act of 1906*, 34 Stat. 768, 21 U.S.C.A. §16 (1972).

11. *National Labor Relations Act of 1935*, 49 Stat. 449, 29 U.S.C.A. §151 (1973 and 1995 Supp.).

12. W. Brooke Graves, "Influence of Congressional Legislation on Legislation in the States," *Iowa Law Review*, May 1938, pp. 520–1. Professor Graves quoted a manuscript loaned to him by Professor Grant.

13. *Ibid.*, p. 420.

14. Jonathan R. Macey and Geoffrey P. Miller, *Costly Policies: State Regulation and Antitrust Exemption in Insurance Markets* (Washington, D.C.: The AEI Press, 1993), p. 35.

15. *NAIC 1994 Annual Report* (Kansas City, MO: National Association of Insurance Commissioners, 1995), p. 3.

16. *Ibid.*, p. 9.

17. *Surface Transportation Assistance Act of 1982*, 96 Stat. 2097, 23 U.S.C.A. §101 (1994).

18. *Interstate Commerce Act of 1887*, 49 Stat. 543, 49 U.S.C.A. §303 (1963) and 71 Stat. 555, 15 U.S.C.A. §§381–4 (1995 Supp.).

19. *Quill Corporation v. North Dakota*, 112 S.Ct. 1904 at 1916 (1992).

20. *Virginia v. Tennessee*, 148 U.S. 503 (1893).

21. Robert H. Jackson, "The Supreme Court and Interstate Barriers," *The Annals*, January 1940, p. 77.

22. *Interstate Horseracing Act of 1978*, 92 Stat. 1811, 15 U.S.C.A. §3004 (1982).

23. *Kentucky Division, Horsemen's Benevolent & Protective Association Incorporated v. Turfway Park Racing Association*, 20 F.3d 1406 (1994).

24. *McCarren–Ferguson Act of 1945*, 59 Stat. 33, 15 U.S.C.A. §1011 (1976).

25. For examples, see *Prudential Insurance Company v. Benjamin*, 328 U.S. 408 (1946), and *Metropolitan Life Insurance Company v. Ward*, 470 U.S. 869 (1985).

26. *Transportation Safety Act of 1974*, 88 Stat. 2156, 49 U.S.C.A. §1801 (1976).

27. Department of Transportation, "Hazardous Materials: Inconsistency Rulings IR-7 through IR-15," *Federal Register*, November 27, 1984, p. 46633.

28. *Social Security Act of 1935*, 46 Stat. 620, 42 U.S.C.A. §510 (1991).

29. *Morales v. Trans World Airlines, Incorporated*, 112 S.Ct. 2031 (1992). See also Joseph F. Zimmerman and Sharon Lawrence, *Federal Statutory Preemption of State and Local Authority* (Washington, D.C.: U.S. Advisory Commission on Interstate Relations, 1992).

30. *National Driver Register Act of 1960* as modified by the *National Driver Register Act of 1982*, 96 Stat. 1740, 23 U.S.C.A. §401 note (1990 and 1995 Supp.). See also 23 CFR 1325 and 1327.

31. *A Report to Congress: NHTSA's Involvement in the National Driver Register* (Washington, D.C.: National Highway Traffic Safety Administration, 1993), p. 43.

32. *Water Resources Planning Act of 1965*, 79 Stat. 244, 42 U.S.C.A. §1962 (1994 and 1995 Supp.).

33. *State Justice Institute Act of 1984*, 98 Stat. 3335, 28 U.S.C.A. §620 and 42 U.S.C.A. §10701 (1995 Supp.).

34. Zimmerman, *Contemporary American Federalism*, pp. 82–102.

35. The information in this paragraph and the following paragraph is taken from Frederick W. Cron, "Touring by Numbers—Why and How," *Public Works*, February 1968, pp. 80–2, 140 and 142.

36. *Atlantic Striped Bass Conservation Act Amendments of 1986*, 100 Stat. 989, 16 U.S.C.A. §1851 note (1995 Supp.).

37. *Atlantic Coastal Fisheries Management Act of 1993*, 107 Stat. 2447, 16 U.S.C.A. §5101 (1995 Supp.).

38. Telephone interview with Ronald Howey of the U.S. Fish & Wildlife Service, July 25, 1995.

39. Letter from Assistant Regional Director (Fisheries) James G. Geiger of the U.S. Fish & Wildlife Service dated July 27, 1995, p. 1.

40. *Clean Air Act Amendments of 1990*, 104 Stat. 2448, 42 U.S.C.A. §7511c (1995 Supp.).

41. "EPA & States to Restore Great Lakes," *EPA Activities Update*, April 17, 1995, p. 1.

42. "Nationwide Crackdown on Funeral Homes that Fail to Provide Required Information Launched by FTC with State Attorneys General," *FTC News Notes* (Federal Trade Commission), July 3, 1995, p. 1.

43. "Electronic Cash Exchange Developed for Trading Recyclable Commodities," *EPA Activities Update*, April 17, 1995, p. 3.

44. Resolution of December 22, 1960, of the Commissioners of the District of Columbia, Chapter 613 of the Maryland Acts of 1959, and Chapter 627 of the Virginia Acts of 1958. Congress granted its consent in 1966. See 80 Stat. 1324.

45. Letter to the author from General Counsel Richard A. Cairo of the Susquehanna River Basin Commission dated July 24, 1995, p. 1. Information in the following paragraph is taken from this source.

46. *Ibid.*

47. See the *North American Free Trade Agreement of 1993*, 107 Stat. 2057.

48. "Federation of State Medical Boards," *Congressional Record*, November 24, 1993, p. E 32052.

49. Graves, "Influence of Congressional Legislation on Legislation in the States," p. 538.

50. Sanford F. Schram and Gary Krueger, "'Welfare Magnets' and Benefit Decline: Symbolic Problems and Substantive Consequences," *Publius*, Fall 1994, pp. 61–82.

Bibliography

Books

Bard, E. *The Port of New York Authority*. Columbia University Press, New York, 1941.

Barton, W. V. *Interstate Compacts in the Political Process*. University of North Carolina Press, Chapel Hill, 1967.

Bird, F. L. *A Study of the Port of New York Authority*. Dun & Bradstreet, New York, 1948.

The Book of the States: 1994–95. The Council of State Governments, Lexington, KY, 1994.

Bradshaw, M. *The Appalachian Regional Commission*. The University Press of Kentucky, Lexington, 1992.

Break, G. F. *Financing Government in a Federal System*. The Brookings Institution, Washington, D.C., 1980.

———. *Intergovernmental Fiscal Relations in the United States*. The Brookings Institution, Washington, D.C., 1967.

Cardozo, B. *The Paradoxes of Legal Science*. Harvard University Press, Cambridge, MA, 1928.

Commager, H. S., ed. *Documents of American History to 1898*, 8th ed. Appleton-Century-Crofts, New York, 1968.

Danielson, M. and Doig, J. W. *New York: The Politics of Urban Regional Development*. University of California Press, Berkeley, 1982.

Deloria, V., Jr. *A Brief History of the Federal Responsibility to the American Indian*. U.S. Department of Health, Education, and Welfare, Washington, D.C., 1979.

——— and Lytle, Clifford M. *American Indians, American Justice*. University of Texas Press, Austin, 1983.

Derthick, M. *Between State and Nation*. The Brookings Institution, Washington, D.C., 1974.

Due, J. F. and Mikesell, J. L. *Sales Taxation: State and Local Structure and Administration*, 2nd ed. The Urban Institute Press, Washington, D.C., 1994.

An Examination of the Tax Incentives and Economic Consequences of Cross-Border Activity. American Legislative Exchange Council, Washington, D.C., 1992.

Farrand, M. *The Records of the Federal Convention of 1787*. Yale University Press, New Haven, 1966.

The Federalist Papers. New American Library, New York, 1961.

Fesler, J. W. *The 50 States and Their Local Governments*. Alfred A. Knopf, Incorporated, New York, 1967.

Frankfurter, F. *The Commerce Clause Under Marshall, Taney, and Waite.* University of North Carolina Press, Chapel Hill, 1937.

Gere, E. A. *Rivers and Regionalism in New England.* Bureau of Government Research, University of Massachusetts, Amherst, 1968.

Graves, W. B. *Uniform State Action: A Possible Substitute for Centralization.* University of North Carolina Press, Chapel Hill, 1934.

Handbook of High-Level Radioactive Waste Transportation. The Midwestern Office of the Council of State Governments, Lombard, IL, 1992.

Handbook of Interstate Crime Control. The Council of State Governments, Chicago, 1942.

Hardy, P. T. *Interstate Compacts: The Ties that Bind.* Institute of Government, University of Georgia, Athens, 1982.

Hellerstein, J. and Hellerstein, W. *State and Local Taxation: Cases and Materials,* 5th ed. West Publishing Company, St. Paul, MN, 1988.

Hines, J. R., Jr. *Altered States: Taxes and the Location of Foreign Direct Investment in America.* National Bureau of Economic Research, Incorporated, Cambridge, MA, 1993.

Implementation of Indian Gaming Regulatory Act: Hearing Before the Select Committee on Indian Affairs, United States Senate, February 5, March 18, and May 6, 1992. U.S. Government Printing Office, Washington, D.C., 1992.

To Improve Cooperation Among the States. The Council of State Governments, Chicago, 1962.

Interstate Compacts: 1783–1970: A Compilation. The Council of State Governments, Lexington, KY, 1971.

Interstate River Basin Development. The Council of State Governments, Chicago, 1947.

Jackson, R. H. *Full Faith and Credit: The Lawyer's Clause of the Constitution.* Columbia University Press, New York, 1945.

Kayne, J. and Shonka, M. *Rethinking State Development Policies and Programs.* National Governors' Association, Washington, D.C., 1994.

Kenyon, D. and Kincaid, J., eds. *Competition Among States and Local Governments: Efficiency and Equity in American Federalism.* The Urban Institute Press, Washington, D.C., 1991.

Kickingbird, K., et al. *Indian Treaties.* Institute for the Development of Indian Law, Washington, D.C., 1980.

Kollin, S. *Interstate Sanitation Commission: A Discussion of the Development and Administration of an Interstate Compact.* Syracuse University Press, Syracuse, NY, 1954.

KPMG Peat Marwick Economic Policy Group. *Effects of Cross-Border Sales on Economic Activity and State Revenues: A Case Study of Tobacco Excise Taxes in Massachusetts, New York City, and Surrounding Areas.* Tax Foundation, Washington, D.C., 1993.

Laski, H. J. *The American Democracy.* The Viking Press, New York, 1948.

Leach, R. H. *Interstate Relations in Australia.* University of Kentucky Press, Lexington, 1965.

———— and Sugg, R. S., Jr.. *The Administration of Interstate Compacts.* Louisiana State University Press, Baton Rouge, 1959.

Leuchtenburg, W. *Flood Control Politics: The Connecticut River Valley Problem 1927–1950.* Harvard University Press, Cambridge, MA, 1953.

Macey, J. R. and Miller, G. P. *Costly Policies: State Regulation and Antitrust Exemptions in Insurance Markets.* The AEI Press, Waldorf, MD, 1993.

Maine Directory of Occupational Licensing. Maine Division of Economic Analysis and Research, Augusta, 1984.

Martin, R. E. *et al. River Basin Administration and the Delaware*. Syracuse University Press, Syracuse, NY, 1960.

McClure, C. E., Jr.. *Economic Perspectives on State Taxation of Multijurisdictional Corporations*. Tax Analysts, Arlington, VA, 1986.

Melder, F. E. *State and Local Barriers to Interstate Commerce in the United States: A Study in Economic Sectionalism*. University Press, Orono, ME, 1937.

Model Regulations, Statutes, and Guidelines: Uniformity Recommendations to the States. Multistate Tax Commission, Washington, D.C., 1995.

Munro, W. B. *The Government of the United States*, 4th ed. The Macmillan Company, New York, 1937.

Murphy, B. M. *Conservation of Oil & Gas: A Legal History, 1948*. Section on Mineral Law, American Bar Association, Chicago, 1949.

O'Brien, S. *American Indian Tribal Governments*. University of Oklahoma Press, Norman, 1980.

Report on Mutual Aid Agreements for Radiological Transportation Emergencies. The Midwestern Office of the Council of State Governments, Lombard, IL, 1993.

Rethinking State Development Policies and Programs. National Governors Association, Washington, D.C., 1994.

Ridgeway, M. E. *Interstate Compacts: A Question of Federalism*. Southern Illinois University Press, Carbondale, 1971.

Rothblatt, D. M. *Regional Planning: The Appalachian Experience*. Lexington Books, Lexington, MA, 1971.

Saxon, J. L. *Enforcement and Modification of Out-of-State Child Support Orders*. Institute of Government, University of North Carolina, Chapel Hill, 1994.

Scott, J. A. *The Law of Interstate Rendition Erroneously Referred to as Interstate Extradition: A Treatise*. Sherman Hight, Publisher, Chicago, 1917.

Selznick, P. *TVA and the Grass Roots*. The University of California Press, Berkeley, 1949.

Shavior, D. *Federalism in Taxation*. The AEI Press, Washington, D.C., 1993.

Smith, A. *An Inquiry into the Nature and Causes of the Wealth of Nations*. The Modern Library, New York, 1937.

Snell, R. K. *Weight-Distance Taxes and Other Highway User Taxes: An Introduction for Legislators and Legislative Staff*. National Conference of State Legislatures, Denver, CO, 1989.

Story, J. *Commentaries on the Constitution of the United States*. Hilliard, Gray, and Company, Boston, 1833.

Sugg, R. S., Jr.. and Jones, G. H. *The Southern Regional Education Board: Ten Years of Regional Cooperation in Higher Education*. Louisiana State University Press, Baton Rouge, 1960.

Suggested State Legislation 1996. The Council of State Governments, Lexington, KY, 1996.

Summary of State Laws & Regulations Relating to Distilled Spirits. Distilled Spirits Council of the United States, Incorporated, Washington, D.C., 1993.

Tax Briefs 1994: Federal and State & Local Revenue Per Gallon of Alcohol, 1992. Distilled Spirits Council of the United States, Incorporated, Washington, D.C., 1994.

Taylor, G. R., Burtis, E. L., and Waught, F. V. *Barriers to Internal Trade in Farm Products*. U.S. Government Printing Office, Washington, D.C., 1939.

Technical Documents and Newsletters. Conference of Southern County Associations Regional Solid Waste/Environmental Network, Atlanta, 1993.

Thursby, V. V. *Interstate Cooperation: A Study of the Interstate Compact*. Public Affairs Press, Washington, D.C., 1953.

Voigt, W., Jr.. *The Susquehanna Compact*. Rutgers University Press, New Brunswick, NJ, 1972.

Voit, K. *Interstate Compacts & Agencies*. The Council of State Governments, Lexington, KY, 1995.

Voting with Their Feet: A Study of Tax Incentives and Economic Consequences of Cross-Border Activity in New England. American Legislative Exchange Council, Washington, D.C., 1992.

Voting with Their Feet II: The Economic Consequences of Cross-Border Activity in the Southeastern U.S. American Legislative Exchange Council, Washington, D.C., 1993.

Zimmerman, D. *The Private Use of Tax-Exempt Bonds: Controlling Public Subsidy of Private Activity*. The Urban Institute Press, Washington, D.C., 1991.

Zimmerman, J. F. *Contemporary American Federalism: The Growth of National Power*. Leicester University Press, Leicester, 1992.

————. *Federal Preemption: The Silent Revolution*. Iowa State University Press, Ames, 1991.

————. *State-Local Relations: A Partnership Approach*, 2nd ed. Praeger Publishers, Westport, CT, 1995.

Zimmermann, F. L. and Wendell, M. *The Interstate Compact Since 1925*. The Council of State Governments, Chicago, 1951.

Zimmermann, F. L. and Wendell, M. *The Law and Use of Interstate Compacts*. The Council of State Governments, Chicago, 1976.

Public Documents

Agency Out of Control. A Critical Assessment of the Finances of the Port Authority of New York and New Jersey. Committee on Corporations, Authorities, and Commissions, New York State Assembly, Albany, 1982.

Barriers to the Development and Expanded Use of Natural Gas Resources. Interstate Oil and Gas Compact Commission, Oklahoma City, 1992.

Child Support Enforcement: Families Could Benefit from Stronger Enforcement Program. U.S. General Accounting Office, Washington, D.C., 1995.

Child Support Enforcement: Fifteenth Annual Report to Congress. U.S. Department of Health and Human Resources, Washington, D.C., 1992.

Child Support Enforcement: Sixteenth Annual Report to Congress. U.S. Department of Health and Human Services, Washington, D.C., 1993.

Cigarette Bootlegging: A State and Federal Responsibility. U.S. Advisory Commission on Intergovernmental Relations, Washington, D.C., 1977.

Cigarette Tax Evasion: A Second Look. U.S. Advisory Commission on Intergovernmental Relations, Washington, D.C., 1985.

Combatting Cigarette Smuggling. Law Enforcement Assistance Administration, Washington, D.C., 1976.

The Commuter and the Municipal Income Tax. U.S. Advisory Commission on Intergovernmental Relations, Washington, D.C., 1970.

The Compact's Formative Years: 1931–1935. Interstate Oil Compact Commission, Oklahoma City, 1954.

Criminal Penalty for Flight to Avoid Payment of Arrearages in Child Support: Hearing Before the Subcommittee on Crime and Criminal Justice, United States House of Representatives. U.S. Government Printing Office, Washington, D.C., 1992.

Department of Agriculture and Markets Annual Report 1992. Albany, NY, 1993.

Directory of Intergovernmental Contacts. U.S. Advisory Commission on Intergovernmental Relations, Washington, D.C., 1994.

Effectiveness of Enterprise Zones: Hearing Before the Committee on Finance, United States Senate. U.S. Government Printing Office, Washington, D.C., 1992.

Establish Federal Standards and Regulations for the Conduct of Gaming Activities Within Indian Country. Hearing before the Select Committee on Indian Affairs, United States Senate on S. 902, June 17, 1986. U.S. Government Printing Office, Washington, D.C., 1986.

Finding Common Ground: Conserving the Northern Forest. Northern Forest Lands Council, Concord, NH, 1994.

Florestano, P. S. *A Survey of the Interstate Compacts in Which the State of Maryland Currently has Membership.* Maryland Commission in Intergovernmental Cooperation, Annapolis, 1972.

The "Full Faith and Credit" Clause of the United States Constitution. The Virginia Commission on Constitutional Government, Richmond, n.d.

Gaming Activities on Indian Reservations and Lands. Hearing Before the Select Committee on Indian Affairs, United States Senate on S. 555, June 18, 1987. U.S. Government Printing Office, Washington, D.C., 1987.

Grade "A" Pasteurized Milk Ordinance. Food and Drug Administration, Washington, D.C., 1993.

The Impact of State Economic Regulation of Motor Carriage on Intrastate and Interstate Commerce. U.S. Department of Transportation, Washington, D.C., 1990.

Implementation of the Indian Gaming Regulatory Act. Hearing Before the Select Committee on Indian Affairs, United States Senate, February 5, 1992, Part 1. U.S. Government Printing Office, Washington, D.C., 1992.

Implementation of the Indian Gaming Regulatory Act. Hearing Before the Select Committee on Indian Affairs, United States Senate, March 18, 1992, Part 2. U.S. Government Printing Office, Washington, D.C., 1992.

Implementation of the Indian Gaming Regulatory Act. Hearing Before the Select Committee on Indian Affairs, United States Senate, May 6, 1992, Part 3. U.S. Government Printing Office, Washington, D.C., 1992.

IMS List Sanitation Compliance and Enforcement Ratings of Interstate Milk Shippers. Food and Drug Administration, Washington, D.C., 1993.

Indian Issues: Eastern Indian Land Claims and Their Resolution. U.S. General Accounting Office, Washington, D.C., 1994.

Industrial Development Bonds: Achievement of Public Benefit is Unclear. U.S. General Accounting Office, Washington, D.C., 1993.

Interjurisdictional Tax and Policy Competition: Good or Bad for the Federal System. U.S. Advisory Commission on Intergovernmental Relations, Washington, D.C., 1991.

Interstate Banking: Benefits and Risks of Removing Regulatory Restrictions. U.S. Government Printing Office, Washington, D.C., 1993.

Interstate Banking: Experiences in Three Western States. U.S. Government Printing Office, Washington, D.C., 1994.

Interstate Child Support: Better Information Needed on Absent Parents for Case Pursuit. U.S. General Accounting Office, Washington, D.C., 1990.

Interstate Child Support: Case Data Limitations, Enforcement Problems, Views on Improvements Needed. U.S. General Accounting Office, Washington, D.C., 1989.

Interstate Child Support: Mothers Report Receiving Less Support from Out-of-State Fathers. U.S. General Accounting Office, Washington, D.C., 1992.

Interstate Child Support Remedies. U.S. Department of Health and Human Resources, Washington, D.C., 1989.

Interstate Child Support: Wage Withholding Not Fulfilling Expectations. U.S. General Accounting Office, Washington, D.C., 1992.

Interstate Tax Competition. U.S. Advisory Commission on Intergovernmental Relations, Washington, D.C., 1981.

Inventory of New York State Compacts. New York State Senate Select Committee on Interstate Cooperation, Albany, 1988.

Local Boundary Commissions: Status and Role in Forming, Adjusting, and Dissolving Local Government Boundaries. U.S. Advisory Commission on Intergovernmental Relations, Washington, D.C., 1992.

Memorandum Report to the Legislature: Interstate Sanitation Commission. New York State Legislative Commission on Expenditure Review, Albany, 1990.

Multistate Regionalism. U.S. Advisory Commission on Intergovernmental Relations, Washington, D.C., 1972.

NAIC 1994 Annual Report. National Association of Insurance Commissioners, Kansas City, MO, 1995.

National Capital Section, American Water Resources Association. *A 1980's View of Water Management in the Potomac River Basin*. U.S. Government Printing Office, Washington, D.C., 1982.

The National Guard: Defending the Nation and the States. U.S. Advisory Commission on Intergovernmental Relations, Washington, D.C., 1993.

New Directions for Regional Planning. The Report of the Governors' Task Force on the Future of the Tri-State Regional Planning Commission, New York, 1981.

A 1980's View of Water Management in the Potomac River Basin: A Report for the Committee on Governmental Affairs, United States Senate. U.S. Government Printing Office, Washington, D.C., 1982.

1986 Annual Report. New York State Senate Select Committee on Interstate Cooperation, Albany, 1986.

1990 Annual Report. New York State Senate Select Committee on Interstate Cooperation, Albany, 1991.

1992 Annual Report. Albany, New York State Senate Select Committee on Interstate Cooperation, 1994.

1993 Annual Report. New York State Senate Select Committee on Interstate Cooperation, Albany, 1995.

1994 Driver License Administration Requirements and Fees. Federal Highway Administration, Washington, D.C., 1994.

Northeast-Midwest Congressional Coalition Financial Statements for 1992 and 1991. U.S. General Accounting Office, Washington, D.C., 1993.

Observations on the FBI's Interstate Identification Index. U.S. General Accounting Office, Washington, D.C., 1994.

Oversight and Reauthorization of the Appalachian Regional Commission and the Economic Development Administration: Hearing Before the Subcommittee on Water Resources, Transportation, and Infrastructure, United States Senate on H.R. 2015. U.S. Government Printing Office, Washington, D.C., 1990.

Participation of the Tri-State Regional Planning Commission in A-95 Project Notification and Review. Governor's Task Force on the Future of the Tri-State Regional Planning Commission, New York, 1980.

Purcell, M. R. *Interstate Barriers to Truck Transportation.* U.S. Department of Agriculture, Washington, D.C., 1950.

Regional Growth: Interstate Tax Competition. U.S. Advisory Commission on Intergovernmental Relations, Washington, D.C., 1981.

Report to Congress on Flow Control and Municipal Solid Waste. U.S. Environmental Protection Agency, Washington, D.C., 1995.

A Report to Congress: NHTSA's Involvement in the National Driver Register. National Highway Traffic Safety Administration, Washington, D.C., July 1993.

Report of the Interstate Commission on Child Support: Hearings Before the Subcommittee on Human Resources, United States House of Representatives. U.S. Government Printing Office, Washington, D.C., 1992.

Report of the Joint Legislative Committee on Interstate Cooperation. Albany, NY, 1962.

Report of the Joint Legislative Committee on Interstate Cooperation to the 1966 Legislature. The Committee, Albany, NY, 1966.

Revenue Diversification: State and Local Travel Taxes. U.S. Advisory Commission on Intergovernmental Relations, Washington, D.C., 1994.

Review and Evaluation of Port Authority of New York and New Jersey Actions Relative to Expense Account Irregularities. Office of the State Comptroller, Albany, 1978.

Should the Appalachian Regional Commission be Used as a Model for the Nation? U.S. General Accounting Office, Washington, D.C., 1979.

Staff of the Joint Committee on Taxation. *Trends in the Use of Tax-Exempt Bonds to Finance Private Activities, Including a Description of H.R. 1176 and H.R. 1635.* U.S. Government Printing Office, Washington, D.C., 1983.

State-Local Taxation and Industrial Location. U.S. Advisory Commission on Intergovernmental Relations, Washington, D.C., 1967.

State and Provincial Licensing System. National Highway Traffic Safety Administration Administration, Washington, D.C., 1990.

State Severance Taxes. Hearing Before the Subcommittee on Energy and Agricultural Taxation, United States Senate. U.S. Government Printing Office, Washington, D.C., 1984.

State Solvency Regulation of Property-Casualty and Life Insurance Companies. U.S. Advisory Commission on Intergovernmental Relations, Washington, D.C., 1992.

State Taxation of Interstate Mail Order Sales. U.S. Advisory Commission on Intergovernmental Relations, Washington, D.C., 1992.

"Supporting Our Children: A Blueprint for Reform:" The U.S. Commission on Interstate Child Support's Report to Congress. United States Government Printing Office, Washington, D.C., 1992.

Targeted Fiscal Assistance for Our Distressed Cities and Towns: Hearing Before the Task Force on Urgent Fiscal Issues of the Committee on the Budget, House of Representatives. U.S. Government Printing Office, Washington, D.C., 1992.

Tax Policy and Administration: California Taxes on Multinational Corporations and Related Federal Issues. U.S. General Accounting Office, Washington, D.C., 1995.

Tax Policy: Internal Revenue Code Provisions Relating to Tax-Exempt Bonds. U.S. General Accounting Office, Washington, D.C., 1991.

Taxation of Interstate Mail Order Sales: 1994 Revenue Estimates. U.S. ACIR, Washington, D.C., 1994.

Technical Documents and Newsletters. Conference of Southern County Associations, Atlanta, 1993.

Toward Quality Water. New England Interstate Water Pollution Control Commission, Boston, 1981.

A Tradition of Consumer Protection. National Association of Insurance Commissioners, Kansas City, MO, 1995.

Unitary Tax: Hearing Before the Subcommittee on International Economic Policy of the Committee on Foreign Relations, United States Senate, September 20, 1984. U.S. Government Printing Office, Washington, D.C., 1985.

U.S. Child Support: Needed Efforts Underway to Increase Collections from Absent Parents. U.S. General Accounting Office, Washington, D.C., 1984.

The Use of Interstate Compacts and Agreements in Illinois. Illinois Intergovernmental Cooperation Commission, Springfield, 1973.

The Volume Cap for Tax-Exempt Private-Activity Bonds: State and Local Experience in 1989. U.S. Advisory Commission on Intergovernmental Relations, Washington, D.C., 1990.

Zimmerman, J. F. and Lawrence, S. *Federal Statutory Preemption of State and Local Authority: History, Inventory, and Issues.* U.S. Advisory Commission on Intergovernmental Relations, Washington, D.C., 1992.

Articles

Abbey, A. B. "Cuomo Intensifies Bank Reform Effort." *Times Union* (Albany, N.Y.). (January 9, 1994), B-1 and B-6.

Abbott, F. C. "College Compacts Lower Costs for All." *State Government.* 63 (July–September 1990), 84–6.

"Act Aiding Sale of State Wines is Struck Down." *The New York Times.* (January 31, 1985), B3.

"Agreement Reached to Restore Long Island Sound." *EPA Activities Update.* (October 3, 1994), 1.

Aldrich, E. "Vt. Officials: There's Progress on Connecticut River Bridges." *The Keene (New Hampshire) Sentinel.* (March 30, 1993), 2.

"Attention Keds Purchasers." *Times Union* (Albany, N.Y.). (November 8, 1993), A-5.

"Attorneys: Interstate and Federal Practice." *Harvard Law Journal.* 80 (March 1967), 1711–29.

Baird, D. C. "Mineral Severance Taxes in Idaho: Considerations for the Legislature." *Idaho Law Review.* 19 (Summer 1983), 607–31.

Baraf, D. L. B. "The Foreign Corporation—A Problem in Choice-of-Law Doctrine." *Brooklyn Law Review.* 33 (1966–67), 219–52.

Batten, J. K. "Tax, Law Aides to Map Cigarette Bootleg War." *Knickerbocker News* (Albany, N.Y.). (August 30, 1967), 3B.

Baucus, M. "Montana Severance Tax—A Supreme Court Defense." *Congressional Record.* (March 25, 1981), S2677–80.

Beaver, J. E. "Common Law vs. International Law Adjective Rules in the Original Jurisdiction." *Hastings Law Journal.* 20 (November 1968), 1–75.

Bennett, J. "States Look to Share Data, Collect More Taxes." *City & State*. 10 (May 24, 1993), 13.

Berhovek, S. H. "Cuomo Turns Down Request to Extradite Cable Officials." *The New York Times*. (June 21, 1990), B4.

Berry, F. S. "State Regulation of Occupations and Professions." *The Book of the States: 1986–87 Edition*. The Council of State Governments, Lexington, KY, 1986, 379–83.

Berry, F. S. and Brinegar, P. L. "State Regulation of Occupations and Professions." *The Book of the States: 1990–91 Edition*. The Council of State Governments, Lexington, KY, 1990, 465–70.

Beyle, T. L. "New Directions in Interstate Relations." *The Annals*. 416 (November 1974), 108–19.

Bigart, H. "Jersey Routs Pennsylvania Spies in Border War on Whiskey Prices." *The New York Times*. (March 5, 1965), 1 and 26.

Blumenthal, R. "Byrne Again Opposes Port Unit: Vetoes Its Plan for Bus Projects." *The New York Times*. (February 11, 1982), 1 and 36.

Borchers, P. J. "Comparing Personal Jurisdiction in the United States and the European Community: Lessons for American Reform." *The American Journal of Comparative Law*. 40 (Winter 1992), 121–57.

———. "The Death of the Constitutional Law of Personnel Jurisdiction: From *Pennoyer* to *Burnham* and Back Again." *U.C. Davis Law Review*. 24 (Fall 1990), 19–105.

Brabner-Smith, J. W. "The Commerce Clause and the New Federal 'Extradition' Statute." *Illinois Law Review*. 29 (1934), 355–60.

Brandon, C. "Butt Smugglers." *Times Union* (Albany, N.Y.). (June 24, 1993), 1 and A-9.

Browne, M. W. "Seizure of Dinosaur Fossil Opens Legal Battle that Could Affect Museums." *The New York Times*. (May 21, 1992), B13.

Bruch, C. S. "The 1989 Inter-American Convention on Support Obligations." *The American Journal of Comparative Law*. 40 (1992), 201–40.

Brutus. "14 February 1778." In Ketcham, R. (ed.). *The Anti-Federalist Papers and The Constitutional Convention Debates*. New American Library, New York, 1966, 302–4.

Bucks, D. R. "Tax Competition: Patent Medicine for Economic Anxiety." *Multistate Tax Commission Review*. (May 1988), 1–4.

Bunch, K. and Hardy, R. J. "Continuity or Change in Interstate Extradition? Assessing *Puerto Rico v. Branstad*." *Publius*. 21 (Winter 1991), 51–67.

"Burns Extradition Refused by Moore." *The New York Times*. (December 22, 1932), 1 and 3.

Carman, E. C. "Should the States be Permitted to Make Compacts Without the Consent of Congress?" *Cornell Law Quarterly*. 23 (February 1938), 280–4.

Carrico, M. L. "'Te Pee' as in Taxpayers: Tribal Severance Taxes—Canvassing the Reservation—Do Tribes Have the Power to Impose Severance Taxes on Minerals Extracted on Non-Indian Fee Lands Within the Reservation?" *Journal of Mineral Law & Policy*. 7 (1991–92), 73–104.

Celler, E. "Congress, Compact, and Interstate Authorities." *Law and Contemporary Problems*. 26 (Autumn 1961), 682–702.

Cerf, C. D. "Federal Habeas Corpus Review of Nonconstitutional Errors: The Cognizability of Violations of the Interstate Agreement on Detainers." *Columbia Law Review*. 83 (May 1983), 975–1028.

Cheit, R. E. "State Adoption of Model Insurance Codes: An Empirical Analyses." *Publius*. 23 (Fall 1993), 49–70.

Chi, K. S. "Interstate Cooperation: Resurgence of Multistate Regionalism." *State Government*. 63 (July–September 1990), 59–63.

———. "State Business Incentives: Options for the Future." *State Trends Forecasts*. 3 (June 1994), 1–31.

"At Cigarette Tax Enforcement Conference, New York City, September 12, 1967." *Public Papers on Nelson A. Rockefeller: 1967*. Office of the Governor, Albany, NY, 1968, 1309–11.

Clark, T. R. "The Effect of Violations of the Interstate Agreement on Detainers on Subject Matter Jurisdiction." *Fordham Law Review*. 54 (October 1986), 1209–38.

Clinton, R. N. "Once Again, Indian Tribes are Losing Ground." *The National Law Journal*. 17 (December 19, 1994), A21-2.

Considine, J. L. "Cigarette Smuggling Big Business." *Knickerbocker News* (Albany, N.Y.). (January 22, 1971), 16A.

"Constitutional Aspects of State Extradition Legislation." *Indiana Law Journal*. 28 (Summer 1953), 662–71.

"Constitutional Law—Full Faith and Credit—Divorce Jurisdiction." *Rutgers Law Review*. 6 (Spring 1952), 615–7.

Cook, W. W. "The Logical and Legal Bases of the Conflict of Laws." *Yale Law Journal*. 33 (March 1924), 457–88.

"Cooperative Agreement on North Branch Potomac Signed." *Potomac Basin Report*. (November–December 1993), 4.

Corwin, E. S. "The "Full Faith and Credit" Clause." *University of Pennsylvania Law Review*. 81 (February 1933), 371–89.

Cox, G. D. "Change of Course: Status Quo Threatened on America's Most-Litigated River." *The National Law Journal*. 16 (September 13, 1993), 1 and 36.

Crihfield, B. and Reeves, H. C. "Intergovernmental Relations: A View From the States." *The Annals*. 416 (November 1974), 99–107.

Croce, B. "Firebirds Moving Home Base to Vermont." *Times Union* (Albany, N.Y.). (May 14, 1994), 1 and A-7.

Cron, F. W. "Touring by Numbers—Why and How." *Public Works*. (February 1967), 80–2, 140, and 142.

Crowe, K. C., II. "Pair to Answer Liquor-Smuggling Charges Today." *Times Union* (Albany, N.Y.). (June 9, 1994), B-7.

———. "State Stockpiling Contraband Liquor." *Times Union* (Albany, N.Y.). (December 9, 1993), B-1 and B-11.

"Cuomo, Puerto Rico Governor Sign Pact." *Times Union* (Albany, N.Y.). (August 16, 1994), B-2.

"Cuomo Warns N.J. to Let Yankees Alone." *Times Union* (Albany, N.Y.). (October 7, 1993), B-2.

Currie, B. and Schreter, H. H. "Unconstitutional Discrimination in the Conflict of Laws: Privileges and Immunities." *Yale Law Journal*. 69 (1969), 1323–91.

Dao, J. "Indians Offer State a Share of Monticello Casino Profits." *The New York Times*. (March 2, 1995), B6.

———. "States Joining in Combating Illegal Guns." *The New York Times*. (April 26, 1993), 1 and B7.

Davidson, D. "Political Regionalism and Administrative Regionalism." *The Annals*. 207 (January 1940), 138–43.

Department of Transportation. "Hazardous Materials: Inconsistency Rulings IR-7 through IR-15." *Federal Register*. (November 27, 1984), 46633.

Diamond, M. "What the Framers Meant by Federalism." In Goldwin, R. A. (ed.). *A Nation of States: Essays on the American Federal System*, 2nd ed. Rand McNally, Chicago, 1974, 25–42.

Dinan, J. P. "Puerto Rico *vs*. Branstad: The End of Gubernatorial Discretion in Extradition Proceedings." *Toledo Law Review*. 19 (Spring 1988), 649–82.

Disney, M. F. "A Municipally Owned Water Company Charging Nonresidents Higher Rates for Water Service than Residents." *Pepperdine Law Review*. 14 (1986–87), 1079–85.

Dodd, E. M., Jr.. "The Power of the Supreme Court to Review State Decisions in the Field of Conflict of Laws." *Harvard Law Review*. 39 (March 1926), 533–62.

Donovan, W. J. "State Compacts as a Method of Settling Problems Common to Several States." *University of Pennsylvania Law Review*. 80 (1931–32), 5–16.

Dougherty, P. "The Yanks Are Going—to Norwich." *Times Union* (Albany, N.Y.). (March 15, 1994), 1 and A-7.

Dunbar, L. W. "Interstate Compacts and Congressional Consent." *Virginia Law Review*. 36 (October 1950), 653–63.

Dunham, A. "A History of the National Conference of Commissioners on Uniform State Laws." *Law and Contemporary Problems*. 30 (Spring 1965), 233–49.

Durant, R. F. and Holmes, M. E. "Thou Shalt Not Covet Thy Neighbor's Water: The Rio Grande Basin Regulatory Experience." *Public Administration Review*. 45 (November–December 1985), 821–31.

"Durational Residence Requirements from Shapiro Through Sosna: The Right to Travel Takes a New Turn." *New York University Law Review*. 50 (1975), 622–80.

Dutton, D. B. "Compacts and Trade Barrier Controversies." *Indiana Law Journal*. 6 (1940–41), 204–19.

Dwyer, J. W. "Conflict of Laws: Full Faith and Credit and Collateral Attack on the Determination of Jurisdiction." *Marquette Law Review*. 48 (1964–65), 102–7.

Eager, B. "Vermont Milk Legal in New York." *The New York Times*. (January 31, 1985), B3.

Earle, R. III. "Northeast Promotes Recycling Markets." *State Government*. 63 (July–September 1990), 64–6.

Egan, T. "Indians of Puget Sound Get Rights to Shellfish." *The New York Times*. (January 27, 1995), A12.

Eichorn, L. M. "Cuyler v. Adams and the Characterization of Compact Law." *Virginia Law Review*. 77 (October 1991), 1387–411.

"Electronic Cash Exchange Developed for Trading Recyclable Commodities." *EPA Activities Update*. (April 17, 1995), 3.

Enos, G. "Big Breaks Lure Plant to Ky." *City & State*. 10 (June 21, 1993), 1 and 22.

"EPA & States to Restore Great Lakes." *EPA Activities Update*. (April 17, 1995), 1.

Epple, D. and Zelenitz, A. "The Implications of Competition Among Jurisdictions: Does Tiebout Need Politics?" *Journal of Political Economics*. 89 (December 1981), 1197–217.

Eule, J. N. "Laying the Dormant Commerce Clause to Rest." *The Yale Law Journal*. 81 (January 1982), 425–85.

Evans, D. "Contest Offers Mislead Entrants." *Times Union* (Albany, N.Y.). (August 25, 1994), C-9.

"The Eyes of Taxers." *Times Union* (Albany, N.Y.). (December 26, 1976), B-1 and B-10.

Faison, S. "Newark Residents Accused of Taking New York Welfare." *The New York Times*. (March 3, 1994), 1 and B2.

Farnsworth, C. H. "Canada Cuts Cigarette Taxes to Fight Smuggling." *The New York Times.* (February 9, 1994), A3.

———. "Smuggled Smokes Make Life for Some in Canada a Bit Uneasy." *Times Union* (Albany, N.Y.). (January 1, 1994), B-12.

Faught, A. S. "Reciprocity in State Taxation as the Next Step in Empirical Legislation." *University of Pennsylvania Law Review.* 92 (March 1944), 258–71.

"Federal Jurisdiction—the Domestic Relations Exception and the Tort of Interstate Child-Snatching: *Bennett v. Bennett*, 682 F.2d 1039." *Creighton Law Review.* 16 (1982–83), 815–33.

"Federal Limitations on State Taxation of Interstate Business." *Harvard Law Review.* 75 (1961–62), 953–1036.

"Federation of State Medical Boards." *Congressional Record.* (November 24, 1993), E 3052.

Fenton, J. H. "Officials of Mass. and N.H. to Study Liquor Price War." *The New York Times.* (December 14, 1969), 73.

Filzer, P. N. "Revenue Sharing Compacts. . . May Help in Getting Approval for Off-Reservation Casinos." *The National Law Journal.* 18 (September 11, 1995), B5–6.

Fowle, F. "Goodman Renews Effort to Life City's Cigarette Tax." *The New York Times.* (January 16, 1976), 31.

Fox, W. F. "Tax Structure and the Location of Economic Activity Along State Borders." *National Tax Journal.* 39 (December 1986), 387–401.

Frankfurter, F. and Landis, J. M. "The Compact Clause of the Constitution—A Study in Interstate Adjustments." *Yale Law Journal.* 34 (May 1925), 685–758.

Franklin, B. A. "Christmas Cheer Is Smuggled Out of Washington." *The New York Times.* (December 24, 1969), 1 and 11.

Freedman, D. "High Court Upholds Global Tax Scheme." *Times Union* (Albany, N.Y.). (June 21, 1994), C-8.

Friendly, H. J. "The Historic Basis of Diversity Jurisdiction." *Harvard Law Review.* 41 (March 1928), 483–510.

Frum, D. "Killing the Goose." *Forbes.* 153 (January 31, 1994), 70–2 and 77–80.

Gallagher, H. R. "Work of the Commissions on Interstate Co-operation." *The Annals.* 207 (January 1940), 103–10.

Goldman, A. L. "Low Fares Cited as Carey Vetoes Path's Budget." *The New York Times.* (February 11, 1982), 1 and 27.

"Governor Supports Bill to Make Interstate Transport of Contraband Cigarettes a Federal Crime." *Public Papers of Nelson A. Rockefeller: 1972.* Office of the Governor, Albany, NY, 1973, 1098–100.

"Governors Sign Fish Ladder Pact." *Community Affairs* (Pennsylvania Department of Community Affairs). (May–June 1993), 3.

Grad F. P. "Federal-State Compact: A New Experiment in Co-Operative Federalism." *Columbia Law Review.* 63 (May 1963), 825–55.

Grant, D. R. "The Government of Interstate Metropolitan Areas." *Western Political Quarterly.* 8 (March 1955), 90–107.

Graves, W. B. ed. "Intergovernmental Relations in the United States." *The Annals.* 207 (January 1940), 1–218.

———. "Influence of Congressional Legislation on Legislation in the States." *Iowa Law Review.* 23 (May 1938), 519–38.

Grodzins, M. "Centralization and Decentralization in the American Federal System." In Goldwin, R. A. (ed.). *A Nation of States.* Rand McNally & Company, Chicago, 1963, 1–23.

Haag, G. L. "The Natural Gas Property Tax/Severance Tax Dilemma: Are They One and the Same?" *Tulsa Law Journal*. 24 (Summer 1989), 661–73.

Hansen, D. A. "State Efforts Toward National Crime Control." *State Government*. 63 (July–September 1990), 72–9.

Hartfield, B. W. "The Role of the Interstate Compact on the Placement of Children in Interstate Adoption." *Nebraska Law Review*. 68 (1989), 292–325.

Hawkins, W. F. "The Lower Mississippi Delta: A Region in Transition." *State Government*. 63 (July–September 1990), 67–70.

Haynes, M. C. "Supporting Our Children: A Blueprint for Reform." *Family Law Quarterly*. 27 (Spring 1993), 7–29.

Hellerstein, J. R. "State Tax Discrimination Against Out-of-States." *National Tax Journal*. 30 (1977), 113–33.

Hellerstein, W. "Commerce Clause Restraints on State Taxation: Purposeful Economic Protectionism and Beyond." *Michigan Law Review*. 85 (February 1987), 758–69.

———. "Complementary Taxes as a Defense to Unconstitutional State Tax Discrimination." *Tax Lawyer*. 39 (1985–86), 405–63.

Helms, L. J. "The Effect of State and Local Taxes on Economic Growth: A Time Series-Cross-Section Approach." *Review of Economics and Statistics*. 67 (November 1985), 574–82.

Henry, D. "Interstate Police Force Urged to Combat Cigarette Smuggling." *The New York Times*. (March 26, 1975), 31.

Heron, K. J. "The Interstate Compact in Transition: From Cooperative State Action to Congressionally Coerced Agreements." *St. John's Law Review*. 60 (Fall 1985), 1–25.

Hill, K. W. and Hurley, P. A. "Uniform State Law Adoptions in the American States: An Explanatory Analysis." *Publius*. 18 (Winter 1988), 117–26.

Hoffer, G. E. and Pratt, M. D. "Taxing Heavy Vehicles: Do State Variations Make a Difference to Interstate Carriers?" *State Government*. 58 (1986), 158–63.

Horowitz, H. W. and Steinberg, L. W. "The Fourteenth Amendment—Its Newly Recognized Impact on the "Scope" of Habeas Corpus in Extradition." *Southern California Law Review*. 23 (July 1950), 441–58.

Humbert, M. "Governor Says Cuomo Letting Personal Bias Drive Grasso Case." *Times Union*. (Albany, N.Y.), B-2.

"Hurley Frees Fugitive." *The New York Times*. (July 28, 1937), 9.

"If the U.S. Collected All Cigarette Taxes." A Letter to the Editor of *The New York Times*. (May 19, 1977), A34.

"Interstate Commerce and State Power." *Virginia Law Review*. 27 (November 1940), 1–28.

"Interstate Compacts as a Means of Settling Disputes Between States." *Harvard Law Review*. 35 (1921–22), 322–6.

"Interstate Rendition: Executive Practices and the Effects of Discretion." *Yale Law Journal*. 66 (1956), 103–15.

Jackson, R. H. "The Supreme Court and Interstate Barriers." *The Annals*. 207 (January 1940), 70–8.

Janson, D. "Iowa is Called Aggressor State: Nebraska Fears Shooting War." *The New York Times*. (July 26, 1965), 1 and 25.

Johnson, L. R. "No Maine Potatoes in Idaho?" *Congressional Record*. (June 15, 1959), A5127.

Judson, G. "Weicher Signs Agreement with 2 Tribes on Casino Gambling." *The New York Times*. (April 26, 1994), B1 and B7.

"Justice Department Sides with NH Workers at Shipyard. . . If It's Not in Maine." *The Union Leader* (Manchester, N.H.). (October 24, 1990), 1 and 8.

Kermani, R. "Smoking Out Counterfeit Cigs: N.Y.'s Biggest Arrest." *Sunday Times Union* (Albany, N.Y.). (November 8, 1981), 1 and A-8.

Kincaid, J., ed. "American Federalism: The Third Century." *The Annals.* 509 (May 1990), 111–52.

Knox, R. A. and Kazamias, M. A. "Tax-Exempt Municipal Bonds—A Viable Alternative." *Mercer Law Review.* 40 (Winter 1989), 621–53.

Knox, W. A. "Prospective Applications of the Article IV Privileges and Immunities Clause of the United States Constitution." *Missouri Law Review.* 45 (Winter 1978), 1–24.

Koselka, R. "The Fight for Jobs." *Forbes.* 153 (January 31, 1994), 68–70.

Leach, R. H. "Intergovernmental Relations in America Today." *The Annals.* 416 (November 1974), 1–169.

Leflar, R. A. "Minimizing State Conflicts of Laws." *Detroit College of Law Review.* 1983 (Winter 1983), 1325–30.

"Legal Problems Relating to Interstate Compacts." *Iowa Law Review.* 23 (1937–38), 618–35.

LePori, S. Y. "The Conflict Between the Parental Kidnaping Prevention Act and the Extradition Act: Naming the Custodial Parent Both Legal Guardian and Fugitive." *St. Mary's Law Journal.* 19 (No. 4, 1988), 1047–82.

Levy, C. J. "2 States to Join in System to Stop Fraud in Welfare." *The New York Times.* (March 30, 1994), 1 and B5.

Lewis, J. J. "Severance Taxes as an Offensive Weapon: The Forbidding Legacy of Wyoming v. Oklahoma." *Journal of Natural Resources and Environmental Law.* 9 (1993–94), 149–66.

Liepas, A. M. "Water Law—Discrimination Against Interstate Commerce in Ground Water for Economic Reasons." *Land and Water Review.* 19 (Summer 1984), 471–83.

Lockhart, W. B. "State Tax Barriers to Interstate Trade." *Harvard Law Journal.* 53 (November 1939), 1253–88.

"Low-Level Waste Controversy." *State Legislatures.* 20 (September 1994), 30–1.

Lueck, T. J. "New York Buys Ads Charging 'Raid' of Company by Connecticut." *The New York Times.* (October 11, 1994), B1 and B5.

———. "Supreme Court Lets Stand Tax on Commuters." *The New York Times.* (June 22, 1993), 1 and B5.

Lyall, S. "New York Battles Oklahoma Over Custody of a Murderer." *The New York Times.* (May 6, 1993), 1 and B10.

MacTaggert, S. "The Neverending Whiskey Wars." *Governing.* 8 (October 1994), 32.

Mahtesian, C. "How States Get People to Them." *Governing.* 7 (January 1994), 44–7.

———. "Romancing the Smokestack." *Governing.* 8 (November 1994), 36–40.

"Maine and NH Say Shipyard Vital to Defense." *The Union Leader* (Manchester, N.H.). (March 18, 1994), 7.

Mannheimer, J. A. "Interstate Rendition Violations and Section 1983: Locating the Federal Rights of Fugitives." *Fordham Law Review.* 50 (October 1982), 1268–91.

Mansfield, H. C. "Intergovernmental Relations." In Fesler, J. W. (ed.). *The 50 States and Their Local Governments.* Alfred A. Knopf, Incorporated, New York, 1967, 158–99.

Martin, J. W. "Tax Competition Between States." *The Annals.* 207 (January 1940), 62–9.

"Mass. Tax is Good News." *The Keene (N.H.) Sentinel.* (January 4, 1993), 1 and 5.

"Massachusetts Reimburses New Hampshire." *Worcester Telegram* (Worcester, MA). (December 5, 1959), 5.

McCabe, J. M. "Uniform State Laws: 1988–1989." *The Book of the States: 1990–1991.* The Council of State Governments, Lexington, KY, 1990, 405–16.

McCool, D. "Intergovernmental Conflict and Indian Water Rights: An Assessment of Negotiated Settlements." *Publius.* 23 (Winter 1993), 85–101.

McCray, S. B. "Federal Preemption of State Regulation of Insurance: End of a 200-Year Era?" *Publius.* 23 (Fall 1993), 33–47.

McCulloch, A. M. "The Politics of Indian Gaming: Tribe/State Relations and American Federalism." *Publius.* 24 (Summer 1994), 99–112.

McGuire, T. J. "Interstate Tax Differentials, Tax Competition, and Tax Policy." *National Tax Journal.* 39 (September 1986), 367–74.

McKinney, S. G. "A Panel Discussion on Interstate Conflicts Over Hazardous Waste." *Natural Resources and Environment.* 4 (Summer 1989), 3–40.

McKusick, V. L. "Discretionary Gatekeeping: The Supreme Court's Management of Its Original Jurisdiction Docket Since 1961." *Maine Law Review.* 45 (1993), 185–242.

McLaughlin, S. "The Impact of Interstate Banking and Branching Reform: Evidence from the Senate." *Current Issues in Economics and Finance.* 1 (May 1995), 1–5.

McLure, C. E., Jr.. "The Exclusive Incidence of the Corporate Income Tax: The State Case." *Public Finance Quarterly.* 9 (October 1981), 395–413.

———. "Severance Taxes and Interstate Fiscal Conflicts." *Texas Business Review.* 56 (July–August 1982), 175–8.

Melder, F. E. "Trade Barriers Between States." *The Annals.* 207 (January 1940), 54–61.

———. "Trade Barriers and States Rights." *American Bar Association Journal.* 25 (April, 1939), 307–9.

Meyers, W. J. "The Privileges and Immunities of Citizens in the Several States." *Michigan Law Review.* 1 (1902–03), 286–308.

———. "The Privileges and Immunities of Citizens in the Several States. II." *Michigan Law Review.* 1 (1903), 364–83.

Miller, F. H. "The Uniform Commercial Code: Will the Experiment Continue?" *Mercer Law Review.* 43 (No. 3–4, 1992), 799–823.

Miller, J. "N.E. Governors, Canadian Leaders Gather." *The Union Leader* (Manchester, N.H.). (June 7, 1995), A7.

Moffitt, D. "More States Cancel Inventory Tax on Items for Sale Elsewhere." *The Wall Street Journal.* (January 15, 1964), 1.

Moore, J. B. *A Treatise on Extradition and Interstate Rendition.* The Boston Book Company, Boston, 1891.

Mott, R. L. "Uniform Legislation in the United States." *The Annals.* 207 (January 1940), 79–92.

Murray, M. N. "The Incentives Game: Win, Lose, or Draw?" *1989 Proceedings of the Eighty-Second Annual Conference.* National Tax Association-Tax Institute of America, Columbus, OH, 1990, 268–74.

Myers, S. L. "Giuliani Says Connecticut Broke Truce." *The New York Times.* (October 14, 1994), B1 and B6.

Nadelmann, K. H. "Full Faith and Credit to Judgments and Public Acts: A Historical-Analytical Reappraisal." *Michigan Law Review.* 56 (1957–58), 33–88.

"Nationwide Crackdown on Funeral Homes that Fail to Provide Required Information Launched by FTC with State Attorneys General." *FTC News Notes* (Federal Trade Commission) (July 3, 1995), 1.

Netzer, D. "An Evaluation of Interjurisdictional Competition Through Economic Development Incentives." In Kenyon, D. A. and Kincaid, J. (eds.). *Competition Among States and Local Governments*. The Urban Institute Press, Washington, D.C., 1991, 221–45.

"New Hampshire Goes to High Court in Lobster Dispute." *The New York Times*. (June 7, 1973), 43.

"New War Between the States." *New England Business Review*. (October 1963), 1–7.

"New War Between the States. Part II: State Loans and Loan Guarantee Programs." *New England Business Review*. (December 1963), 1–7.

"New War Between the States. Part III: Municipal Bonding for Private Industry." *New England Business Review*. (July 1964), 2–7.

"New War Between the States. Part IV: Tax Exemptions and Concessions." *New England Business Review*. (October 1964), 2–7.

"NH, Maine, Vt. Joining Forces on Health Care." *The Union Leader* (Manchester, N.H.). (November 11, 1993), 9.

Nice, D. C. "State Participation in Interstate Compacts." *Publius*. 17 (Spring 1987), 69–83.

Nickerson, C. "Smuggling Surge Roils Canada." *The Boston Globe*. (February 16, 1994), 1 and 14.

Nimmer, R. T. "UCC's Art. 2 Gets Revised to Fit the Information Age." *The National Law Journal*. 14 (November 15, 1993), 32–4.

North Carolina–South Carolina Seward Boundary Agreement." *Congressional Record*. (September 29, 1981), H6667–8.

Norton, R. "Albany's Toxic Taxes." *City Journal*. 4 (Autumn 1994), 10–8.

Novack, J. "Torture by Tort." *Forbes*. 155 (November 6, 1995), 138 and 140–1.

"N.Y.P.D. Freebie." *Forbes*. 155 (April 10, 1995), 22.

Oates, W. E. and Schwab, R. M. "Economic Competition Among Jurisdictions: Efficiency Enhancing or Distortion Inducing?" *Journal of Public Economics*. 35 (April 1988), 333–54.

"Official Recommendations of the United States Commission on Interstate Child Support." *Family Law Quarterly*. 27 (Spring 1993), 31–84.

Olsen, D. and Butcher, W. R. "The Regional Power Act: A Model for the Nation?" *Washington Public Policy Notes*. 12 (Winter 1984), 1–6.

"The Original Jurisdiction of the United States Supreme Court." *Stanford Law Review*. 11 (July 1959), 665–719.

Papke, L. E. "Subnational Taxation and Capital Mobility: Estimates of Tax-Price Elasticities." *National Tax Journal*. 40 (June 1987), 291–304.

"Pataki Unveils Plan to Fight Welfare Recipients' Double-Dipping." *Times Union* (Albany, N.Y.). (September 10, 1995), D-4.

Perlman, E. "Buying It Better." *Governing*. 8 (August 1995), 61–2.

———. "Dancing Around the Dumps." *Governing*. 8 (August 1995), 48–51.

———. "Taxing Travelers to the Hilt." *Governing*. 8 (December 1994), 20–1.

Petersen, J. E. "Interstate Meat Markets: The High Price of Buying Jobs." *Governing*. 7 (October 1993), 60.

Pielemeier, J. R. "Why We Should Worry About Full Faith and Credit to Laws." *Southern California Law Review*. 60 (July 1987), 1299–341.

Plaut, T. R. and Pluta, J. E. "Business Climate, Taxes and Expenditures, and State Industrial Growth in the United States." *Southern Economic Journal*. 51 (July 1983), 99–119.

Plungis, J. "Nations Within a State." *Empire State Report*. 19 (October 1993), 31 and 33–5.

Powell, T. R. "Indirect Encroachment of Federal Authority by the Taxing Powers of the States. II." *Harvard Law Review*. 31 (1917–18), 572–618.

Quint, M. "Met Life Asked for $10 Million." *Times Union* (Albany, N.Y.). (February 7, 1994), B-5.

Rankin, R. S. "Fugitives from Justice." In Rankin, R. S. (ed.). *Readings in American Government*. D. Appleton-Century, New York, 1939, 389–94.

Redburn, T. "New Flare-Up in Region's Border Wars Kills an Oft-Ignored Truce." *The New York Times*. (October 16, 1994), 37 and 42.

Reese, W. L. M. "The Status in this Country of Judgments Rendered Abroad." *Columbia Law Review*. 50 (1950), 783–800.

Regan, D. H. "The Supreme Court and State Protectionism: Making Sense of the Dormant Commerce Clause." *Michigan Law Review*. 83 (May 1986), 1091–287.

"Regional Education: A New Use of the Interstate Compact?" *Virginia Law Review*. 34 (1948), 64–76.

"Renew Extradition Row." *The New York Times*. (May 28, 1938), 3.

Rheinstein, M. "The Constitutional Bases of Jurisdiction." *The University of Chicago Law Review*. 22 (Summer 1955), 775–824.

Riggs, R. W. "Radioactive Waste Compacts for the Northeast States." *State Government*. 63 (July–September 1990), 80–2.

"Roadblocks Used by State to Shut Off Tax-Free Liquor." *Knickerbocker News* (Albany, N.Y.). (February 9, 1966), 6A.

Robbins, W. "3 Million Chickens Destroyed in Bid to Halt Spread of Virus." *The New York Times*. (November 28, 1983), 1 and B11.

Rohter, L. "Rich Debtors Finding Shelter Under a Populist Florida Law." *The New York Times*. (July 25, 1993), 1 and 26.

Ross, G.W.C. "'Full Faith and Credit' in a Federal System." *Minnesota Law Review*. 20 (1935–36), 140–90.

Routt, G. C. "Interstate Compacts and Administrative Co-operation." *The Annals*. 207 (January 1940), 93–102.

Royster, J. V. and Fausett, R. S. "Control of the Reservation Environment: Tribal Primacy, Federal Delegation, and the Limits of State Intrusion." *Washington Law Review*. 64 (July 1989), 581–659.

Sagan, J. R. "Severance Taxes and the Commerce Clause." *Wisconsin Law Review*. 1983 (No. 2, 1983), 427–52.

Samborn, R. "OLC to Meet—for 100th Time." *The National Law Journal*. 13 (July 29, 1991), 3 and 36.

Samson, J. J. and Kurtz, P. M. "UIFSA: An Interstate Support Act for the 21st Century." *Family Law Quarterly*. 27 (Spring 1993), 85–90.

Santa, D. F., Jr.. "The Incomplete Complete Auto Transit Test: Commerce Clause Analysis in Commonwealth Edison Co. v. Montana." *Columbia Journal of Environmental Law*. 8 (1982), 185–210.

Schram, S. F. "Post-Positivistic Policy Analysis & the Family Support Act of 1988: Symbols at the Expense of Substance." *Polity*. 24 (Summer 1992), 633–55.

Schroeder, D. W. "The Right to Travel: In Search of a Constitutional Source." *Nebraska Law Review*. 55 (1975–76), 117–32.

Schwinn, E. "Moynihan Sees States Warring Over Welfare." *Times Union* (Albany, N.Y.). (July 22, 1995), 1 and A-8.

"Senecas to Evict Leaseless Tenants." *Times Union* (Albany, N.Y.). (September 22, 1994), B-2.

Shannon, J. "Federalism's 'Invisible Regulator'—Interjurisdictional Competition." In Kenyon, D. A. and Kincaid, J. (eds.). *Competition Among States and Local Governments*. The Urban Institute Press, Washington, D.C., 1991, 117–25.

Shores, D. F. "State Taxation of Interstate Commerce: Quiet Revolution or Much Ado About Nothing?" *Tax Law Review*. 38 (Fall 1982), 127–69.

"Sick Chickens Force Quarantine in PA." *Knickerbocker News* (Albany, N.Y.). (November 5, 1983), 2A.

Sims, C. "Port Authority Seeks $1 Rise in Bridge Tolls." *The New York Times*. (November 21, 1990), B1 and B6.

Simson, G. J. "Discrimination Against Nonresidents and the Privileges and Immunities Clause of Article IV." *University of Pennsylvania Law Review*. 28 (November 1979), 379–401.

Smith, M. E. "State Discriminations Against Interstate Commerce." *California Law Review*. 74 (July 1986), 1203–57.

Specht, L. B. "State Jurisdiction in Divorce Actions Involving a Non-Resident Spouse." *St. Mary's Law Journal*. 16 (No. 1–2, 1984–85), 211–31.

Spengler, J. J. "The Economic Limitations to Certain Uses of Interstate Compacts." *The American Political Science Review*. 31 (February 1937), 41–51.

Spindler, C. J. "Winners and Losers in Industrial Recruitment: Mercedes-Benz and Alabama." *State and Local Government Review*. 26 (Fall 1994), 192–204.

Stankee, G. A. "Residents' Property Tax Exemptions: A Model Analysis Under the Privileges and Immunities Clause." *Notre Dame Law Review*. 69 (1984), 878–96.

Starr, J. R. "Reciprocal and Retaliatory Legislation in the American States." *Minnesota Law Review*. 21 (March 1937), 371–407.

"State Attorneys General Launch Investigation of Cable Industry." *Times Union* (Albany, N.Y.). (November 18, 1993), D-8.

"State Pioneers Tax Change for Visiting Athletes." *Times Union* (Albany, N.Y.). (August 4, 1994), B-2.

"State Won't Become N.J.'s Power Broker." *Times Union* (Albany, N.Y.). (July 22, 1995), B-2.

"States Act to End Long Oyster War." *The New York Times*. (June 14, 1964), 55.

"States Agree to NOX Reductions: Benefits to the Bay are Uncertain." *Bay Journal*. 4 (November 1994), 4.

"States Impose Quarantines on California Produce." *The Keene (N.H.) Sentinel*. (July 20, 1981), 5.

"Status of Indian Gaming Compacts." *Governors' Bulletin*. 27 (December 6, 1993), insert page.

Stevens, W. K. "Taxes by Energy States Causing East–West Split." *The New York Times*. (October 15, 1984), B12.

Stewart, R. B. "Interstate Resource Conflicts: The Role of the Federal Courts." *Harvard Environmental Law Review*. 6 (1982), 241–64.

Tannenwald, R. "Massachusetts' Tax Competitiveness." *New England Economic Review*. (January/February 1994), 31–49.

Tatarowicz, P. M. and Mims-Velarde, R. F. "An Analytical Approach to State Tax Discrimination Under the Commerce Clause." *Vanderbilt Law Review*. 39 (May 1986), 879–960.

Tenenbaum, D. "Whose Trash is This? Flow-Control War May Get Costly." *City & State*. 11 (January 1994), 30.

"Thomas v. Washington Gas Light Company (100 S.Ct. 2647): A Reexamination of the Constitutionality of Supplemental Worker's Compensation Awards Under the Full Faith and Credit Clause." *Ohio Northern University Law Review.* 8 (July 1981), 447–65.

"Thompson v. Thompson (108 S.Ct. 513): The Jurisdictional Dolemma of Child Custody Cases Under the Parental Kidnapping Prevention Act." *Pepperdine Law Review.* 16 (January 1989), 409–30.

Tibbets, D. "NH Wooing of Mass. Liquor Buyers Blasted." *The Union Leader* (Manchester, N.H.). (June 23, 1993), 6.

Tilley, J. W. "Michigan's Oil and Gas Severance Tax Versus Royalty Interest Holders." *Michigan Bar Journal.* 78 (December 1993), 1288–91.

Towns, W. R. "The Extradition Clause: Asylum from the Warrant Requirements of the Fourth Amendment." *Houston Law Review.* 16 (Nos. 4–5, 1979), 975–1005.

Toy, H. S. and Shepherd, E. E. "The Problem of Fugitive Felons and Witnesses." *Law and Contemporary Problems.* 1 (October 1934), 415–23.

"230-Year Border Fight Settled by Maine and New Hampshire." *The New York Times.* (July 11, 1974), 18.

"Two States Clash on Liquor Sales." *The New York Times.* (December 14, 1969), 73.

"Uniform Interstate Family Support Act (with Unofficial Annotations by John J. Sampson)." *Family Law Quarterly.* 27 (Spring 1993), 93–173.

Van Alstyne, W. W. "International Law and Interstate River Disputes." *California Law Review.* 48 (1960), 596–622.

Vawter, W. R. "Interstate Compact—The Federal Interest." In Task Force on Water Resources and Power. *Report on Water Resources and Power.* U.S. Commission on Organization of the Executive Branch of the Government, Washington, D.C., 1955, 1683–1702.

Verhovek, S. H. "Cuomo Turns Down Request to Extradite Cable Officials." *The New York Times.* (June 21, 1990), B4.

Vetter, W. V. "Tribal and State Taxation of Property and Activities Within the Exterior Boundaries of Indian Reservations." *South Dakota Law Review.* 31 (Summer 1986), 602–26.

"Virginia General Assembly Takes Steps to Leave ASMFC." *Bay Journal.* 5 (March 1995), 13.

Voit, W. K. *Interstate Compacts & Agencies.* The Council of State Governments, Lexington, KY, 1955.

von Falkenhausen, B. "Full Faith and Credit to Statutes of Sister States: *Hughes v. Fetter.*" *Cornell Law Quarterly.* 37 (1951–52), 441–58.

"Vt. Benefits from NY, Mass. Taxes." *The Union Leader* (Manchester, N.H.). (June 22, 1993), 7.

Wald, M. L. "California Car Rules Set as Model for the East." *The New York Times.* (December 20, 1994), A16.

———. "E.P.A. Urges Compromise on Auto Pollution Rules." *The New York Times.* (September 14, 1994), B4.

Wasylenko, M. "The Location of Firms: The Role of Taxes and Fiscal Incentives." In Bahl, R. (ed.). *Urban Government Finance: Emerging Trends.* Sage Publications, Beverly Hills, CA, 1981, 155–90.

Watson, D. J. and Vocino, T. "Changing Intergovernmental Fiscal Relationships: Impact of the 1986 Tax Reform Act on State and Local Governments." *Public Administration Review.* 50 (July/August 1990), 427–34.

Weinberg, L. "Choice of Law and Minimal Scrutiny." *University of Chicago Law Review.* 49 (1982), 440–88.

"Whopping Tax Reduces Bay State Cigarette Purchases." *The Union Leader* (Manchester, N.H.). (November 19, 1993), 22.

Wilkins, D. E. "Breaking Into the Intergovernmental Matrix: The Lumbee Tribe's Efforts to Secure Federal Acknowledgement." *Publius.* 23 (Fall 1993), 123–42.

Williams, S. F. "Severance Taxes and Federalism: The Role of the Supreme Court in Preserving a National Common Market for Energy Supplies." *University of Colorado Law Review.* 53 (Winter 1982), 281–314.

Williamson, R. A. "Divorce Recognition—A Two Headed Monster: Full Faith and Credit and Due Process." *Ohio State Law Journal.* 30 (Spring 1969), 311–31.

Wrightson, M. T. "The Road to *South Carolina*: Intergovernmental Tax Immunity and the Constitutional Status of Federalism." *Publius.* 19 (Summer 1990), 39–55.

Zimmerman, J. F., ed. "Interstate Relations." *Publius.* 24 (Fall 1994), 1–114.

———. "Federal Preemption." *Publius.* 23 (Fall 1994), 1–121.

———. "Child Support: Interstate Dimensions." *Publius.* 24 (Fall 1994), 45–60.

———. "Introduction: Dimensions of Interstate Relations." *Publius.* 24 (Fall 1994), 1–11.

Zimmermann, F. L. "Intergovernmental Commissions: The Interstate–Federal Approach." *State Government.* 42 (Spring 1969), 129–30.

———. "The Role of the Compact in the New Federalism." *State Government.* 43 (Spring 1970), 128–35.

———. "A Working Agreement." *National Civic Review.* 58 (May 1969), 201–5 and 232.

——— and Leach, R. H. "The Commissions on Interstate Cooperation." *State Government.* 33 (Autumn 1960), 233–42.

Unpublished Materials

"Air Quality Planners Release List of Potential Emission Control Regulations." A news release issued by the Metropolitan Washington Council of Governments, July 1, 1993.

Clark, J. M. "Original Jurisdiction and the Supreme Court: Suits Involving States." A research paper prepared for a Seminar in American Federalism, Graduate School of Public Affairs, State University of New York at Albany, December 1993.

"Comparative Cigarette Tax Collections, Per Capita Cigarette Tax Collections, Per Capita Cigarette Consumption by States, 1972." Federation of Tax Administrators, Chicago, 1973.

"Conflicts and Child Support: A working paper prepared for the Commission on Interstate Child Support by Professor William L. Reynolds, University of Maryland School of Law, November 29, 1990."

"Excerpts of Remarks by Governor Nelson A. Rockefeller Prepared for Delivery at the Cigarette Tax Enforcement Conference, New York, New York, September 12, 1967." A press release from the Office of the Governor.

Florestano, P. S. "Interstate Compacts: The Invisible Area of Interstate Relations." Paper presented at the 1993 Annual Meeting of the American Political Science Association, Washington, D.C., September 3, 1993.

Green, T. S., Jr.. "State Discriminations Against Out-of-State Alcoholic Beverages." Presented at the National Conference on Interstate Trade Barriers, Chicago, April 5–7, 1939.

Hill, J. P. *Managing the Nation's Water Without Washington: The Interstate Compact Experience*. Unpublished Ph.D. Dissertation, Michigan State University, East Lansing, 1992.

Hines, J. R., Jr.. "Altered States: Taxes and the Location of Foreign Direct Investment in America." National Bureau of Economic Research, Incorporated, Working Paper No. 4397, July 1993.

Lee, S. H. *Federal Preemption of State Truck Size and Weight Laws: New York State's Reaction and Preemption Relief*. Unpublished Ph.D. Dissertation, State University of New York at Albany, 1994.

Letter to Governor Christine Todd Whitman of New Jersey from Governor Mario M. Cuomo of New York, dated March 6, 1994. Available in the Executive Chamber, Albany, New York 12224.

"Memorandum to the Commission on Interstate Child Support from Professor Lea Brilmayer, Yale Law School, December 4, 1990."

"Memorandum to the Commission on Interstate Child Support from Professor Paul M. Kurtz, School of Law, University of Georgia, re: Jurisdiction, State Standards, Notice, November 29, 1990."

"Memorandum to the House Ways and Means Staff from Professor Patrick J. Borchers, Albany Law School, re: Recommendations of the United States Commission on Interstate Child Support, November 9, 1992."

"News release from the Office of Governor Mario M. Cuomo of New York, February 23, 1983."

"A 100-Year Tradition of Excellence." Unpublished fact sheet issued by the National Conference on Uniform State Laws, Chicago, n.d.

Press release issued by the Office of Governor Nelson A. Rockefeller, Albany, N.Y., September 29, 1972.

Press release issued by the Office of Governor Nelson A. Rockefeller, Albany, N.Y., February 11, 1973.

Reynolds, K. "Federal Preemption of State Action in the Area of Native American Hunting and Fishing and On-Reservation Gambling Activities." A paper prepared for a seminar on American federalism, Graduate School of Public Affairs, State University of New York at Albany, December 12, 1990.

Reynolds, W. L. "Conflicts and Child Support: A Working Paper." University of Maryland at Baltimore School of Law, November 29, 1990.

Roeskin, E. "Doing Business in Other States: Taxation Problems." An address presented at the Sixth Annual Institute of House Counsel, Madison, Wisconsin, n.d.

"Uniform State Laws: What Are They?" Unpublished fact sheet issued by the National Conference on Uniform State Laws, Chicago, n.d.

Zimmerman, J. F. "Child Support: Interstate Dimensions." Paper presented at the 1993 Annual Meeting of the American Political Science Association, Washington, D.C., September 3, 1993.

Index

Abbey, Alan B., 159 n.28
Ad hoc cooperation, 197–8, 219
administrative agreements, 50, 193–97
Ad valorem property tax, 174
advisory compacts, 41
affect crime, 105
agricultural compact, 42
aid to families with dependent children, 72, 77
Airline Deregulation Act of 1978, 124, 138 n.46, 180 n.6, 197, 227
Akwesasne Reserve, 167
Alaska v. Arctic Maid, 139 nn.87–88
Alaska Packers Association v. Industrial Accident Commission, 81 nn.22–25
Alcan Aluminum v. Franchise Tax Board of California, 176, 183 nn.97–98
alcoholic beverage taxation, 168–70
Aldrich, Eric, 210 n.59
Allgeyer v. Louisiana, 81 n.19
Allied-Signal, Incorporated v. Director, 175, 183 nn.94–95
Ambach v. Norwick, 101 n.60
Alabama Bar Association, 187
American Association of Motor Vehicle Administrators, 203
American Association of State Highway Officials, 230
American Bar Association, 187
American Refrigerator Transit Company v. Hall, 183 n.76
American Trucking Association v. Scheiner, 139 n.100, 174–75, 183 nn.88–92
Andrews v. Andrews, 82 n.41
Antieu, Chester J., 89, 91, 99 nn.6, 13

Appalachian Regional Commission, 47, 54, 57 n.61
Appleyard v. Massachusetts, 115 n.39
Arizona v. California, 25, 30 n.44, 31 n.62
Arizona v. New Mexico, 29 n.8, 30 nn.33, 35
Arizona Public Service Company v. Snead, 184 n.103
Arkansas v. Oklahoma, 26, 31 n.69
Armco Incorporated v. Hardesty, 134, 139 n.99, 177–78, 184 n.109
Articles of Confederation and Perpetual Union, vii, 2–3, 5–6, 17, 33, 59, 88, 114, 117, 126, 214, 216
Associated Industries of Missouri v. Lohman, 140 nn.121–22
Association of State and Interstate Water Pollution Control Administrators, 202
Atlantic States Marine Fisheries Compact of 1942, 38, 40, 44–45, 55n.19
Atlantic Striped Bass Conservation Act Amendments of 1986, 56 n.54, 230–31, 235 n.36
Atherton v. Atherton, 82 n.39
Austin v. New Hampshire, 94, 99 n.8, 100 nn.35–37
Automotive Information Disclosure Act of 1958, 124, 137 n.44
Axelrod, Donald, 51, 58 n.86

Bacchus Imports Limited v. Dias, 132, 139 n.101, 168, 182 n.45
Baldwin v. G.A.F. Seelig, Incorporated, 129, 139 n.79
Baldwin v. Montana Fish & Game Commission, 96, 100 nn.41, 43

Bank of Augusta v. Earle, 81 n.16, 92, 99 n.19
Bank Holding Compact Act of 1956, 138
   nn.54–5
Bankruptcy, 15 nn.34, 137 nn.40–41
Barclays Bank, 176, 183 n.99, 233 n.8
Barringer v. Griffes, 184 nn.112, 116
Batten, James K., 180 n.9
Bell v. Bell, 82 n.40
beneficial services, 95–96
Bennett, Julie, 210 nn.69, 71
Berhovek, Sam H., 114 n.17
Bibb v. Navajo Freight Lines, Incorporated, 100
   n.22
Biddinger v. Commissioner, 115 nn.37, 43
Bigart, Homer, 182 n.51
Bingham v. Bradley, 115 n.42
Blackmun, Harry A., 95, 152
blood-alcohol-content (BAC) standard, 206
blue laws, 169
Blumenthal, Ralph, 58 n.87
Board of Liquidation v. McComb, 115 n.49
Bona vacantia suits, 27–28
Borchers, Patrick J., 79, 83 n.61, 85 nn.112, 114
Boston Tax Exchange v. State Tax Commission,
   177, 184 n.106
Boulder Canyon Project Act of 1928, 38, 55 n.22
boundary compacts, 42
boundary suits, 23–25
Bradley, Bill, 82 n.54
Bradwell v. Illinois, 97, 100 nn.48–50
Brandon, Craig, 180 n.16
*Braniff Airways, Incorporated v. Nebraska State
   Board*, 183 n.83
Brennan, William, 152
Brieant, Charles L., 120
Brilmayer, R. Lea, 79, 85 n.115
Brown v. Board of Education, 115 n.50
*Brown-Forman Distillers v. New York State
   Liquor Authority*, 139 n.102
Brown v. Maryland, 136 n.2, 138 nn.62–63
Bruch, Carol S., 81 n.1
Brutus, 89
Burns, Robert E., 108
Burtis, Edgar L., 136 n.17
Bus Regulatory Reform Act of 1982, 124, 138
   n.46, 233 n.3
business development corporations, 144
Butcher, Walter R., 57 n.64
*Butchers' Benevolent Association v. Crescent
   City Live-Stock and Slaughter House
   Company*, 99 nn.14–18
Buttlegging, 163–68

*C & A Carbone, Incorporated v. Town of
   Clarkstown*, 140 nn.119–20
Cabazon Band of Mission Indians v. California,
   48, 57 n.67
cabinet secretaries, 230–31
Cairo, Richard A., 232, 235 n.45
California v. Nevada, 31 n.54
California v. Southern Pacific Company, 29
   n.8
California v. Texas, 30 nn.29–32
California v. West Virginia, 30 n.33
Canadian Commissioners on Uniform Provincial
   Laws, 187
Cardozo, Benjamin, 60, 81 n.2
Carroll v. Lanza, 81 n.27
Case of the State Freight Tax, 180 nn.7–8
Casey, Robert P., 196
*Central Greyhound Lines, Incorporated v.
   Mealey*, 183 n.81
Chafee, John H., 54
Charlton v. Kelly, 115 n.41
*Chemical Waste Management, Incorporated v.
   Hunt*, 140 n.114
child support, 68–80; enforcement amendments,
   73; recovery act, 74, 79–80
Cheever v. Wilson, 82 n.38
Cheit, Ross E., 192, 208 nn.29–32
Chi, Keon W., 145–47, 159 nn.15–18, 196, 209
   n.51
*Chicago and Alton Rail Road v. Wiggins Ferry
   Company*, 81 n.18
Child Support Recovery Act of 1992, 74, 84
   n.86, 215, 233 n.4
Chisholm v. Georgia, 14 n.16, 30 n.39
cigarette tax enforcement conference, 163
*City of New York v. United States Department of
   Commerce*, 209 n.58
civil defense compacts, 42
Clark v. Paul Gray, Incorporated, 139 n.73
Clean Air Act Amendments of 1990, 205, 210
   n.78, 231, 235 n.40
Clifford, Nathan, 93
Clinton, Robert N., 11, 15 n.26
Coalition of Northeastern State Governors, 192,
   202
Coe v. Coe, 82 n.49
Collector v. Day, 152, 160 n.42
Colorado River Compact, 38, 40, 56 n.37
Comitas jurisdictionum, 59
Commager, Henry S., 14 nn.3, 5
Commercial Drivers License Act of 1986, 51, 58
   n.85

Commercial Motor Vehicle Safety Act of 1986, 14 n.11

Commission on Intergovernmental Relations, 199

Commonwealth Edison Company v. Montana, 182 n.68, 183 n.69, 233 n.7

compensatory tax, 135, 178

competition for tourists, sports franchises, and business firms, 141–60; tourists and gamblers, 142–43; industry, 141–49; assessing tax and other incentives, 149–51; congressional regulation, 151–53

Complete Auto Transit Incorporated v. Brady, 171, 182 nn.64–65

concurrent power, 163

Congress, 2–4, 17, 24, 29, 33, 36–46, 54, 61–63, 69, 72, 78, 104, 120, 123–27, 135–36, 141, 161–63, 164, 166–68, 179, 186, 203–6, 213, 218–19, 224–29, 232–33

Connecticut v. New Hampshire, 30 n.18

Connecticut River Bridge Advisory Committee, 198

Considine, John L., 180 n.11

consistency rulings, 226

constitutional convention, vii, 3–4, 33, 60–61

Contagious Disease Act of 1903, 120, 137 n.24

Continental Congress, 2, 6–7, 59

Contraband Cigarette Act of 1978, 166, 181 n.29, 233 n.6

Cooley v. Board of Wardens, 127, 138 n.66

Corfield v. Coryell, 95, 99 n.10

Coughlin, Thomas A., III, 112

council of state governments, 123, 191, 198–99

Coyle v. Smith, 14 n.15

Cretien, Jean, 167

Crichfield, Brevard, 57 n.59

crime control and corrections compact, 42

Crime Control Consent Act of 1934, 57 n.56, 210 n.73

Croce, Bob, 158 n.9

Cron, Frederick W., 234 n.35

cross-over sanctions, 205

Crowe, Kenneth C., II, 181 n.32, 182 nn.49, 56

Cuomo, Mario M., 12, 107, 113, 143, 193

Currie, Brainerd, 87, 99 n.1

Cuyler v. Adams, 39, 56 n.31

Dalton, John, 198

Dao, James, 14 n.22, 209 n.48

Davidson, Donald, 49–50, 57 nn.74, 78–80

Dean Milk Company v. City of Madison, 139 n.86

Deficit Reduction Act of 1984, 160 n.53

Delaware v. New York, 21, 28, 30 n.27, 31 n.78

Delaware River Basin Commission, 27, 36, 46

Delaware River Joint Toll Bridge Commission v. Colburn, 39

Department of Revenue v. Kuhnlein, 137 n.27

Derthick, Martha, 53, 57 nn.76–77, 58 nn.98–99, 57 nn.76–77, 58 nn.98–99

Diamond, Martin, 2, 14, n.6

discretionary original jurisdiction, 17–22; parties, 18–20; justiciable controversy, 21–21; appropriateness, 21–22

Dinan, Jay P., 111, 115 n.53

diversity of citizenship, 17

divorce proceedings, 64–68

doctrine of equitable apportionment, 25, 214

doctrine of prior apportionment, 25

doctrine of riparian rights, 25

doctrine of *stare decisis*, 190

domicile problem, 65–68

dormant commerce clause, 133, 214

Dougherty, Pete, 158 n.8

Douglas, William O., 68, 82, 107

dual judicial system, 17

dual sovereignty, vii

Due Process of Law Clause, 64, 89, 133, 176

Dunham, Allison, 208 n.11

Dunn v. Blumstein, 82 n.33, 96, 100 n.43

Eager, Bill, 137 nn.20–21

economic competition, 217

economic protectionism, 117–36, 216

education compacts, 42

Egg Products Inspection Act of 1970, 124, 137 n.44

eight amendment, 110

Elazar, Daniel J., 190, 208 nn.23–25

electoral college voting system, 21

eleventh amendment, 6, 39

Elrod, Linda H., 83 n.71

Emergency Highway Energy Conservation Act of 1974, 211 n.83

energy compact, 42

Energy Policy and Conservation Act of 1975, 211 n.84

Enos, Gary, 158 n.1

Epp v. State, 84 n.101

equal protection of the laws clause, 64, 89, 94, 126, 178, 226

Ervien v. United States, 14 n.14

Escheats, 27–28

Estin v. Estin, 82 n.50

Evans, David, 209 n.54
Ex Parte Spinney, 100 n.46
Ex Parte Young, 56 n.33

facilities compact, 42
Faison, Seth, 15 n.29
Family Support Act of 1988, 73–74
Farnsworth, Clyde H., 181 nn.34–36
Farrand, Max, 14 n.8, 81 n.9
Federal Aviation Act, 174
Federal Coal Leasing Amendments of 1974, 172, 183 nn.70–71
Federal Fire Prevention and Control Act of 1974, 206
Federal Gun-Free School Zone Act, 74
Federal Income Tax Refund Offset Program, 73
federal-interstate compacts, 46, 231–32
Federal Reserve Bank of Boston, 144
federalist papers, 33, 81 nn.5, 10–11, 88, 99 nn.2–4, 117–18, 136 nn.3–7
Federation of Tax Administrators, 202
Fenton, John H., 182 n.47
Field, Stephen J., 90–91
fifth amendment, 41, 78
Finney, Joan, 48
Fleischer, Malcolm L., 164
Flood Control Act of 1936, 210 n.73
Florestano, Patricia S., 41, 52, 56 nn.40–42, 58 nn.93–94
Florida v. Georgia, 37, 55 n.14
Foley v. Connelie, 101 n.59
foreign judgment, 82 n.57
formal and informal cooperation, 185–207; uniform state laws, 186–92; formal administrative agreements, 193–97; ad hoc cooperation, 197–98; intergovernmental relations commission, 198–99; national and regional associations, 199–203; federal promotion, 203–6, 219
formula apportionment, 173–77
Fort Gratiot Sanitary Landfill, Incorporated v. Michigan Department of Natural Resources, 140 n.113
fourteenth amendment, 29 n.17, 78–79, 87, 89, 91
Fowle, Farnsworth, 181 nn.22–23
Frankfurter, Felix, 46, 51, 55 nn.1–2, 57 n.58, 58 n.82, 67, 174
Friendly, Henry J., 60–61, 81 nn.6–8
Fugitive Felon and Witness Act of 1934, 104–5, 114 n.6
full faith and credit, 6–7, 59–85; origin, 60–61;

congressional clarification, 51–62; supreme court clarification, 62–64; divorce proceedings, 64–68; child support, 68–80, 98, 185, 215–16
Full Faith and Credit for Child Support Orders Act of 1994, 75, 81 n.15, 215, 233 n.4
Fulton Market Cold Storage Company v. Cullerton, 100 n.22
Fulton, Robert, 127
Fur Products Labeling Act of 1951, 124, 137 n.43

Gallagher, Hubert R., 137 n.32, 198, 210 n.63
gambling on reservations, 9–11
Garcia v. San Antonio Metropolitan Transit Authority, 152, 160 n.47
General Agreements on Trade and Tariffs of 1994, 232
Geiger, James G., 235 n.39
General American Tank Car Corporation v. Day, 139 nn.74–75
Georgetown v. Alexander Canal Company, 41, 56 n.39
Gibbons v. Ogden, 127, 138 n.61
Gillis, Ronald, 63
Gillis v. State, 82 n.30
Goldman, Ari L., 58 n.88
Goldman v. Sweet, 183 nn.92–93
Goodman, Roy M., 165
Governors, 233
Grain Standards Act of 1968, 124, 137 n.45
Grant, J.A.C., 222
Grasso, Thomas, 46, 112
Graves, W. Brooke, 14 n.2, 137 nn.30–31,37, 222, 233 n.12, 232–33, 234 n.14
Green v. Biddle, 37, 55 n.3
Green v. Van Buskirk, 81 n.17
Gregg Dyeing Company v. Query, 139 nn.76–77
Guiliani, Rudolph W., 151

Hall v. State, 114 n.8
Haddock v. Haddock, 82 n.42
Hamilton, Alexander, 3, 61, 81, 117–18
Harlan, John M., 128
health compacts, 42
Healy et al. v. Beer Institute, 139 nn.103–4
Heart of Atlanta Motel v. United States, 78
Heath v. Alabama, 82 n.31
Heisler v. Thomas Colliery Company, 182 nn.60–61
Heisler triology, 171, 173
Hellerstein, Walter, 172, 183 n.73

Hemphill v. Orloff, 99 n.20
Henry, Diane, 181 n.21
Heron, Kevin J., 57 n.64
Hess v. Port Authority Trans-Hudson Corporation, 39, 56 n.30
Hicklin v. Orbech, 97, 101 n.56
Hill, Jeffrey S., 56 n.50
Hill, Kim Q. 190, 192, 208 nn.19–22, 26
Hindlider v. La Plata River and Cherry Creek Ditch Company, 39, 56 n.28
Hines, James B., 159 n.27
Hinson v. Lott, 138 n.67
Holmes, Oliver W., 119
Holtzman, Elizabeth, 40
homestead exemption, 13
H.P. Hood & Sons v. Du Mond, 139 n.72
Hope Natural Gas Company v. Hall, 182 n.60
Hotel and Motel Fire Safety Act of 1990, 211 n.93
Hours of Service Act of 1907, 137 n.42
Howey, Ronald, 235 n.38
Hughes v. Alexandria Scrap Corporation, 139 n.92
Hughes v. Fetter, 82 n.29, 207 n.2
Hughes, Charles Evans, 38, 122
Hughes, Howard, 21
Hunt v. Washington Apple Advertising Commission, 139 n.93
Hunt, Guy, 107
Hurley, Charles F., 108
Hurley, Patricia A., 190, 192, 208 nn.19–22, 26
Hyatt v. New York, 115 n.34

Illinois v. City of Milwaukee, 29 n.11
Illinois v. Kentucky, 24, 31 n.55
Illinois ex rel. McNichols v. Pease, 115 n.40
Imperium in Imperio, 8
Indian country, 170
Indian Trade and Intercourse Act of 1790, 168, 181 n.38
Indian Trader Act of 1876, 168 181 n.38
Indian Gaming Regulatory Act of 1988, 9–11, 14 n.20, 57 n.66
Indian nations, 8–11
Indian Tribe-State Gaming Compact, 48
industry, competition for, 143–58
in personam jurisdiction, 78
in re King, 84 n.102
in re Strauss, 115 n.36
intergovernmental relations commission, 198–99
internal consistency test, 132
Internal Revenue Act of 1913, 152

internal free trade, 7–8
International Association of Milk Control Agencies, 199
International Fuel Agreement, 125
interstate agreement on detainers, 45–47, 57 n.62, 111–13
Interstate Banking and Branching Efficiency Act of 1994, 126, 138 n.57
Interstate Bus and Truck Conference, 123
Interstate Commerce Act, 187, 208 n.7, 234 n.18
interstate commerce clause, 78, 89, 92, 98, 121, 126, 133, 170, 176, 178, 226
interstate compacts and agreements, 6, 12, 24, 33–58, 186, 215; negotiation and ratification, 34–36; congressional consent, 36–40; amendment and terminations, 40–41; number and types, 41–49; other regional agencies, 49–50; administrative agreements, 50; assessment, 50–54
Interstate Compact for Out-of-State Parolee and Probationer Supervision, 107
interstate compact on pest control, 44
interstate economic protectionism, 117–40; trade barriers, 118–22; removal of barriers, 122–35, 216–17
Interstate Horseracing Act of 1978, 134–35, 140 n.123, 234 n.22
Interstate Oil and Gas Compact of 1935, 38, 55 n.19
interstate sanitation compact, 45
interstate suits, 23–28; boundary, 23–25; water, 25–27; tax, 27, bona vacantia, 27–28

Jackson, Robert H., 60, 81 n.3, 128, 139 n.71, 225
James v. Dravo Contracting Company, 38, 55 n.21
Janson, Donal, 13 n.1
Jenkins Act of 1949, 164, 181 n.17, 233 n.5
Johnson, Lester R., 136 nn.18–19
Judd, Harold T., 20
Judiciary Act of 1789, 29 n.3
Justice Improvement Act of 1988, 29 n.2
justiciable controversy, 20–21

Kansas v. Colorado, 30 nn.42–43, 31 n.61, 56 n.35
Kansas v. Finney, 48, 57 n.69
Kaufman v. Kaufman, 82 n.43
Kayne, Jay, 160 nn.38–40
Kennedy, Anthony M., 175

Kentucky v. Dennison, 22, 30 n.40, 107–8, 110–11, 115 n.21
Kentucky Division, Horsemen's Benevolent & Protective Association, Incorporated v. Turfway Park Racing Association, 140 n.124, 234 n.23
Kenyon, Daphne A., 159 n.14
Ketcham, Ralph, 99 n.5
Kickapoo Tribe of Indians v. Babbitt, 48, 57 n.70
Kincaid, John, 14 n.2, 159 n.14
Kohn v. Melcher, 96, 100 nn.44–45
Krueger, Gary, 235 n.50
Kuffner, Charles, 112–13
Kulko v. California Superior Court, 70, 78, 83 n.62
Kurtz, Paul M., 79, 85 nn.116–17, 119, 121

Landis, James, 46 ,51, 55 nn.1–2, 57 n.58, 58 n.82
Lascelles v. Georgia, 115 n.33
Laski, Harold J., 51, 58 n.83
Lawrence, Sharon, 234 n.29
Leach, Richard H., 14, n.2
Lee, Seung-ho, 138
Lehman, Herbert H., 36
lex domicilii, 65
lex loci contractus, 62
licensing and taxing powers barriers, 121–22
Livingston, Robert R., 127
long arm statute, 70
Long, Henry F., 169
lottery compact, 42
Louisiana v. Mississippi, 24, 30 nn.33, 36, 31 nn.51–52
Louisiana v. Texas, 19, 29 n.14
Loving, Susan B., 112
Low Level Radioactive Waste Policy Act of 1980, 35, 38, 42, 55 nn.6, 20, 56 nn.49–50, 203, 210 n.74
Lueck, Thomas J., 159 nn.34–36

Macey, Jonathan R., 224, 234 n.15
MacTaggert, Stacy, 182 n.52
Madison, James, 60, 81 n.5, 88, 118
Magnolia Petroleum Company v. Hunt, 81 n.12
Mahon v. Justice, 115 n.32
Mahtesian, Charles, 142, 158 nn.2–4, 159 nn.29, 31
Mail Fraud Act of 1909, 165, 181 n.19
Mansfield, Harvey C., 53, 58 n.100
marketing and development compacts, 42

Marquette National Bank v. First of Omaha Corporation, 138 n.58
Marshall, John, 117, 127
Marshall, Thurgood, 175
Maryland v. Louisiana, 27, 31 n.71, 131, 139 nn.97–98, 183 n.74
Massachusetts v. Missouri, 30 n.26
McCarron-Ferguson Act of 1945, 92, 100 n.24, 126, 130, 138 n.59, 178, 186, 207 n.4, 226, 234 n.24
McCool, Daniel, 11, 15 n.28
McCray, Sandra B., 207 n.5
McCready v. Commonwealth, 95–96, 100 n.40
McCulloch, Anne M., 14 n.20
McCulloch v. Maryland, 151–52, 160 n.41
McFadden Act, 125, 138 n.53
McKesson Corporation v. Division of Alcoholic Beverages & Tobacco, 140 n.105
McKusick, Vincent L., 18, 20, 22–23, 30 nn.37–38, 47
McLaughlin, Susan, 138 n.57
Mediterranean fruit fly, 21
Melder, F. Eugene, 122, 137 nn.25, 28
Melia, Robert, 74
Memorial Hospital v. Maricopa County, 82 n.33
Merrion v. Jicarilla Apache Tribe, 182 n.58
Metropolitan Life Insurance Company v. Ward, 100 n.23, 184 n.110, 234 n.25
metropolitan problems compacts, 42
Milhelm Attea & Brothers, Incorporated v. Department of Taxation and Finance, 181 nn.41–42
Miller, Geoffrey P., 224, 234 n.14
Miller, Jerry, 210 n.70
Miller, Samuel F., 91, 97
Mills v. Duryee, 62, 81 n.16
Mineral Lands Leasing Act of 1920, 172, 183 nn.70–71
minimum contacts, 133
Minnesota v. Barber, 139 n.70
Mintz et al. v. Baldwin, 139 n.78
Miranda v. Arizona, 110, 115 n.46
Mississippi v. Louisiana, 31 n.53
Mississippi River Commission, 49
Missouri Death Tax Act, 122
Missouri v. Illinois, 29 n.4, 30 n.46, 31 n.59
model for improved relations, 213–35
Model Toxic Toxics in Packaging Act, 192
Modern Woodmen of America v. Mixer, 81 n.20
Moe v. Confederated Slaish and Kootenai Tribes of Flathead Reservations, 168, 181 n.39
Moore, A. Harry, 108

Moffitt, Donald, 159 n.21
Moorman Manufacturing Company v. Iowa, 174, 183 n.84
Morales v. Trans World Airlines, Incorporated, 209 nn.55–56, 234 n.29
Motor Carrier Act of 1980, 124, 138 n.46, 180 n.6
Motor Carrier Act of 1991, 125, 138 nn.50–51
Motor Carrier Safety Act of 1984, 125, 138 n.49
motor vehicle compacts, 44
Mott, Rodney L., 189–90, 208 nn.15–18
Multistate Tax Commission, 180, 192, 219, 227
Murdock v. City of Memphis, 56 n.32
Munro, William B., 127, 138 n.64
Murphy, Blakely M., 56 n.53
Murphy, Shelly, 180 n.3
Murray v. Clough, 115 n.35
mutual aid compacts, 44

Nadelmann, Jurt N., 60, 81 n.4
Napoleonic Code, 190
National Association of Insurance Commissioners, 192, 199
National Bellas Hess, Incorporated v. Department of Revenue, 140 nn.107–8
National Committee for Uniform Traffic Laws and Ordinances, 229
National Conference of Commissioners of Uniform Laws, 34, 186, 207, 219, 222
National Driver Register, 203, 210 n.75, 219, 228, 234 n.30
National Governors' Association, 124–25, 151, 158, 199, 224, 229
National Labor Relations Act of 1935, 222, 233 n.11
National Minimum Drinking Age Amendments of 1984, 211 n.85
natural resources compacts, 44
Nebraska v. Wyoming, 26, 31 nn.63–65
necessary and proper clause, 89
Netzer, Dick, 150, 153, 159 n.30, 160 n.57
New England confederation, 103
New York v. Connecticut, 23, 30 n.49
New York ex rel. New York Central & Harlem Rail Road v. Miller, 183 n.78
New York State Department of Environmental Conservation, 45
New York State Legislative Commission on Expenditure Review, 52
Nickerson, Colin, 181 n.37
Noble Bank v. Haskell, 136 n.14

North American Free Trade Agreement of 1993, 232, 235 n.47
Northeast Bankcorp v. Board of Governors, 138 n.56
Northeast-Midwest Coalition, 229
Northeast-Midwest Senate Coalition, 229
Northeastern Interstate Forest Fire Protection Compact, 37, 55 n.18
Northern Forest Lands Council, 47–48, 57 n.65
Northwest Airlines, Incorporated v. Minnesota, 183 nn.79–80
Northwest Ordinance, 2
Northwestern States Portland Cement Company v. Minnesota, 46, 57 n.57, 180 n.5
Nutrition Labeling and Education Act of 1990, 124, 137 n.44

Office of Child Support Enforcement, 74
Ohio v. Wyandotte Chemicals Corporation, 30 n.33
Olsen, Darryll, 57 n.64
Oklahoma v. Arkansas, 29 n.13
Oklahoma Tax Commission v. Jefferson Lines, Incorporated, 183 n.96
Oklahoma Tax Commission v. SAC and Fox Nation, 15 n.23
Oliver Mining Company v. Lord, 182 n.60
Ontario Flue-Cured Tobacco Growers' Marketing Board, 167
opt-out statutes, 221, 229
Oregon Waste Systems, Incorporated v. Department of Environmental Quality, 140 nn.115–18
Orient Insurance Company v. Daggs, 99 n.19
Ott v. Mississippi Valley Barge Line Company, 183 n.82
Ozone Transport Commission, 205, 219

Pacific Employers Insurance Company v. Industrial Accident Commission, 81 n.26, 207 n.2
Pacific Northwest Electric Power and Conservation Planning Council, 47, 57 n.63
Pacileo v. Walker, 115 n.45
Parens patriae, 19–20, 27, 95
Parental Kidnapping Prevention Act, 78
Pataki, George E., 9, 11, 15 n.31, 113, 150
Paul v. Virginia, 90–91, 99 nn.11–12, 207 n.3
Pennover v. Neff, 55 n.4
Pennsylvania v. New Jersey, 29 n.15
Pennsylvania v. New York, 28, 31 n.77

Pennsylvania v. Wheeling and Belmont Bridge Company, 40, 56 n.36

People ex rel. Bernheim v. Warden, 114 n.9

People ex rel. Halvey v. Halvey, 82 n.37

Pettibone v. Nichols, 115 n.38

Philadelphia v. New Jersey, 140 n.112

Pielemeir, James R., 62–63, 81 n.21, 82 n.28

Pike v. Bruce Church, Incorporated, 171, 182 n.63

Piper v. Supreme Court of New Hampshire, 101 nn.52–53

Plant Quarantine Act of 1912, 126, 138 n.60

political culture, 199

police power, 119–21, 226

Pollock v. Farmers Loan & Trust Company, 152, 160 n.43

Port Authority of New York and New Jersey Compact, 35–36, 38, 40, 52, 223

Port Authority Trans-Hudson, 52

Preemption, vii, 123–26

President, 229–30

Prigg v. Pennsylvania, 114 n.5

Private Truck Council of America, Incorporated v. Secretary of State, 140 n.126

Private Truck Council of America, Incorporated v. State of New Hampshire, 140 n.125

privilege doctrine, 171

Privileges and Immunities, 7, 87–101, 126; origin of guarantee, 88–89; judicial clarification, 89–98, 216

product liability statutes, 186

proprietary powers barriers, 121

Prudential Insurance Company v. Benjamin, 234 n.25

Puerto Rico v. Branstad, 110–11, 115 nn.48, 51–52, 54

Puerto Rico v. Iowa, 29 n.12

Pullman's Palace Car Company v. Pennsylvania, 183 n.75

Pure Food and Drug Act of 1906, 233 n.10

Quint, Michael, 209 n.57

Quill Corporation v. North Dakota, 133, 135, 140 nn.109–11, 127, 225, 234 n.19

Rakowsky, Judy, 84 n.87

Randolph, Edmund, 3

Reciprocity, 122–23, 135

Reeves, H. Clyde, 57 n.59

Reeves Incorporated v. State, 139 n.94

regulatory compacts, 44

Rehnquist, William H., 132, 134

Removal of Causes Act of 1920, 29, 56 n.34

rendition, 7, 17, 103–16, 216; state statutes, 105–7; act of 1793, 104–5, 114 n.5; supreme court clarification, 107–11; interstate agreement on detainers, 111–13

Republican River Compact, 39

reserved powers, 4

res judicata, 66

Revenue and Expenditure Control Act of 1968, 152, 160 n.50

Revised Uniform Reciprocal Enforcement of Support Act, 70

Reynolds, William L., 77–78, 84 n.106, 85 n.118

Ridgeway, Marian E., 52–53, 58 nn.95–96

Riker, William H., 14 n.7

river basin conpacts, 45

Rivers, Eurith D., 108

Roberts v. Reilly, 115 n.31

Rockefeller, Nelson A., 163–65

Rohter, Larry, 15 n.33

Roosevelt, Franklin D., 38–39

Santa Clara Pueblo v. Martinez, 8, 14 n.17

Scalia, Antonin, 175

Schaefer, William D., 196

Schram, Sanford F., 235 n.50

Schreter, Herma H., 87, 99 n.1

Schwinn, Elizabeth, 15 n.35

Scott, James A., 114 nn.2, 4

Seabrook case, 19–20, 27

seal of quality program, 118–19

Sealy, Frank, 112

Selznick, Philip, 57 n.75

service compacts, 45

severence taxes, 170–73

Shaffer v. Carter, 93, 100 n.28

Shapiro v. Thompson, 82 n.33

Sherman Anti-Trust Act of 1890, 187 208 n.7

Sherrer v. Sherrer, 67, 82 n.48

Shiras, Oliver P., 96

Shonka, Molly, 160 nn.38–40

Sims, Calvin, 55 n.7

Simson, Gary J., 100 n.39

sin taxes, 163

sixteenth amendment, 152

slaughterhouse cases, 91

Smith, Adam, 117, 136 n.1

Smith, Michael E., 129–30, 139 nn.80, 91

Social Security Act of 1935, 234 n.28

Sossello, Pedro, 193

South Carolina v. Baker, 152, 160 nn.45–46

South Carolina State Highway Department v. Barnwell Brothers, 129, 139 nn.81–82

South Dakota v. Dole, 205, 211 n.86

Sosna v. Iowa, 64, 82 nn.32, 35–36

special matter, 18–20, 26

St. Louis v. Missouri, 138 n.52

Stanley Studies, Incorporated v. Alabama, 139 nn.89–90

State Board of Transportation v. Jackson, 137 n.26

state's business climate, 145–49

State Commission on Interstate Cooperation, 123, 219

State v. Creditor, 100 n.47

State Justice Institute, 228–29, 234 n.34

State v. Randolph, 100 n.46

State ex rel. Stephan v. Finney, 14 n.21

state legislatures, 221–23

Stephan, Robert T., 48

Sterns v. Minnesota, 14 n.14

Stevens, John Paul, 131, 175, 197

Stevens, William K., 182 nn.57, 59

Stone, Harlan F., 128–30

Streitwolf v. Streitwolf, 82 n.40

Sturgis v. Washington, 100 n.38

substantial nexus, 133

suggested state legislation, 191–92

supremacy of the laws clause, 123, 162

Supreme Court of New Hampshire v. Piper, 97, 100 n.51, 101 nn.51–55

Surface Transportation Assistance Act of 1982, 124, 129, 138 n.47, 224, 234 n.17

Surface Transportation Efficiency Act of 1991, 125

Susquehanna River Basin Compact, 46–47

Sweeney v. Woodall, 115 n.44

Tandem Truck Safety Act of 1984, 125, 138 n.49

Taney, Roger B., 22, 127

Tannenwald, Robert, 159 n.26

tax compacts, 46

tax credits, 177–78

Tax Equity and Fiscal Responsibility Act of 1982, 205, 211 n.87

tax exemptions, 145–50

tax exportation, 161–80

Tax Injunction Act of 1937, 176

Tax Reform Act of 1976, 19, 177, 180 n.6, 184 n.104

Tax Reform Act of 1986, 152–53, 160 nn.53–54

Tax revenue competition, 161–84, 217–18; tax differential problem, 163–70; exportation of

taxes, 170–73; tax apportionment, 173–76; taxation of multinational corporations, 176–77; tax credits, 177–78

tax sanction, 205–6

tax suits, 27

Taylor, George R., 136 n.17

Ted Weiss Child Support Enforcement Act of 1992, 84 n.84

Tennessee Valley Authority, 49–50, 57 n.73

tenth amendment, 4–5, 54, 111

Texas v. Florida, 30 n.28

Texas v. New Jersey, 27–28, 31 nn.75–76

Texas v. New Mexico, 23–24, 29 n.6, 31 nn.66–68

Thalweg, 24

thirteenth amendment, 104

Thomas, Clarence, 27

Thurlow v. Commonwealth of Massachusetts, 138 n.65

Thursby, Vincent V., 51, 56 n.34, 58 n.84

Title IV-D, 72–74, 77

Tobin v. United States, 38, 55 n.24

Toomer v. Witsell, 99 n.9, 100 n.30

Transportation Safety Act of 1974, 226

Travellers' Insurance Company v. Connecticut, 93, 100 n.27

Travis v. Yale and Town Manufacturing Company, 93, 100–1 nn.29–30

Trinova Corporation v. Michigan Department of Treasury, 184 n.117

Tully, James H., Jr., 165

Tuscarora Indian Reservation, 166

twenty-first amendment, 120, 132, 169

Tyler Pipe Industries v. Washington Department of Revenue, 184 n.111

ultra vires, 13

Uniform Close Pursuit Act, 105–6, 114

Uniform Commercial Code, 188–89

Uniform Criminal Extradition Act, 105, 114

Uniform Division of Income for Tax Purposes Act, 192

Uniform Enforcement of Foreign Judgments Act, 69

Uniform Interstate Family Support Act, 70–71

Uniform Reciprocal Enforcement of Support Act, 69–70, 83 n.60, 107

Uniform Residential Landlord and Tenant Act, 188

uniform state laws, 186–92

Union Refrigerator Transit Company v. Kentucky, 183 n.77

unitary tax system, 175–77, 179
United Building & Construction Trades Council v. Mayor & Council of Camden, 101 nn.57–58, 139 n.96
United States Advisory Commission on Intergovernmental Relations, 52, 58 n.89, 144, 148, 154, 159 nn.24, 22–25, 164, 166–67, 180 n.12, 181 n.28, 191, 199, 219
United States Bankruptcy Court, 13
United States Commission on Interstate Child Support, 70–73, 75–79
United States Constitution, 3–9, 12, 15 n.32, 17–19, 22, 29 n.17, 33–34, 40, 59–60, 71–72, 87–88, 103–4, 106–11, 114, 118, 123, 126–27, 151, 162, 172, 206, 215, 224
United States Environmental Protection Agency, 25–26
United States General Accounting Office, 83 nn.65–66, 69, 77, 84 n.85, 153, 160 nn.58–60
United States v. Harris, 99 n.7
United States Office of Child Support Enforcement, 68
United States v. Lopez, 84 n.90
United States v. Schroeder, 84 n.89
United States v. South-Eastern Underwriters Association, 207 n.4
United States Steel Corporation v. Multistate Tax Commission, 37, 55 n.17
United States Supreme Court, 4–9, 11, 13, 17–28, 33–34, 39–40, 54, 61–68, 77–78, 90–98, 117–18, 121, 125–35, 163, 168, 170–76, 179, 206, 214–15, 217–18, 226
Utah Power & Light Company v. Pfost, 182 n.62

Vanderbilt v. Vanderbilt, 82 n.51
Vawter, Wallace R., 36, 55 n.9
Vincent, Fred M., 89
Virginia v. Tennessee, 37, 55 nn.15–16, 234 n.20
Virginia v. West Virginia, 22, 30 n.41
Virginia-Kentucky Interstate Compact of 1789, 37
Voit, William K., 56 n.42

Wabash Valley Compact, 38, 55 n.23
Wald, Matthew L., 211 nn.80–81

Walling v. Michigan, 138 nn.68–69
Walters, David, 112
Ward v. Maryland, 93, 100 nn.25–26
WardAir Canada, Incorporated v. Florida, 183 nn.85, 87
Washington, Bushrod, 90, 95
Washington v. Confederated Colville Tribes, 168, 181 n.40
Washington, George, 104
Washington Metropolitan Area Transit Regulation Compact, 38, 55 n.23
Water Quality Act of 1965, 203
Water Resources Planning Act of 1965, 228, 234 n.32
water suits, 25–27
Waugh, Frederick V., 136 n.17
Webb-Kenyon Act of 1913, 168, 182 n.44
Weeks Act of 1911, 37, 55 n.11, 210 n.73
Weissert, Carol S., 56 n.50
Wendell, Mitchell, 34, 36, 38, 55 nn.5, 10, 25
Western Live Stock v. Bureau of Revenue, 139 n.83
Whitman, Christine Todd, 12
Wickard v. Filburn, 78
Wilkins, David E., 14 n.19
Wilkins v. State, 100 n.47
Williams v. North Carolina, 67–68, 82 nn.44–47
Williams, Stephen F., 172, 183 n.72
Williams v. Vermont, 184 nn.113–14
Willis Committee, 192
Wilson Act of 1890, 168, 182 n.43
Winters v. United States, 11
Wool Products Labeling Act of 1940, 124, 137 n.43
Worcester v. Georgia, 9, 14 n.18
Worldwide Military Locator Service, 74
Wyoming v. Oklahoma, 27, 29 n.6, 31 nn.72–73

Zimmerman, Dennis, 153, 155, 160 nn.51, 55–56
Zimmerman, Joseph F., 14 nn. 4, 10, 56 n.43, 85 nn.111, 122, 137 n.39, 207 n.1, 208 n.6, 210 n.77, 233 nn.1–2, 234 nn.29, 34
Zimmermann, Frederick L., 34, 36, 38, 55 nn.5, 10, 25

About the Author

JOSEPH F. ZIMMERMAN is Professor of Political Science at the State University of New York at Albany. He is the author of over 20 books, including *Contemporary American Federalism* (Praeger, 1992) and *State-Local Relations, Second Edition* (Praeger, 1995).